A Casebook of
COUNSELING

THE CENTURY PSYCHOLOGY SERIES

RICHARD M. ELLIOTT, *Editor*

KENNETH MacCORQUODALE, *Assistant Editor*

ROBERT CALLIS
University of Missouri

PAUL C. POLMANTIER
University of Missouri

EDWARD C. ROEBER
University of Michigan

A Casebook of
COUNSELING

Appleton-Century-Crofts

NEW YORK

PRINTED IN THE UNITED STATES OF AMERICA

To

Our Wives

Preface

THE *Casebook* is an outgrowth of a counseling program with which we have been associated for a number of years. In a very real way, the program consists of three parts—teaching, research, and service. As will be seen, each of these parts is dependent upon, and supportive to, the other parts of the program. Three years ago the staff and several advanced graduate students (serving as counselors in the counseling service) began a series of seminars for the purpose of outlining a group of research studies. We expressed our discontent with the dearth of tested knowledge about counseling, particularly about the counseling process. We lamented the fact that many students in counseling avoided doing research on counseling *per se* and chose instead to do their research in "safer" areas such as test construction and validation. With the assurance by the professors in the group that they would tolerate and even encourage research that might be tenuous and somewhat nonrigorous in experimental design, several of the graduate students made bold by deciding to venture, research-wise, into this ambiguous and relatively uncharted area of endeavor called counseling.

We started with the idea that to study counseling we must consider what actually happens in counseling through verbatim recordings of interviews, not what the counselor reports, or remembers. Vice-President T. A. Brady, Dean L. G. Townsend, and Dean Elmer Ellis of the University of Missouri were quite helpful to us in thinking through the ethical considerations involved in recording interviews in the counseling service. Our first efforts were then directed toward identifying and objectifying some of the important variables in counseling. Our hope was to examine the manner in which these variables function and determine the nature of some of their properties. Actually, we have made only a small beginning on this ambitious endeavor.

From the first series of studies two things became apparent which are of interest to us here. First, the case materials which were gathered for tne studies were soon recognized as possessing high value as instructional materials. Consequently, the organization of our "Methods and Techniques of Counseling" course was revamped around four or five sets of case materials rather than around a content-topical outline. After more than two years of experience with the course so organized, we are of the firm opinion that we teach more "reality" about counseling than was true prior to the introduction of case materials into the course. Secondly, we are beginning to believe that some of the important and possibly crucial variables in the counseling process are not reflected by the methods of classifying interview data which have been used by Covner, Raimy, Porter, Seeman, Dipboye, Rundquist, Proff, Chappell, and others. This belief has come in part from the research findings, but more importantly from studying the case materials in classes and seminars, and from tryout of new ideas in the practice of counseling.

We have found that the interstimulation which occurs among the three parts of the counseling program—teaching, research, and service—has whetted the frontier of our knowledge of counseling into a sharp, sensitive, growing edge. The *Casebook* represents one stage in our search for understanding of counseling. In fact, it may be a stage beyond which we are now ready to move. For example, we are now considering an hypothesis that can be stated something like this: The relationship which obtains between counselor and client may be the most important and fundamental factor in counseling, a factor to which other accouterments, such as giving information, interpretation, clarification, catharsis, etc. may be appended according to a variety of specific clients or situations. Relationship is a living, dynamic "organism." Unlike rapport, it cannot be "established" once and for all by a cheery "good morning" and a spirited "What did you think of the ball game last night?" It can become sick and recover, it can grow stale and flourish, all within the hour. It may be the most powerful tool which the counselor has at his command. To present this hypothesis as we have suggests that it is something which we have discovered. In a sense this is true even though the abstract concept has been described by many others. To understand something as an abstract concept is one thing; to *discover* how an abstract concept displays itself in real life situations may be quite another thing. Learning to apply theory to the practice of counseling embodies an elment of discovery on an institutional level as well as for the individual counselor. Our point is this: training programs, like individuals, grow and develop—partly through understanding abstract concepts and partly through discovering for themselves how abstractions manifest themselves in real behavior. The brief historial sketch mentioned above is to show how a program may grow and develop in much the same way as an individual does.

The reader may observe justifiably that there is little in the *Casebook* that has not been presented elsewhere in the professional literature. True as this may be, our experience has convinced us that the gap between didactic learning of theory and application of theory in practice is too great for many students to bridge without the aid of some intermediary instrument such as the *Casebook*. This is our justification for the *Casebook*.

Many persons have contributed to the production of this book. We express our appreciation to them. Especially do we want to acknowledge with professional and personal gratitude the services rendered by the five clients who consented to appear anonymously in the *Casebook*. Without their willing co-operation, this book would not have materialized.

The research seminars out of which many of our ideas originated included the following persons (with their present locations indicated): Mrs. Marjorie K. Blank, Kansas City, Missouri; Dr. Wilbert J. Dipboye, Syracuse University: Dr. Fred C. Proff, University of Illinois; Dr. Richard M. Rundquist, University of Kansas; Dr. George K. Shoemaker, Buick-Pontiac-Oldsmobile, Kansas City, Kansas; Dr. J. W. Yates, State Teachers College, St. Cloud, Minnesota; and Dr. Tolan C. Chappell, Miss Janeth J. Turner, and Dr. JT Winslow of the University of Missouri. Members of that group made significant contributions to the counseling program and thus to the *Casebook*.

Dr. Fred McKinney, Dr. Kenneth B. Brown, and Dr. Guy A. Renzaglia of the Psychology Department, University of Missouri, and Mr. George E. Mowrer, State of Missouri Department of Education have read and criticized various parts of the manuscript. We are highly appreciative of their help.

The following tests publishers have granted us permission to reproduce certain test profiles: The Psychological Corporation; Science Research Associates; Stanford University Press; and Mr. E. J. Hankes of TESTCOR. Their permission has made it possible for us to present test data in the form which counselors are accustomed to using. We are grateful for the contribution of these publishers.

Finally, we express our sincere appreciation to Dr. Arthur H. Brayfield of Kansas State College for his initial and sustained encouragement to produce this book.

R. C.
P. C. P.
E. C. R.

Contents

CHAPTER 1

An Orientation to

THE CASEBOOK

THE EDUCATION of a counselor involves a blend of the understanding of counseling theory and the skills of putting such theory into practice. The instructional gap between the teaching of theory and practice with real clients has been all too great. Students who master didactic courses sometimes fail to see how counseling theory applies to real-life counseling situations. One method of bridging this gap has been the use of case materials, recordings, and typescripts of actual counseling interviews. Rogers (281) provided a complete set of interviews for one case in order to illustrate his concepts of the counseling process. This was one of the first such cases in book form. A greater variety of case materials was presented by Snyder, *et al.* (353). However, these cases were mostly reconstructed from the counselor's notes or were excerpts from actual counseling interviews. In their publications, both Rogers and Snyder emphasized one point of view regarding counseling methodology, nondirective or client-centered therapy. As witnessed by recent publications, other individuals who are engaged in counselor education have been using typescripts of counseling interviews in order to improve the application of theory to practice; and many others, who lack the facilities for developing their own typescripts, evidence interest in the use of such materials with didactic classes.

This *Casebook of Counseling* has been developed as a means of studying counseling theory as it relates to actual practice in an educational setting. It is *not* concentrated upon a single theoretical concept of counseling methodology but recognizes contributions from several, and sometimes diverse, points of view. It contains a variety of counseling cases and presents some of the common problems encountered in the counselor's day-to-day activities. It reflects degrees of counselor preparation and experience; and, as a consequence, the *Casebook of Counseling* purposefully includes counseling at varying degrees of effectiveness.

ORIGINS OF MATERIALS FOR THE CASEBOOK

The setting for the counseling cases is a university counseling service which caters to the needs of university students, and to secondary school students who are invited to the campus for counseling during the summer. This latter counseling service for secondary school students encourages participation by clients who do not expect to attend college as well as those who may eventually enter some college or university. The university counseling service maintains equipment and facilities for recording interviews; and these facilities serve a twofold purpose: (1) occasionally, as data for research are needed, they are used to collect recordings which can be transformed into verbatim typescripts; and (2) they provide a check upon the progress of counselors-in-training as they work with role-playing or real clients in counseling interviews. Each client who makes an appointment at the counseling service is given the appointment slip shown in FIGURE 1.

```
+-----------------------------------------------------------+
|                                                           |
|            UNIVERSITY  COUNSELING  BUREAU                 |
|       Name _____       |
|                                                           |
|       Your appointment is with _____         |
|                                                           |
|       at_____          |
|                                                           |
|       A.M. P.M. on _____           |
|                                                           |
|       N.B.—Occasionally the staff of the Counseling Bureau|
|            records interviews for research purposes. If you|
|            prefer not to have your conferences recorded,  |
|            please indicate this to your counselor.        |
|                                                           |
+-----------------------------------------------------------+
```

FIGURE 1

If any client objects to the possibility of a recording being made, the recording equipment is not used. Clients, though, rarely offer any objections. On the same campus there are a psychiatrist and clinical psychologists in the health service; and consequently the cases handled at the counseling service represent the usual adjustment problems of normal, adequately-functioning individuals.

In order to study counseling, concerted efforts were made to collect consecutive recordings of a limited number of counseling cases. Seventeen cases were completely recorded during the early part of one academic year. Recording of several other cases was started but had to be abandoned because of technical difficulties with recording equipment. Insofar as possible, the seventeen cases, therefore, represented a sample of the day-to-day work performed by the counselors. There was no attempt to discard a case simply because it did not represent adequate counseling techniques. These cases ranged from two to eleven interviews per case with a median of approximately three interviews per case. Using this pool of data, four doctoral candidates studied client responses, counselor responses, counselor style, and selected criteria of counseling effectiveness (*77, 115, 264, 306*). Typescripts of other cases were added eventually to the original pool of counseling interviews. The *Casebook of Counseling* drew three cases from the original seventeen and two from subsequent additions to the typescript pool.

Of the cases finally selected for this *Casebook of Counseling*, three represented the efforts of second-year graduate students and two the work of Ph.D. counseling psychologists. As a result, some of the interviews reflect the inexperience of the beginning counselor, while others are examples of the experienced counselor at work.

After the recordings had been typed as completely as possible, they were proofread by the counselor who handled the case. Any words or names which might identify the client were then removed or changed. These typescripts, while originally intended for research purposes, suggested further uses as counselor-training materials. After a final check that all identifying data had been removed, some of the cases were used with graduate students in the study of counseling theory and practice as points of departure for classroom discussions. The verbatim typescripts, though, had a few limitations with respect to use in the classroom: (1) they were sometimes difficult to read with the same meanings as intended by the clients; (2) they had to be selected carefully in order to avoid wasteful repetition and to bring out a variety of counseling situations; (3) they placed excessive responsibility upon the instructor for selecting critical incidents in the counseling interviews and for stimulating adequate discussions of the incidents; and (4) reader attention was frequently distracted by minor points, such as grammar, and drawn away from the fundamental dynamics of counseling.

As an outgrowth of the aforementioned experiences, the authors decided to select a few cases and develop them into more suitable classroom materials. The five cases finally developed for this purpose did not illustrate any one set of counseling concepts. The major criterion for selection was the extent to which any given case contributed to the study of counseling techniques, regardless of how the counseling techniques might be rated on a scale of effectiveness. A portion of a case could, therefore, demonstrate a common error made by counselors. To select only "effective" counseling cases and those which always placed the counselors in the most favorable light would not always lend itself to a discussion of "good" and "bad" practices. It seemed more important to illustrate some of the down-to-earth interviews which might occur from day-to-day and exemplify rather fundamental concepts and issues.

In preparing the cases for more effective classroom usage, the authors edited the materials only when it enhanced the reading and understanding of the materials. With the exception of the *Case of John Battle* which encompassed eleven interviews, the cases are reported with only minor editing. The *Case of John Battle* was too long for inclusion in its entirety, so the authors cut out extraneous materials which might divert the reader's attention from salient features of the case.

The data for each case are presented sequentially as they became known to the counselor. For example, the *Case of Bill Davis* begins with a summary of Bill's freshmen placement tests, the results of which were available to the counselor prior to the first interview. Next is the verbatim first interview, followed by the counselor's notes made immediately after the interview. Bill then took the Strong Vocational Interest Blank for Men, the Kuder Preference Record-Vocational, and filled out a personal data blank. These materials follow the counselor's notes for the first interview. The case closes with the second interview and the counselor's notes on that interview. All materials, therefore, are presented, as they occurred, in the exact time sequence. At the close of each case there is an addendum which was devised by the authors. These summary statements of client behavior and counseling techniques were, of course, not a part of the original case materials.

Editorial remarks, which are interspersed throughout all cases but one, were developed through a variety of procedures. After the materials for each case had been edited whenever it was absolutely necessary, and had been arranged sequentially, the counselor handling any given case went over the materials carefully pointing out what he considered to be critical incidents. The authors read the cases individually and collectively and found other critical incidents. As a final check on the usefulness of the editorial comments the cases were used in several classes of graduate students. One student read the responses of the counselor and one read those of the client. The instructor listened and interrupted the role-playing whenever he desired or at the request of any class member. The instructor might interpret or explain comments; or he might listen to reactions of class members and thereby find need for further editorial comments. Advanced graduate students in seminars also discussed each case and made their contributions to editorial comments. As a result, all editorial comments which appear in the cases have been developed out of actual practice and have been found useful in the training of counselors. In these comments reference is made to items in the professional literature which are appropriate to the editorial remarks and have proved useful in classroom discussion. Effort was made to include only the most essential references in the professional literature. One case, the *Case of John Battle,* contains few editorial remarks and references to professional readings. The case is presented in this manner so that readers of the casebook can use it to test their understanding of counseling theory and develop an independence of critical thinking with respect to counseling techniques.

In order to adhere to accepted ethical practices, each client was asked to read his complete case, including editorial comments, in its final form and was given the opportunity to give or refuse permission for publication. Each client was also given the opportunity to edit the material. In no instance did any one of them make significant changes in the meanings of the materials. Every effort was made to present the materials as a professional project and yet in no way to coerce a client into granting such permission. The counselors were also asked whether they would grant permission for publication. Neither the five clients nor the five counselors expressed any resistance to the methods used in developing the casebook or the rights to publishing the materials. All of them gave their permission to publish the material as it is presented here. Fictitious names are used throughout all case material.

DESCRIPTION OF CASES

Readers may better understand the rationale of the *Casebook of Counseling* by examining both the data for each client and the authors' purposes for selecting each of the five counseling cases. It was intended that the learnings emphasized in the first case would be reinforced, as well as supplemented, by later cases. The pivotal or first case, therefore, is the *Case of Bette Morgan.*

The Case of Bette Morgan

Miss Morgan sought counseling services as an aid to arriving at some feasible educational and vocational plan. After several exploratory educational and work experiences, she had found it difficult to find anything that really appealed to her. Much of her dissatisfaction seemed to center upon difficulty in establishing satisfying interpersonal relationships.

The *Case of Bette Morgan* was chosen as the introductory case because of several factors:

1. It involves a variety of counseling techniques and, therefore, can be used to introduce a wide range of topics for discussing both theory and practice.
2. It indicates the relationship which frequently exists between problems of educational and vocational planning and so-called personal problems.
3. The counseling contact was maintained until there were positive signs of learning and until the client seemed more able to make her own choices and plans.

The Case of Bill Davis

Bill Davis, an engineering student who expected to graduate soon, came to the counseling service, possibly at the suggestion of an instructor. Mr. Davis expressed some concern over which phase of engineering work he might enter after graduation. His measured interests were not typical of engineering graduates. The prospect of service in the armed forces added to his uncertainties. With this discrepancy between measured interest and academic field, it is interesting to speculate what course of action the client would have taken had he consulted a counselor when he was a freshman. In fact, it is equally interesting to speculate as to whether he will remain in the engineering field as a vocation.

The *Case of Bill Davis* was appropriate to this type of casebook for these reasons:

1. It demonstrates the ease with which a counselor can assume that he understands the client's problem and yet understands very little about it at the close of the case.
2. It involves a client whose measured and expressed interests are in an area different from his actual preparation during four years at the university.

The Case of Tom Smith

Tom Smith entered college on the basis of tests. His opportunities for reality testing with respect to scholarship had been limited. He sought counseling services because of scholastic difficulties. Actually, Mr. Smith was able to adjust readily his aspirations in accordance with his experiences in the university. That is, when he found that he was unable to achieve a particular goal, he rather realistically adjusted his aspirations to a more appropriate goal. Mr. Smith's goal in attending the university was for the purpose of self-improvement and not necessarily to obtain a degree, or earn credits or grades. The counselor did not readily understand and appreciate this motivation.

This case was chosen for the casebook for the following reasons:

1. It portrays a counselor who finds it difficult to comprehend the needs and values of a client.
2. It illustrates the problem involved with a client who is less verbal than most college students.
3. It demonstrates the futility of the counselor trying to change a client's level of aspiration when the client is not ready to change without further reality testing.
4. It demonstrates some inadequacies in judging counseling effectiveness upon the basis of immediate criteria. Subsequently, the client attained success as measured by his *own* standards.
5. It shows a faulty referral which the counselor did not clarify.

The Case of Ruth Brook

Miss Brook had completed the eleventh grade in a relatively large high school and had demonstrated a high level of scholarship. Her interests were broad and more highly developed in artistic activities. One of her major concerns seemed to be the lack of a dominant and a pervasive type of interest. Her excellence in such a variety of school and other activities has also been troublesome at times when it was necessary to choose between activities. She has reached the stage of adolescence when it is difficult to distinguish between her friends and her dates. Running through the interviews is the question of whether some masculine interests may hinder her in playing a feminine role. Her presented problem was one of attempting to explore educational and vocational plans in order to choose a college as well as to obtain a scholarship.

The *Case of Ruth Brook* became a part of the casebook for the following reasons:

1. It provides an illustration of a counselor and client attempting to use occupational and educational information as a means of examining the client's self-concept.

2. It portrays counseling as it might be carried on within a secondary school setting.

3. It represents a glimpse of a normal adolescent girl who is encountering some of the common problems of adolescence. As a result, the concept of normality can be discussed concurrently with other aspects of the case.

4. It shows some of the problems of attempting to crowd several interviews into a short span of time—and the limitations of such a procedure.

The Case of John Battle

John Battle was a transfer student who had attended several colleges and universities. He was referred to the counseling service by a counselor in another university.

Mr. Battle's presented problem was one which involved vocational planning. However, as was true in the *Case of Bette Morgan,* it was necessary to consider problems of interpersonal relations as an integral part of the case. Some will say that the problem of interpersonal relations was the core or central problem. This is true. However, the counselor did not overlook the practical aspects of vocational choice that were present in the case. That is, quite frequently a counselor will become preoccupied in trying to understand the dynamics of an individual and lose sight of the somewhat mundane reality that an individual tries to be economically self-sufficient and vocationally productive in order to be a satisfied person. In this case we see how the two concepts—dynamics of the individual and vocational choice—are inextricably interwoven.

The *Case of John Battle* does not include many editorial comments or references to the professional literature. It provides the reader an opportunity to serve as his own critic and to develop his own powers of discrimination regarding client behavior and counseling techniques. The case was especially appropriate to this usage for the following reasons:

1. It covers a wide range of discussion topics, interesting and varied client behavior, and several counseling techniques.
2. It shows a client who manifests personal problems and yet finds it difficult to face them.
3. It is longer than other cases in the casebook and requires more careful reading and analysis in order to understand its rationale.
4. It reflects client learnings, some of which occur outside the counseling hour.
5. It demonstrates a technique of handling a referral case.

This case raises several important questions about the nature of cases which the counselor should accept as clients. If the problem is obviously one which should be dealt with by another profession, the counselor should not accept the case. Unfortunately, such decisions are not clear-cut in all instances. As the field of counseling develops, it becomes increasingly apparent that many academic and vocational problems are a resultant of affective disturbances. This is not to say that the academic and vocational problems are not real or important. They are real and they are important, but their solution lies fundamentally in better affective adjustment. In considering a case of this sort, the counselor must make a decision regarding (1) the severity of the affective disturbance and (2) his own competence to deal effectively with the person. The counselor may not be able to make the appropriate decision until after one or more interviews. In the *Case of John Battle* the counselor's decision was that the client's affective disturbance was not beyond the counselor's competence to deal with effectively. The counselor's judgment in this instance was exonerted (at least in part) by the fact that the client, subsequent to counseling, was able to complete a college degree, a feat which he had failed to accomplish in three or four previous attempts. Also, the client has demonstrated vocational competence subsequent to his graduation from college. There is relatively little follow-up information, however, concerning his affective and social adjustment.

CHAPTER 2

The Case of

BETTE MORGAN

★ THE CASE consists of four interviews which were phonographically recorded. At the time of the first interview the counselor knew only that there was no record for the client in the files of the counseling service.

The counselor of this case had earned a doctor's degree in educational psychology and had had three years post-doctoral experience in counseling, college teaching, and administration of a college counseling service at the time of this case.

The client was a self-referral for counseling, i.e., she was not referred by anyone else, such as her adviser, dean, etc. She indicated that she had learned of the services of the counseling center through friends.

FIRST INTERVIEW

S1—I'm wondering whether I'm in the right field of study, and I thought an aptitude test might help.

C1—Mm-huh. (*pause*) Can you give me a little background now on your thinking about the kinds of things that you would like to go into, what you have thought about to date?

S2—Well, I'm in Education, I just started this semester—and I got to thinking about it the other day, and I thought maybe I wouldn't want Education too much anyway, because I never did like school too much. (*pause*)

C2—Mm-huh.

S3—So I thought, well, I'd better be sure about it, and the only way to find out is to take tests.

★ It is not unusual for students to conceive of counseling as consisting essentially of aptitude testing. The counselor could have taken this opportunity to structure the interview, i.e., explain to the client what she could expect from counseling and what the process would be. However, the counselor in this case felt that it was too soon for structuring; that structuring should come *after*

9

the problem has been developed. This procedure gives the counselor the opportunity to structure according to the problem presented in the specific case at hand. Also, this counselor is prone to devote a minimum amount of time to formal structuring. In fact, **C40, C41, C45,** and **C107** are the only counselor responses which deal with structuring to any significant extent.

C3—Yes. (*pause*) How far are you in your college work now?

S4—Well, I should graduate a year from February.

C4—Mm-huh, a year from February. (*pause*) Can you go back and—well, begin in high school and trace this interest of yours, your thoughts all this time, what you at various times have thought you wanted to go into, and some ideas as to why, and why you changed?

S5—Well, in high school I always liked art quite a bit, and then I wanted to go into art. But when I got to thinking about that, I realized that there weren't too many open fields in that, and that I wasn't above average, I mean, in my class. I mean, I wasn't superior in art ability although I did like art. So I didn't think that I, in competing in such a field of competition, that I wouldn't—ah—have much future in art; then I decided to go into social work, so I went to College A and took some social work courses; and then I transferred here. I didn't like social work too much because it seemed awfully involved, and I just wasn't interested in it. I mean, I took some of these courses that were just as boring as they could be, and some of these teachers that were just as boring as they could be; and I just decided that I didn't like that, because it was too boring. (*pause*) Then I quit school and decided to try office work, maybe I'd like that, I didn't care for office work at all. (*pause*) So I came back to school thinking I would go into Education because it was something that I could do and something that I thought that (*pause*) I might be able to (*pause*) like (*pause*) if I gave it a chance. Lately I began to wonder about that.

C5—What particular field in Education?

S6—Elementary.

C6—Elementary Education. (*long pause*) What courses have you had, or what has been your experience that has now made you doubt that Education is—

S7—Well, it's just the fact that I don't like school.

C7—You don't like to go to school, you mean?

S8—Mm-huh.

C8—Mm-huh. (*pause*)

S9—I wouldn't want to do anything I would feel like I had to do, I mean, like going to school. It would be drudgery if I didn't like school.

C9—Mm-huh. (*pause*) Now, of course, you came to college, I presume, because you had something you wanted to get from college, then you dropped out a while, and now you're back. Can you tell me something about the contrast there—what you liked and what you didn't like, what you wanted to get from college, and apparently you haven't, or has there been always a dislike for school? (*pause*)

S10—Well, (*pause*) I never did really dislike school. It's just that I didn't see any point to it. I mean, I had to have a reason for everything I did, and I just couldn't see that there was any point to it, some of the courses that I took.

> ★ The client indicates that she has no particular goal in going to college, but the counselor fails to recognize this thought. Then the client repeats it in **S12**, the counselor only partially recognizes it in **C12**, and in **C16** the counselor changes the topic of discussion without having developed the question of goals in an adequate manner.

C10—Now is that particularly college, or is that high school, or general—

S11—No, it's not high school. College.

C11—Mm-huh. It's mostly college that you're not liking, apparently.

S12—Well, it wasn't exactly that I didn't like college; I couldn't see where I was going. I didn't know where I was headed, and it was just useless as far as I was concerned. I mean, I *tried* to make grades, but I didn't have a future goal in mind like that.

C12—Mm-huh. (*long pause*) In high school you really didn't need to have much of a goal.

S13—Well—(*Counselor interrupts*).

C13—In the same kind of thing that you're meeting here.

S14—I didn't think much about a goal in high school.

C14—That's what I mean.

S15—I just took it for granted. It's something I had to do.

C15—Yes. (*pause*)

S16—Really didn't have a choice. (*long pause*)

C16—Well, how is your college outside of the classroom? How is that to your liking?

S17—Well—(*Counselor continues talking*).

C17—How have you found it here or at College A?

S18—Well, I liked College A better than I do the university. I think that the university is quite large, and it's, ah—(*pause*) I think it's, I don't know, it's so different from what I would like it to be.

C18—Now, how long have you been here?

★ The counselor completely ignored feeling or content of S18. It would have been better to have responded to the idea that the client finds her experiences at the university different from what she would like them to be.

S19—I've been here for about two and a half years.

C19—Mm-huh. (*long pause*) And how long were you at College A?

S20—One and a half.

C20—Mm-huh.

S21—When I changed my major, I decided to go here. I was in the College of Arts & Science. (*pause*) Then I found out something just recently that startled me quite a bit. I found out that I had an I.Q. of 127, and I've never made above average grades. Never!

C21—What sort of grades have you—

S22—Well, in Art in high school, I think I made better grades in high school than I did in college—I made S's and (*pause*) and at College A I made S's in Art, but my college has all been M's mostly.

C22—Where have you gotten this information about a 127 I.Q.?

S23—Well, there's a girl in the house that had been giving I.Q. tests. She's taking this course in testing, and she has to give her own I.Q. tests, and the test was checked by her instructor.

C23—Mm-huh. Well, that would put you up, oh (*pause*)—compared with people in general, rather high; compared with college freshmen, it's well above average; compared with college seniors, it's just about average for people who actually graduate. (*long pause*) Many college seniors, or people who graduate, usually have somewhat above an *M* average, not an *S* average, but something that's between an *M* and *S* average at least. That's a pretty high score. (*pause*)

★ The last statement—"That's a pretty high score"—was intended to be a statement of fact and agreement with client's understanding of the meaning of the test score. The tone of voice used was more matter-of-fact than reassuring.

S24—I think that I've been worrying a little bit to think that I could've done so much better and I didn't, you know.

C24—How do you account for it?

S25—I really don't know, except that I'm not motivated. (*laughs*) (*long pause*)

C25—What are some things that you do like to do, in terms of—oh—it might be the work experience you've had, or it might be any, any sort of thing that you get satisfaction from, that you like to do, that you enjoy (*pause*) in your recreational work, or what have you?

★ This is a tangential response to S25. It might have proved more productive to respond directly to the client's ideas about her motivation.

S26—Well, I like recreation quite well, folk games, and activities on campus quite well, and I enjoy music. I mean, I'm not good in music; I just enjoy it for music's sake. And art, naturally, but I'm not good in, you know, extremely good in any of it, I just enjoy it. (*pause*) But office work bores me stiff.

C26—What was your office work like?

S27—Well, my first job was a filing job. I did nothing but file all day. Now, that could have been something too; and I felt like a machine could do just as well as I could, you know, without any training or anything, same thing. (*laughs*) Then I had a job working with invoices, which was a varied job, and it was a little better. (*long pause*)

C27—How much of your dislike for office work do you suppose stems from doing a job that didn't really challenge your ability?

★ **C27** is actually an interpretation response but in the form of a question.

S28—Quite a bit. That's one reason I decided to come back to school.

C28—Mm-huh. Then you wouldn't necessarily reject office work, the whole field of office work, but it's mostly a rejection of the routine. (*long pause*)

S29—I always had the feeling that there was (*pause*), I don't know, something better to work for than just get up, go to the office, and come back. Something higher.

C29—Then a job that has some intrinsic—

S30—Mm-huh.

C30—. . . satisfaction to it. (*long pause*) What do you have in mind doing when you do get out of college?

S31—Well, I had thought of teaching first grade, it's what I had in mind. One thing, I thought it would keep me on my toes, I'd have to be a step ahead of them all the time, and I would enjoy teaching. I realize that, when I was down in the grades, I didn't get some of the basic things that are necessary like reading ability and spelling. I've always been a poor speller and poor reader; and I thought, well, that would be one thing that I could further that interest in them, you know; but then I got to wondering, if I'm a poor speller and poor reader, could I help them at all? (*long pause*)

★ The client expressed some feelings of inadequacy here which the counselor could have reflected rather than asking a question about future plans. Also these feelings of inadequacy or futility are mentioned or implied in **S5, S21** and **S24.** Frequently client statements are "double-barrelled," that is, they contain two aspects— one relating to feelings about himself and another relating to planning or content. The counselor must decide to which aspect he will respond. Actually, there is no clear-cut evidence as to which is the more appropriate response. A good rule-of-thumb might be—when in doubt, respond to feeling.

C31—Had you intended to make whatever work that you go into your career or is that employment for a limited period of time before you plan to get married, or what?

★ This is almost a universal question to be considered by women in making vocational plans. Frequently a strong "career" interest in women is indicative of personality deviation (not necessarily personality maladjustment). In any event, the relative strength of career and marriage motivation and goals needs to be considered and understood. This idea is brought into play by the counselor in **C56.**

S32—Well, it was my career. (*long pause*) So far as I know now.

C32—I was not thinking of any specific plan, but the general idea that maybe you would teach for three or four years or something before you get married.

S33—Well, no, that hasn't been my plan. I think even if I got married, I'd probably want to keep on with it. (*long pause*)

C33—What do you think that you need to know about yourself, and about, oh, jobs or various job opportunities to help you see your way more clearly?

S34—Well, I wanted to know where my ability lies really, that's what I really wanted to know, so I can work for something and improve myself.

C34—Mm-huh. (*long pause*) Can you tell me now a little bit more about your experience with education courses or the curriculum? What has been to your liking or satisfaction there?

S35—Well, I've just taken it this semester, and I like it except that it seems so far away; I mean, of course I haven't really gotten into it yet—

C35—Mm-huh.

S36—. . . and, I know it requires a lot of patience, but—I realize that you have a lot to learn before you can go into it. I've been taking History of American Ed., and Ed. Psych., American History.

C36—Then this is your first semester with Education courses?

S37—Mm-huh. (*long pause*)

C37—I was wondering—more specifically, why you doubt Education as of now, what sort of ideas you have run into, and your—

S38—Well, in History of American Education, the professor explained that there were a lot of teachers who were incompetent, and I just got to wondering if I wouldn't be incompetent in teaching, and the fact that the community places so much stress on school teachers, what they should conform to—

> ★ Here again the client expresses feelings of inadequacy to which the counselor fails to respond. She expresses essentially these same feelings in several other responses (First interview: **S5, S9, S12, S31, S38, S47, S56**; Third interview: **S27, S66, S70, S73, S81**; Fourth interview: **S36, S59**). The counselor should have responded to these feelings directly. The fact that expressions of these feelings occur repeatedly when not responded to is indicative of their importance to the client.

C38—Mm-huh.

S39—. . . and I'm just not one of those people who can conform. But if I'm expected to conform, I just run the other way; and I know I wouldn't like that, if I had to be pinned down to some standard, I just wouldn't like that.

C39—What are some of the things you think the community might expect or demand of you that you wouldn't want to—that wouldn't be a part of your usual style?

S40—Well, nothing particular. I mean, as far as I can see, I would fit in perfectly with what the community would expect; but just the idea that, I don't know—(*long pause*) In a way, if I made it a point to get in a *city* school, I may not have that at all.

C40—Mm-huh. (*very long pause*) Well, here's what I have in mind at the moment as far as that test battery is concerned. Vocational interest will be one of the big factors in determining what kind of work, or what areas you would be most satisfied in working in (*pause*). We'll get at that through two different tests, approaching it from different frames of reference. I think for your own information we might have a recheck on intelligence (*pause*)—using a different test that should come out with essentially the same answer except that it is specifically designed for adults, whereas the one that you took starts with, oh, maybe three-year-olds and goes up to adults, too. (*pause*) You will come out with a different I.Q., because there's a greater spread, a different interpretation for I.Q.'s on the Stanford-Binet for adults than there is for the Wechsler-Bellevue. We can actually equate those, and see what they would come out to be, for instance that 127 on the Binet, oh, might run (*pause*) maybe 120 to 125 somewhere in there on the Wechsler. You don't get quite as wide a spread of scores on the Wechsler as you do on the Binet, and that doesn't mean any difference in ability. We have a teacher-attitude inventory which should get at essentially how well you would get along with children in the classroom, how you'd feel about teaching and about children.

S41—I think that is one of the things I need.

C41—Yes. It may be a part of vocational interest, I don't know, at least it's specifically designed at teaching and how well you get along with children. Of course, if your attitude is such that you will not be apt to get along with children, then you're not going to be as satisfied with that kind of work as if you did get along with them well. (*pause*) I think it would be well for us to get a check on some sort of personality measure, and see how that fits in. I was wondering if there is any feeling of need for a check on reading? You say you were a pretty slow reader and speller. Is there any need at this stage of the game for a measure of that sort?

★ Methods of test selection in counseling have not been very clearly delineated in the literature. Bordin and Bixler (53) describe two methods which are in use so far. In the traditional method, the counselor assumes full responsibility for selecting the tests which the client is to take. In the other method, which Bordin and Bixler had been developing, the client is given full responsibility for choosing the tests which he wishes to take after the counselor has described in nontechnical language the tests which are available and appropriate.

Basic differences in counseling style, orientation, and philosophy are inherent in these two methods of test selection. If the counselor is to use tests in his counseling primarily for the purpose of furthering his own understanding of the client which he may in turn use in helping the client to increased self-understanding, he probably would use the traditional procedure in test-selection. Implicit in this procedure is that the counselor assumes the responsibility for conducting the counseling in such a manner that he gains maximum diagnostic information about the client. The fact that the counselor chooses the manner in which the counseling process will be conducted is not to be construed to be an attempt to control or direct *client behavior or choices.* All counselors—including those of nondirective orientation—dictate the manner in which the counseling process will be conducted. The fact that the counselor retains the responsibility for directing the counseling process does not contraindicate the counseling being client-centered. In fact, any counseling worthy of the name is client-centered.

If, on the other hand, the counselor chooses to have the client select the tests, he must also be willing to accept gaps in diagnostic information about the client. However, if the counselor chooses the tests, he has little opportunity to get client reaction to the tests chosen; for example, there is little opportunity for the client to reject the idea of taking a particular test, which in itself is diagnostic information. The counselor should be aware of these implications in choosing a method of test selection.

In **C41** the counselor is deliberately brief and vague in indicating what a personality test might show. He has found that this is especially desirable in using the Minnesota Multiphasic Personality Inventory, where the client may be disappointed with a "normal" profile because he perceives it as yielding no information. Discussion of personality tests at this time may make the client wary and defensive in taking the test. On the other hand, a rather full discussion of personality tests may bring out the rationale in using personality tests and thereby permit the client's reactions on the test to be more overt.

S42—No, I don't think so. I think I've a pretty good idea about that.

C42—Mm-huh. (*pause*) Do you have any questions about these that I've mentioned, whether they are going to be the things that you wanted to know?

S43—I think they are.

C43—Is there anything else that you might want? (*pause*)

S44—No, I think that covers it. (*long pause*)

C44—Now, do you have any questions about the more specific information about the job, what teaching is actually like, what the opportunities are; what the job is going to be like—salaries, advancement, that sort of thing about teaching or any other kinds of jobs that you might be considering? (*pause*)

S45—Well, (*long pause*) I don't have any real pertinent questions that I can think of.

C45—Well, maybe that's a little premature until we do get a better idea of the general area which to consider; and then maybe we'd better go to more specific information about what the current field is like, whatever field it might be. We have drawn together that sort of information about a variety of jobs and occupations; so that once you decide on an area, you can find out what the jobs are like in that area and what the opportunities are. (*long pause*) Are you thinking about whether you should stay in Education this next semester or not? (*pause*)

S46—Well, I was. Mm-huh. I don't want to go on with it anymore. There's no future in it if I can't do it. I don't like children.

C46—Mm-huh.

S47—Don't know how to handle them. (*pause*) It's just a waste of time. Feels like a waste of time now, but I may be mistaken over it. (*long pause*)

C47—Let me go back to a point you mentioned earlier. What seems to be the difference between College A and the university (*pause*) as far as you are concerned?

> ★ **C47** ignores **S47**'s rather strong feeling that she should not be in Education; however at this point in the interview, the counselor was not satisfied that the problem had been developed fully. Presumably the counselor was preoccupied in analyzing some of the other material and did not attend to **S47**; witness **C47**.

S48—Well, College A was a smaller school, and you got to know a lot more people, and there weren't so many people you didn't know. The whole college did things together; you know, I mean, just a group thing, everybody did everything together. If anybody was in on it, everybody was; and here it's not so much that way, I mean, they don't seem to be so much of a center of interest, it's more like little tiny groups here, I mean—

C48—Mm-huh.

S49—And usually a little group will form, and there's nothing you can do about going into a different group, or a group that you would like better, because you're not associated with them; you don't know what they do, you know. I mean, you're usually associated with people that you go to class with, and people that you live with.

C49—Yes. It's tough—(*client continues talking*)

S50—You can't do anything about it, I mean, you're completely powerless in the situation, at least I think so. For other people, I mean, they maybe have a different personality, and more contacts, it might be different. (*pause*)

C50—You feel that you don't have as many contacts with other students here as you would like?

S51—Well, that's not it. I have lots of chances, or opportunity for contacts; but they just don't seem interesting, they just don't have any meaning for me.

C51—Mm-huh. (*long pause*) Now is that a different kind of experience than you had at College A?

S52—Well, it seems that there was always something exciting going on, I mean, there was always some group starting something new, I mean something different all the time, and I always liked different things, you know—

C52—Mm-huh. (*pause*)

S53—For instance, weather like this, the kids would go out and go sleigh riding. I mean, something you don't see very often; but they just get a notion to do it, so they do it; (*pause*) and you're just a part of it, so you do it, too. (*long pause*)

★ The counselor could have reflected the attitude expressed in this and preceding statements which seem to point up the client's central problem. She wants to be wanted and to have something to live for—a goal in which she feels she is making a worthy contribution and is thereby accepted and liked.

C53—Your ideas from your History of Education class (*pause*) about whether you're going to be a good teacher or not, does that stem pretty much from what the instructor has said, or is that tied in with any of the questions you've had about the field earlier, as far as teaching is concerned? Or is that a—

S54—Well, I—

C54—. . . another new idea?

★ During the first interview and in particular during the first part of the first interview the counselor has a choice between two general procedures depending on his "style" of counseling. He may choose to follow closely and intensively the topics which the client introduces and not introduce any topics for discussion himself. This procedure has the advantage of permitting the client to discuss fully the topics which seem most important to him at the time.

The other procedure is of the nature of a survey. After having the client develop his problem to some extent, the counselor introduces a series of topics for discussion which to some degree survey various areas of client behavior and thought—vocational plans, educational history, family relations, financial status, etc. This procedure probably would be used by the counselor who tries to understand the client in some diagnostic sense of the word.

The counselor of the present case was following the latter procedure. There are several counselor-initiated shifts in topic of discussion (**C16, C40, C47, C53, C67, C81**) in the first part of this interview. Later in the case, however, the counselor-initiated shifts are less frequent.

S55—. . . hadn't thought about it at all before. When I came back to school, that's what I was going to do. Nothing was going to change my mind.

C55—Mm-huh.

S56—And I just hadn't given it much thought. I'd just taken it for granted that that's what I wanted to do, and at last I'd found something that I wanted to do, you know. And then, all of a sudden I just wondered if I could do it, and I wanted to really know whether I could or not. (*long pause*) And I don't think there's any use in going into it blind, when I can know more about it. (*pause*)

C56—Now in terms of test results that are based on experience of others, (*pause*) we tend to be able to, oh, very roughly classify women students —(as much as we can classify any groups of people)—the women students break into two kinds of interest groups. That is, you can't just say black and white, but it's essentially a breaking into two kinds of interests. One is essentially a professional career interest that is the predominating interest, and the other is essentially a homemaking interest that is primary. (*pause*) A girl who is interested essentially in being a homemaker (*pause*) in addition may want to develop certain skills to work or to have a potential earning power, but that may be secondary interest. I wonder, in that sort of a classification, how you would perceive yourself, where you think your interests and ideas fall?

S57—Well, I think they probably fall in the homemaking section more than the other one, I mean, I have a feeling that I'm a mixture.

C57—Mm-huh. . . . you would be able to work for a while, or maybe continue working after you're married (*pause*) whether you tend to give that the priority of interest. As an example, most women who are doing office work, as far as their interests are concerned, are essentially homemakers; and there is a big turnover among the office workers. (*pause*) They may work until they get married, or after they're married. It seems that most of their interests are essentially homemaking. Many of them don't like it anymore than you liked it; that's typical for the group.

S58—Well, I think I'm a little different in that I have a reason for what I'm doing. I can't just do it expecting something later. I've got to get something out of it for what it is.

> ★ In view of later developments, the client's statement—"I can't just do it just expecting something later"—is probably referring to her doubts whether she can make a satisfactory marriage. The next client response reflects this same idea—". . . there's no use counting on something you're not sure of."

C58—Yes.

S59—And the way I look at it, you might as well prepare for something. I mean, you never can tell what might happen, or anything. And there's no use counting on something you're not sure of.

C59—Well, that was one of the things I think that you'd expressed a little better than I did, that the potential earning power is sort of an insurance policy, that you have the earning power if and when you need it.

S60—And, with me I don't think it's so much the earning power, just having an interest.

C60—Mm-huh. Something that you consider important to do.

S61—That's right. I think the interest is much more important than the money you make. (*long pause*) And that's one reason I think that probably if I got married I'd probably want to work anyway, I mean, still feeling like I'm using some creative talents.

C61—Mm-huh. Yes, if you didn't need the job for the earning power itself, if you should have a home, maybe some of these other, more creative interests that you have, that you say you don't have skill to actually make any money with, those might well take over, as far as your primary interests are concerned. Interior decorating, or—

S62—Mm-huh.

C62—Art work, that sort of thing, in terms of hobbies or recreation—you can have a shift after you're married. That is, when you didn't need to be doing something like that for an income.

S63—That's why I think that—

C63—If that is your essential or primary interest, you may have to go to a secondary interest as far as a job for pay is concerned. You don't want to forget about those primary interests, because they're still there, whether they're used in your work or not, they need to be used for your own satisfaction. (*pause*)

S64—Then I think in college—that is one of the least ways where you can use it, I mean, you've got to use every bit of your knowledge and your energy on studying something; and perhaps it's not what you're interested in at all.

C64—In your relatively free time there must be time to pursue some of the other interests that aren't part of your curriculum.

S65—Well, naturally you like to go out, mm-huh, you go to a show or do something in the evening when it wouldn't be the least bit creative.

C65—Mm-huh. (*pause*) You think that possibly your major interest, as you now feel, is essentially in creative areas.

S66—I think so.

C66—You mention art and music, what about writing?

S67—Well, as I said before, I'm not doing anything that I enjoy, I mean, just for my own self, you know, in comparison with anyone else. (*long pause*)

C67—Is there any other background of ideas that we need to fill in to get at the basis from which to evaluate your test results? (*long pause*)

★ Thus far the client has indicated a tendency toward drifting from one activity to another, seeking some field of study or work which is both interesting and in line with her capabilities. She rebels somewhat from conforming to relatively fixed standards or codes of behavior, desiring excitement and the opportunity to express herself creatively and socially. School has been tolerated, because it is accepted and respectable, but it has also been without any purpose or goal for her. She has not been able to find satisfactory outlets for creative or social expression either at College A or the university. Marriage is desirable but an uncertain event, so she wants to be "safe"—she is seeking an interesting area for work and for expressing herself. In summary, she sums up her difficulty as "I'm not motivated" (S25).

The client feels that she can overcome her lack of motivation by finding some area of study or work which at present is not perceived and extremely elusive. Actually she has indicated only a façade or symptom of the true problem. The counselor, realizing that there was some reason why the client lacked drive toward some goal, was searching for further clues in **C67.**

S68—Well, (*pause*) in doing anything creative I've always had a feeling that I couldn't do it. I don't know why, where it stems from, whether it's inherited or what, but studying for a course or anything, I have a feeling that I can't do it. (*pause*)

C68—And yet you feel maybe that's not a reality but it's something—

S69—It's just something that I've conjured up, anyway I don't know. (*long pause*)

C69—You say that you're not sure whether it's inherited, you mean that there might be other people in your family who have the same kind of a—

★ This is a critical point in the interview. The counselor has had the feeling for sometime that there was something which was disturbing the client but which she was not mentioning. At the same time the client was telling him subtly that she lacks confidence in herself as a woman and the counselor was not sufficiently sensitive to these expressions of feelings and attitudes.

S70—Well, my mother is like that to a great extent, I mean, she could be very intelligent if she wanted to; but she keeps saying "can't do this, can't do that," and she really has not encouraged me too much to do things. She's satisfied if I am a happy child, and I am.

C70—It's what you tried to be?

S71—Yes.

C71—How would you describe your family, and your family life? (*pause*)

S72—Well, in what way?

C72—Well, mainly, what would portray it to me? (*pause*)

S73—Well, my father is very intellectual, very interesting to talk to, but he's hard to get to know. I mean, he's one of these people that's always right. Once you get started talking to him it's okay, but you kind of have a feeling of fear when you're around him. He's got a temper, and if you know how to approach him, you can enjoy talking to him; but it is just knowing how to go about it, which way to go about it, that won't set off a bomb keg or something. And mother is awfully easy to talk to, but she— (*pause*) she kind of says some things that just rub you the wrong way, I mean, she can say it in an indirect way that you just get the idea what she means, and—(*pause*) lots of times we don't agree anymore and she won't come out and disagree with you; but she'll just let me know how she thinks about it, and then I don't get a chance to explain my position.

> ★ There is quite a bit of content and some tentative negative attitudes which the counselor ignored in his next response. **C73** would be judged to be a very inadequate response to **S73**. However, the counselor first inquires about other members of the family and then, in **C76**, summarizes the client's feelings toward her father *and* mother.

C73—Are there any other children in your family?

S74—Yes. I have a brother that's eighteen.

C74—Where is he now?

S75—He's at College B. (*long pause*)

C75—How well do you get along with him? What's been your relationship with him?

S76—We get along very well. (*pause*) Sometimes of course we have arguments, but on the whole we get along pretty well. (*long pause*) Lots of times I don't agree with the way mother handles him. I think I've done my own little job of handling him, (*pause*) pointing out different things to him that I don't agree with. (*long pause*)

C76—You think your mother may be a little more lenient with him than you think she should be? (*long pause*) In other words, as I see your description of your father, he does have a pretty positive attitude toward you; but he is a little bit touchy to approach, a little hard to feel free around, and yet essentially positive in attitude toward you. But you are a little different with your mother, where it is easy to talk with her; but still, basically, you're farther apart than you are with your father.

> ★ **C76** is actually a response to **S73**. The effectiveness of **C76** is shown in **S77**, where the client expresses her feelings toward her mother more definitely than she did in **S73**.

S77—Well, in fact, I don't think we could ever agree on anything, really, basically.

C77—-Does that give you much concern?

S78—Well, it has, but lately I just decided that she has her own ideas, and I have mine, and oil and water just don't mix; and as long as we keep our opinions away from each other, it'd be okay. But I haven't been too successful in staying away from touchy subjects so far. One thing I don't know exactly how to do—I mean, going home for Thanksgiving and Christmas and whatnot. I mean, you just naturally start talking about things, and it's always about something that I'm interested in, or she's interested in, and we always have a difference of opinion on whatever we're interested in; and it starts all over again, and I just have to take it for what it is and try to forget it. (*pause*)

C78—What are some examples of the things that you have different ideas about particularly? (*long pause*)

★ It is interesting to note the counselor's use of pauses or silence as a technique of counseling. In **C78, C79,** and **C80** the counselor waited until the client was able to verbalize a response. This was apparently a sore spot, and the client needed time to decide whether to give an answer, to decide how much to tell the counselor, or to decide how to formulate the answer. An eager counselor might have tried to explain the question or to change the topic of discussion. In either case the client might have escaped from verbalizing some of her inner feelings. Note the counselor's attempts to use pauses in the early stages of this interview and how the client did not respond as well to early pauses as this present series of pauses.

S79—Well, (*pause*) almost anything, anything at all. I express an idea and she will take the opposite viewpoint; and anything that she would have an idea on, well, I would take the opposite viewpoint.

C79—What seemed to happen in those you had in mind, that you recall? (*long pause*)

S80—Well, one thing which has always been a sore spot is my cousins. I have three cousins my own age, and my mother and their mother are very close. Any time my cousins do something outstanding, well, she comes home and tells about it. I mean, they just talk on the telephone all the time and speak to each other quite often; and they're always talking about their children, I mean, that's the main subject; and she always comes and tells me some story about what they've done, or this or that; and for some reason, I've never felt like I'm exactly what mother expected me to be, because I haven't measured up to these cousins. The other seems to build up her children, but my mother doesn't. I mean, she, she—I noticed that any time I bring home a girl friend, she's always *so* much nicer to my friends, she takes on a wonderful personality while she wants to have one, and she's so much nicer to my friends than she is to me. I mean, she's just, just honey all over the place, you know, and she does it for me in a way; but still she doesn't give me any satisfaction, because she doesn't treat me like that. She's always saying for me to bring my friends home sometimes, because I can tell that—and she sews quite a bit for me, and things like that; and I know she loves me or she wouldn't do things like that, because she tries to show her love for me; but she doesn't do it in the right way. And then she throws these cousins up to me, and I have a feeling, of course she is what—they have quite a bit more money than we do, and they've had lessons of all kinds, and they've had all kinds of clothes, and I've never felt like we could be compared, because I didn't have as much money as they did, and not as much clothes as they did, and look as nice as they did, and that's been the main background of everything so far.

C80—Essentially then you feel that your mother actually, as far as what you can feel, is rejecting you. She does more physical things and material things for you, but as far as affections and feelings, you just don't feel you've got any from her. (*long pause*) Makes it a little rough. (*long pause*)

> ★ This is a good summary of the feelings and attitudes expressed in S80, enough so that the client continues in S81 to relate an incident in her childhood in which her mother hurt her very deeply.

S81—I can remember one time, when I was real small, something that hurt me quite a bit; and I was never able to forget it. We were waiting for dad to come home from work, and I must have been about five or six, and mother was eating an apple, and I took a bite out of the apple, and I can remember that mother just was *so* hurt, that she made me feel *so* little, and *so* small, for taking a bite out of her apple. (*long pause*)

C81—Now, how about this feeling of relationship between you and your father? (*pause*) Do you feel that you get affection from your father?

> ★ After several long pauses the counselor shifts the discussion to the father. This was probably an error since the client comes back to the attitudes toward the mother to develop them further.

S82—Well—I feel that he loves me,—but he's unapproachable; I mean, I haven't got what you'd call affection exactly, but I have the feeling of security when I'm with him. I know that he loves me, and I know that he is *for* me, you know.

C82—Mm-huh. But you can't be sure of this with your mother.

S83—Mm-huh. (*long pause*)

C83—Now has that been a pretty general pattern for about as long as you remember? (*pause*)

S84—Well (*pause*) yes, mm-huh. I didn't, I didn't mind it—. . . so much in high school because I had a bunch of kids that I went around with, and we just had pecks of fun all the time, and I just didn't let it get me down, I didn't notice it so much; but any time I would—I had a real close girl friend, and mother didn't like her especially. She just did everything she could—I mean, she didn't go too much out of the way, but just little nags here and there about her, and (*pause*) then she went to a different college than I did, and I didn't have a real close girl friend for a long time. And she was remarking about how I don't have any friends. I mean, she nags me because of the friends I do have, and then because I don't have any friends, well, then she nags even worse.

C84—You can't win for losing. (*long pause*) Well, that just kind of shuts off (*pause*) or restricted your opportunity to get the kind of affection that you want.

S85—Yes. It seemed like I can't get what I want, I mean, she's always blocking me off. I would tell her something about something I wanted to do, and she'd find a reason why I couldn't do it. (*pause*) And I don't think it's intentional at all. I think that's just, just our attitudes to each other. I must have done something to hurt her quite a bit, and it's just— the feeling's just gone (*pause*) because we have had quite a few just *terrific* arguments.

C85—Now, her attitude toward your brother is quite different, I presume.

S86—Oh yes, mm-huh. She's quite proud of my brother. He's very cute, and he's something to be proud of; but I think sometimes it's best not to give him too much conceit. (*long pause*)

C86—Do you feel that you've had restriction in your opportunities to develop ways of expressing affection in the home—ah—in growing up? What I'm leading up to here is, what effect has that had on your opportunities to learn to experience an exchange of affection, how has that transferred over into your relation with boyfriends, and dating?

> ★ Again this is interpretation through a question. This response leads the client somewhat rather than follows her. Apparently this response is not too far ahead of the client, since she agrees with the interpretation and expands on it.

S87—Well, it has quite a bit. (*pause*)

C87—Quite frequently?

S88—I never feel real, completely at ease with someone in expressing myself, and if I date, I kind of restrain myself.

C88—You just haven't learned how to exchange affection in the home, and since you haven't, well then you're a little bit lost with your boyfriend. (*pause*) Have you felt that much of a restriction so far in your dating? Have you come up to a point where you think you would like to exchange more affection, but you don't feel that you know how, or are capable to, or quite trust yourself to it?

S89—Well, (*pause*) my trouble has been that I haven't found anyone that I would want to show a whole lot of affection to; and I sometimes wonder if I'm really not capable of loving anyone (*pause*) enough to want to show that affection to. (*long pause*) But I have been in love before, but with somebody that I didn't date and (*pause*) had no way of showing affection. (*long pause*)

> ★ The client's statement, "My trouble has been that I haven't found anyone that I would want to show a whole lot of affection to" raises the question, Why? The most probable answer is that she has difficulty entering into an exchange of affection rather than lack of opportunity to do so.

C89—That fits into a general pattern here. I mean, in terms of the priority you give to a vocation. (*long pause*) If you did change in that respect so that you are able to deal on an affectional level more freely than you feel that you are able to at present, (*pause*) the priority of job over marriage —that relationship could change. (*pause*) At present, apparently you're thinking that maybe your job is going to take a higher priority (*pause*) because you haven't been able to find a great deal of satisfaction in your dating so far that is going to lead immediately to marriage. Have I interpreted you right?

> ★ This is a rather strong interpretation which is probably ahead of the client's thinking at the moment, or possibly is just hard for her to face squarely. However, with additional re-interpretation (**C92** and **C93**), the client begins to understand and accept the interpretation. The counselor was attempting to make an important point: that the client's difficulty with interpersonal relations— family and boyfriends—and her vocational choice problems are highly related. The counselor felt it to be important to make this association in the first interview.

S90—I have a little bit. I don't think that my wanting to have my interest outside of myself has anything to do with the fact that (*pause*) I don't have the affection that I might.

C90—Well, it doesn't rule it out at least. It might—

S91—It can go with—

C91—Yes.

S92—And I think that if you love someone that you should strengthen that outside of you, (*pause*) do it together, for that. (*long pause*)

C92—Now I want to go back to this point: you said you wondered whether you were capable of loving someone else. I wonder whether it's actually a capability or whether it's more based on your experience in the home as you grew up (*pause*) in having few opportunities actually to learn how to express affection (*pause*) in a more safe environment.

S93—I imagine that's what it is.

C93—And you get into a situation where you're, oh, let's say, playing a little more for keeps, it isn't quite as protected as the home, that you haven't learned the skills, or learned to trust your affections to others that you might have, and probably would have if there was a freer situation at home particularly with your mother. Well, with your mother and father both, because there you have two different situations with both of them, you have some block as far as affection is concerned. (*pause*) And that's essentially where we learn to deal with our emotions and our affections and that kind of thing, in the family.

S94—I've had quite a bit of Sociology and Psychology courses, and I've realized that, and it's *so* hard to go home and know all of this. (*pause*)

C94—Yes. You'll have to come around to the point, I think, of this: you're not going to change your parents (*pause*) as they grow older, get, as they say, "more set in their ways." (*pause*) It's a matter of taking a neutral position, I think, with your family, rather than attempt to change them or to reject them, (*pause*) as such. You mentioned that it is kind of hard to do because you might be able to say you do that, but what you actually feel may be a different thing. (*pause*) And that means if you do really feel that, you're establishing a neutral position, (*pause*) just developing a feeling of independence and security outside of the family. Perhaps your home base then moves from the family to some position outside the family, and that must be a secure and satisfying base for it to stick.

S95—I came away to school.

C95—That has not been very satisfying?

S96—No. (*laughs*)

C96—So that's one of the difficulties in attempting to move away from the family. You still haven't been able to establish a home base outside it. (*long pause*) What usually happens is that your boyfriend—that relationship—takes care of that, (*pause*) but you're hampered somewhat in establishing that sort of secure relationship. (*pause*)

★ By this time the general style of counseling has become apparent. It is essentially the same procedure as that suggested by Thorne (400). First the counselor helps the client to develop her problem as fully as she is able to at this time. The counselor may use a variety of techniques to do so—neutral or ambiguous questions, questions about specific points, acceptance, reflection and clarification of feelings and thoughts. When the counselor has reached an understanding of some aspect of the problem, he interprets this to the client (**C76, C80, C88, C89, C92** and **C93** for example). The interpretations are made in such a way that the client feels free to accept, reject, or modify the interpretation. Frequently interpretation is sufficient to produce insight and self-understanding which leads to more desirable and satisfying client planning and behavior. Occasionally additional techniques are employed, such as suggesting courses of action as in **C94.** This cycle is repeated with variations until the client feels she can make satisfactory adjustments without the aid of a counselor.

S97—I feel like I have to know a boy pretty well before I go with him; and here you don't have too much of a chance to, unless you have a class with him every day or every other day; (*pause*) and even at that, you don't get to know him very well. (*pause*) Everything here seems so disconnected from what I'm used to at home, the principles I was brought up on, and things like that. (*long pause*)

C97—What do you mean by that? I have an inkling, but maybe you can tell me a little bit more.

S98—Well, I was brought up to believe in not smoking, and not to drink, and here most everyone accepts it. And of course, there's always a few people that don't; but it's quite hard to find the few people, I mean, (*pause*) I have gone out with quite a few people that don't, but they don't seem to have the other qualities that I want. (*laughs*) (*pause*) And, when I do find someone that I think is pretty nice and whatnot, I don't exactly know how to take them. I don't know, I can't take them for what they're worth, I mean, I have that difficulty, not knowing exactly where *I* stand. (*long pause*)

C98—How much of a problem has it been to you, the changing moral base from what you grew up on and what you find here?

S99—I haven't noticed it to be such a problem at all, you know, it just— maybe I suppressed it or something, and didn't realize what it was.

C99—Well, what I was wondering was whether it was much of a chore for you to fit into groups here (*pause*) which at least seems to now have some different ideas from what you grew up on.

S100—Well, I haven't had too much trouble in high school fitting into groups, I mean, especially if I was interested in what they were doing and whatnot; but lately I've found that I can't, because I'm not interested. I mean, I don't have the frame—ah—for instance, they'll be interested in something that they've done before, something that one of these kids has done before, and I didn't know about it, and I had no connection with it, and hence I'm not interested in it.

C100—You mean before you came to the campus?

S101—Yes. Mm-huh. Before, I started to be interested in certain groups. (*pause*) Seems that I just started to be interested in that—. . .

C101—Now, did I catch what you were talking about a while ago—that the people who now appear to have the kind of, let's say, moral values that you were brought up on may be a little less interesting to you than some of the others who are "smokers and drinkers?" (*long pause*)

S102—Again I realize that's just a difference in personality; and I mean that I could meet someone that did just as well, and that wouldn't have any effect on it.

C102—Of course, many of the other students contend that they were brought up the same way that you were, and had to change after they came to college. Of course, they may have swung the pendulum away over while they are here, too. And after they have had a chance to explore, the pendulum will swing back somewhat. (*pause*)

S103—I think I can't change my ideas until I get right down (*pause*) into doing something, and then I can't be able to participate in—I mean, I'll have to be participating in it to really get the most out of it; and if I don't want to participate in it, I'm not going to. I haven't. (*pause*) Now lately I've just kind of been sliding along and, whatever comes along (*pause*) I do have fun and all that, but there's just something, something always fails. It's not what I want, I mean, I enjoy it to a certain extent, but I know that I could be enjoying something so much better.

C103—Isn't it essentially acceptance that you're looking for, in a general sort of way; and it may come from the group, it may come from an individual; but being just a lttle bit starved on that side, and you may be looking for it a little bit more, or needing a little bit more than any other in the group.

S104—And then I think perhaps I haven't gone about it in the right way, gone about seeking it the right way.

C104—And I think part of that, that we've mentioned before, comes from (*pause*) the lack of experience in dealing on an affectional level. As yet, your experience with that hasn't been particularly successful, you haven't developed those skills that the others have. (*pause*) I think it tends to work in a vicious cycle, no skill, no affection; no affection, no skill.

S105—And all the time I can see it, I can't do anything about it.

C105—You can't quite get your fingers on it. (*long pause*) As was mentioned before, and it's important enough that it would be well to mention again, I think it has a direct bearing on the general course of events for you from here on, and just what general pattern are you going to take? Is it going to be essentially a career; (*pause*) is it going to be essentially marriage? Now, of course, both can go together. (*pause*) Which "inside of you" seems to be the thing that you want most, the thing you're going to need in the long haul most, and probably base some of your plans on that?

S106—What consideration for instance?

C106—I think career and non-career are essentially the things I'm driving at. It may make no difference in what you actually do in the training program, in terms of areas or the job that you prepare for, but in terms of your own thinking of what should take priority. (*pause*) If it is home and family (*pause*) that you consider to be pretty essential for your own satisfaction and happiness, then some of these ideas of relation with other students, particularly boyfriends, is a pretty important consideration now too. (*pause*) I think you just indicated, (*pause*)—"when I don't see the answers I'll just kind of forget about it, just let it alone,"—isn't going to solve anything.

S107—I know.

C107—And now—if that does seem to be a fairly important thing for you in the long run, a part of your plan, then it should be considered along with the idea of vocational plans; then we'll see what we can work out on the other, too.

S108—Actually, when you come right down to it, you've got to face it, you've got to face it.

C108—Yes. I think it will be easier to face *now*, to work out in a college environment, than it is to wait until after you're out and in a "more adult" set-up. (*pause*) It would be easier for you to do it here, where you have groups that you feel closer contact with, people your own age and group experience.

S109—That's another reason I came back, because I didn't have any contacts at all, working.

C109—It's harder to make contacts in a general community.

S110—It really is, with all the kids going to college.

C110—So you have a big group to practice on here.

S111—Mm-huh.

C111—You have a big social supply.

S112—Could I ask you what time it is?

C112—I have 9:15. Do you have a 9:00 class? (*client nods affirmatively*) (*pause*) When would you like to start your tests?

S113—Could I start them this afternoon?

C113—Okay. (*pause*) Do you want to wait until all your tests are in before we talk about these further, or do you want to come in before some of your tests are ready?

S114—Well, I'll probably wait until they are all finished.

C114—Okay. That will be right after vacation. You check after vacation, see how my appointment book is. I'll give this check sheet to the psychometrist right out here. Whenever you're ready, you just come in there, and she'll take care of you for your testing.

S115—Okay.

C115—You check my appointment book and then make an appointment when you finish your testing.

★ At this time it is essential that a counselor take another look at his client. He sees here a client who feels she has lacked affection in the home. She sees her father as difficult to approach and yet more understanding than her mother. She believes her mother has found it difficult to accept her as a daughter by comparison with her cousins. The client can see no basis of comparison because of the advantages enjoyed by the cousins over her. This lack of affection in the home has made it difficult for her to express affection to others, such as friends, dates, etc. She is afraid that this condition will negate any efforts toward marriage. She sees a portion of her difficulty and in S105 first indicates a feeling of futility toward any attempt to resolve the difficulty. She also realizes that she can't avoid facing the problems (S108).

This interview raises several points concerning counseling techniques and procedures. The client presented a vocational choice problem and requested aptitude tests in order to solve the problem. After some preliminary exploration, the counselor was convinced that information from aptitude tests alone would not afford a satisfactory solution to the presented problem. The counselor then decided to explore other areas to see if the problem was in fact broader than the one presented, rather than accept the problem as presented. In order to explore other areas, the counselor ignored several opportunities to follow up ideas and feelings expressed by the client (C16, C40, C47, C53, C67, C81). In the latter part of the interview when it became apparent *to the counselor* that the presented problem of vocational choice was related to if not a product of difficulty in interpersonal relations, the counselor was then faced with the task of developing client understanding of the relationship between these two problems. This is not an unusual situation in vocational counseling. Generally, in the beginning, the client prefers to deal solely with aptitude-test data rather than with the broader issues of self-concept as it affects other areas of living as well as vocation. See Super's (383) article on self-concept.

COUNSELOR'S NOTES ON THE FIRST INTERVIEW
(*Dictated Immediately after the Interview*)

★ The client came in to take some aptitude tests. She is considering whether or not she is in an appropriate field of study.

In high school the client's major interests were art and music. She went to College A for two years and a half and for some reason she became disinterested in college work and quit school. She worked for about a year in general office work as a file clerk and later on inventories and vouchers. She studied social work either at College A or here—I'm not sure which—and found the course work as such uninteresting. Then she changed to elementary education.

She's been at the university a year and a half and this semester is her first semester for professional course work in Education. She is taking a course in History of American Education from Dr. North. Some of the ideas that he has put out in the course concerning teachers, particularly incompetent teachers, have raised the question in the client's mind as to whether she will be a good teacher or not. That at least is a precipitating idea which caused her to come to the counseling service.

In the course of our conversation, the client indicated that her major interest was essentially directed toward a career, with only secondary priority placed on marriage and a family of her own. As the interview developed, we discussed her home and family to some extent. She described her father as a person difficult to talk with, at least she doesn't feel perfectly free in her relations with him, but does feel that essentially he loves her and "is for her." She feels that she has learned how to deal with him so that their relations are quite smooth. She said that he feels in the discussions that he is always right; but if she approaches him properly, there is no strain in the relationship. On the contrary, her mother does many material things for her; but the client feels that her mother rejects her as far as feeling and affection is concerned. Her mother criticizes her a great deal and holds her up to an unfavorable comparison to some of the client's girl friends. The relationship between the client and her mother is quite strained although there is nothing acute about the relationship.

The client has a brother who is 18 years old and enrolled in College B. The mother is quite fond of the brother and praises him a great deal. The client says she likes her brother very much and gets along with him rather well, although he is a little spoiled. From the discussion of the family relations, I then moved the conversation to the question of how this experience in the home along the affectional line enters into her relationship with other students on campus, particularly with her boyfriends. She says that it does definitely, and she has not made particularly close friends. She is unable to get the satisfactions that she would like to get from membership in various groups, and she has never found boyfriends with whom she felt easy and secure enough to express much affection for them. She raised the question of *whether she was capable of loving someone.* I pointed out the relationship between this concept and her lack of opportunity to learn how to express affection in her home environment and feel secure about it. She seemed to grasp the idea and thought that she was going around in circles here. She was somewhat concerned about it but recently has attempted to simply avoid the idea and just, as she put it, "muddle along."

I then pointed out the relationship between her ideas about boyfriends and her friends in general and her questions about vocational choice. I told her that apparently a prime consideration was whether she was essentially interested in a *career or in marriage.* They were not mutually exclusive but in terms of her own satisfaction over a long period of time that was the major question; and she seemed to agree or understand, although I wasn't absolutely sure. I suggested that in addition to trying to find out what her vocational goals should be it was equally, and possibly, more important to consider her relations with her boyfriends and what she wanted or could do about it. She seemed to understand this point; but I didn't have a chance to develop it because at that time she asked what time it was and she was already 15 minutes late for a class. So the interview ended. She said she would come back for another appointment after she had completed her testing.

SECOND INTERVIEW

(6 Days after the First Interview)

★ This was an unexpected interview, i.e., the client had not scheduled an appointment. In her first response, which was not recorded, the client asked about the results of the test she had taken.

C1—Let's see, you've taken only one test so far.

S1—Yes.

C2—That one hasn't been scored yet. That's the interest test. It's sent off to be scored, and it takes about a week to come back; so it might be better to wait until later to discuss the tests.

S2—Mm-huh.

C3—Was there anything that you wanted to talk about this morning other than the tests?

S3—Well, not that I know of. (*pause*).

C4—Did you want to spend any time this morning on the rest of your test battery?

S4—Well, I really won't have time. That's the trouble.

C5—Mm-huh.

S5—(*pause*) Could you explain something about the tests, the rest of the tests?

C6—Mm-huh. You've taken one interest test, vocational interest, and there are two here. I just mentioned another one, and it appraises interests in a little different way, so that you get both of them there. This is an intelligence test, individual intelligence test, and both of these you can call personality tests, and this is the teacher attitude test.

S6—Mm-huh.

C7—Is that what you meant?

S7—Yes. That's what I mean, Mm-huh.

C8—Well, it'll be after vacation before you get around to do any more on these; and as soon as you have finished these, then make an appointment with me and let's go over them.

S8—Mm-huh.

C9—Now, are you going to be faced with a decision to be made before next semester, such as the possibility of a change of college or something?

S9—Well, (*pause*) yes, I think so. I would like to know what I'm going to do.

C10—Mm-huh. Yes, pre-registration starts just as soon as you get back. Mm-huh.

S10—Mm-huh. I guess so.

C11—Mm-huh. You get back on Thursday, and the following Monday advance registration starts. (*pause*) I guess that runs for about two weeks. (*pause*) So then you'll still have time.

C11—I'll have to plan to take the tests as soon after I get back as possible.

C12—Well, probably within a week after you get back. (*pause*) Mm-huh. That will still give you a week of the advance registration period to work on it.

S12—Mm-huh. Yeah. I was kind of interested in knowing before vacation what it would be.

C13—Yes. It's kind of hard to take just one of the tests alone and have it make much sense for you, but of course you can get some material out of it. Usually, particularly in terms of vocational interest, the area in which your interests seem to be focused, you get a better understanding by taking both of them—

S13—Mm-huh.

C14—. . . which attempt to measure interest in two different ways, you get better information by taking both at the same time.

S14—Well, I'll come back then.

C15—Okay. Now, you know that you come here for the testing whenever you want. You don't have to make any prior arrangements, except for this one test. You'll have to schedule that one, the rest of them you take whenever you come over.

S15—Mm-huh. Okay.

C16—The one you need to make an appointment for is the individual intelligence test. Then when you finish all your testing, make an appointment with me.

S16—Okay. That'll be good.

C17—Mm-huh. I'll see you later then. (*pause*) Are you going home for Christmas?

S17—Yes. If I can get home, that is. Are you going out of town for Christmas?

C18—I expect to stay here.

S18—Mm-huh.

C19—We are trying to cajole some relatives into coming here.

S19—I can't imagine Christmas in this town.

C20—Merry Christmas to you.

S20—The same to you.

COUNSELOR'S NOTES ON THE SECOND INTERVIEW
(*Dictated Immediately after the Interview*)

★ This was a very short interview. The client had taken only the Strong Vocational Interest Blank, and the results of it were not ready. She plans to take the remainder of the battery after vacation and then see me again. The client came in today hoping to get the results of the Strong before vacation. I was not at all satisfied with this interview. Probably the client had something on her mind which was not brought out. I didn't give her an opportunity to do so.

PERSONAL DATA SHEET

★ Between the second and third interviews the client filled out a one-page personal data sheet. Following is a summary of the information from the personal data sheet:

Client:—Age: 21 years.
        Born in a metropolitan area in the state.
        Home Address: A suburb of the same metropolitan area.
        Marital Status: Single.
        Graduated from high school four years ago.

Attended College A for two years, major field was sociology.

At present is a junior in the College of Education, major field is elementary education.

Is not earning any of college expenses except for some work during vacations.

Occupational Plan: elementary school teacher.

Work Experience: (1) Nurse's aide in hospital during summer vacation two years ago. (2) Filing clerk in manufacturing company for four months about a year ago. (3) Invoice clerk in retail store for three months immediately following the filing clerk job. (4) Plans to work in a retail store during this Christmas vacation.

Leisure Time Activities: Dancing, skating, movies.

Family:—Both parents are living and still married.

Father: Age 54, completed one year of college, employed as a foreman.

Mother: Age 53, completed 2 years of college, housewife.

Brother: Age 18, enrolled in College B.

RECORD OF TEST DATA

Tests Administered:

(1) Strong Vocational Interest Blank, Form W—see profile sheet.

(2) Kuder Preference Record—Vocational, Form CM—see profile sheet.

(3) Minnesota Multiphasic Personality Inventory, Booklet Form—see profile sheet.

(4) Rotter Incomplete Sentences Blank, College Form—see Blank.

(5) Minnesota Teacher Attitude Inventory, Form A, Raw Score—27, Percentile Rank—22, Norm Group—beginning education juniors (academic majors).

(6) Wechsler-Bellevue Intelligence Scale, Form I—see profile sheet.

The testing was done by professionally qualified psychometrists.

THIRD INTERVIEW

(25 Days after Second Interview with the Christmas Holiday intervening)

C1—How are you this morning?

S1—All right. (*long pause*)

C2—Well let's see, where did we (*pause*) get to?

★ An opening response such as this gives the client wide latitude in choosing a topic to discuss. The counselor had expected to discuss rather fully the test results with the client in this interview. However, through a series of rather neutral counselor responses, the client was permitted to choose the topic for discussion; and she chose to ignore the test results. In fact, it was the counselor who introduced the rather meager discussion of the test data later in the interview (Third interview **C47** ff.). The reader may question the advisability of having the client take a battery of tests and then not discuss them fully with the client. However, all of the test results were used. Although there was little "formal" discussion of the test results *per se,* the results were woven into the interpretations which the counselor made throughout the interviews. See especially **C32** in the fourth interview in which the results of the MMPI were the basis for the interpretations made. Actually this is a more defensible procedure. Any interpretation which the counselor makes should be based on all data available, not just test data alone.

S2—Well, I think I've taken all the tests now. (*pause*)

C3—Yes. Would you repeat for me now the various questions you had as we ended last time?

S3—Well, what I wanted to know is whether I'd be suited for a school teacher or not; and if not a teacher, what else? (*long pause*)

C4—What's been your thinking since our last talk (*pause*) in regard to that question?

S4—I am a little undecided whether I'm going to come back to school next semester, (*pause*) so I'm just waiting to see what, how this,—I don't imagine this will have a whole lot of weight, because I know what I like.

C5—Mm-huh.

S5—But I think it might tell me something that I want to know.

C6—Tell me a little bit about the question, coming back or not next semester. I think that is new as far as I'm concerned.

S6—Mm-huh. Well, I thought I might take a commercial art course and really go on with it, I mean, if I like it. It's at least worth trying for, whether I succeed or not. If I enjoy doing it, I think it'll be worth it. (*long pause*)

C7—Yes. How about commercial art schools compared with art that you get here at the University?

S7—Well, one of my majors has been art, and I've taken a few courses,

HANKES REPORT FORM FOR—

STRONG VOCATIONAL INTEREST TEST - WOMEN

SEE OTHER SIDE FOR EXPLANATION

OCCUPATION	C	C+	B-	B	B+	A
STANDARD SCALE	0 10 20	30		40		50 60 70
ARTIST	-200 -150 -100 -50	0	50	100	150 200 250	
AUTHOR	-200 -150 -100 -50	0	50	100	150 200 250 300	
LIBRARIAN	0		50		100 150 200	
ENGLISH TEACHER	0	50		100		150
SOCIAL WORKER	-50	0	50		100	150
PSYCHOLOGIST	0	50		100	150	200
LAWYER	-50		50		100	150
SOCIAL SCIENCE TEACHER	-50	0	50		100	150
Y.W.C.A. SECRETARY	0	50	100	150	200	250
LIFE INSUR. SALESWOMAN	-50	0	50		100	150
BUYER	-50	0	50		100	150
HOUSEWIFE	-100	-50	0	50	100	150
ELEMENTARY TEACHER	-50	0	50		100	150
OFFICE WORKER	-150 -100	-50	0	50	100	150
STENOG.-SECY.	-100	-50	0	50	100	150
BUSINESS ED. TEACHER	-100	-50	0	50	100	150
HOME ECON. TEACHER	-50	0	50		100	150 200
DIETITIAN	-50	0	50		100	150
PHYSICAL ED. TEACHER	-50	0	50		100	150 200
OCCUP. THERAPIST	-50	0		50		100
NURSE	-50	0		50		100
MATH.-SCIENCE TEACHER	-50	0	50		100	150
DENTIST	-100	-50	0	50		100
LABORATORY TECHNICIAN	-50	0	50		100	150
PHYSICIAN	-50	0	50		100 150	200

STANDARD SCALE	75 70 65 60 55 50 45 40 35 30 25
FEMININITY-MASCULINITY	F -100 -50 0 M

NOTES

ENGINEERS NORTHWEST   MINNEAPOLIS 1, MINNESOTA   FORM WRB

NAME — MORGAN, Bette

AGENCY OR SCHOOL

AGE — 21

DATE

NUMBER

39

NAME __MORGAN,__ __Bette__ _____ AGE __21__ SEX __F__ Code __50'73--9'42__ _____ DATE OF TEST _____
Print   Last   First   Initial   M or F

First Revision, February 1951

SELF-INTERPRETING

PROFILE SHEET

for the
KUDER PREFERENCE RECORD
VOCATIONAL

Form C

MEN and WOMEN

DIRECTIONS FOR PROFILING

1. Copy the V-Score from the back page of your answer pad in the box at the right.   **41**

   If your V-Score is 37 or less, there is some reason for doubting the value of your answers. 〔I〕 your other scores may not be very accurate. 〔If〕, *your V-Score is 45 or more,* you may not have understood the directions, since 44 is the highest possible score. *If your score is not between 38 and 44,* inclusive, you should see your adviser. He will probably recommend that you read the directions again, and then that you fill out the blank a second time, being careful to follow the directions exactly and to give sincere replies.

   If your V- Score is between 38 and 44, inclusive, go ahead with the following directions.

2. Copy the scores 0 through 9 in the spaces at the top of the profile chart. Under "OUTDOOR" find the number which is the same as the score at the top. Use the numbers under M if you are a 〔m〕an and the numbers under F if you are a 〔wom〕an. Draw a line through this number from one side to the other of the entire column under OUTDOOR. Do the same thing for the scores at the top of each of the other columns. If a score is larger than any number in the column, draw a line across the top of the column: if it is smaller, draw a line across the bottom.

3. With your pencil blacken the entire space between the lines you have drawn and the bottom of the chart. The result is your profile for the *Kuder Preference Record—Vocational.*

	0 45	1 22	2 19	3 37	4 31	5 49	6 18	7 19	8 50	9 34
	OUTDOOR	MECHANICAL	COMPUTATIONAL	SCIENTIFIC	PERSUASIVE	ARTISTIC	LITERARY	MUSICAL	SOCIAL SERVICE	CLERICAL

Published by SCIENCE RESEARCH ASSOCIATES
228 South Wabash Avenue, Chicago 4, Illinois
Copyright 1951, by G. Frederic Kuder. Copyright under International Copyright Union. All rights reserved under Fourth International American Convention (1910). Printed in the U.S.A. Copyright 1951 in Canada.

Please use code number 7-299 when reordering this profile.

T-21-X

Reprinted with permission of the publisher,
Science Research Associates.

The Minnesota Multiphasic Personality Inventory

Starke R. Hathaway and J. Charnley McKinley

Scorer's Initials _____

Name _____ MORGAN, Bette

Address _____

Occupation _____ Student _____ Date Tested _____

Education _____ College junior _____ Age 21

Marital Status _____ Single _____ Referred by _____ self

NOTES

The experimental scales—Re, St, and Do were not available to the counselor at the time of this case. They are reported here for the interest of the reader.

F

Female

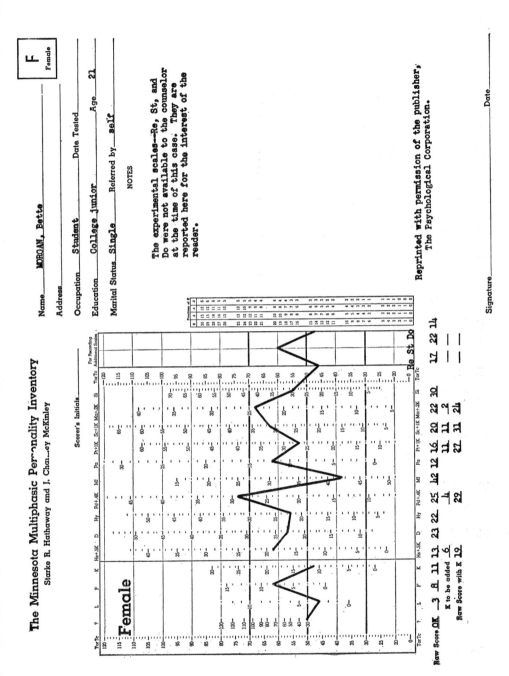

Female

Raw Score OK −3 8 11 13 23 22 25 12 12 16 20 22 30   17 22 14

K to be added 6   4   2   — —

Raw Score with K 12   22   11 11 27 31 24   — —

Re St Do

Reprinted with permission of the publisher,
The Psychological Corporation.

Signature _____ Date _____

INCOMPLETE SENTENCES BLANK — COLLEGE FORM

Name **Bette Morgan**   Sex **F**   Age **21**   Marital Status **Single**

School **Education**   Class **Junior**   Date

Complete these sentences to express your real feelings. Try to do every one.
Be sure to make a complete sentence.

1. I like **to dance.**

2. The happiest time **I've had can't be distinguished from my other happy times.**

3. I want to know **more about music, ballet, art politics and world affairs.**

4. Back home **I hope to be in four weeks.**

5. I regret **having gone to school after my first year at College A.**

6. At bedtime **I try to set aside the cares of the day in hope for a new chance tomorrow.**

7. Boys **are full of wild stories and overgrown ideas but they also have an unconquerable spirit for life that is undeniable.**

8. The best **can be found in any situation if you know what to look for.**

9. What annoys me **is the uncertainty of purpose while going to school.**

10. People **are interesting if you take time to understand them.**

11. A mother **is responsible for not only the care but the love of her child.**

12. I feel **the spring in the air.**

13. My greatest fear **is loneliness.**

14. In high school **the clique was all important and I managed to hold my head above water.**

15. I can't **do all the things I'd like to do but I would be satisfied if would do the things I can do.**

(TURN PAGE OVER AND CONTINUE)

Printed in U. S. A. 50-111 AS

JULIAN B. ROTTER, AUTHOR

16. Sports _____I like._____

17. When I was a child ____I had a rip rore!en time with the kids I knew._____

18. My nerves ____are about the same as they are in other people._____

19. Other people __are like me in nature some with more and some with less of what____
    I have yet we differ in experience and that's what makes people so interesting.

20. I suffer ____because I'm not doing what I want to._____

21. I failed __many time but realize that I have the potential to succeed at something.

22. Reading ____one of my handicaps since I read slowly._____

23. My mind __is as good as any one else's (if not better)_____

24. The future __seems uncertain but there will be a future regardless of what it is_
    that needs to be prepared for.

25. I need __friendship and love and a sense of usefulness._____

26. Marriage __is the happiest result of love._____

27. I am best when __I forget myself._____

28. Sometimes ____I wonder why I spend the lonely nite._____

29. What pains me __is the temperature in this room._____

30. I hate ____being an outsider._____

31. This school ____is far from perfect._____

32. I am very _____

33. The only trouble _____

34. I wish ___I could travel._____

35. My father __can be very nice when he wants to be._____

36. I secretly _____

37. I ___don't know whether I'm in love or not._____

38. Dancing ____is fun._____

39. My greatest worry is __what I will do next semester._____ _____

40. Most girls ____get married._____

WECHSLER-BELLEVUE INTELLIGENCE SCALE
FOR ADOLESCENTS AND ADULTS

RECORD FORM I

NAME **MORGAN, Bette** AGE **21** EDUC. **Jr.** DATE OF EXAM_____ NO____
OCCUP. **Junior--Education** NAT._____ BIRTHDATE_____ COLOR **W**
PLACE OF EXAM. **Counseling Center** EXAM. BY **T.C.** PREVIOUS EXAM. **Stanford-Binet**

TABLE OF WEIGHTED SCORES†

RAW SCORE

Equivalent Weighted Score	Information	Comprehension	Digit Span	Arithmetic	Similarities	Vocabulary	Picture Arrangement	Picture Completion	Block Design	Object Assembly	Digit Symbol	Equivalent Weighted Score
18	25	20		14	23-24	41-42	20+		38+			18
17	24	19	17	13	21-22	39-40	20		38	26		17
16	23	18	16	12	20	37-38	19		35-37	25	66-67	16
15	21-22	17		11	19	35-36	18	15	33-34	24	62-65	15
14	20	16	15		17-18	32-34	16-17	14	30-32	23	57-61	14
13	18-19	15	14	10	16	29-31	15		28-29		53-56	13
12	17				15	27-28	14	12	25-27	20-21	49-52	12
11	15-16	12-13	13		13-14	25-26	12-13		23-24	19	45-48	11
10	13-14	11	12	8	12	22-24	11	11	20-22	18	41-44	10
9	12	10	11	7	11	20-21		10	18-19	17	37-40	9
8	10-11	9			9-10	17-19	9	9	16-17	16	33-36	8
7	9	8		6	8	15-16	7-8	8	13-15	14-15	29-32	7
6	7-8	7	9	5	7	12-14	6	7	11-12	13	24-28	6
5	6	5-6			5-6	10-11	5		8-10	12	20-23	5
4	4-5	4	8	4	4	7-9	4	6	6-7	10-11	16-19	4
3	2-3	3	7	3	3	5-6	2-3	5	3-5	9	12-15	3
2	1	2	6		1-2	3-4	1	4	1-2	8	8-11	2
1	0	1		2	0	1-2	0	3	0	7	4-7	1
0		0	5	1		0		2		5-6	0-3	0

SUMMARY

TEST	R.S.	WT.S.
INFORMATION	19	13
COMPREHENSION	14	12
DIGIT SPAN	10	7
ARITHMETIC	9	12
SIMILARITIES	21	17
(VOCABULARY)	( )	( )
VERBAL SCORE*		61
P. ARRANGEMENT	10	9
P. COMPLETION	13	13
BLOCK DESIGN	30	14
OBJECT ASSEMBLY	22	13
DIGIT SYMBOL	43	10
PERFORMANCE SCORE*		59
TOTAL SCORE		

*Proration is necessary if four or six Verbal tests are given or four Performance tests.

		I.Q.
VERBAL SCALE	61	117
PERFORM. SCALE	59	111
FULL SCALE	120	116

†Clinicians who wish to draw a "psychograph" on the above table may do so by connecting the appropriate raw scores; however, one must recognize the relative unreliability of these subtest scores when they are thus treated.

TEST ANALYSIS AND OBSERVATIONS   The examiner feels that this is a good estimate of the client's intelligence. Nothing unusual was observed in the examination.

but they haven't been commercial courses, been more fine art courses; and there's not many commercial courses offered here, and this correspondence course that I was thinking of is strictly commercial. It's commercial advertising.

C8—Where is this school? Where is it located?

S8—(client states the name and location of a commercal art correspondence school). (*long pause*)

C9—And then you would live at home? (*pause*)

S9—That's the only hitch. (*laughs*)

C10—Mm-huh. (*long pause*) Well, is part of that the result of dissatisfaction with school here?

S10—Well, I have been going with a fellow who is going to be stationed at Army Camp A, and he'll be coming home quite often.

C11—Mm-huh.

S11—And I think that will probably help quite a bit, (*pause*) but I don't know whether it would be satisfactory or not.

C12—Now, what would be satisfactory?

S12—Well, the fact that he'll be there on weekends.

C13—Mm-huh. (*long pause*) Well, what are your questions about it, whether it will be satisfactory?

S13—Well, whether I could stand the family during the week, you know. (*pause*) Sounds terrible to say it this way, but—(*long pause*)

C14—You are wondering if (*pause*) getting to see your boyfriend weekends (*pause*) is enough to balance off the staying home during the rest of the week? (*long pause*) What is the nature of the relationship (*pause*) with your boyfriend?

S14—Well (*pause*) I don't know. It would be—(*pause*) I can't seem to —he asked me to marry him, but I don't know how it will turn out yet.

C15—How do you feel about him?

S15—Well, it's hard to say. I really don't know. I think sometimes I'm in love with him, and sometimes I'm not sure. (*long pause*)

C16—What are your doubts, and what raises the question?

S16—Well, (*long pause*) I've been going with him for a long time, and he's always liked me quite a bit, but I never had given him a second thought, you know. I just haven't looked at him in the same light, (*pause*) but he doesn't think I'm sincere, and I sometimes wonder if I am. (*laughs*) He can't understand it, and I can't explain it to him. I don't know how it will work out. (*pause*)

C17—How recent is this development?

S17—Since Christmas. (*long pause*)

C18—Then it came as more of a surprise to you? You weren't expecting it?

S18—No, not exactly. After we'd talked, I kind of thought, well, I should do something about what we talked about; and I knew that Bill would probably call at Christmas, and he did. (*long pause*).

> ★ This is some evidence of the effectiveness of the first interview in stimulating the client to thought and action about her difficulties in interpersonal relations. Self-planning and action outside of the interview are good criteria of the effectiveness of counseling. One might wonder if her actions are premature or immature at this point. The counselor approaches this question in his next response.

C19—Are you wondering if (*pause*) going with Bill may be an escape from your family?

S19—It could possibly be.

C20—And is that one of your doubts, one of your questions about your feeling towards him? (*pause*)

S20—No, I don't think I would let that, that *entirely* make up my mind. (*pause*) That is, it does have weight though. (*long pause*) I realize that there are parts of things that I have to overlook, (*pause*) and, I hadn't. (*pause*) We went together when we were in high school; and afterwards he went to College B, and I went to College A; and then I transferred to the University. And we hadn't really been together a whole lot since then, and I just feel I have to get to know him before I can make any statements. People can change.

C21—What did you have in mind when you said things that you need to overlook? (*pause*)

S21—Oh, well, they're just little insignificant things. I mean, (*laughs*) nothing too great I would say. (*long pause*) He's always been rather— (*pause*) Oh, he's the type that you get the impression that he's awfully sure of himself, and he actually does have a feeling (*pause*) of confidence in himself. (*pause*) It seems like underneath all that veneer that he's entirely different than what he really is, I mean, what he shows to people that he is. (*pause*)

C22—And how well do you think you understand what's underneath the veneer? Is that one of your questions?

S22—That's one of the questions. (*long pause*) Get the impression that he's very—ah—might say, aggressive in a way; and yet (*pause*) he likes to have logical reasons for everything. (*pause*) New Year's Eve was the last time I saw him. We decided that we would wait before we—we wouldn't see each other until the end of the semester, and then he would know whether I really (*laughs*) cared for him or not. (*pause*) But as far as I can understand, it's not something you can just decide yes or no. You just have to understand the situation. And yet, we don't seem to get any place when we're together because it's just something that we just— we just can't express ourselves too well so that the other one can understand us.

C23—So that you get a feeling of being close but at the same time, one of distance.

S23—No, it's not that. It's (*pause*) I just can't express how I feel. I get all—I have a feeling that he wouldn't think that I was—oh, I don't know. Just, he kind of sets up an attitude—this can't be; too good to happen, you know, not logical. In fact, Christmas—we went out Christmas eve and, he called when I wasn't home, Wednesday, and I called him Thursday; and I actually didn't think he was going to call me back Christmas, and so I told him just—I don't want him to give me anything that— (*pause*) I mean, I really was sincere; so I called him back, and he said that—I was real mad about it because he hadn't called back and hadn't trusted me that much; and he said, well he thought it was hypocrisy to go on. He's the type that thinks quite a bit about things, you know. He gives the impression that he doesn't care, when he really does. (*pause*) I know that—at least I *feel* that he loves me. I mean, I can just sense that, I mean, I know he does, and yet I know that he's kind of down on the whole thing. (*pause*)

★ The client was finding it difficult to express herself here; witness the pauses, the incomplete sentences, the "backing-and-filling," and the conflicting and ambivalent expressions. It would have been better if the counselor had summarized the expressions in S23 rather than go on to another idea as he did in C24. When a client is laboring with some difficult expressions it behooves the counselor to stick close to the topic at hand until the client is able to verbalize it more freely.

C24—How well are you able to express your affection for him, to show him what your feelings are?

S24—How what?

C25—How well?

S25—Pretty well. (*laughs*)

C26—You don't find yourself being unable to express your own feelings to him.

S26—No, except in words. I mean, I can't tell him why I like him now when I didn't before. (*long pause*) Would you think that perhaps that going out with him and seeing him quite often might, might improve the situation?

C27—I was wondering how well you felt you knew each other, and then how much you've been together, how much you've had a chance to get to know each other?

★ The counselor avoided answering the client's direct question by asking in return a rather ambiguous question designed to further expression by the client.

S27—Well, I've had a very good chance to get to know him. I mean, what he's really like, and what he thinks. He's very outspoken, and he doesn't keep things to himself. (*pause*) I think I know him pretty well, except that it seems like he's done *so much* in the last four years, that I haven't had any experience, you know, he always has a lot of girlfriends, and whatnot. And I sometimes wonder if I could measure up to all the girls he's gone with.

C28—Measure up to your competition. (*client laughs*) How would you describe this fellow that I'd get a picture of him, what he's like . . .

★ The phrase, "How would you describe (someone)," has proved to be a very effective *nonspecific* stimulus to client expression about someone else—mother, boyfriend, etc. The client can be as impersonal about the description as he feels he needs to and yet feel free to discuss the person.

S28—Well, that's real hard to say. (*pause*) He gives the impression of being a man of the world, always telling jokes and things, and—(*long pause*) I don't know, but it seems to me like he always has a good time, he always watches out for himself, he's always going to get somewheres no one else does. He went into the Army after he graduated from College B; and he made top grades at College B, was in a good fraternity, always had a girlfriend, and was the top in everything; and I thought, well, I'd bet he'll meet his Waterloo in the Army, you know, because he's just not Army type. But he was in the Army, and he became ill after his first few weeks in the Army. But he came out of the hospital, he's head of his platoon now, and gets off week ends. He's being transferred to another army camp—for further training, and is being commissioned a second lieutenant. (*long pause*) He's the kind that's very logical and has to have a reason for everything; and I think that's one thing I admire about him. (*long pause*)

C29—Had you dated him much when he was at College B?

S29—No, except during vacations; and I didn't go to College B at all. (*long pause*)

C30—How ready do you think he is to get married?

S30—I really don't know. Sometimes I think he's seen the world and knows what he likes and is ready to settle down and get married; and he has said himself that he doesn't think he's ready to settle down and get married. All our friends are married. We have a lot of friends in common, and just all of them are married. And yet he goes on, "We won't be ready to get married for ten years yet." (*pause*) So I don't know. That's what he says, but I think he wants to get married, too. He wants to, and yet I don't think he's really ready. (*long pause*)

C31—How about you?

S31—Oh, I'm ready. (*laughs*) (*pause*) At least, I think I am, may not be. (*long pause*)

C32—Why your home town rather than here, as far as your being away from Bill?

★ An alternative response here could have been—"Would you like to talk about this?"

S32—Well, (*pause*) it's more or less been a problem. (*pause*) Of course, he'll have to spend part of his time in our home town, and that means just part of his time here. And he does have quite a few girlfriends in our home town. And I *just don't* like the University very well at all. I may like it better than I do home, and I have a feeling that maybe being on campus would keep me on my toes a lot more than when I'm at home, because I'm always better in an environment where I am inspired to be better. (*long pause*)

C33—How will it be at home, if you go home next semester? (*long pause*)

S33—Probably very boring. (*pause*) I'll have my art, I mean, I'll have something to do; (*pause*) but it's pretty boring all right. (*pause*) Christmas I know it was, just sitting around waiting for the telephone to ring, I thought I'd really go mad. (*long pause*) My family just isn't very creative. They like to listen to the radio a lot, and Sunday afternoon we'd turn the radio on, read the paper, and never budge; and that just kills me. Oh, I love to go out and do things; and then when I don't have anyone to go out and do things with is when I feel kind of hateful, sometimes. (*long pause*)

★ The client indicated some understanding that she may be partially responsible for the poor relations with her family when she stated—". . . when I don't have anyone to go out and do things with is when I feel kind of hateful, sometimes." Prior to this point she has placed almost all of the blame on her mother.

C34—Now about the University, what is it you find that is not interesting to you here?

S34—Well, the main reason's because I don't have a crowd to go around with.

C35—Mm-huh. Then you have a crowd to go around with at home?

S35—Well, I do have some friends, not a crowd. I mean, I have friends scattered . . .

C36—Will it be better in that respect?

S36—Mm-huh. (*long pause*)

C37—I think I would question, until I got more information, the correspondence work in commercial art.

> ★ Some counselors would denounce this introjection of counselor opinion. Arguments can be advanced to support both sides of the issue. Some would contend that the client is entitled to counselor opinions when they can be supported by facts or sound judgment. Others would contend that actually we are not dealing with "facts" but with the affect. The counselor in the present case expressed his opinion in order to block a premature and possibly an immature decision and to cause the client to consider further the issue. Dollard, *et al.* (*118*) would call this "challenging the client's story."

S37—I thought it might add—(*counselor interrupts*)

C38—Not commercial art, but correspondence work.

S38—That's what dad said. He said don't just go by the advertisement, but try to find out all about it. So I wrote in to one of the magazines for a reference, and they look into college standards.

> ★ Note the planning and action taken since the last interview: client considered going into commercial art training and has investigated some of the opportunities.

C39—We have some kind of a directory here. Let me see if I can find it. (*long pause while the counselor asks another counselor to search for the directory.*) Can't seem to locate it at the moment. It isn't too (*pause*) refined in evaluation, but it does clean out some of the complete "gyp-joints."

S39—Mm-huh.

C40—Now, even if it were a good correspondence school, our art department, anyway, seems to think that there are very few correspondence schools that can actually give adequate instruction in art. Now, I was just wondering, if you're interested at all in it, whether you might be able to get what you want and need better at College C (in home town).

S40—Mm-huh.

C41—Possibly evening school.

S41—That's an idea.

C42—College C does have a rather extensive evening school, and I would think they would have commercial art work.

S42—Mm-huh. The only thing about College C is it's an awfully stiff school unless you're real good, they try to flunk you out. And, if you've graduated from there, you can feel like you've done something; but I don't know whether I can do it, and I don't want to, I mean just be—

C43—Well, it may be that their evening school is a little different from regular day school. They seem to make a difference. (*knock at door*) Pardon me. (*Another counselor brings in the correspondence school directory.*) What was the name of the school?

S43—(*client gives name of the art school.*)—(*long pause while counselor searches directory*).

C44—Yes, it's on the list. (*pause*) Approved private correspondence school by this agency. Now, that does not mean that it's necessarily really high class, but at least it does meet the minimum standards. Here is a picture of the building for that school.

S44—Hmmm. Not a very pretty building.

C45—You might take a look at College C's evening classes. Some of them are college credit classes, and some of them are not. You may or may not be wanting to get college credit out of it, and that of course makes some difference in the standards they will hold you to, or how practical a course you're interested in, or how theoretical you're interested in. You might find that they have the course you want there. You can then get the face-to-face instruction which would appear to me to be pretty important in art instruction, that you have a chance to see some of the work of the instructor and have him criticize your work, what you've done.

S45—Mm-huh. I see.

C46—You can check the telephone directory and find a listing there. You might find a commercial art school in your home town that you can attend. (*pause*)

S46—Well, I know that College C night school is supposed to be a lot easier than the day school.

C47—Yes. You have many people there who are not caring about grades in the night school, who are taking it just for the same reason that you're taking it; and they do gear their work then according to what the students want. (*long pause*) Before we get too far along, let's see what we've got here. (*Referring to test data*) (*long pause*) Here is the one vocational interest test. (*shows the client the profile*) (*pause*) That compares your interests with people who are doing those various kinds of occupations. They have been with the work for, oh, three years or more. That is, they're not just beginners who may leave the field immediately. They've been in it long enough that we presume they like the work. (*pause*) The scores out there in the "A" bracket would indicate that your vocational interests are quite similar to those particular people; "B+" then is also quite similar. As you go on down, your interests get more and more different from those people, until you get in the "C" area there, then your interests are probably somewhat different from artists or home ec. teacher, or whatever the particular group is. (*pause*)

S47—Guess in artist I'm "B—" (*pause*) I thought one time I would like to go into occupational therapy; and I guess I've tried just about everything. (*long pause*)

C48—This is the other test that will go along with it. Now here, it is more of a preference within your own frame of reference. Seems that you tend to prefer artistic kinds of activities more than any of the others, and you tend to reject clerical work more than any other. The rest of them fall pretty much around the average. (*pause*) Now, that's a little different from this (*Strong VIB*) actually, where you have the office worker and steno-secretary scores coming out a little.

S48—I wondered about that.

C49—Well, it doesn't necessarily disagree because you'll probably find many people doing clerical and secretarial work who have no more interest for it than you do, because your interests can be similar to that group of people. (*long pause*) You notice housewife comes out to be one of your stronger interests.

S49—Mm-huh. (*long pause*)

C50—Elementary teacher does, (*pause*) social worker, housewife, occupational therapist, and the general office worker.

S50—The elementary teacher comes out farther than the others, doesn't it?

C51—Just about the same, actually. (*long pause*) These artists represent a variety of artists: portrait, landscape, still life painters, sculptors, and commercial artists. (*pause*)

S51—I wonder if I'd be taking too much of a chance to do that, after all the schooling I'd have. The logical thing would be to go on to school and graduate, with only a year to go. (*pause*)

C52—Yes. It seems like, that if you do, that you would be throwing away—

S52—A lot.

C53—Your goal of getting a degree in college.

★ The counselor's assumption that the client wanted to get a college degree is an error which is frequently made. This is an example of the counselor's assuming that the client has the same values and goals as the counselor.

S53—I've never had that goal. Some people do, but I never did have. I don't know why.

C54—Yes. (*long pause*) It depends somewhat on what you think you want. Actually, a degree, as such, for general cultural purposes (*pause*) wouldn't be worth much more to you than the three years which you'd have. (*long pause*)

S54—But it'd be better if I went on with art work. I'd be doing something that I really like. And, I don't know, I have a feeling that if you really do what you're interested in, even though you fail at it, you know you're doing what you want to do.

★ Here the client expresses motivation and determination which was lacking in the first interview. This is very tentative, as the client indicates in her next response.

C55—Yes. (*pause*) Are you thinking of art work primarily for your own use, or are you planning to do commercial art work? (*pause*)

S55—Well, I haven't set any definite aim, and that's my trouble. I can't set definite aims, what I'm aiming at. I thought I'd take the course, and then see where it leads.

C56—What have you had here in practical art work?

S56—Oh, I've had Oil Painting, and Design (*pause*) and that's about all. (*long pause*) (*Counselor refers to university catalog.*)

C57—There is quite an array of courses in painting and drawing, (*pause*) many in art crafts; about four courses in basketry, toy making, bookbinding, weaving, pottery; three courses in pottery; a couple in jewelry. (*long pause*) I keep wondering if you go home and take the commercial art course (*pause*) whether you're actually (*pause*) going to have enough to keep you interested, (*pause*) whether working alone on an assignment is going to be particularly appealing to you?

S57—Mm-huh. I know what you mean. I feel like I might lack interest in it, too. I might let it slide and not finish it.

C58—Actually only about three per cent of the people who enroll in commercial correspondence courses ever complete them.

S58—Is that all?

C59—About three per cent. (*pause*)

S59—And I have a feeling that my family won't be too inspiring to do a whole lot. I don't know enough. I have to be inspired, I can't work under conditions when I'm not at my best.

C60—Where does that come from, that come mostly from within yourself, or is that from stimulation from other students and teachers?

S60—What, the inspiration?

C61—Mm-huh. (*pause*)

S61—Well, possibly it comes from within myself.

C62—You mean you thought you need other people to check on your ideas, to get ideas from—

S62—Yeah. I'm sure—

C63—Will you be missing a good bet just working alone on your work?

S63—I think I probably would. (*long pause*)

C64—Is this of secondary importance (*pause*) or, is being in your home town your main goal right now, that is, being there weekends?

S64—No, I don't think that's the main reason. (*long pause*) Bill is the kind that needs inspiration himself, and I realize that I'm going to have to be on the ball to—not to hold him exactly—but to make things interesting. And if I'm going to be dull myself, it's not going to be worth anything. (*long pause*)

C65—Now how does what you do next semester fit in with that idea? (*pause*)

S65—I don't think I understand what you mean. (*long pause*)

C66—How does your consideration of art work or what you get here at the university—how does that fit into whether you're going to be somewhat of an inspiration to Bill? (*pause*)

S66—Well, I realize that I have to be enjoying what I'm doing; and I know that this semester I certainly haven't felt satisfied with my accomplishments at all. (*pause*) Of course, if I had a different attitude about it—(*pause*) Like last night, I was reading History, and I just couldn't get anything out of it. It just stared me in the face, and I just couldn't read it. And then I thought if I had an object in reading it, I thought, well, there's a discussion class. I'm very slow in saying things in discussion, and I thought, well, why don't I read it and just see how many things I can discuss in class and give my own viewpoints on them. So I read it, and I felt like I had a goal in mind. I could do it, but as far as just doing it for no reason at all, I just can't. (*pause*) And perhaps I won't have any goal at all when I'm home. Perhaps I'll just disintegrate.

C67—I think, the more you describe the situation, that you're apt to have even less than you have here.

S67—Mm-huh.

C68—(*pause*) What are the things that are interesting to you, that you enjoy doing, that you get a bang out of, that make you, yourself, feel good?

S68—Well, I don't really know, I haven't thought about it too much. (*long pause*) I guess being around people and expressing my viewpoints and whatnot, and sharing ideas.

C69—Mm-huh.

S69—And I possibly wouldn't get that, I don't know—(*pause*) I think as you say there's more opportunity, if I can find it here; but it's up to me to find it.

★ Here the client accepts a fairly realistic evaluation of her situation, and, what may be more important, indicates that the responsibility for action is hers and an apparent willingness on her part to accept this responsibility; yet there is an implication of futility about the whole situation.

C70—Well, at the same time apparently you haven't found it, certainly not to the present—

S70—That's the way I feel about it. I've gone to school so much, and I haven't found it. I wonder if I ever will. (*pause*)

C71—There's another alternative that we haven't mentioned yet; and if you go back to your home town, and that is to get a job.

★ Note that the counselor did not respond to the feeling of futility and despondency which the client expressed in **S70**. He has acted in this same manner in several other instances. This probably is the major weakness in the whole case. Is he not sensitive to the feelings and attitudes being expressed? Probably he is aware of them. Then, why does he not respond to them? A real possibility is that the counselor does not feel able to accept and work with the feelings and attitudes expressed. If the counselor has not yet learned to recognize and accept his own feelings, the client's expression along these lines may cause him to feel uncomfortable and anxious and thus be threatening to him. This may also explain the strong emphasis in this counselor's behavior on gaining information about the client. He may feel more comfortable in dealing with cognitive material, and therefore concentrates his efforts in that area.

S71—Oh, well, I wanted to get a job and do the correspondence work on the side. I was considering getting a contact job at an office. It's a good paying job and doesn't require a lot of typing which I don't like, and I would make contacts that way. (*pause*)

C72—Well, how does your job fit into your social satisfaction?

S72—Well, if I can accomplish something in a job, it would—

C73—Is that apt to be more satisfying to you than going to school? (*long pause*)

> ★ In this and subsequent responses the counselor has the client evaluate the merits of the alternative courses of action.

S73—Maybe it is. I had worked before, as I said, but I never had felt like I really accomplished anything on my job. I'd just go to work and come back, and that's all. (*pause*)

C74—Well, would this job you have in mind be different? (*long pause*)

S74—It may be, if I meet some nice people, and really make the most of it. (*long pause*)

C75—We come back again to this idea of meeting people, making friends and that sort of thing, where you haven't been able to do that sort of thing to your liking here or in previous jobs that you've had. Now, is there any indication as to how things are going to *change* (*pause*) either here or at home with a job?

> ★ The counselor puts the issue up to the client. It is as if he had said —"you have floundered from home to school to job without much personal satisfaction. Now you have been proposing to continue in this same kind of behavior hoping that another change in environment will bring personal satisfaction when similar changes in the past have not. Isn't it possible that the change must be in you and not your environment?" Perhaps it would have been better if the counselor had made this response.

S75—I've given it quite a bit of consideration, too, and I don't know. (*pause*) I really don't know—I don't know what it takes to go ahead and—(*long pause*) About the only thing I know is the negative side. I don't know how to overcome it.

C76—Now is it the same thing occurring in several different settings, more a function of *you* than of the situation?

> ★ To be able to make as frank a statement as this and have it accepted by the client (**S76**) is indicative of good rapport. The counselor has to judge when to be openly frank with the client. If it is wrongly timed, the client will become defensive as she does slightly in **S76** but the relationship is not disturbed and **C76** actually aids progress.

S76—It seems that way. But in a way I wonder if—In high school, I didn't have any trouble, too much—I know, with the church people—

C77—Mm-huh. Well now, what's different?

S77—Well, it's the difference being that I was a part of that group; and I don't seem to be a part of anything, and I don't have the qualities to make myself a part of anything. I don't know, I just build up a feeling that I'm outside of everything, and I'm just way down underneath.

★ In this and her two preceding responses the client summarizes some rather disturbing feelings about her social adjustment. In the next response she indicates an interest in trying to make a better adjustment and lists some of her abilities which will help her do so.

C78—Mm-huh. (*long pause*)

S78—If there was something I could put my finger on, or something I could work for, those I could overcome because I have worked for things and accomplished things, and maybe I can. I do have quite a bit of determination when I'm working for something. (*long pause*)

★ In S78 the counselor has a choice between two expressions to respond to: (1) "There is something wrong with me or my adjustment. I don't know what it is." or (2) "I have to find something of value to work for." The counselor responded to the second. The first alternative would help the client gain insights concerning herself; the second would help her get answers but which perhaps would be only partially understood.

C79—Of course, right now you have two or three conflicting possible goals: (*pause*) what is your answer to Bill going to be, what your attitudes seem to be toward work and school, and how important those things are to you. (*long pause*) Such that you are torn two or three different ways. (*long pause*) Does that seem to be the key to the questions that you had in mind?

S79—Mm-huh. (*long pause*)

C80—What answer have you given Bill? (*long pause*)

S80 Nothing definite. I said that I'd better think about it awhile. I thought there's an awful lot to consider. It's not that I didn't think that Bill wasn't in love with me or think that I don't know how it would turn out and I didn't trust him—(*long pause*)

C81—How strong is the physical attraction between you two? (*pause*)

★ Here the counselor shuts off the client's beginning explorations of her adjustment to others. Simple encouragement to continue seems indicated.

S81—It's pretty strong. (*long pause*) I think I've had the feeling it wouldn't last, that (*pause*) while he attained so much in high school that I'd probably disappoint him. He seems to have had so much, and can explain so much, and been on top so much; and I don't seem to find myself. I'm just wandering around someplace somewhere. I don't have the same popularity, the same kind that I had before. And yet it seems like I can understand Bill, that I know him. I can see what he needs and, although I don't seem to have exactly what it takes to meet him right now, I think maybe I will.

★ After expressing rather strong negative attitudes about herself, the client indicates that if she just can have a little time she believes she can work things out satisfactorily. This air of hopefulness which is now appearing in the client's responses is encouraging.

C82—What you're looking for, I gather, is then a few months to work out your own ideas, and what it's going to take—ah—inner satisfaction. And that's the idea of delay. Then the questions come of what is the best setting, how to go about that. (*long pause*) What are the things that you need to make a decision on pretty soon, or before the end of the semester? You have to decide whether you're going to stay in school or not. (*pause*) Then there are some other things.

★ The counselor has *repeatedly* failed to reflect the client's feelings of inadequacy and has directed his responses toward consideration of more external and current problems. In general, it is a moot question as to which should be done, but in this case the client has repeatedly brought up her feelings of inadequacy.

S82—Well, let's see. There's Bill and me—(*pause*)

C83—(*Counselor looks at his watch*) There are a good many things here to be considered. I think maybe we'd better take a little more time on them. Let's see what my schedule is. Do you have Wednesday at this time available?

S83—Mm-huh.

C84—Let's see if we can begin to piece some of the things together Wednesday. Maybe we won't get it all done. The main question, as I see it, is what are the things you need to have a chance to explore or experience to develop your own self, utilizing your resources and have some goal and know what you're working toward, that are satisfying to you. And in what sort of a setting are those best met. What you need to do to work them out.

S84—Yes. That's exactly what I need.

C85—I guess we've gathered most of the information that you need to consider, and it's a matter of piecing it together.

S85—. . . (*this response was not audible from the recording*).

C86—Well, sometimes we need to get another person in on the discussion to help us see the things a little more clearly than just thinking about it alone.

S86—Well, it certainly has paid. It seems that I have pieced a lot together that before I had never realized. Just pieces here and there—

★ This seems to be a sincere expression of satisfaction with the results of counseling so far. However, it may only be an example of what Hathaway (*182*) describes as "hello-goodby" behavior.

C87—Well, we'll pick it up again on Wednesday at 10:00. (*pause*)

S87—Thank you for talking with me.

C88—Okay, well, I'll see you Wednesday.

S88—Okay. Goodbye.

★ The client exhibits ambivalent feelings toward her boyfriend, displaying difficulties in expressing affection toward him. She senses that this feeling handicaps her efforts. Future plans are affected by her capabilities and motivation to learn how to express affection toward others. She begins to show signs of wanting to resolve the problem, although she is not positive that she can.

COUNSELOR'S NOTES ON THE THIRD INTERVIEW
(*Dictated Immediately after the Interview*)

★ The client came in today after having completed the various tests prescribed in the first interview. There seemed to be additional complications in the case that were brought out today. Over Christmas holidays the client's boyfriend, Bill, asked her to marry him. Bill is a graduate of College B and a former acquaintance and boyfriend of the client from high school days. They had seen each other occasionally weekends during the time that he was going to College B. He is now at Army Camp A completing basic training and is going into advanced special training. He is to receive a commission of second lieutenant soon. I did not learn a great deal of the relationship between the two; however she describes Bill as someone who is quite energetic and forceful and somewhat of a leader, particularly during his time at College B.

The client also is very seriously considering dropping out of school at the end of this semester and returning home. She thinks she could get a job possibly at some kind of contact office work and take correspondence school courses in commercial art. However, she is quite uncertain as to how she would fare living again with the family. She thinks that would be a poor situation at best. Apparently she doesn't get along too well with her parents and her interests in recreational activities seem to be quite different from those of her family. On the other hand, she has received very little satisfaction from school mostly because she has not been able to make friends and feels out of place in that respect. She feels a lack of any goal in her educational work, too.

We discussed very briefly the results of the Strong and the Kuder, but there was little except confirmation of her expressed interest there. We didn't go into any other test results today.

I suggested that we continue the discussion on Wednesday of this week.

FOURTH INTERVIEW

(*2 Days after Third Interview*)

C1—Where do we pick up from here?

★ The counselor gave the client the opportunity to decide what is to be discussed. It is particularly important to open an interview in this manner in order to give the client the opportunity to introduce new material resulting from his thinking and experience since the last interview. S2 is an example of this: "I had thought of one other alternative. . . ."

S1—Let's see. We're trying to find where I'm going to be next semester.

C2—Yes. As I recall, none of the choices were completely (*pause*) to your liking, either staying here or going back to your home town.

S2—I had thought of one other alternative, and that is to take Home Ec. I don't know how to cook, and I could take an interior decorating course, and a costume design course, and so on.

★ The client continues her attempts at constructive planning outside of the interview.

C3—Are you familiar with the Home Ec. (*pause*) major in Arts and Science, that is, through the College of Arts and Science?

★ The counselor is introducing information relevant to the point in question which the client needs to have in order to consider the problem intelligently. One of the goals in counseling is intelligent, rational post-counseling behavior. Therefore, a decision-making experience in which facts and information are brought to bear on the point in question is properly included in the definition of counseling. Feelings and attitudes which are basic to the development of a realistic and personally satisfying self-concept should, in most instances, be given first priority in the counseling process. Vocational counseling may be viewed as a process of aiding a client to develop a concept of himself which is personally (psychologically) satisfying and which is in harmony with the realities of his environment.

S3—No, not really.

C4—Well, they have set up a (*pause*) Home Ec. major in Arts and Science which is a nonprofessional major. The bulk of the students in Home Ec. in the College of Agriculture are those essentially interested in professional courses in Home Ec. Now there may be some courses that you can't get if you enroll in Home Ec. in Arts and Science, but those are mostly professional courses; and I think it's a little bit easier in terms of prerequisites and required courses if you take it through the College of Arts and Science.

S4—Mm-huh.

C5—You're already in Arts and Science, aren't you?

S5—No, I'm—(*counselor interrupts*).

C6—No, that's right, you're in Education. Well, you may still be able to take those courses. (*pause*) I don't know about Education, though. What I am looking for is a place where you have pretty free choice. You might be able to do it in Education, or maybe you'd have to transfer to Arts and Science or Home Ec. (*long pause*) Now, how would that (*pause*) make this town any more palatable?

S6—Well, I don't know about it except—something I thought, and I more or less just discarded it and had kind of decided to go home, just temporarily decided that unless something comes along to change my mind. I mean, I have to decide on something, and I think the easiest way is to decide on something, until something comes along to change my mind; and if I had a reason enough to stay, well then I'll stay.

C7—Mm-huh. (*long pause*)

S7—Except for the fact that I don't know how to cook, and I'll have to either get the experience at home or take a course in it. Still there's dress design—(*pause*) it will be interesting, too, as well as interior decoration. But the trouble is I have to have a lot of requirements for that. I have to take Textiles, and Design I and II in Home Ec. I did have Design in Arts and Science—(*pause*)

C8—Let me see what I can find out from Home Ec. (*counselor dials phone—telephone conversation with Home Economics instructor*). Well here's what seems to be available. There's a course in Foods, which is a laboratory course. Then there's another Foods course, which is lecture, neither of which requires Chemistry because they're essentially for non-majors.

S8—Mm-huh.

C9—There's a beginning course in Design that is a prerequisite to any of the Interior Decorating courses.

S9—I've had that.

C10—Then there's the course in Clothing Construction, Textiles, Home Nursing and Health, and Family Relations which has some prerequisites, I think Psychology or Economics or something which you probably have had. (*long pause*) You've had some Psychology and Sociology?

S10—Yes.

C11—Well, then, Family Relations would be open to you. Have you had a course in General Economics?

S11—Yes.

C12—That's about the array. There are about half a dozen courses there that you can choose from. (*Gives list of courses to client.*)

S12—Mm-huh.

C13—Do you think that is what you're looking for, some more interesting course work, or is that apt to make a great deal of difference?

★ After having supplied the client with some technical information about course offerings which was necessary in order for the client to consider this course of action, the counselor raised the question of whether to stay in school or not. That is, the client needed this information before she could consider the alternatives intelligently.

S13—I think that would make quite a bit of difference, because the interesting course work in itself is interesting. I don't know whether I can even take what I wanted to, though. I mean, I'm interested in Design, but I've had so much Design in Arts and Science. I've had three courses in it in Art.

C14—Well, could be by talking to someone in Home Ec., you might be able to go into some of the Interior Decorating courses now.

S14—Mm-huh.

C15—I think for that you'd probably have to talk to someone in Home Ec. to see if they would permit it.

S15—You know something else I was wondering about—whether I could take Textiles and Costume Design at the same time. Textiles I think would be fun. No, I don't believe I could. That's a requirement for Art in Textiles. (*long pause*)

C16—What was that last?

S16—Costume Design. (*pause while counselor looks at college catalog*).

C17—I would think so. It says—prerequisite is Advanced Design. (*long pause*) Are you interested in the courses that are essentially practical application?

S17—Yes. Mm-huh. (*long pause*)

C18—There are five courses that you could go into, I believe. The Foods lecture and lab., two separate courses, Clothing Construction, Textiles, and Costume Design. (*pause*)

S18—What about Interior Decoration? That requires Design, doesn't it?

C19—Yes. Let me check. (*long pause while counselor looks at college catalog*). The first course is offered, Interior Design, then Interior Decoration, which is the continuation. Both of them are offered this time. Now, that might be a possibility, too. Then there was Design I that you've had in Arts and Science in Art, the kind of background you need for the course. And maybe you could get, if you wanted, a full schedule of Home Economics courses. It might mean registering as a special student, (*pause*) that is, not a candidate for a degree. Of course it is also possible that you might want to transfer to Arts and Science as a candidate for a degree with a major in Home Economics, (*pause*) even though you didn't intend to complete a degree.

S19—Mm-huh.

C20—I think that would all fit under the program.

S20—Mm-huh.

C21—I think you can always register as a special student.

S21—What does that include? I mean essentially?

C22—That means, essentially, that you're not a candidate for a degree. You take about what you want to take.

S22—Well, even if I did this, I would just go for one more semester, and that's all. (*long pause*) Of course that means I kind of lose my chances of coming back and taking my degree in Education.

C23—Well, it would (*pause*) really mean that time would be lost as far as applying it to a degree here, most of it would be lost. (*pause*)

S23—I wonder if it's so important that I have to decide right away. Couldn't I just stay on a semester, and see how things work out? If I decide to come back next year, well, I'll graduate in February; and there's not much chance of getting a teaching job in the second semester.

C24—Well, I don't know. As I understand the labor market, there is a teacher demand. There probably are about as many jobs opening up in February as there are people graduating to fill them. There are fewer jobs, fewer people. In June there are more jobs, and more people. (*pause*) What about your major in Elementary Education? How much do you have by way of electives?

S24—Well, I have every hour taken up. I mean, every hour is a requirement. (*long pause*)

C25—What seems to be (*pause*) the crucial points in your decision of whether to stay or not? (*long pause*)

S25—Well, I think personally that I would somewhat be interested, regardless of Bill, I mean, and I'd still have to know what I wanted to do. And I realize that I have to (*pause*) prepare myself for something, I mean, I can't just trust it to luck. (*pause*) Oh, I feel like that I need to see what I can do about it. I mean just for the heck of it, rather than plunging myself into teaching which I'm not sure of.

C26—Then you say you want to try out, you mean, (*pause*) in courses or in actual work.

S26—Well, in courses and to see what I can do with it professionally.

C27—Mm-huh. (*long pause*) Would you say that would be (*pause*) more important or less important than what you work out with Bill? (*long pause*)

S27—Well, I guess, to say offhand that what I work out with Bill would be more important, but I'm not sure of it now. I mean, if I were sure of it, I would know whether that would be the most important thing, but I'm not, I can't count on it.

> ★ This response just about summarizes all of the client's confusion. She considers her relation with Bill as primary but is afraid that it will not lead to a satisfactory marriage—"I can't count on it." Consequently, she attaches major importance to the selection of a vocation and preparation for it. A career seems more attainable now even if it would be less interesting than a satisfactory marriage.

C28—Mm-huh. (*long pause*) How much of not being sure how you work out things with Bill—how does that tie in with what you've seen in your own family set up?

S28—I don't know, but I don't think I feel too much, too strongly,—that I would let that affect me too strongly. Now, it might, but (*pause*) I think it does have an effect.

C29—I was wondering if it might cause you to be uncertain. (*pause*)

S29—Well, I'm not uncertain about myself, but I'm rather unsure about what Bill feels about it; and I'm not sure whether it'll work out, because of that. I think that is the only reason for my feeling this way.

C30—Are you thinking maybe his ideas about getting married are somewhat impulsive?

S30—Yes. Mm-huh. (*pause*) Except not too much. In a certain sense they are. (*long pause*) I always pictured him as the type that was rather fast and would date you and leave you; but Christmas, I—maybe it's because I've seen something different, but he's not like that at all, and that's one reason that caused me to change my mind. (*pause*) I think he's just as sincere as anybody that I would meet, and yet he doesn't want to feel tied down.

C31—Well, are you saying that you wonder whether you can be as free and uninhibited as he is? (*pause*) Do you feel that you would be sort of dragging your feet with him? (*pause*)

S31—No, I don't know whether that's true or not, either. That is the way I feel now, but I hope to change; I mean I hope that—(*long pause*) I don't—I'm more or less sure and maybe blindly confident that when I find something that I really like to do, that if I want to do it badly enough, I can do it. The trouble is that I just haven't found the thing I want to do badly enough.

C32—Let me take another look. (*Looks at client's folder, the MMPI profile in particular.*) (*long pause*) Let me make a guess. See how it strikes you, how it fits. In terms of your present and past ideas, you mentioned that your relations with other students and groups of friends haven't worked out as well as you think they should. (*pause*) Has that been mostly because you think they should and not because you necessarily think they're highly important and highly satisfying to you? The important associations that you want—are they in terms of the fellows that you date rather than more casual groups of friends? (*pause*) Have you been trying to focus on wider social contacts because you think you should, rather than what you feel like doing?

★ Here the counselor was trying to develop an hypothesis about the client from an MMPI profile whose critical characteristics are a high Pd score and a low Mf score. In our clinical experience we have found that a marked Pd "spike" on the MMPI for college counseling cases many times is associated with an early home environment which is lacking in real affection and acceptance. The home may be a "broken" one in fact or in its affective impact on the children. Also, we find that the dating life of many of these students is a shallow one. They may date as often as other students, but their attention is rarely concentrated on any one person for long. Usually they will date one person two or three times and then "lose interest" and move on to another. It would appear that they are unable or unwilling to trust their affections to another. They are afraid to put themselves in a position where someone might reject their bid for affection and acceptance. This interpretation of a high Pd score coupled with what may be a more than usual feminine make-up (low Mf) suggests that the client may have a strong need for affection and acceptance on a personal and intimate basis but is thwarted in attempting to satisfy this need by an inability or unwillingness to enter into "entangling" emotional relationships.

S32—I think quite often I do a lot of things that I don't want to.

C33—Well, I was wondering if that would be one of the things you think you should do, and actually there isn't much drive to go out with groups.

S33—That's very true. I've more or less built up an idea of what I should do, and what I should be, and (*pause*) I seem to push myself when I don't really want to, and I think, why did I do that? (*pause*) It seems like I have a feeling I should be a leader, and actually I really think that I'm probably a much better follower than I am a leader. Not a follower in all respects—a leader for myself (*pause*) but not an obvious one, I mean, not one like I try to be. I mean a leader different, knowing that I'm doing what's right for myself, and yet in that respect, but not leading a crowd. (*pause*) I've been expecting a lot of swell things from myself and expecting something I really don't want.

C34—Would you say that your interests are pretty definitely nonprofessional in terms of long term goals? (*long pause*)

S34—What do you mean by nonprofessional?

C35—Noncareer. Your interests are essentially in marriage, and family, and a home? (*pause*) Are those pretty strong in terms of your own interests and desires?

S35—Yes. I think they are. (*pause*) I think I could be perfectly content to stay home and fix up the house and clean—of course I'd have to have an automatic dishwasher (*laughs*)—I hate to do the dishes. (*pause*) I like to go out quite a bit, and keep up with the latest in styles, and talk about the latest in music, and keep up with classical music. (*long pause*)

★ The client is now able to accept some of her interests and motivations which earlier she was not. She still is not very comfortable with these ideas because she cannot be sure that she can implement them. However, this is some progress toward developing a self-concept which is apt to yield more personal satisfaction.

C36—Well, let me raise this question again that I raised a while ago. How much did your family relations in terms of difficulties that you encountered there as dissatisfaction (*pause*) sort of dampen or inhibit or raise a question about how well you can carry on the role of a housewife as you think you'd like to?

S36—I really don't know whether it's damaging in respect to being a housewife or not, but in every other respect it has. I mean, I just don't seem to have enough in back of me to have the confidence that I can do something. I did when I had a group back of me, and I thought—well, that I had lots of friends that really liked me for what I was, you know.

C37—Mm-huh.

S37—But since I lost contact with that group, I know I've lost it. (*long pause*)

C38—Have you tended to be pretty careful, (*pause*) maybe more hesitant at times, in getting emotionally involved? (*pause*) Afraid you might get hurt? (*long pause*)

S38—Yes. I think so, as far as dating, I think so, except with someone I really like, I just, well, I become—

C39—Would you say again?

S39—If there's someone I really like, I just shut up like a clam; and it doesn't usually inhibit me as far as dating, and that's one way I think that—I can like Bill, I mean, it's just something that's grown, and it's so easy—

C40—In a relationship that you can trust.

S40—Mm-huh.

C41—Well, I think you're caught in two cross purposes here. One is apparently a rather strong feminine drive, maybe a little stronger than most women, which tends to highlight your relations with Bill, or any other fellow that you might like a great deal. It's that kind of a relationship which would be suggested as being the most important for your general activity, and general satisfaction, and then, of course, that would tend to minimize the need for satisfaction from broader, more casual groups. That suggests, then, a pretty strong personal, intimate relationship with some man, and having your life pretty well centered around men. Also this suggests some things you've said that the difficulty in being able to set up easy, emotional, affectional relationships in the home has caused you to be pretty wary and cautious in your own dealings with men, and bringing the two together, you come out with two or three things. One is that your relationship with Bill has sort of broken through that barrier of protecting yourself from being hurt as you think that you might be from what you've grown up with; and having broken through that in establishing your relationship with Bill, the social activity around campus and elsewhere is pretty minor in terms of satisfaction and interest; that if you are pushing yourself in that direction, you may be pushing yourself against what you really are.

★ Here the counselor is interpreting to the client his ideas as outlined in the comment following C32. It is essentially correct and comprehensive with the exception of the idea concerning the importance of groups *per se*. Her fundamental need here is for acceptance whether by an individual or by groups. Associated with the need for acceptance is a need for a feeling of personal worth.

S41—I don't know, I've always liked to have a good time.

C42—Yes.

S42—I know when I'm with a group that I can feel comfortable; and I just enjoy it and have a good time, I know.

C43—A group that you feel accepted by, for what you are, and not necessarily what you do.

S43—Mm-huh.

C44—In that respect your needs haven't been as well satisfied as most people's have been in your family life as you grew up.

S44—I've always had a fear of not being accepted, and that fear just sets up a wall between me and the crowd, I mean, I have a hard time breaking into it.

> ★ S44 and S45 indicate a significant degree of self-understanding. The rather basic psycho-social need for acceptance and a feeling of personal worth and dignity which has not been fully satisfied to date seems to be the cause of much of the client's difficulty.

C45—Because you're afraid that they may not accept you, they may hurt you, and you don't want to put yourself in the position of being hurt. (*pause*) So that if you do find a group that is very accepting, that you feel a part of, that's wonderful.

S45—To me that's very satisfying. Mm-huh. And when I get that, *I'm just in the clouds.* I know, in my church group at home, when I first found this group, and started going with one of the fellows in the group, I thought: Can this be me; it can't be possible!

C46—Then Bette blossomed?

S46—Yes! (*laughs*) (*long pause*)

C47—Well, is that the essential dynamics of your situation? Is that the crucial elements of it?

S47—I believe it is. (*pause*)

C48—Now this general fear of being hurt by others until you're sure. Is that some of the things that are holding you back, making you delay a little bit with Bill? (*pause*) Although you can't put it directly on him, it's just those generalized fears?

S48—Well, it might be. And, it might be a fear of not living up to his standards. (*long pause*) One thing I don't particularly care about Bill for, he's very socially minded; and he thinks that we should do this, and we should do that; and one of the things he thinks incessantly of is partying. He said that I had rather narrow beliefs when I was going to high school, and he said that one reason that he couldn't ask me to marry him before was because he didn't think I would fit into his, his— ah—he would not be able to take me anywhere, you know, and drink, and a drinking party situation and feel that he was perfectly at ease with me, you know; and he said at Christmas (this year) he thought he could do that. He said I'd changed a lot. He said it seemed like that I'm *alive* a little bit. (*laughs*) (*pause*)

C49—Well, are you saying that you're wondering if Bill is going to make demands on you in terms of being socially outgoing, that you might not be able to meet? He works into a group very easily, and for you it takes longer and a little more work. And in that respect you may be dragging your feet as far as he sees it—(*pause*) which is again this fear of not being accepted by the groups. As far as you and Bill are concerned, things are going smoothly.

S49—Mm-huh. Just about.

C50—That's the way you see it. Except when he begins to push you out into groups, you're not sure how fast you can assimilate that. (*pause*) That all fits in together.

S50—Yes. Seems to me like that as soon as I know that I have to do something, that I'm put in a situation where I *have* to do it I get scared and just sort of run as fast as I can in the other direction. (*pause*) That's the way I feel about it, I just want to take out. (*pause*) And yet, I, you might say, submerge it and try and make out that I don't feel that way at all.

C51—Mm-huh.

S51—I really do, and I know it. (*pause*)

C52—And then you probably appear to others somewhat tense?

S52—Mm-huh.

C53—And inhibited, and not free, because well, you actually aren't. You've got forces there that you've got locked together and you can't be free.

S53—And I know that, I mean, I can't make a very good impression and it's no wonder that I haven't (*pause*) done what I've wanted to do. (*long pause*)

C54—Well, what have we to do yet? (*pause*)

S54—Just find whether I'm going into Home Ec., or go home. I can see where I'll need to learn how to cook, and I'm willing to take a chance on it, because I'll have to learn how to cook sometime anyway.

★ This is an interesting response. The client shifted the topic of discussion back to the question of what she is to do in the immediate future (within the next two weeks). Whether she is rejecting the counselor's interpretations or finds the discussion of interpersonal relations too uncomfortable or whether the pressure to decide whether to stay in school or not was the reason she made the abrupt shift in topic of discussion is not known.

C55—The question I've had right along, is whether going home will be any more satisfying to you than here. Now, I'm not trying to keep students for the university; but if it's good for *you* to go home that's where you should go, and I'd be the first one to say it. Have you been thinking mostly in terms of your social life in groups and so forth? (*pause*) What you have said suggests that being readily available to meet Bill, whenever he is free, would be maybe most important. Then some of these other things, how are they patterned out? What would you suggest, where you should be?

S55—Also, I know that I'm going to have to keep on my toes to have something else just beside Bill. I mean, if that becomes the whole thing, well then I'll just gradually deteriorate. That's the way I look at it. It may not be that way, but it seems like that would happen. (*long pause*)

C56—Yes. I think gradually you will want to be able to work towards keeping pace with him, which means that as you find that you can really trust other people to like you, you'll be more outgoing; but that has to come more or less at *your* pace, how fast you can assimilate that sort of thing, how fast you can be sure.

S56—I know the way I'm going on now down here for me, I haven't, you really have to organize yourself; and you have to realize what you can take, and what you can't take.

C57—Yes.

S57—And as long as I go along not knowing what to do about it, well, it won't get any better.

C58—Of course, until recently you haven't had the "core" with Bill to work around. (*pause*) That is, you haven't had the important "core." (*long pause*)

S58—Right now, I don't exactly really know where I stand with him. I know that he likes me pretty well, and yet I don't know whether that's what he really wants, or not, because I do know he dated some other girls at Christmas. I know that he has quite a few opportunities, and he says he has been on the verge of marriage several times, given his pin away I think four times; and when he asked if I didn't want the pin, I said, "yes," but then he said the next time we went out he didn't bring it with him because, he said, "It'd been given away four times," he said, "he wanted this one to last." (*laughs*) (*long pause*)

C59—Well, do you seem to have any real doubts about how you feel toward Bill?

S59—No, I don't believe I do. (*pause*) Once in a while I really get to wondering. (*long pause*) One thing that I am a little worried about—(*pause*) I knew one of the girls whom he knew quite well, and she was (*pause*) well, she was just—she was glamorous and knew just how to handle Bill and all that; and as far as competing with her, I don't know whether I can or not. I mean, I know that he still likes her. Of course she's married now, and he was very serious. He told me that it might be embarassing for me sometime if he should happen to meet her on the street, and I don't know whether I can measure up to—I mean, he might keep that back in his mind; and if I'm not as glamorous (*pause*) don't wear my clothes as well or something, well then—(*pause*)

C60—That's kind of his choice to make. (*pause*) Which apparently he has. (*long pause*)

S60—I don't think he's too sure of himself though. (*pause*) That might be just my own idea about it.

C61—Well, if you're pretty sure of your own feelings for him, I think you ought to give him an opportunity to test out how he feels for you. If he reciprocates and there seems to be a stable feeling for you, (*pause*) I think you may have a tendency to hold back and not express yourself until you're very sure how he feels; (*pause*) and he may be doing the same thing.

S61—I think that's what the situation is. (*laughs*) (*pause*) I'm afraid he doesn't think that I really know how I feel, and I don't think he knows how he feels; (*pause*) and I have learned just recently (one of the girls in the house is married to a fellow that is stationed at this army camp, and I think he went in about the same time Bill did;) he won't get out of basic for another month yet, so that means that I won't see him until then. Means I'll have to wait for him to come to me. (*pause*)

C62—Yes. Of course, you can do some things in letters.

S62—Well, he decided that he would not write. At least I'm giving him a four weeks' cooling off period.

C63—You can always write him.

S63—Well, I don't have his address. (*pause*) And all the time, it's just as bad for him as it is for me. I mean, well then that's what he said. (*long pause*) I don't give the impression that he's not very fond of me. (*long pause*)

C64—(*Counselor looks at watch*). Do you think we need to spend another session discussing this? (*pause*)

S64—Well, I don't really think we do. Do you?

C65—I don't know how you feel about it. I think in the last ten or fifteen minutes we, at least to me, seemed to come to the most important factors in the situation, and if you think you can go ahead and plan pretty well without discussing it further, why then that's all that's necessary.

S65—Well, you think it would actually be better to come back and take Home Ec. then? (*long pause*)

C66—Well, my general tendency would be not to move unless you're sure that it's for the better—and that's the thing that I can't fully see— how going home is better.

S66—Mm-huh.

C67—It certainly may be no worse. I'm not sure how it would be any better.

S67—Well, after our first talk, when you said that I should be with my parents and take a more or less indifferent attitude toward them, I went home, you know; there were lots of things that I couldn't talk to them about; and it seems to me when you understand a person better, you understand why they are like that. It doesn't affect you as much.

> ★ This kind of client response is a good indication of the effective-
> ness of counseling. The client tried out the counselor's suggestion
> and found that it worked to her satisfaction.

C68—It is a sort of a middle of the road attitude: "they are my parents and I like them, and we're going to get along so long as we don't try to force each other into our own individual patterns. We can be in-dividuals and still get along and be different."

S68—And yet I realize that there's—I have lots of aunts, and cousins that like to talk quite a bit; and at the same time I hate being talked about. Oh, *I hate that*, and lots of times I get in on it, you know, and of course they don't realize it, I guess; and that's something that's really hurt me, that is something I'm going to have to overcome eventually, and I thought one way to do it is to try associating with them and getting used to it.

> ★ Planning for the future with an optimistic outlook is another in-
> dicator of the effectiveness of counseling and an indication that
> the client is about ready to terminate the counseling contacts.

C69—You're also building up a reservoir and a balance of satisfaction in terms of experiences coming in (*pause*) and then I think if things work out well with Bill, that *there* is going to be your major source of satis-faction. (*pause*) You may be a little reluctant to put yourself out, let's say lead in terms of your own feelings at the moment. But if that's the way you feel, it's what you should do. (*pause*) If he responds as you think he will, then everything's fine. At least you will have been able to say to him: here's the way I feel about it and show him that. (*pause*) Otherwise he may wonder himself, have the same feeling, will be as equally reticent, because of your own holding back what you really feel.

S69—Mm-huh. (*pause*) That's one thing that I can feel lots of times; but I can't do anything about it but the fact that— (*pause*)

C70—Yes. They may just be waiting for you to make the first move, which Bill has already done. (*pause*) Well, let's put it this way. If you want just to talk about some of these things before the end of the semester, why, just give me a buzz and make an appointment.

S70—Okay.

C71—And if you don't have any questions, why all right.

S71—Well, I certainly am glad that I've had a chance to talk to you.

C72—Yes, sometimes you stew around in your own ideas; and when you get a chance to talk to somebody else about them, they just pattern out beautifully.

S72—Yes. (*pause*) Bye.

C73—Bye.

★ The client in the fourth interview gives further evidence of her need for affection and approval. There are indications that she is developing self-understanding (S33, S35, S36, S39, S44, S45, S50, S59), is trying to apply some of her understandings (S2, S6, S23, S25, S67, S68), and is going to try to work out the solution alone (S64).

The client during the course of the interviews, passed through a period of exploration, then a period of putting pieces together in new relationships (or self-understandings), and finally a period of attempting to practice some of the new learnings.

COUNSELOR'S NOTES ON FOURTH INTERVIEW

(*Notes Dictated Immediately after the Interview*)

★ The interview today went very haltingly for the first half or more. We discussed the question of what she should do next semester and didn't seem to be able to get hold of any real questions pertaining to her choice. She had considered the possibility of remaining here and taking Home Economics courses— foods, clothing, textiles, interior decoration. I checked on courses that would be available to her; but this was not a very strong desire on her part, that is, it conflicted with her idea that she didn't like to live here. I raised the question as to whether going home would be any better than staying here, indicating that

I could see no strong points in favor of going—of course, I could see some disadvantages of staying here, too. It was after this sort of discussion that we began to discuss what I would consider basic points in the case.

According to our test data and what the client has related so far, she has strong feminine interests and desires; but these are countered to some extent by a rather emotionally barren home background which is described in previous interview notes. I interpreted these two points to her and then went on further to say that her desire to engage more in group activities may be actually forcing herself into a kind of activity which is really not in keeping with her own make-up. She qualified this to some extent by saying that that was somewhat true, although when she did find a group that did accept her for what she was, that she became quite elated about it and almost "soared into the clouds." I interpreted it that this fit into the general picture very well, that one of her strong needs was to be accepted and have feelings of personal worth as far as others are concerned, most particularly in terms of some man; but, in general, she wanted to be accepted by other people, that she had had difficulty in this before and mostly it stemmed from a lack in the home background in being able to form close emotional attachments. She seems to have been able to form a satisfactory emotional relationship with her boyfriend, Bill, but she has some doubts about this—not about Bill, himself. He seems to be a rather gregarious, outgoing individual, who meets people well and enjoys social contacts; but she was afraid that the demands that he may make on her in terms of socialization may be more than she is able to handle at the moment, that is, trying to force herself into groups that may not be accepting of her. She has been rather hesitant to express her feelings toward Bill so far; and the situation at present is that he has given her four weeks or so to make up her mind, and she cannot write to him even because she doesn't know his specific address. I encouraged her to feel free to express her actual feelings to Bill so that he might know what they were and could respond to them as he felt. This of course is a little counter to her general tendency of being reluctant to express her feelings in fear of getting hurt. However, she seemed to feel that she would be able to do so, although she had been reticent to do so so far.

I believe she understood the various interpretations I made, and I asked her if there was anything more we needed to do. She seemed to think there was no need for further contact, although she asked me directly, was it true that I thought she should come back here or stay here and take Home Economics? I again reiterated my previous point that, in absence of any strong evidence that she should change, I would think that she would be better not to make any move; but I couldn't see any positive factors one way or the other, and I thought the question of leaving or staying was, for the most part, of minor importance. She was quite interested in learning how to cook and learning about clothes, and this she could get here by taking Home Economics courses, possibly as a special student. The interview ended with no plans for further contact unless she felt that she wanted to talk with me further. If she does, she will call for an appointment.

* * * * *

The client came in seven days after the fourth interview for just a few minutes to report that she had decided to stay in school the Spring semester and major in art education. Almost all the courses she took for the elementary education can be applied to the art education major. She was pleased with this choice.

* * * * *

Follow-up interview. About a year after the first interview a contact was made with the client to determine what had happened in the meantime. She had not continued in college as she had planned to do. During the year she was out of school she worked at a variety of jobs, sometimes living at home and sometimes living in other cities. She then returned to college and pursued a combination art and elementary education major. She obtained part-time work as a commercial artist while attending college.

She was more confident of her educational and vocational plans than she had been before. Her attitudes about her family were more positive; enough so that she was quite accepting of her family. But she no longer dated Bill and had no steady boyfriend.

At this time she was given an opportunity to read the manuscript of her interviews. At first it was disturbing to her, but in a short time she was able to use it as a guide in noting changes in attitudes that had taken place.

ADDENDUM

In the Case of Bette Morgan we find a young lady who has drifted from one activity to another. Her present question is concerned with the feasibility of continuing in education. This shifting she blames upon her lack of motivation. She came to the counselor in hopes that she could find some unexplored area of study and eventual work that would be interesting to her, and thus she could overcome her feeling of boredom.

As client and counselor explored the problem in greater detail, we see the client as an individual who has found it difficult to identify herself completely with either her father or her mother. Her father is difficult to approach and yet more understanding than her mother, who has been unable to accept her daughter for what she is. This seeming lack of affection in the home has handicapped her in her expression of affection toward dates, friends, etc. In other words, she has never been able to practice in a "safe" environment and now finds it difficult to operate on an affectional level anywhere in her environment. Test data verify the fact that she is a very feminine woman who wants the companionship of men, and yet she lacks the faith and skill necessary for establishing affectional relationships. She seeks the complete approval of others and yet cannot accept them completely herself. She desires marriage and yet cannot completely accept anyone as a potential partner.

The counselor in working with Bette used an approach characterized by the introduction of several topics related to general areas of living and adjustment. After accepting the client's statement of her problem, the counselor discussed various home and school topics which gradually yielded a picture of her. The cyclical process which accompanies this procedure gradually focuses the attention of the client and counselor upon the client's "real" problem—and the shifts in discussion topics become less and less frequent.

Bette's immediate question of remaining in elementary education, leaving school, or finding another major, remained in the picture until the very end of the case. Her inability to operate affectionally would probably hinder success in any three of the above alternatives. One of the counselor's major problems in this type of situation was to help her see that the immediate problem is a part of a larger problem. Bette's future satisfactions had to be built upon the resolution of the larger problem.

The counselor aided Bette in relating the immediate and "real" problems through a series of tentative interpretations with which she could agree, disagree, or modify to suit herself. These interpretations were verbalized in such a way that neither the client nor the counselor was forced into a defensive role.

Although "complete" closure was not obtained in this case, the client indicated signs of wanting to overcome the handicap and a few signs of actual growth. The client's growth in these respects was fostered by the use of tentative interpretations by the counselor.

CHAPTER 3

The Case of

BILL DAVIS

THE CASE consists of two interviews which were phonographically recorded. The counselor of the case had completed a master's degree in counseling and educational psychology and was in his second year of experience as a part-time counselor at the time of the case. At the beginning of the first interview the counselor knew only that the client had entered the university in the college of engineering about three years earlier and had taken freshmen placement tests at that time. The test results were as follows:

(1) A.C.E. Psychological Examination for College Freshmen, 1942 Edition

	Raw Score	Percentile Rank
Quantitative	35	28
Linguistic	71	73
Total	106	56

(2) Cooperative English Test A: Mechanics of Expression, Form S   142   62

(3) Cooperative English Test B2: Effectiveness of Expression, Form S   42   74

The norm group in this instance was freshmen who had entered the university the two previous years.

FIRST INTERVIEW

C1—What's on your mind, Bill?

S1—Well, here's what I had in mind. Of course I may be a little late for this, but it's probably never too late to find out some things. I'd like to take—a set of examinations to find just what,—you know, what department if I start out in a business I would be best suited to work in. I did not take those examinations when I first came here, you know, which I probably should have done. But I didn't know until last year that there was such a thing.

C2—You're in Engineering School, is that right?

S2—Yes.

C3—And you're going to graduate.

S3—In June.

C4—You'd like to know, what aspect of engineering or business that you should—

S4—Well, yes, mm-huh. Of course, I believe that when you have a certain type of degree that, ah, it doesn't mean you're going to stay in it all your life anyway.

C5—What are your future plans?

S5—Well, I'll probably stay in engineering for a while or, if I go back into the service—of course, I don't know what the start will be there—but, eventually I think I'd like to go into business for myself.

C6—What type of—(*client interrupts*)

S6—Would have to spend a little money for that. Well, I don't know yet, I mean, it all depends on the breaks, I guess.

C7—Would it be something in connection with your engineering?

S7—Probably small. No, not in connection with engineering because it's very hard to get along in engineering in your own business. And, I like engineering for the information it gives you. I'll probably stay in it for quite a while, but you never can tell what you'll end up doing.

C8—That's right. You want to use it as a stepping stone to your own business?

S8—That's what I'd like to do. (*pause*)

C9—Well, I'll tell you about these tests then. We can give you some idea of what your interests are like. We can give you some idea of what your mental ability is like, although having gone as far as you have, you ought to have a pretty good idea what your mental ability is like to begin with. We can give you a little idea about personality, not a great deal from these tests.

> ★ Here, the counselor breaks into the development of the problem with a structuring response. Sometimes the counselor needs to structure with regard to the present problem rather early in the interview in order for the client to feel free to develop the statement of his problem more fully. It seems too early for structuring here, however. Typically, structuring is important when the client is expecting some service not consistent with counseling, i.e.; *the* answer to his problem from *a* test, a nonprofessional relationship with the counselor, a nonprofessional service, or a naiveté toward the purpose and procedures of counseling (*100, 278*).

S9—Well, I think that kind of information will help out. Just, ah, how conclusive are your tests? I mean, ah—

C10—They aren't going to give you any answers. They'll give you some indications perhaps.

S10—Well, that's what I mean.—They're more or less indications.

C11—Yes. You would probably get more out of the interest tests than you would anything else. (*pause*) How have your grades been since you've been in engineering?

S11—Oh, I have about a 2.2 average. They aren't outstanding.

★ Grade point averages are computed from assigned weights as follows: A or E = 4.0; B or S = 3.0; C or M = 2.0; D or I = 1.0; F = 0.0.

C12—What aspect of engineering are you in? Chemical? Civil?

S12—Civil engineering. It approaches a broader viewpoint, than the other types of engineering, and,—

C13—You were a little less restricted?

S13—Yes. I guess you could call it that. It probably is a little less analytical sort of engineering, you know.

C14—Mm-huh.

S14—Whereas mechanical and chemical engineering, I guess are more what you'd call engineering. A civil degree, I don't think, prepares you for too much. I don't suppose, any engineering degree does, well, prepare you for lots of money—if that's what you're interested in, just doesn't do it.

C15—Mm-huh.

S15—But, — an education isn't conducive to making lots of money. (*laughs*) It's the breaks.

C16—That's true.

S16—Anyway that's—I just wanted to find out, without wasting a lot of time when you go out into business. I imagine, stuff like that can sort of lead you along, can't it?

C17—Yes. That will give you some indication of where, where—

S17—(*client interrupts*) I mean, I know quite a bit about my myself, but I find there is an awful lot I don't know yet.

C18—Yes, maybe it will help fill in the gap.

S18—And, maybe I've got the wrong idea about some things.

C19—Possibly.

S19—I took a three-hour course in psychology over there and that's where I found out about all this.

C20—Did you take it this semester?

S20—No, I took it last semester. It was an interesting course. I enjoyed it.

C21—I think you can learn something from these tests if you think about them as you take them, about the response that you make to certain things like that. They bring up points that you hadn't thought of before. Now in business, would you like to be in some kind of business where you make contacts with people or in something more of a technical nature, or just what?

> ★ The counselor is attempting to bring the testing *per se,* into a more obvious relationship with the counseling process by suggesting to the client that he keep in mind the question he wants answered by the tests while he is actually taking the tests.

S21—Well, that's kind of hard to say. (*laughs*) I don't know.

C22—What work experience have you had?

S22—Well, I've worked three summers for a civil engineer, worked on streets and things like that, you know. Of coures, I missed so much. I'm taking accounting and a sociology course because I want to find out, ah—

C23—(*Counselor interrupts.*) You are getting a little far afield for an engineer, aren't you?

> ★ Recognition of the feeling expressed in S22 would have been better and perhaps more meaningful to the client, but as it turned out he proceeded in spite of the counselor.

S23—No, I don't think, ah—

C24—I don't mean it exactly in that sense of the word. But usually you engineers are loaded down with physics, etc. all the way through.

S24—Well, you've gotta take 12 hours of humanistics; but then I could have taken a technical elective instead of this accounting, or at least they call them technical, but I could have taken something in civil engineering. But, after you've had three years of engineering or three and a half years of strictly engineering, you gotta get a little of something else because you just can't narrow your field down—it's too narrow. When you get out in life, you have to be able to know a little bit about something else when you talk to people.

C25—That's right. Of course, it's so seldom we hear of an engineer taking a sociology course, or accounting, or anything like that.

S25—Well, I don't know, I know a couple of engineers—of course, they're getting a business degree besides. But what I would like to do—it takes quite a while longer to get a degree—about two years.

C26—That seems to be a favorite combination now.

S26—It is. It is a fine combination—or law. But of course, law is very rare for an engineer and lawyer. It takes so long. But business is something you can combine with engineering. But I don't know just how well these tests can help you out. I guess, you can try to tell me more after I've taken then probably.

C27—Yes. Then, like I said before, they're not going to come out with any answer—you should do this, you should do that.

★ Further structuring concerning tests is taking place because the counselor felt that the client was over-emphasizing what the tests could do for him.

S27—I wouldn't expect that.

C28—There will be some indications of interests along certain lines.

S28—Mm-huh.

C29—In that respect they may be able to give you some ideas that you may not know already. Now, this one interest test is a test that compares you to people out in the field working in these various occupations, areas of work. They are happy and successful with what they are doing.

★ Although it is technically correct that the men in Strong's criterion groups were "successful," it is doubtful whether they should be labeled "successful" here, since it might imply to the client that interest is tantamount to ability.

S29—(*Client interrupts*) It's a—

C30—Not an aptitude test though—purely an interest test.

S30—Well, this interest test, does it compare you with all occupations?

C31—No, not all of them.

S31—Only specific ones.

C32—Maybe I can find a copy of it, to give you an idea of what it's like. (*Counselor finds copy of Strong Profile sheet.*)

S32—There are probably related questions to different professions.

C33—Here is a profile.

S33—Oh, I see.

C34—It will measure you in these areas. This is called a biological science area. This is the physical science area. Production manager is by itself. A technical area,—people who like to work with their hands are found in this area frequently. Social service area for those people interested in helping others in some way or another. Musician is by itself. C.P.A. by itself. This area is business detail and this is business contact. A linguistic area, then president of manufacturing concern by itself. Business detail and business contact differ in that in business contact a person is aggressively going out to contact others in a business situation.

S34—Or an extrovert type.

C35—Well, yes it might be if you want to put it that way. That's one way of putting it. The business detail is, oh, it's more or less a technical thing using certain knowledge working with certain things but you're not necessarily working with people in the same sense that you would in business contact or sales area. People are coming to you in many cases. Now, that's what the test is like. That's the Strong. The other one is different. It takes your likes and your dislikes, more or less of an internal thing— how you feel about certain types of activities. This doesn't necessarily compare you to people in those jobs.

S35—Well, I see.

C36—Now, will there be anything other than those two that you would like to go ahead and work on?

> ★ Essentially, the choice of tests is being left to the client, however, the counselor has indicated earlier (**C9**) what he thinks would be most valuable in terms of the presented problem.

S36—Well, course I don't know how many you have or what different types you do have.

C37—Here's a list of the tests. You can take a look at them.

S37—I'll take a look at them. Let's see, you were speaking of the general interest test, and the personality test. Is that the two you were speaking of?

C38—Well, if you're interested—yes. That personality area is a tough one to test. The Minnesota Multiphasic is a—you may have heard of it in your psych. course. It's a screening device. That's about all it is. As far as diagnosing you as to what your personality is like, it won't do that.

> ★ It would appear that the counselor is reflecting uncertainty on his part in dealing with the MMPI in counseling situations. It is doubtful that "screening device" and "personality aberrations" (in **C39**) have much meaning for the client. Abstruseness and abstractness in counselor talk suggests that the counselor may feel uncomfortable about an idea or attitude or is not well skilled in handling it.

S38—Mm-huh.

C39—It may give you an indication of any personality aberrations that are present.

S39—That personality is such a funny—

C40—Yes.

S40—I mean it's such a funny thing. It has so many different aspects to it.

C41—Most of those other tests wouldn't be particularly valuable to you, I don't think.

(*Pause, while client looks at test record*)

S41—Oh, Kuder Preference Record and Strong Vocational Interest—those are two different tests in the general interest part. Well, I think that those two would probably do me,—probably be what I'm looking for, I guess.

C42—All right.

S42—It can't do any harm.

C43—It takes a week to send the Strong away and have it scored. Do you have time this afternoon?

S43—Well, let's see, how long will it take?

C44—About an hour. Not an hour for both, an hour on each one.

S44—Well, let's see. I guess I could. Yeah.

C45—All right. Now you want to get the Strong out of the way and send it off and then a week from tomorrow you could come in and it will be ready for you. Then we could talk about it further.

S45—All right. A week from tomorrow.

C46—Okay, Bill, let's go back and I'll take you to meet the psychometrist.

COUNSELOR'S NOTES ON THE FIRST INTERVIEW

(*dictated immediately after the interview*)

★ Mr. Davis came to the counseling service for the specific purpose of taking some tests. At the present time he is a senior in the College of Engineering and will graduate in June. He had heard about the tests available here, and he thought he'd like to take them to see if he could get a better idea of what aspect of business or engineering he'd enter. He said that he didn't plan to stay in engineering for the rest of his life, but he thought that the engineering background would be a good stepping stone to the management of a business of his own. I explained to him what the function of the counseling service was, what the tests could do and what they couldn't do, the fact that he wasn't going to receive any pat answers here and he seemed to accept that. Mr. Davis heard about the counseling service during the process of taking a course in psychology. His work experience consists of summer work for three years with a civil engineer. This should prove valuable to him should he go on into civil engineering in which he is getting a degree. He sounds a little bit disappointed in his engineering course. The past couple of semesters he's been taking some course work outside of engineering, and it's proved very interesting to him. Mr. Davis was mainly interested in taking two interest tests and those were the only tests selected. After completing the test battery, he will return later for further counseling.

PERSONAL DATA SHEET

Between the first and second interview the client filled out a one-page data sheet. Following is a summary of the information from the personal data sheet:

Client:—Age: 23 years.

> Born in a metropolitan area; present home address is in this same metropolitan area.
>
> Marital Status: Single.
>
> Graduated from high school in metropolitan area about four years ago.
>
> Upon graduating from high school he entered White University and attended for one summer and one semester. Then he transferred to this university. At White University he studied civil engineering.
>
> At present is a senior in the college of engineering, majoring in civil engineering.
>
> Spends about 18 hours/week studying. Is not working while attending the university.
>
> Work experience: Worked for an engineering firm during the past three summers.
>
> Leisure Time Activities: Reading, dating occasionally, dancing.

Family:—Father, age 60, occupation not indicated. Mother, age 60, housewife.

> Both parents living; parents still married. No siblings.

REPORT OF TEST DATA

Test administered:

(1) Freshmen placement tests consisting of—

    (a) American Council on Education Psychological Examination for College Freshmen, 1942 Edition.

    (b) Cooperative English Test A: Mechanics of Expression, Form S.

    (c) Cooperative English Test B2: Effectiveness of Expression, Form S.

The results of these three tests are reported at the beginning of of the case.

(2) Strong Vocational Interest Blank, Form M—see profile sheet.

(3) Kuder Preference Record, Vocational, Form CH—see profile sheet.

STRONG VOCATIONAL INTEREST TEST—MEN

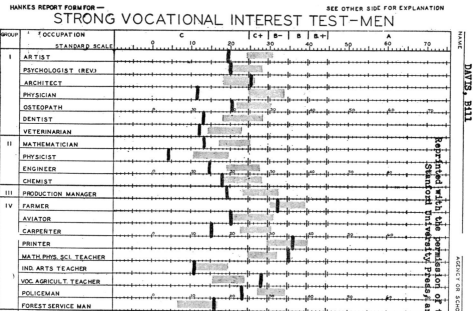
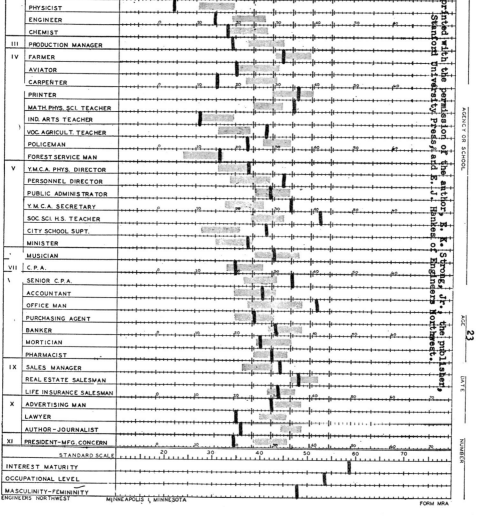

GROUP	OCCUPATION
I	ARTIST
	PSYCHOLOGIST (REV.)
	ARCHITECT
	PHYSICIAN
	OSTEOPATH
	DENTIST
	VETERINARIAN
II	MATHEMATICIAN
	PHYSICIST
	ENGINEER
	CHEMIST
III	PRODUCTION MANAGER
IV	FARMER
	AVIATOR
	CARPENTER
	PRINTER
	MATH. PHYS. SCI. TEACHER
	IND. ARTS TEACHER
	VOC. AGRICULT. TEACHER
	POLICEMAN
	FOREST SERVICE MAN
V	Y.M.C.A. PHYS. DIRECTOR
	PERSONNEL DIRECTOR
	PUBLIC ADMINISTRATOR
	Y.M.C.A. SECRETARY
	SOC. SCI. H.S. TEACHER
	CITY SCHOOL SUPT.
	MINISTER
	MUSICIAN
VII	C.P.A.
	SENIOR C.P.A.
	ACCOUNTANT
	OFFICE MAN
	PURCHASING AGENT
	BANKER
	MORTICIAN
	PHARMACIST
IX	SALES MANAGER
	REAL ESTATE SALESMAN
	LIFE INSURANCE SALESMAN
X	ADVERTISING MAN
	LAWYER
	AUTHOR—JOURNALIST
XI	PRESIDENT—MFG. CONCERN

STANDARD SCALE C   C+ B- B B+ A

INTEREST MATURITY

OCCUPATIONAL LEVEL

MASCULINITY—FEMININITY

ENGINEERS NORTHWEST   MINNEAPOLIS I, MINNESOTA   FORM MRA

NAME **DAVIS,** **Bill** _____ AGE **23** SEX **M** Code **4670--3812** _____ DATE OF TEST _____
Print   Last   First   Initial   M or F

SELF-INTERPRETING

PROFILE SHEET

for the

KUDER PREFERENCE RECORD
VOCATIONAL

Form C

MEN and WOMEN

DIRECTIONS FOR PROFILING

1. Copy the V-Score from the back page of your answer pad in the box at the right. **[43]**

" *your V-Score is 37 or less,* there is some __son for doubting the value of your answers, l your other scores may not be very accurate.

, , your V-Score is 45 or more, you may not have understood the directions, since 44 is the highest possible score. *If your score is not between 38 and 44,* inclusive, you should see your adviser. He will probably recommend that you read the directions again, and then that you fill out the blank a second time, being careful to. follow the directions exactly and to give sincere replies.

If your V-Score is between 38 and 44, inclusive, go ahead with the following directions.

2. Copy the scores 0 through 9 in the spaces at the top of the profile chart. Under "OUTDOOR" ⌐ d the number which is the same as the score ⌐ he top. Use the numbers under M if you are ⌐an and the numbers under F if you are a woman. Draw a line through this number from one side to the other of the entire column under OUTDOOR. Do the same thing for the scores at the top of each of the other columns. If a score is larger than any number in the column, draw a line across the top of the column: if it is smaller, draw a line across the bottom.

3. With your pencil blacken the entire space between the lines you have drawn and the bottom of the chart. The result is your profile for the *Kuder Preference Record—Vocational.*

Published by SCIENCE RESEARCH ASSOCIATES
228 South Wabash Avenue, Chicago 4, Illinois
Copyright 1951, by G. Frederic Kuder. Copyright under International Copyright Union. All rights reserved under Fourth International American Convention (1910). Printed in the U.S.A. Copyright 1951 in Canada.

Please use code number 7-299 when reordering this profile.

First Revision, February 1951

	0 51	1 32	2 24	3 23	4 60	5 23	6 30	7 19	8 25	9 42
	OUTDOOR	MECHANICAL	COMPUTATIONAL	SCIENTIFIC	PERSUASIVE	ARTISTIC	LITERARY	MUSICAL	SOCIAL SERVICE	CLERICAL

Reprinted with permission of the publisher,
Science Research Associates.

SECOND INTERVIEW

(*27 Days after First Interview*)

★ The Strong Vocational Interest Blank came back from the scorer without a name on it. The counselor could not be sure that it belonged to this client, so, he asked this client to take the Strong Vocational Interest Blank again which the client did. This is what they are referring to in the first few responses.

C1—Well, it must have been right the first time, Bill.

S1—Yes. You mean it's the same as the one before?

C2—It surely is.

S2—Well, that might be.

C3—Looking at the Kuder I think probably, that there is more reason to believe that it is.

S3—Is that the second one that I took? This one here, is that the Kuder?

C4—Yes. You'll notice here for instance—these things measure interest in two different ways. I mean, the Kuder is more or less your frame of reference—how you feel about different activities—which you prefer. And this one, as I explained before, actually gives you these things to respond to and then compares you with people who are out in the field active on the job and content, happy with what they are doing.

★ Both client and counselor are studying the profile. Some counselors prefer to interpret test data without showing the client the profile. In doing so the counselor must either rely on his memory solely, or, by looking at the profile without showing it to the client, run the risk of having the client feel that he is not being allowed to co-operate in the venture as much as he might like to. Most clients participate much more actively in the discussion of test data if they are allowed to look at the test records while the counselor explains it than if they are not. This is particularly important when the test results may be "bad news" for the client. By placing the test record on the desk in front of the client, the counselor can appear less identified with the data and the client feels freer to reject or distort the data without rejecting the counselor in doing so.

S4—Um-huh.

C5—Now—you'll notice here most engineers—I'll show you a typical engineering profile in a minute. Here, this is called physical science area, this area right here. Your interests are practically in every case dissimilar.

S5—Oh, I kind of thought that that was the way it would come out in a way. I mean, I sort of had that in mind. Lots of my answers, I don't know it seemed to, you know, when you weigh one against a certain group and then later down the paper you find it again and then you weigh it against that group. And, in that respect that's where I thought they might be a little dissimilar.

C6—The same way here in the biological science area, practically all dissimilar. In the technical area most engineers come out here farther than you have. You have some that are indefinite, some that are slightly similar but most of them are very weak.

S6—How do they grade the indefinite ones?

C7—Well, it's a matter of responding to these different things that, statistically they point out a pattern and if you respond to so many in such a way, why, it gives you a more typical pattern, more typical score for some things than for others. You don't have much interest we'll say in this technical area in which you will find quite a bit of interest with engineers. A little, but not much interest here in the social service area, that area in which people are interested in helping others, a B+ rating. In fact, you have nothing on the whole profile but B's, nothing higher that a B+ rating.

> ★ **C7** is an inadequate answer to the client's question about the
> meaning of scores in the "shaded" area on the profile. However,
> in **C29** the counselor does give a definitive answer to this question.

S7—(*Client interrupts*). In other words, I didn't put enough answers down there, or positive answers.

C8—For any one of those particular scales, yes. You didn't respond in the way that people who are out on these jobs would respond.

S8—Um-huh.

C9—And the same way here in business detail. There is a little interest indicated here but even that is very slight. You have a profile here which, ah,—

S9—Doesn't show a whole lot.

C10—It doesn't show a whole lot, but people who have profiles like that quite frequently wind up in business. Which, as I remember, is something that you're rather interested in. Eventually, some sort of business, isn't that the idea.

S10—Um-huh, eventually, I think. I don't know—

C11—And, that (*profile*) is typical of people who go into business. They don't show much of a differentiated profile a lot of times. (*pause*) Now let's look at—

S11—(*Client interrupts*). I had a hard time taking that quiz in a way. And, I took this one again, and by that time after I've seen the answers one time you should know just about, you shouldn't have to deliberate on any of them. These up here, now, if your score would come out up here it would mean that you were intensely interested in it, is that right?

C12—It would mean very strong similar interests to people in that group. For instance, on an engineer's scale where you scored in the C ratings—

S12—Um-huh.

C13—a typical engineer will score somewhere out in here, B+ or A. He'll be quite far out there on the chemist scale usually, too.

S13—Um-huh.

C14—When you score out in here, that means that you respond to those questions just about like the average engineer does—the man who is out on the job and is happy with what he is doing. But you didn't. You answered those items the opposite way from what an engineer would. Let me show you a typical engineer's profile that was worked out in a doctoral dissertation. (Pause, while counselor gets out a Strong Vocational Interest Blank profile which shows interest pattern of students who were in their third year in the engineering school contrasted with that of students who had entered the engineering college as freshmen but later transferred to another college in the university and were in their third year in college.) The black are the engineers. The crosshatch are the non-engineers.

S14—Um-huh.

C15—Here the engineers' median score was a B+ but they ranged everywhere from an A down to a B, nothing below that. On the chemist scale, his median was almost a B+, and they range from the A's to the B's. Farmer scale median score, B, and lot of them you'll find out here in the A's. So you can see that the profile juts out here in this technical area.

S15—Um-huh.

C16—And, there is considerable interest in these two areas, engineer and chemist. Now, it drops back here, median scores do, which isn't too much different from what you have here. But the big difference is in the engineer and chemist scales and in all of these jobs in the techincal area. You just don't have a typical engineer's pattern. (*pause*)

★ The counselor is drawing upon research data and clinical use of the Strong Vocational Interest Blank. In **C14**, he was referring to Saddler's unpublished doctorial dissertation (*307*) made at the University of Missouri in which all students in the study had entered the College of Engineering in September, 1946 and were studied two years later. Saddler contrasted the group of students who were still in engineering in September, 1948 with a group of students who were no longer in engineering at that time but were enrolled in some other division of the University. These two groups were called Engineers and Non-Engineers. In Appendix A a composite profile showing the differences Saddler found between the two groups in interest patterns is presented. Saddler noted that those who remained in engineering had significantly different interest patterns from those who left engineering but continued to succeed in college. The Engineer and the Chemist Scales differentiated the two groups sharply. In the study, civil, chemical, electrical, and mechanical engineering students were treated as one group without regard to specialization. Significant differences were found between the two groups of students on other variables studied even though precollege backgrounds of the two groups were quite similar.

The contrast between Bill Davis' S.V.I.B. Profile and Saddler's engineering students profile is evident. By looking at both of them, one can understand the statements made by the counselor in **C14, C15,** and **C16.** Bill Davis does not have an engineer's profile.

S16—I see. (*pause, while client looks at profile sheet*).

C17—Now, you know more about yourself, how do you feel about those things? You've indicated a little bit to me last time that engineering wasn't what you wanted to do for the rest of your life.

> ★ The counselor started to have the client relate the test data to how he perceives himself but negated the effect of this when he continued with another idea. It would have been better if he had stopped after the first sentence of this response.

S17—Um-huh.

C18—And this would tend to back that up.

S18—Why do I have to have such a high rating in that?

C19—Actually it's in the shaded area.

S19—Oh, I see.

C20—You see the shaded areas are more or less inconclusive, they are not strong one way or the other, just kind of there. (*pause*) Social service —you have, let's see, four scales in the social service area that are similar and one that is quite strong, a B+ on it,—high school teacher.

S20—How come I get such a low rating on C.P.A. while on senior C.P.A. I'm up here in the B+?

C21—Those are two different jobs. The C.P.A., works for himself, you see this scale is in an area by itself.

S21—Um-huh, yes.

C22—But the senior C.P.A. is considered in the business detail area.

S22—I see, um-huh.

C23—This is the person who owns his own business, his own certified public accounting business.

S23—I see.

C24—This fellow works for somebody else and in that way they differ.

S24—Um-huh.

C25—They are a different breed of animal I guess, for some reason they are. You show some interest in that business detail area.

★ This discussion of C.P.A. and Senior C.P.A. demonstrates the value of a good "working knowledge" of the characteristics of various norm groups of tests being used. This is essential in test interpretation, particularly with empirically derived tests (*147*, *413*).

S25—I show some interest as far as, what would you say my median is? I mean, as far as interest and non-interest, or can you draw a conclusion?

C26—Well, you can draw a little bit of a conclusion there. I mean, you can't get anything strong, for instance. But look up here in the biological science area. You can say pretty well that your interests are dissimilar in that area.

S26—Um-huh.

C27—The same way in the physical science.

S27—Um-huh.

C28—They are pretty much different.

S28—Um-huh.

C29—Your marks on this side of the gray indicate dissimilar interest. Where it is above it would be similar interest in varying degrees.

S29—Um-huh, yes.

C30—Now here in this technical area they are either inconclusive or they're dissimilar practically, except here on Vocational Ag. teacher, another teaching job, there is a little bit of interest there. Now, here in the social service area you have four that are definitely more similar than dissimilar and yet they are all rather weak except this one right here which is a teaching job. Business detail—they are either inconclusive or similar. The senior C.P.A. and this office man are similar but this is the only one that's really significantly similar.

S30—Um-huh.

C31—This linguistic area shows dissimilar interest. Business sales, contact with people, selling of something is inconclusive. Except for this one which isn't—

S31—I kind of thought that was the way it would come out. I don't know, I just sort of had the feeling.

C32—Uh-huh. Maybe we can relate these two here, Bill (*referring to the Kuder and Strong tests.*)

★ Sometimes the beginning counselor feels that the results of the Kuder Preference Record and Strong Vocational Interest Blank can be related to each other only when the test results agree with each other. A good illustration of this attitude was the counselor-in-training who came up with what appeared to be inconsistencies between the Kuder Preference Record and Strong Vocational Interest Blank for a client and remarked, "which one of these tests should I throw away?" As a matter of fact, discrepancies between any two tests may yield significant information for both client and counselor.

S32—Let's try.

C33—Scientific way down, very little interest which is indicated right here. In other words you think about yourself in what you prefer and do not prefer in the same way that you measure out over here when compared with people who are actually doing the job. You show considerable interest in this persuasive area. Now, that doesn't quite go along with what we have here in sales, when it is actually compared with people doing the work. Did you ever have any contact with sales work?

★ By using a coding system similar to the one proposed by Hathaway (*181*) for the MMPI, the profiles for various occupational groups reported in the manual for the Kuder Preference Record—Vocational can be converted into readily usable data. Each scale is assigned a number: 0—outdoor, 1—mechanical, 2—computational, 3—scientific, 4—persuasive, 5—artistic, 6—literary, 7—musical, 8—social service, 9—clerical. The numbers representing the scales on which significantly high scores were obtained are placed to the left of a dash and the numbers representing the scales on which significantly low scores were obtained are placed to the right of the (*69*).

The code for the profile representative of a group composed of various kinds of engineers is '32—'8, indicating that engineers typically have peak scores on the scientific and computational scales. Contrast this with the code for the client's profile, 467'0—381'2, in which both scientific and computational scores are low.

The prime (') is used in coding to differentiate the high scores from the near high scores, and the low ones from the near low ones (*69*).

S33—Well, I'll tell you what. Well, no, I haven't done any selling. The reason might be that some of the questions over here, I wasn't thinking of selling in terms of, ah, I wasn't thinking in terms of selling as far as persuading is concerned.

C34—Um-huh. What were you thinking of, your contact with, the men on the job?

S34—Well, no, I don't think so. 'Course the only real experience I've ever had in persuading people has been on jobs that I've had like in a fraternity or something like that. And that would be what I was thinking of—jobs like that or, in the service sometime persuading someone into something. And, I used to have pretty much luck on that. Of course, as far as selling is concerned now, I don't know. Is persuading necessary to selling?

C35—Usually you'll find that people in sales will score pretty high on that persuasive scale. Now, engineering sales is a little different I suspect from most sales work because it is a rather technical sales. Isn't that right?

★ Some of the groups which have peak scores on the persuasive scale are: sales managers, 4'—'102; filling station managers, 4'—'; salesmen and sales agents (except to customers), 4'—'1; retail store managers, 4'—'210; sales engineers, 4'—9'7.

S35—Yes.

C36—You've got a certain technical knowledge here about your product and you're going to use that in order to sell them something. It isn't so much a matter of giving them a smooth line of oil, you have to show them what you've got here and you present it in a rather technical manner. So it is a different type of sales actually.

S36—The way I look at it—sales—the reason I think I scored so low there is that in a selling job, you have such a good product that if the person has a need for it he's going to buy it. Of course, a good salesman is one that has more sales than the other fellow.

C37—Yes.

S37—The other one will have the persuasion ability to go with it. That's the way that I look at selling.

C38—Yes, I think you've got something.

S38—As far as I'm concerned if a salesman approaches me, if I need the object I'll buy it regardless of how much persuasion he might use.

C39—Um-huh.

S39—Now, that is probably different with other people.

C40—If you don't have use for it, you're not going to buy it regardless of what he is selling. Look here, as far as the sales manager is concerned, it shows some similarity in your interest, a B— which is pretty weak, but nevertheless some similarity whereas here in the other two it's in that inconclusive area. You don't know.

S40—Um-huh.

C41—And there is a difference between sales managers jobs and the real estate salesman and life insurance salesman. Those people are contacting customers, selling in that respect but the sales manager is doing something a little different than that. He is working with a group of salesmen, more or less in a technical capacity as a salesman. That might have some relationship to this. The only significant areas are here in persuasive, literary, musical. This is the average range between here and here and these are pretty far down the line. But you do pop up there in that persuasive area. What do you think about these?

S41—I haven't had much, ah,—I don't know.

C42—Do you like to read?

S42—I don't spend a lot of time reading, no, except just for studying.

C43—But you do like to read?

> ★ Here the counselor is referring to the literary scale of the Kuder Preference Record, Vocational. His implied interpretation of the literary scale is rather tenuous. Some of the occupational groups who have peak scores on the literary scale are: lawyers and judges, 6'—1'; advertising agents, 64'7—21'39; authors, editors and reporters, 6'7—123'0; musicians and music teachers, 7'6—123'4. It would have been better if the counselor had referred to the data in the manual for the test.

S43—Yes.

C44—Well, these can very easily be avocational interest showing up like that. The same way with music. Do you like music? Good music?

S44—Well, I've never studied any, if that's what you mean.

C45—No, but you do like to listen to it?

S45—Oh, yes.

C46—That's what I mean by avocational interest, that sort of pops up here. In your case about the only one that we could really relate to your problem, your going out and getting a job, is the persuasive area. In other words, you would prefer that type of activity more than you would any of the others here. Social service is way down.

> ★ The interpretation of the literary and musical scales is inadequate. It is "forced" and the counselor gave the client no opportunity to react to it, i.e., test it against his concept of himself. In making an interpretation of test data, the counselor should do it in such a way that the client is given the opportunity to and feels free to agree, disagree, or distort the information in any way he needs to. Only in this way can the test information be integrated into the

self-concept of the individual. In cases where discrepancies are quite evident, the counselor feels no obligation to defend the test but simply uses test results to explore the reasons for such a discrepancy with the client.

S46—It seems to be a little different from this over here, doesn't it? (*referring to the Strong Vocational Interest Blank*)

C47—A little. (*pause*)

S47—I think quite a few of these questions on social service had to do with clinical work and things like that, didn't they? I'm not sure.

C48—They were slanted toward helping other people, pretty definitely.

S48—Yes.

C49—There wasn't much doubt in your mind at what they were driving at perhaps.

S49—Um-huh. Interesting to say the least.

C50—What do you think about it, Bill?

S50—Well, I'll tell you, that's probably one reason I came to see you.

C51—What do you mean by that?

S51—What's this masculinity—femininity? (*The client had just noticed the M-F scale.*)

C52—That indicates masculine or feminine interest as far as the vocation is concerned.

S52—Oh. Um-huh, I see.

C53—You scored about average here which is probably a little less than most engineers because they seem to come up right around in here.

S53—Um-huh.

C54—For engineers.

S54—What's this interest maturity?

C55—I won't even try to interpret it to you. It doesn't make any difference.

S55—Occupational Level?

C56—Oh, interest maturity! Occupational level was what I was thinking of. Interest maturity gives us an indication of whether your interests have crystallized or not. When you were in high school up to about the time you were about 18 why your interests are pretty much in a state of flux. I mean, you'll be interested in one thing for a while and then turn a little while later and be interested in something entirely different. Between 18 and 25 they feel that your interests pretty well set themselves into a pattern that you'll hold probably the rest of your life. There is an indication there that your interests have stabilized, that they are not necessarily in a state of flux. When that thing goes down low, then that is a pretty good indication that the measure that you have here is not a good measure, that is could change in, say, six months or so.

★ This is an essentially correct statement about the interest maturity scale. However, we have a few cases which suggest that a high I-M score cannot be completely trusted to indicate stability of interest. From clinical experience we have found that persons with high I-M scores who are changing their concepts of themselves and their environment, as far as socio-economic status is concerned, by virtue of higher education, can have a radical shift in pattern of vocational interest. The counselor should be very cautious in helping a client make long term educational and vocational plans if the client is highly intelligent and comes from low socio-economic background. His vocational interests may change markedly as new "horizons" come within his perceived realm of possibilities.

S56—I see. Well, if this thing runs down here quite a ways it would mean that these things are a little—

C57—(*Counselor interrupts*). I wouldn't put my faith in the profile.

S57—I see.

C58—But, there are people like you who just don't have an outstanding interest pattern on that; and they have found through research, that those people many times wind up in some business capacity of some sort.

S58—Um-huh. Well, this thing doesn't show anything outstanding then does it?

C59—No, it doesn't (*pause*) It probably shows more interest in business detail than it does in any other field there.

S59—Um-huh. (*pause*) Social science high school teacher.

C60—Um-huh. You've been taking this course in sociology and getting in your humanities requirements, haven't you? You said that you had gotten a kick out of it.

S60—Well, they're interesting courses, yeah.

C61—Yes. (*pause*) Maybe that influenced your scores somewhat.

S61—It possibly did. (*Pause, while client looks at profile sheet.*) Um-huh. This is your interest. What did you say this showed?

C62—It is also another interest test but it is from a preference angle rather than comparing you directly to people who are out on the job working.

S62—What do these numbers refer to up here, 60 and—?

C63—That's a raw score, I believe. (*pause*)

S63—I thought that 35 ran along all the way through.

C64—No. That's a raw score and then that gives you your percentile rank over here on the side.

S64—Well, they were interesting to take.

C65—Do you think that you learned anything about yourself by taking it?

S65—I think so. Well, ah, I don't know. I did learn something about myself but I don't believe that I learned too much that I didn't know, probably.

> ★ At this point in an interview the counselor usually would like to have the client summarize what he has *learned* from the interpretation of test results. A question such as: "How would you describe what these test results mean to you?" usually produces the desired result. Gaps in and distortions of the test data can be very glaring in these summaries. The counselor gets at this in **C68**.

C66—Yes, confirmed it.

S66—I think probably (*pause*)—

C67—In other words you had a feeling all along that, that your interest was not definitely in engineering.

S67—Well, primarily, yes. That's why I wanted to take these tests. (*pause*)

C68—What do you think these things will mean to you in terms of going out and getting a job?

S68—Well—. (*pause*) I don't know, that's a good question.

C69—Well, let's look at it this way, Bill, in respect to the different areas in engineering where jobs are available. Which one of these areas do you think that you would fit in best? (*pause*)

S68—Well, from the looks of this (*pause*) it would probably be in, I don't know, in the detailing or something like that.

C70—What do you mean by detailing, Bill? I don't think I've heard of that term.

S70—Well, a detailer is a draftsman in a way. A designer. He actually designs say a bridge and so forth, and the detailer actually works with the detail of the thing.

C71—How about production?

S71—Well, do you mean from the standpoint of this or—

C72—Um-huh. (*pause*)

S72—Well, I could be interested in that. 'Course my scale fell down here to—where was it?

C73—Yes. But now let's look. In production what are you doing? You have more contact with people in production probably than you do . . .

S73—Yes.

C74— . . . in any of the other things except sales and that doesn't show up too well in sales, does it? In production you are working with men on a job aren't you?

S74—Well, if you're in a factory or something like that.

C75—Yes, let's say so.

S75—Producing something.

C76—Here's the thing about design or research and development. Your scientific interest is probably not great enough for you to enjoy a job like that, is it?

S76—Not for too long, that's true.

C77—Sales, we don't know exactly. It is possible that you will do all right in that area but we don't know really. There is more to indicate that something like production would be of more interest to you than any of the others that you would tease out of that thing, don't you think? (*pause*)

S77—You mean taking both of them together and the persuasive part of it and this over here.

C78—The interest there is business detail. (*pause*)

S78—Yes, well perhaps you're right.

C79—I don't know, I'm just throwing it out—

S79—Well, I guess this interest thing, you don't know exactly where— you don't find any real outstanding interest. You don't know exactly what kind of conclusion to draw do you?

> ★ The client is expressing some disappointment with the fact that his vocational interests are not strongly focused in some area. This is a common reaction when interests are relatively undifferentiated. Probably it would have been better to recognize this feeling, rather than to reiterate the interpretation made previously.

C80—Well, one conclusion that you can draw is that many people with a profile like that do go into business. (*pause*) The very absence of the pattern leads you to draw that kind of conclusion.

S80—I see. (*pause*) Well, I guess I've taken up enough of your time.

C81—Well, that's what I'm here for.

S81—But, I'll think about this.

C82—Well, that's the main value to give you something to think about. Like I said before you can't get any pat answers from these things. You've got to relate them to yourself and how you feel about these things and then they become valuable.

S82—Um-huh. I think I'm just about four years too late in taking this thing, but,—

C83—I wouldn't say that.

> ★ This attempt at reassurance probably is inappropriate. A response something like this would have helped the client clarify his thinking on this matter: "Do you suppose you would have done anything differently four years ago if you knew then what you know now?"

S83—'Course, it's never too late.

C84—No. (*pause*) Have you looked into any job possibilities?

S84—I have had some interviews and some offers and the conclusion that I can draw from that is that I'll never be highly successful in say, chemical engineering or something like that. Is that right according to what that shows?

C85—Well, let's not put it that way because, these are not aptitude tests. Remember that. It's an interest test.

S85—An interest test.

C86—Let's say, you probably wouldn't be too happy with a job in this area because—

S86—I see, yes.

C87—Because of the fact that your interests are not there. I mean, interest is a big factor in your success, that's true.

S87—It is. I think it is in every respect.

C88—And as interest affects success you can say that, yes. In other words, you would be more happy doing something else rather than a research or design job in engineering. It's quite possible that you would have much more interest and get along quite satisfactorily in an aspect of engineering that wasn't concerned with design or research; something more of a business-like nature.

> ★ This is a good summary of the implications of the test data for the client. It is difficult to know from the client's response how well he understands and accepts this information about himself.

S88—I see. Well, I'll keep these things in mind.

C89—Okay.

S89—And, I want to thank you for your trouble.

C90—I hope it gives you some leads, something to think about.

S90—Do you keep these on file over here?

C91—Yes.

S91—Well, I guess this will close my case for a while. (*laughs*)

C92—Do you have any other questions? Why, fire away.

S92—All right, I'll do that. I can't think of anything else right now.

C93—Did I show you the Occupational Information Library when you were in here the last time?

★ This statement might have begun.—"Have you become familiar with various jobs in Engineering." Then—"Did I show you the Occupational Information Library when you were in here the last time?"

S93—No.

C94—You might be interested in looking through it. I'll show it to you and if you'd like to, why, you can look through it.

S94—Something like this sort of confirms an idea that I've had. I don't know whether you've read this article by Hutchins, who used to be at Chicago.

C95—Robert Hutchins, Yes.

S95—He says the way to get an education is to enroll in liberal arts and just take courses that you want to take and spend time in the library reading books. I've sort of, the last six months or so, it has seemed a lot clearer but, you're not going to college,—and college isn't going to fix it so you can make a million dollars or anything like that. It's just mostly luck anyway.

C96—Um-huh.

S96—I'm beginning to realize that now, I mean, that sort of shows up in these tests.

C97—All the way through, Bill, in your engineering training, as you think back now, were you particularly interested in your course?

S97—Well, that's what is so unusual, I'm surprised that I didn't come in before.

C98—Because you have felt a certain dissatisfaction with the courses.

S98—Well, I didn't think that I felt any more dissatisfied than somebody else who talks about his courses, about how rough a course is. I've gotten along all right. I know what I'm doing.

C99—Um-huh.

S99—But as long as I'm here I may as well get a degree that possibly is going to mean more than a liberal arts degree or something like that, but I see that now it doesn't as far as education is concerned. My ideas have changed a lot in the last few years I think.

C100—The last few years.

S100—(*Client interrupts*). When I came up to college I thought that I knew absolutely what I wanted. And, I went into engineering just "whole-hog." I haven't gotten an "I" in school yet. Of course my grades haven't been too high either, but they are above average.

C101—You've hit the more specialized training here in the last couple of years. It has become a little sterile to you, is that right?

★ Exploring the idea of why he was so certain as a freshman might have opened new areas for consideration—family pressure, friends, changing self-concept, motives at that time, etc.

The present discussion was not too productive. Reflection of the feeling rather than content might have produced better results.

S101—Well, I don't know. You see in Engineering School you can't take a whole lot of—. It's not like the business curriculum where you stay in the Arts College for the first two years. In engineering school you start right out and I suppose never do get into much of that to really get enough of a taste of it.

C102—The little taste you've had here lately has kind of—

S102—(*Client interrupts*). Yes, perhaps that's one of the reasons. I don't know.

C103—Given you a taste for more.

S103—Maybe. (*laughs*) It's hard to decide.

C104—Yes.

S104—In college you can get out and get just about as much out of a good library as you can get out of taking courses here in school. But, after I get out of here, I don't know, I'd better get into a field. Ah, being happy, it kind of correlates—Being happy on your job and the amount of money that you are making, I don't believe is necessarily—

C105—One involves the other.

S105—True, true.

C106—That depends upon the person of course. There are some people where making a good deal of money is absolutely essential to a job as far as they are concerned in order to be happy. With others, the job itself is enough to make up for a good deal of money that they don't have if they are happy with what they are doing.

S106—It seems in any job to make a good salary you've got to spend a lot of time on it. Most men if they're successful spend more time out of the office than inside. They do work at home and on the week ends when they're starting out.

C107—Um-huh. (*pause*)

S107—Well, I've taken enough of your time, I think.

C108—Well, if you have any other questions, Bill, feel free to come back in.

S108—Well, I'll do that. It's been a great help in taking those tests. I'm glad that I had the opportunity.

C109—I'm glad we could give them to you. I'll show you the Occupational Information Library, just in case you're interested.

COUNSELOR'S NOTES ON THE SECOND INTERVIEW
(Dictated Immediately after the Interview)

★ Mr. Davis came in today for a test interpretation. The Strong Vocational Interest Blank showed a flat pattern, one that is similar to those people in college who go on into business at some time or another. This tends to back up what he had talked about the first time he had come in, that eventually he wants to go into business instead of engineering. The results of the Strong didn't seem to surprise him any. In fact, he said he'd been rather expecting something similar to this to show up. Most of our discussion today was concerned with the two interest tests and a rather thorough interpretation of the two. The client asked a lot of intelligent questions about how the two were made up and just what they consisted of. He seemed to arrive at the conclusion that the tests confirmed the fact that his real interest was not in engineering as such. We seemed to arrive at the conclusion that should he go on into engineering that something in the line of production would probably be of most interest to him. Mr. Davis also expressed a few more of his ideas on the engineering curriculum, the fact that he probably wishes now that he had had more information about himself and his interests earlier in his scholastic career. He seems to be, as he brought up in the first interview, a bit disappointed in his college work. I showed him the Occupational Information Library before he left, but we made no further contacts.

ADDENDUM

★ The first concern of the counselor in any given counseling situation is that of clarifying and developing the client's problem(s). There are many ways of working toward this goal. Thorne (*400*) and others have recommended that early phases of the first interview be given over to the discussion of topics introduced by the client, utilizing counselor responses, such as general leads, simple acceptance, structuring, and reflection of feeling. In many cases, client problems are complex and interrelated, one (or more) assuming primary importance with another problem area of lesser importance serving only as a symptom. The first interview is usually used to aid the client in sensing these problem areas and placing them in the proper perspective to each other.

The Case of Bill Davis is an example of counseling without any clarification of the client's problem. Bill is a senior in the engineering college. Evidence seems to indicate that his interests at least are quite dissimilar to graduates in engineering. He presented his problem in S1 as wanting to take some tests so that he could discover what direction to take in business. The counselor accepted this statement at face value. Without clarifying the client's stated problem, the counselor launched into a series of responses which led to the selection of tests to be taken. The first and second interviews did not clarify the client's original statement of his problem. Neither did they accomplish much in terms of client growth and understanding. Although the interviews yield interesting material, there is no closure in the case—nor is there any way to determine whether the client actually had a problem.

The beginning counselor might well be on guard against a similar error. He might easily find himself trapped in several ways, such as accepting a problem without further exploration or clarification, assuming that the client is seeking some particular service, taking referrals in the terms outlined by a referral agency, permitting his own needs and biases to interfere with the client's expession of his problem, or assuming that test data will clarify and isolate the client's problem.

CHAPTER 4

The Case of

TOM SMITH

★ THE CASE consists of five interviews; the first three were phonographically recorded. The first three interviews occurred within a span of three weeks. The fourth and fifth interviews occurred four months and a year later, respectively.

The first four interviews were conducted by one counselor and the fifth one by a different counselor since the original counselor was no longer on the staff of the counseling center. The original counselor of the case had earned a master's degree in counseling and guidance and had had about six months of part-time counseling experience at the time of the case.

The client was referred to the counseling center by the university psychiatrist with the following comment on the referral form, "Mr. Smith is having difficulty scholastically, especially in mathematics."

At the time of the first interview the counselor knew that the client had entered the university in the College of Agriculture two months earlier. Data from the following tests administered at the time the client entered the university were available:

A. *Freshman Placement Tests*

(1) Cooperative English Tests, Form S—

	Raw Score	Percentile Rank
A: Mechanics of Expression	66	3
B2: Effectiveness of Expression	1	1

(2) Hundred Problem Arithmetic Test, Form V—	42	11

The norm groups were university freshmen for the English tests and high school seniors for the arithmetic test.

B. *Tests of General Educational Development, College Level*
(*for purposes of establishing advanced standing college credit*)

	Standard Score	Percentile Rank
Test 1: Correctness and Effectiveness of Expression	41	1
Test 2: Interpretation of Reading Material in the Social Studies	43	3
Test 3: Interpretation of Reading Materials in the Natural Sciences	43	1
Test 4: Interpretation of Literary Materials	44	2

The norm group for the G.E.D. tests was college freshmen or sophomores who had just completed a comprehensive introductory or survey course related to the subject matter of the test. Norms are available for three types of colleges; Type II norms were used here.

FIRST INTERVIEW

(The First Few Responses were not Recorded)

C1—Can you tell me a little more about how you seem to be held back? For instance, what subjects do you seem to have the most difficulty with?

S1—Well, mathematics mostly.

C2—Mm-huh. How does that affect you?

S2—Well, I haven't done very good on the tests in taking them.

C3—Mm-huh. (*pause*) Could you tell me a little bit about your background, where you are from, what you plan to do and so forth?

S3—Well, I'm from (name of town).

C4—Yes.

S4—Have you ever been there?

C5—No. But I know where it is.

S5—I'm in pre-vet. school. I'd like to take up veterinary medicine, if I can make the grade.

C6—Mm-huh.

S6—That's my only trouble.

C7—When did you decide on veterinary medicine?

★ It might have been better to recognize the client's feeling that he may have difficulty "making the grade" in veterinary medicine. Failure to respond to this feeling at this time may have "set the stage" for much of the difficulty he encountered in later phases of the case. The counselor could have said, "Would you like to talk about that?"

S7—Well, I've been kind of interested for some time. I live on a farm and I work a lot with livestock.

C8—Do you know any veterinarians?

S8—Well, yes, our local veterinarian.

C9—Mm-huh. And you'd like to do the work he seems to be doing at the present time?

S9—Yes.

C10—You haven't worked with him though while he is working with animals, or anything like that?

S10—Well, yes, I've worked some.

C11—Have you?

★ Counselor responses in the early stages of the first interview frequently are quite crucial to the development of the problem. Two general principles can be followed to advantage: (1) pay unusually close attention to what the client is saying in terms of both content and feeling; and (2) use nondirective responses for the most part. The counselor has failed to implement either of these principles so far.

S11—Mm-huh.

C12—What made you choose veterinary medicine as the field you wanted to go into?

S12—Well—(*Counselor interrupts*)

C13—Was it any one person or just working on the farm?

S13—Working on the farm and there are a lot of demands for that now.

C14—Had you considered any other possibilities?

S14—You mean taking something else?

C15—Yes, going into some other field.

S15—Well, that could be agriculture.

C16—You could work on a farm then if it didn't pan out that you could make it in vet. medicine?

S16—That's right. A person could use all that knowledge on a farm anyway.

C17—That's right.

★ In the previous four responses the counselor seems to imply that the client should choose some field of endeavor other than veterinary medicine. Even though this may be "correct" it is too early in the case to suggest it. The client is not ready for it; at least the counselor has no evidence to suggest that the client is ready for it. The counselor should encourage the client to express his feelings about himself at this time.

S17—In fact, we have one in veterinary medicine school who is planning on going back after he graduates.

C18—Oh.

S18—Treat all the livestock.

C19—Mm-huh. Use his knowledge that he has with vet. medicine for his own stock and not necessarily for applying it as a doctor, is that right?

S19—Well, yes, and he can take some local calls.

C20—Oh, I see. (*pause*) Well, can you tell me a little bit more about yourself? As far as your high school work is concerned and perhaps how you stand with the Army and something along that line?

★ At this particular time there was considerable unrest among the male students due to the uncertainty of draft deferment policy. Many students were taking a "what's the use" attitude toward school work.

S20—Well, you see, my high school—I never really did go to high school. They gave me G.E.D. tests and I completed an agriculture course, that is, in correspondence. I made good grades on that, but I had a lot of time, you know, I could just study whenever I'd feel like it.

C21—Yes.

S21—I served in the armed forces for two years.

C22—It doesn't look as though you will be called up then?

S22—Well, not for a while.

C23—You're not in the reserve, are you?

S23—No.

C24—Sometimes the indecision and the fact that you don't know how you stand with the Army holds some people back in their academic work. (*pause*) As I understand it then you feel that testing will perhaps give you information that you want about yourself. To know perhaps where you would be best fitted and something about the reasons for your difficulties, is that right?

S24—Yes, in fact, that's what Dr. Block (*psychiatrist in student health service*) recommended.

C25—How did it happen you went to Dr. Block? Was he recommended to you by some of your friends?

★ The counselor asked a question which could have elicited some valuable information about why the client consulted the psychiatrist and how he felt about it. However, he blocked any possible free response to his question by continuing with another question which suggested a specific answer. Vague, unstructured, ambiguous questions are very useful in helping the client develop his problem in that such questions have a stimulus value similar to projective techniques, provided such questions are not followed by simple, structured questions. It would seem important to have the client develop more fully his reasons for consulting the psychiatrist and the nature of that contact in relation to being referred to the counselor. However, the client seems somewhat reluctant to do this (S27 and S28). A response such as, "Can you tell me a little more about that?" might have proven more pro-

ductive than **C28**. Then the counselor made a rather serious
error in **C28**. Having failed to develop the problem adequately,
he proceeded to a structuring response concerning tests. Such
structuring is quite premature.

S25—Well, yes. (*pause*)

C26—Did you feel that he was the person who might be able to help you
or not?

S26—Well, I just decided to see him for the curiosity of it.

C27—Mm-huh. What did you find out ?

S27—Well, he just asked me some questions and then he recommended
me to come over here and take some tests. (*pause*)

C28—Mm-huh. Well, I'll be glad to suggest some tests that will at least give
us some information about you. We ordinarily suggest for students who
have difficulty, a battery of three or four tests to get sort of an overall
picture to help you see yourself as compared with other individuals.
For instance, we like to get a picture of your interests, the range of your
interests, where your interests seem to lie, how your interests compare
with other people on particular jobs. We like to get some indication of
your scholastic aptitude. How you compare with other students, how
much capacity you have, how well you're working up to the capacity and
something along that line. Something about your personality to see
whether or not there may be some personal factors that may be holding
you back in doing your school work, and finally something in the way of
reading to give an indication as to whether or not perhaps ability to read
and comprehend might be part of your difficulty.

S28—How do you test a guy if he lies or not?

C29—If he lies?

S29—Yes, sir.

C30—Well, It's a little difficult to do although the personality test will
pick that up somewhat. Why did you ask?

S30—I just had that down on your list and I just wondered.

C31—Oh, you mean you were wondering if the personality test would
pick that up?

S31—Yes.

★ The client's question about "lying" is rather puzzling. One guess
as to its significance at this time is that it reflects some sort of
uncertainty concerning the suggested tests. Another guess as to
the significance of the client's question about "lying" is that it
may be an expression of hostility. Since the psychiatrist referred
the client to the counseling center, the client may have felt it
necessary that he consult the counselor in order to keep in "the

good graces" of the university. He may have been saying in effect, "I have kept this appointment but you can't force me to participate." The ensuing discussion of lie detectors may be a façade, a retreat from subtle expression of resistance and hostility.

C32—Of course, we don't have anything,—you mean something comparable to the lie detector that they use in court or something like that?

S32—Well, not necessarily, I just thought about it.

C33—Well, let me say this, that as far as any test is concerned, the information the test will give you will be only as meaningful to you as you are honest. If you attempt to change a test one way or another, to make yourself out to be someone that you're not, let's say, some tests just won't pick that up. I mean, it's all right, but we don't feel that we are here to try to pick that up necessarily. People who come over here do so pretty much on their own steam and we feel that they want as good information as they can possibly get. And, so we don't worry too much about whether or not they lied because if they do show up on a test one way or another we feel that they are cheating themselves. Does that seem to be logical to you?

S33—Yes, sir. I just asked it, I just wondered if the test—ah—is actually testing very well.

C34—Mm-huh.

S34—How do you test on this here—ah—how do you say, these tests they use in courts?

C35—As I understand it in court they find that when a person lies, deliberately lies, knowingly lies, that one thing a person's hand will sweat a little bit more than it ordinarily will or his blood pressure will rise a little bit above the normal level. It doesn't seem to be a great change and perhaps outwardly the person may be just as calm and collected apparently as can be, but I would say that those are the two main ways that they have of telling, that the blood pressure seems to rise or perhaps they seem to perspire more.

S35—What if he gets excited, then what? The blood pressure would rise then wouldn't it?

C36—Yes, but if a person is just excited or nervous about having to answer questions, shall we say, they can detect the difference between that nervousness and the nervousness from making a deliberate lie.

S36—Oh, I see.

C37—It's a matter of degree. Let's say that you are ordinarily a very calm and collected individual and you go in and someone starts asking you questions, he'll ask you a lot of irrelevant questions like what is your name, was it raining outside when you came in, or did you see anyone in the hall when you came in. Just questions that don't have a lot of mean-

ing just to establish a level of your nervousness under the question procedure. After he's established that, then he asks some pertinent questions
like where were you on the night of June 13th or something like that and
he can tell whether or not blood pressure or whether perspiration seems
to increase. It's rather an intricate system. There's always a lot of scientific research, of course, we don't have any such test here, but I guess
certain state agencies have the equipment that can do that.

S37—Well, it wouldn't help you in your work anyway.

C38—No, I don't suppose it would. Do you feel as though there are times
when you're not as honest with yourself as you would like to be?

S38—No. I'd like to have myself tested to see how honest I'd turn out.

C39—When have you felt that perhaps you weren't being quite as honest as
you should?

S39—Well, at no particular time.

C40—Mm-huh.

S40—Can you analyze on your handwriting?

> ★ This may be a further indication of resistance or it may indicate
> a need for structuring concerning what the client can expect from
> counseling and in general what the process will be. (See **S55**.)
> Is the client being defensive about something which he does not
> want to reveal to the counselor and is afraid that "tests" may do so
> against his wishes?

C41—Well, I haven't gone into that study very much, but as far as I
know you can't.

S41—You can't?

C42—No. Do you feel that your handwriting is different now than it was
some while ago?

S42—No. It's a funny thing, I kinda got shaky with my hands.

C43—Mm-huh.

S43—My writing is generally pretty good but sometimes I get shaky.
I kinda blur my writing.

C44—Mm-huh.

S44—Do you feel that is due to nervousness?

C45—When do you notice that type of thing?

S45—Well, when I get rushed up. Like taking a test, you know, kinda
get excited.

C46—Mm-huh. (*pause*) In other words if there is a little bit of pressure
put on you why you get a little upset, is that right?

S46—Yes, sir. (*pause*)

C47—Do you feel that if you were less nervous, more calm and collected when taking a test that you would perhaps make a better grade and do a better job on the test?

S47—Yes, sir. That's my trouble. I get nervous and jammed up.

C48—Mm-huh.

S48—Especially that part of the time.

C49—Mm-huh. Do you feel that when a test is all over and you look over your answers and your mistakes that you made, that you really know the answer perhaps as well as the next person but just because you were nervous you couldn't write down the right answer?

S49—Well, not exactly. If the question was a little complicated, it would take a little bit more thinking. I'd probably miss it on that account.

C50—Mm-huh. (*pause*)

S50—I get along with most tests all right.

C51—In other words, you feel that if the test doesn't require too much complicated thinking, and you can just follow it right through, you make out all right. But if it requires a lot of complicated thinking, you get a little mixed up, is that right?

S51—Mm-huh.

C52—Well, do you feel that you can do complicated thinking when you're not in a test situation?

S52—Yes, sir.

C53—But it's just this test situation that seems to (*client interrupts*).

S53—Mar it all.

C54—Well, you're not alone on that, I'll assure you that there are many other students who have similar difficulties. I might point out that we do have a reading and study clinic which might be able to help you on part of your difficulty, as far as study techniques are concerned and in reading ability to improve yourself. So if you do feel after testing, it's indicated that the reading clinic might help you, why we can see that you get help in that area. (*pause*) Do you feel that you know very much about our counseling service here? You were referred over here by Dr. Block (Psychiatrist). I don't know whether you're too well aware of our services or not.

★ From the test data available at the beginning of the interview the counselor knew that the client had limited scholastic achievement compared with other college freshmen. This, in turn, suggests limited ability to do college work. In **S49** the client indicates that he has some awareness of these limitations. The attempted reassurance and the implication that improved reading and study skills may compensate for lack of mental ability and scholastic achievement has probably hindered the client in developing self-understanding and self-acceptance. **C54** probably indicates that the counselor does not feel comfortable dealing with clients who are apt to fail scholastically in college. This is an attitude displayed frequently by beginning counselors. They seem to have difficulty identifying with clients who aspire to do college work but lack the mental ability to do so. It is as if the scholastically successful student feels that he cannot "afford" to associate with or be identified with the scholastically failing student. It appears that other students feel that to identify with the failing student is to place their own status and feeling of security in jeopardy. These attitudes probably carry over into the work of the beginning counselor.

S54—No, sir, I didn't know anything about it until he suggested it.

C55—I see. Well, let me explain the things that we do. Now you are going to take a battery of tests. That is one of the things we do here. We also spend a lot of time just talking with students to help them explore their personal attitudes, their outlook on the future, educationally, and job-wise to help them explore their future plans as much as we can, to see if just talking won't help people get their feet on the ground a little bit better, be able to work a little better in school. We have an occupational library which explains job possibilities in a number of different areas. If you're interested in the area of veterinary medicine, we have information about that particular area so that you can see a little better how you might fit after you finish, if you are able to finish your training and work into it. You can see how you would fit into the world of work as a veterinarian—something of your duties, pay, hours, in other words, just to help you see how you would fit into the world of work. So, those are the three main areas I suppose you might say that we have; the counseling, the testing, and the occupational information service, in addition to the reading and study skills clinic that I mentioned. Does that give you any better picture of perhaps what we may have to offer that can be of help to you?

S55—Oh, I see what you're getting at now.

C56—Well, how do you feel then that we can help you in addition to the testing? Do you think that there is any other area that we can help you or do you feel that testing will help you understand yourself well enough so that you can—

S56—Well, I might try testing and see how I come out.

C57—All right. Fine. Well, let me suggest some tests for you. I mentioned the interest tests, one of mental ability, the personality inventory and a reading test. Now I have an idea that it will probably take about four hours. You don't have to do it all at once, just take your time, you know, just whenever you have a free hour or so to complete the testing and then when you get through I think it will give you some valuable information about yourself. When do you have some free time so that you can drop by and take some of these tests?

S57—Let's see, I'll be off at three o'clock.

C58—Okay, well, that's fine. That will give you a couple of hours then this afternoon. You can work the rest whenever it seems convenient for you.

S58—Okay.

C59—Then when you get all through with your testing, we'll look over the tests and discuss them and see how that helps you and we can see where we will go from there after we get through with them. Well, do you have any other comments or questions you'd like to ask me about the service we have here.

S59—Not that I know of.

C60—All right, fine. I'll introduce you to the psychometrist who is the person who will give you the tests.

★ In analyzing initial interviews, we find rather typically several "errors" in counseling. Most often these so-called errors are instances in which the counselor has not been aware of or has not responded to significant statements of the client. However, it seems that if the counselor is attentive to the main stream of client thought and feeling, counseling proceeds satisfactorily without any real hindrance resulting from these errors. It would appear that so long as the client perceives the counselor as being a person who is accepting and understanding of him and who is intent on helping him reach a satisfactory solution to his problem, the counselor can make many technical errors without noticeably affecting the counseling process. Rogers emphasizes essentially this same point (291). This does not mean that appropriate attitude is sufficient; counseling skill is also necessary.

Usually, in the initial interview, the client produces so much potentially significant material that it is nearly impossible for the counselor to respond to all of it. This does not seem to be so much of a problem in later interviews. We have found that in supervising beginning counselors we need to guard against over-emphasizing technical errors, especially those occurring in the first interview.

The initial interview with referrals from another agency can be a little tricky, especially if the motivation for the referral comes essentially from the referring agency and not the client. We have come to believe that the person making the referral should do a great deal more than is usually done in making a referral. "I think you should see Mr. Block," usually is not suffi-

client. In the present case there are indications that the client did not understand very well what he could expect from the counselor. The momentary flare of hostility and resistance could be a result of this lack of understanding. The counselor attempted to handle this situation through passive acceptance of the client's feelings of hostility and then explaining the nature of the counseling relationship and what the client could expect from it. However, in light of subsequent developments, the client seems to persist in the idea that tests would solve his problem. Perhaps this idea is less threatening to the client than one which might suggest a change in the manner in which he perceives himself.

COUNSELOR'S NOTES ON THE FIRST INTERVIEW
(*Dictated Immediately after the Interview*)

★ Mr. Smith came to the counseling service at the suggestion of the university psychiatrist. (In a telephone conversation the psychiatrist indicated to the counselor that this man's problem was not an emotional problem as much as it was one of lack of academic success.) Mr. Smith said that he had been having serious difficulty scholastically, particularly in mathematics. He appeared to be a retiring individual and indicated nervousness and blocking on tests. The counselor's hunch is that it is lack of scholastic aptitude, especially in view of the freshman placement test scores. He is a preveterinary medicine student. His interest in vet medicine stems from his farm background and association with the local veterinarian. The university psychiatrist suggested a test battery and Mr. Smith felt also that this would be helpful to him. He will return at a later date for interpretation of the test data and further discussion.

PERSONAL DATA SHEET

Between the first and second interview the client filled out a one-page personal data sheet. Following is a summary of the information from the personal data sheet:

Client:—Age: 23 years.
　　　　Born in or near a small town in the state; present home address is this same small town.
　　　　Marital Status: Single.
　　　　Did not graduate from high school but was granted a high school equivalency certificate on the basis of High School G.E.D. Tests.
　　　　At present he is a freshman in the College of Agriculture enrolled in a preveterinary medicine curriculum.
　　　　Spends about 20 hours per week in study.
　　　　Works about 16 hours per week on the university farm; earns about half of his college expenses.

Work Experiences: General farming and feeding live-
stock for 8 years.
Attending college under the G.I. Bill (P.L. 346).
Leisure Time Activities: Reading.

Family:—Father living; mother dead.
Father's Occupation: Farming.
One brother, age 25, completed 8th grade, farmer.

TEST DATA

In addition to the test data available at the beginning of the first
interview (freshman placement tests and G.E.D. Tests), the following tests were administered between the first and second
interview with the following results:

(1) Strong Vocational Interest Blank, Form M, see profile.
The score on the interest maturity scale (IM) was a
standard score of 33, which is below the first percentile
rank compared with 23 year old men. See Strong (365, p.
263, Table 68). Also this IM score is well below the mean
IM score of any of Strong's criterion occupational groups;
the group of artists scored lowest on the average with a
mean IM score of about 46. The mean IM score for the
group of 23 year old men was about 53. It is our opinion
that the IM score of 33 is so deviate in terms of any appropriate norm group that it invalidates the remainder of
the profile as far as inferences customarily drawn are concerned. Since the IM score of 33 could have occurred by
chance answering much less than one time in a hundred,
we may conclude that it has some real meaning. Just what
this real meaning is is not known.

(2) Minnesota Multiphasic Personality Inventory, Booklet
Form, see profile.
This MMPI profile, characterized by a spike on the Sc
scale is a difficult one to interpret. Marked elevation on the
Sc scale suggests severe affective disturbance. A search of
the literature reveals no profile characteristic of psychiat-
rically diagnosed groups that is similar to this one. MMPI
profiles typical of various groups of psychotics and severe
neurotics are characterized by elevations on the neurotic
triad as well as on the psychotic scales. Groups classified
as mild or moderate neurotics achieve profiles with elevations on the neurotic triad and the Pt scale. Typical profiles for groups classified as conduct disorders, psychopathic personalities, constitutionally inferior personalities,
and psychopathic deviates have been reported in the
literature but these profiles seem to vary according to the
varying definitions of these groups. However, in no instance

STRONG VOCATIONAL INTEREST TEST—MEN

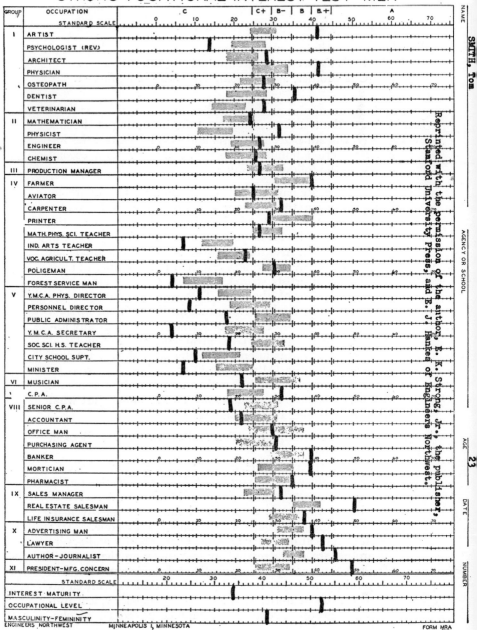

Reprinted with the permission of the author, E. K. Strong, Jr.; the publisher, Stanford University Press, and E. J. Hankes of Engineers Northwest.

NAME   SMITH, Tom

AGENCY OR SCHOOL

AGE   23

DATE

NUMBER

GROUP	OCCUPATION	C	C+	B-	B	B+	A
I	ARTIST						
	PSYCHOLOGIST (REV.)						
	ARCHITECT						
	PHYSICIAN						
	OSTEOPATH						
	DENTIST						
	VETERINARIAN						
II	MATHEMATICIAN						
	PHYSICIST						
	ENGINEER						
	CHEMIST						
III	PRODUCTION MANAGER						
IV	FARMER						
	AVIATOR						
	CARPENTER						
	PRINTER						
	MATH. PHYS. SCI. TEACHER						
	IND. ARTS TEACHER						
	VOC. AGRICULT. TEACHER						
	POLIGEMAN						
	FOREST SERVICE MAN						
V	Y.M.C.A. PHYS. DIRECTOR						
	PERSONNEL DIRECTOR						
	PUBLIC ADMINISTRATOR						
	Y.M.C.A. SECRETARY						
	SOC. SCI. H.S. TEACHER						
	CITY SCHOOL SUPT.						
	MINISTER						
VI	MUSICIAN						
	C.P.A.						
VIII	SENIOR C.P.A.						
	ACCOUNTANT						
	OFFICE MAN						
	PURCHASING AGENT						
	BANKER						
	MORTICIAN						
	PHARMACIST						
IX	SALES MANAGER						
	REAL ESTATE SALESMAN						
	LIFE INSURANCE SALESMAN						
X	ADVERTISING MAN						
	LAWYER						
	AUTHOR-JOURNALIST						
XI	PRESIDENT-MFG. CONCERN						

STANDARD SCALE

INTEREST MATURITY

OCCUPATIONAL LEVEL

MASCULINITY—FEMININITY

The Minnesota Multiphasic Personality Inventory

Starke R. Hathaway and J. Charnley McKinley

M Male

Name SMITH, Tom

Address

Occupation _____ Date Tested _____

Education College freshman _____ Age 23

Marital Status Single _____ Referred by _____

NOTES

The experimental scales — Re, St, and Do — were not available to the counselor at the time of this case. They are reported here for the interest of the reader.

Scorer's Initials _____

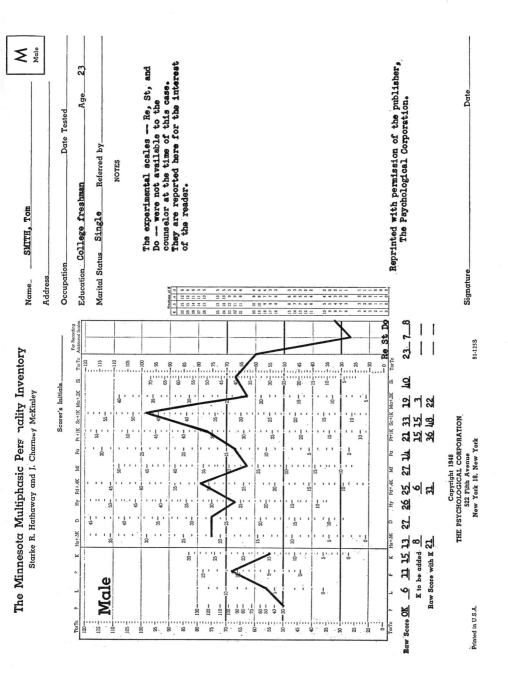

	L	F	?	K	Hs+.5K	D	Hy	Pd+.4K	Mf	Pa	Pt+1K	Sc+1K	Ma+.2K	Si		Re	St	Do
Raw Score	OK	6	11	15	13	27	26	25	27	14	21	33	19	40		23	7	8
K to be added					8			6			15	15	3			—	—	—
Raw Score with K	21				31			36			48	22						

Copyright 1948
THE PSYCHOLOGICAL CORPORATION
522 Fifth Avenue
New York 18, New York

Reprinted with permission of the publisher, The Psychological Corporation.

Printed in U.S.A.

51-125S

Signature _____ Date _____

117

does any of these profiles resemble that of Tom Smith. It must be remembered that all of these reports deal with *hospitalized psychiatric patients.* Our clinical experience strongly suggests that we cannot make direct inferences about nonhospitalized clients from data on hospitalized patients.

MMPI profiles characterized by an elevation on the Sc scale are encountered rarely among hospitalized psychiatric patients but often enough among male clients (college students) to warrant serious effort to construct hypotheses as to the meaning of such a profile. We have attempted to develop such an hypothesis. It is based on very limited experience in terms of the numbers of cases studied and the intensity of the case studies. Data on the cases consisted of MMPI profiles, Rorschach records, case histories and counseling records.

Some of our ideas and guesses as to the meaning of an Sc spike are as follows: The person maintains contact with the realities of his environment which differentiates him from the "schizophrenic" who tends to withdraw from contact with his environment. However, the person's perception of his environment is *distorted* by pressing affective needs. He is dissatisfied with his social adjustment, his personal relations with others. More often than not this dissatisfaction centers around heterosexual relations in which he feels inadequate to play an organized aggressive male role which our culture expects of him but is accompanied by a desire to do so. We might expect him to have had difficulty in identifying with his father in his developmental years. Identification with the mother has been neither highly positive nor negative. His concept of himself is not satisfying. He fears any self-role which requires putting to a test his capacity to be a self-assertive, decisive, "manly" individual. He may have strong feelings of aggression and hostility which he finds unacceptable because they are a threat to his needs for acceptance, affection and dependency. The result is an immature and insecure person whose attempts to adjust by passive or aggressive dependency and through fantasy are not very satisfying.

The level of mental ability may have an important influence on the prognosis in counseling with persons of this sort; the high ability person may be able to develop insights more readily. Also related to prognosis is the elevation on the D-scale in relation to Hs and Hy. If D is elevated over Hs and Hy, there probably is anxiety present which can be used to further therapeutic progress. However, even at best these cases tend to be long term ones with mediocre progress. The person's adjustment is apt to continue to be marginal. In an informal follow-up of a small group whose MMPI showed a marked Sc spike it was found that even though many of them seemed near a psychotic break at times, none of them actually had such a break. Our experiences with clients of this sort suggest that the central theme in therapy would revolve around the clients feelings of inadequacy to assume a mature, well organized, male role.

(3) (Triggs) Diagnostic Reading Test, Survey Section, Form A:

	Raw Score	Percentile Rank
Rate of reading	191 w.p.m.	1
Story comprehension	4	1
Vocabulary	12	1
Total comprehension	4	1
Total	16	1

The norm group was Arts and Science College freshmen.

(4) Wechsler-Bellevue Intelligence Scale, Form I:

	Raw Score	I.Q.
Verbal scale	44	96
Performance scale	43	89
Full scale	87	92

SECOND INTERVIEW

(*13 Days after the First Interview*)

S1—Well, what was the result?

C1—Well, we have quite a bit of testing, haven't we?

S2—Yes, sir.

C2—I was wondering, though, before we got into the testing if perhaps we could fill in some of the gaps in my own information—as to your background, your aspirations, what you want to do and—well, your view of your success so far, something along that line. I just feel that I don't know quite enough about you to make an intelligent interpretation of the test so far. Do you see what I mean? (*pause*) You went to school in (name of town), is that right?

★ In light of later developments it would have been better to deal with the test data here and then have the client relate the data to how he views himself. Perhaps the client's defensiveness would have been less if he then saw how other data about himself were necessary to "make sense" out of the test data.

S3—No. See, I completed a general agriculture correspondence course.

C3—I see. (*pause*) Well, at what level was that program?

S4—At college level.

C4—Then where did you attend high school?

★ Early in the first interview the client indicated that he had not attended high school but obtained a high school equivalency certificate on the basis of G.E.D. Tests. The counselor neither put this information in his notes nor did he remember it. This points up the importance of keeping adequate notes and refreshing one's memory by studying the case folder before each interview. Even though the counselor failed to put this bit of information in his notes and failed to remember it, the information was on the Personal Data Sheet which the client filled out between the first and second interview. Apparently the counselor did not study this information before the interview. The information *per se* might not be very important to the case. However, the client's *feelings* about it are very important here. The fact that he didn't go to high school and "doesn't have as good a background" as other students is a sore point with the client. The client feels somewhat handicapped because he didn't go to high school and is irritated by **C4, C15** and **C16**.

S5—See, I don't have a very good high school background. I'm here on G.E.D. Tests.

C5—Yes.

S6—You see, this agriculture course, that was all agriculture. I mean, I didn't have mathematics much to deal with.

C6—Yes. (*pause*) Were you satisfield with the work you were doing there? Was it the type of thing you wanted?

S7—Yes, sir.

C7—Mm-huh. Tell me a little bit about it. I don't feel that I quite understand the type of course that it was.

S8—Well, you see, it's a correspondence school and I had an examination on every chapter and then a final exam on the book.

C8—Mm-huh.

S9—And, then my requirement was to hand in two or three lessons during the week, which I did.

C9—Mm-huh.

S10—And I made *A's* on all my examinations.

C10—Now, what type of courses were those?

S11—Well, I had farm planning.

C11—Mm-huh.

S12—You want me to go on and name them?

C12—Yes.

S13—Modern fruit growing, vegetable growing, poultry farming. That gives us four—livestock raising, elements of dairy, principles of veterinary science, and field crops.

C13—Now, were those courses that you took there accepted by the University here when you came down?

S14—They won't okay correspondence courses.

C14—Oh, I see. Do you feel that the background that you have though as a result of the correspondence work has been of help to you here? It sort of fills in the information that you want here. It should help you here at the University, is that right?

S15—Yes, sir. It was a regular college text. (*pause*)

C15—Well, you didn't finish high school then, I take it.

S16—No, sir.

C16—Oh yes, I recall that.

S17—Well, I never attended any high school except—I did some work with just another correspondence school.

C17—(*pause*) You've been working for your father for some time, is that right?

S18—Mm-huh.

C18—How do you like working on the farm?

S19—Pretty well.

C19—Do you (*pause*) Are you planning to work with your father this coming summer?

S20—Yes, if I don't continue school.

C20—There is a possibility that you might stay in school this summer?

S21—Yes, sir. (*pause*)

C21—Well, can you tell me a little bit more about your background? Tell me something about your home life. You've lived with your parents until you came down here, is that right?

S22—Yes, sir, besides the two years I put in the service.

C22—Mm-huh.

S23—Of course, my mother—ah—deceased here a year ago.

C23—(*pause*) Was that somewhat unexpected?

S24—Well, not too much.

C24—(*pause*) How would you describe your mother? (*pause*) What was she like? (*pause*)

S25—Well, she liked farming and liked associations—one thing and another.

C25—Did she have many church activities?

S26—No, just goin' to church is about all. I mean, she never took up many activities.

C26—She devoted her life pretty much to the farm?

S27—Yes, sir.

C27—How about your father? How would you describe your father?

S28—Well, he's pretty old now. He farmed all his life, too.

C28—Mm-huh. (*pause*) How did you get along with your folks? How did you get along with your father when you were working with him?

S29—Well, he kind of had old ideas.

C29—That right? How is that now? How would you describe his old ideas?

S30—Well, he figured what he'd done a number of years back he should re-do now, that is, you know, more,—well, not too much, but to a certain extent he does.

★ This conflict over the old and the new in farming methods frequently reaches "fever pitch" between father and son. The conflict is accentuated when the son attends college for the purpose of learning modern methods of farming and returns to the farm and tries to apply them. It's as if the father wants his son to "get a college education" and yet, paradoxically, he appears *not* to want his son to learn anything at college! This conflict between father and son is so frequent that it is almost the rule rather than the exception. In fact, some agricultural authorities believe that this conflict is a major reason why such a small proportion of graduates of colleges of agriculture return to actual farming. Many agriculture graduates take jobs in related agricultural work such as county agent work, rural insurance, farm implement manufacturing, etc.

C30—Can you give me an example of that?

S31—Well, he likes to use old methods. That is, he don't very well approve of modern ways.

C31—Mm-huh. Do you mean in the type of farming you do or the way you do it?

S32—Yes, sir.

C32—Well, what are some of the new ways of farming that he hasn't followed? I'm not too familiar in that field.

S33—Well, (*pause*) the modern way of feeding is one thing, but to a certain extent he is, and then again he isn't. That is, he always used fertilizer and that's modern as far as that goes, and lime. (*pause*)

C33—Does he use up-to-date machinery on the farm?

S34—No, not too much.

C34—What type of machinery do you think would be helpful to him that he hasn't been using?

S35—Well, (*long pause*) well, I think he likes to use the horses too much. That is, we have the horses and tractor both.

C35—Mm-huh.

S36—Well, we use tractors, too, but he prefers the horses much as he can. (*pause*)

C36—I see. How do you feel about using horses?

S37—Well, it was all right at that time, but it's too far back now.

C37—Mm-huh. (*pause*) Why do you think that your father has some of those old-fashioned ideas?

S38—Well, one thing, he didn't keep up.

C38—Mm-huh. Why do you suppose that was? (*pause*)

S39—Well, I think they keep changing to new methods. He just kept the old ones.

C39—Mm-huh. Do you think that he felt that the old way was the best way?

S40—Yes, sir.

C40—Mm-huh. Was there any particular reason why he felt the old way was the best way? Was he a successful farmer the old way?

S41—Well, I wouldn't say that.

C41—What would be your explanation of it then? (*pause*)

S42—I don't believe I know.

C42—Mm-huh. Well, if you're going to go back to the farm and you were able to change things, what sort of changes would you like to see on the farm? Let's say your father would allow you to make any changes that you felt were necessary. What changes would you like to see? (*pause*)

S43—Well, I'd improve the livestock a little.

C43—Mm-huh.

S44—And the way we feed them and so forth.

C44—Mm-huh. Now, how would you go about that?

S45—Well, one thing, pull up the standard of breeding.

C45—Will you explain a little bit more about that. I'm not quite as familiar with that type of thing as I should be. Tell me in terms that I can understand just how you would improve the breed of your stock.

S46—Well, I'd get better breeds and not—

C46—Mm-huh. Buy better stock—

S47—Yes, sir.

C47—. . . to begin with. What breeds would you buy?

S48—Well, I like Herefords, as far as that goes.

C48—Mm-huh. Well, what change would you make then?

S49—Well, I'd be wanting to make a higher grade or registered cows.

C49—The ones you have aren't registered?

S50—No, sir.

C50—What advantage would there be to having registered cows?

S51—Well, we could sell them at a higher price.

C51—I'm not too familiar at all, what does registering cattle indicate? Who does the registering?

S52—Well, you have to have a registered cow and steer (*sic*) to start out with. And then you just send in—ah—register the new calves.

C52—Mm-huh. Who registers them?

S53—Well, it's a special organization, like the Hereford Installation.

C53—Mm-huh. (*pause*) Do you think your father knows about these registered animals?

S54—Yes, sir. He always registers his steers but he don't care about his cows.

C54—I see. (*pause*) Does that make a lot of difference, in your estimation?

S55—Well, it doesn't so much in our calves. They grow up okay, but the cows—ah—some are not purebred.

C55—Mm-huh.

S56—Of course, there isn't too much difference as long as you sell them on the market. It don't make any difference whether they're registered or not.

C56—Mm-huh.

S57—In fact, breeding stock is about the only thing that needs to be registered.

C57—Mm-huh. In other words, you wouldn't get any more if you're going to sell them as slaughter cattle, is that right?

S58—That's right.

C58—Mm-huh.

S59—Just that if you purchase a steer that is registered it costs a little more than one that's not. They sell for a higher price. (*pause*)

C59—Now, you're planning to go through school here and if everything works out well you'd like to get into veterinary school, is that right?

S60—Yes, sir.

C60—Well, tell me a little bit more about your desires to become a veterinarian. When did you first decide to take that line of work?

S61—Well, I was kind of interested in taking care of stock when they get sick.

C61—Mm-huh. (*pause*) When did you first enjoy that type of work?

S62—Well, I don't know, it's been so long ago. I always did kind of like it.

C62—Mm-huh.

S63—You see, my uncle, he does veterinary work and I like to watch him.

C63—Is that right? Is he there in your community?

S64—Yes, sir.

C64—Have you talked to him very much about it?

S65—Well, yes, sir.

C65—What does he have to say?

S66—Well, he likes to talk mostly about the bad spots in it.

C66—Mm-huh. Well, what are some of the good and bad spots about it?

S67—Well, you have to put in long hours. That is, you'd probably be called up and out at night.

C67—Mm-huh. (*pause*) Well, now are those good or bad features about it?

S68—Well, being called out at night is a bad feature.

C68—Mm-huh. What would be a good feature about it?

S69—Well, it's a pretty good paying job.

C69—Is that important to you, that you have a job that is going to pay pretty well?

S70—Well, I'd like a job to pay enough to make a living, that's about all.

C70—Mm-huh. If you could have a job that would pay you a living, would you be satisfied with something other than being a veterinarian?

S71—Well, yes, sir.

C71—Mm-huh. What other types of jobs would you like to have if they pay you a good living? (*pause*)

S72—Well, they would be more or less in the line of farming, taking care and feeding stock.

C72—Mm-huh. You'd like that type of work? You'd like to have a farm of your own or would you like to work for your father?

S73—Well, I'd rather farm my own.

C73—Mm-huh. (*pause*) You have a brother, is that right?

S74—Yes, sir.

C74—Is he working with your father on the farm?

S75—Yes, sir.

C75—And if you went back that would make three of you doing the farming, is that right?

S76—Yes, sir.

C76—Do you get along pretty well with your brother and your dad when you're doing the farming? (*long pause*) I notice here that your brother completed about eight years in school—ah—but you can't remember just how many you've completed. When you did drop out of school, what was the reason for your dropping out?

S77—Well, I didn't like school and didn't see any use out of it at that time.

C77—Mm-huh. What did you do after you dropped out?

S78—I worked there with my dad.

C78—Mm-huh. What did your dad think about your dropping out of school?

S79—Well, he didn't say anything about it. He didn't think much of education, anyway.

C79—Mm-huh. How do you feel about it?

S80—Well, if I had to do it over, I would work a lot harder on it and kept agoing.

C80—What benefit do you think it would have for you to have completed high school, regular high school?

S81—Well, I'd be a lot better at special work.

C81—Mm-huh.

S82—Fact they have a lot of GI classes, around there in the community where they go to school part of the time and farm the other part.

C82—Mm-huh. Did you ever participate in any of those classes?

S83—Well, not yet. See, I just got to come to the University to take up vet medicine.

C83—Mm-huh. (*pause*) How do you like the University so far?

S84—I like it okay.

C84—Mm-huh.

S85—I like the people and so far I'm getting along with the teachers.

C85—Mm-huh. But you have been having a little difficulty, is that right in some of your classes?

S86—Yes, sir.

C86—What classes have been giving you the most difficulty?

S87—Well, English and Math, that's all.

C87—Mm-huh. Now, then what math course are you taking?

S88—Agricultural math.

C88—Agricultural math.

S89—Yes, sir. (*long pause*)

C89—What do you feel is your difficulty in your course?

S90—Well, I'm kinda slow at picking things up, my main trouble.

C90—Mm-huh. Do you think that you have more trouble than some of the rest of them in the class?

S91—I think so.

C91—Why do you think that you are a little slower than the rest?

S92—Well, some of them get their work quick and I have to work about twice as long.

C92—Mm-huh. But, why do you think that you have to work kind of slow?

S93—You mean why I think I have to work twice as long?

★ Here is a young man whose formal education included no high school work. Test data suggest that he is a poor academic risk for college work. We might say that he has an unrealistic concept of himself; his aspirations are not in line with his abilities. Why? In the usual course of events in a person's education, he is able to test constantly his abilities against the requirements of the education program. Generally speaking, the progression up the educational ladder is gradual enough that we are able to develop concepts of ourselves which are in keeping with the demands of the educational environment without confusion and without trauma. In other words, we learn about how far we can go and can accept this with good graces. Not so with this client. *He has not had the opportunity to test his self-concept* (ability) to do college work) *against the reality of his environment* (high school curriculum). The result is an unrealistic self-concept caused in part by a large gap in his experience sequence. The concept of differential ability to do academic work is not very clear to him. It would appear that this case is qualitatively different from ones of *chronic* "overaspiration" which have some surface similarities with this one. See Ginsberg, *et al.* (*158, 159*) and Super (*383*) for a more complete discussion of the development of a realistic self-concept.

C93—Mm-huh.

S94—Well, I know I put in a lot more time studying than my roommate. Looks like he does better on the test than I do.

C94—Mm-huh. Why do you think your roommate does better than you on the tests?

S95—Well, anyway, he completed high school work, that is, he had a lot of more—

C95—Do you feel that if you had completed high school you'd be in a better position to—

S96—Yes, sir.

C96—Mm-huh.

S97—And another thing, I have a lot more to learn than he does.

C97—Mm-huh. You feel then that your background isn't quite as adequate as his would be for—

S98—Yes, sir.

C98—. . . college work. (*pause*) Do you think that the fact that you haven't had high school will limit you in what you will be able to do?

S99—Well, no, not on the farm.

C99—Mm-huh.

S10—Fact, I've done a lot better than quite a few high school graduates have.

C100—I see. In what way have you been more successful than they have?

S101—Well, in doing actual work. Looks like they have more trouble than I do.

C101—Mm-huh. What kind of work do they have difficulty with?

S102—How to operate and run the machines.

C102—Mm-huh. You feel then, that you have an advantage over them in that?

S103—Yes, sir.

C103—Mm-huh. Where did you pick up your skill at operating machinery?

S104—Well, I mostly pick up from my brother. He is good at that type of work.

C104—Mm-huh. You learned quite a bit from your brother?

S105—Yes, sir. He figured out the instruction books and one thing and another.

C105—Mm-huh. Can you figure out from the instruction books how to work machinery?

S106—Yes, sir.

C106—Mm-huh. You seemed to have sort of a knack for that type of thing?

S107—Yes, sir.

C107—Mm-huh. Well, now, the reason I've been asking a lot of these questions, I want to fill in my background to understand you better. But, I want you to understand that our purpose here is to help you. We don't benefit particularly from asking various questions. We feel that we can be of better assistance to you if we understand you better. Understand what I mean?

S108—Yes, sir.

C108—Mm-huh. We want you to feel that we are helping you in the best way we can. I want you to feel that—well, you can feel at home here. I don't want you to feel strange at all. I mean, I notice that you say "yes, sir" quite a bit. Well, that's nice that you do, but it isn't necessary at all. We're just pretty much on the same level that you are. We don't feel that we have anything that we can hold above your head or anything like that. I mean, we don't feel that we are any better than you are. Do you feel that we are?

★ The counselor finds himself in a difficult position. He feels that he does not understand the client well enough yet to make a discussion of the test results meaningful for the client. Attempts to have the client elaborate about himself have resulted in a stilted question-answer session. The counselor felt that a recognition of this situation and some re-structuring might help. However, as Robinson (278) suggests, when the counselor finds it necessary to re-structure in the later phases of a case, it is more likely that his own techniques are inappropriate than that the client needs to be set straight.

S109—Well, yes.

C109—Do you? How is that? How do you feel that—

S110—Well, first of all you talk better than I can.

C110—Mm-huh. Do you feel that you are handicapped then by the manner of speech that you have?

★ The counselor misinterpreted the client's remark and thereby passed up an opportunity to discuss the client's feelings.

S111—Well, to a certain extent.

C111—Mm-huh. (*pause*) Tell me about that. How do you feel other people react to you?

S112—Well, (*pause*) looks like I'm always. . . .

C112—Do you feel that if you are able to use better English than you do at the present time that you would be better accepted?

S113—Well, yes, sir.

C113—Mm-huh. You want to be better accepted?

S114—Yes, sir.

C114—Mm-huh, (*pause*) What would you like to have other people think of you if you could change the way things are right now?

S115—Well, I just want to be an average guy. That is, I wouldn't want to be a, a—

C115—Mm-huh. You don't feel that you're average now?

S116—Well, not quite enough. I don't talk enough.

C116—Mm-huh. In other words, you feel the fact that you can't talk quite as well as someone else handicaps you?

S117—Yes, sir. And then I have trouble expressing things a little bit more.

C117—Mm-huh. (*pause*) Somewhat of a strain for you to get an idea across to someone else?

S118—Yes, sir.

C118—Mm-huh. (*pause*) Do you feel that by becoming a veterinarian that you'll be pretty much of an average guy?

S119—No. Depends on what kind of work I do.

C119—Mm-huh. Do you think you could do the type of work your uncle does?

S120—Yes, sir.

C120—Do you feel that you understand enough about the work with the training that you'd be able to do it?

S121—Yes, sir. (*pause*)

C121—Tell me something more about your uncle. How would you describe him?

S122—Well, he, he can talk good and express his ideas, make them forceful.

C122—Mm-huh. You would like to be able to do that?

S123—Yes, sir. He does a lot of good work.

C123—Mm-huh. You don't feel that you would be able to do the type of work he is doing unless you would be able to express yourself on those points?

S124—Yes, sir. (*pause*)

C124—Do you think that your difficulty in English is a result of your difficulty in expressing yourself?

S125—I think it's mostly English.

C125—Mm-huh. You are having difficulty in English courses, is that right?

S126—Yes, sir. (*pause*)

C126—Have you talked to the instructor about that?

S127—Well, yes, he said I am improving.

C127—Mm-huh. How do you feel about it? Do you think you are?

S128—Well, yes, to a certain extent quite a bit.

C128—Mm-huh.

S129—I tell you I know a lot more about it now than I did before I came up here.

C129—Mm-huh. What courses are you having more success in than you are in English and Math?

S130—Oh, animal husbandry—that seems a lot easier.

C130—Mm-huh. Do you feel that your farm background and so forth is helping you there?

S131—Yes, sir. And, then the past education I had in that agriculture course.

C131—Mm-huh. (*pause*) You're a little reticent to talk aren't you? When you speak, you just give it a quick answer and let it go at that. Isn't that the way you do quite a bit?

S132—I think so.

C132—Mm-huh. You must be thinking a lot of things when we're talking here that you don't express, is that right?

S133—Yes, sir.

C133—Well, what have you been thinking about while we've been talking here that you haven't expressed?

S134—Hmmm. I don't know—(*pause*)

C134—Mm-huh. I hate to feel that I'm asking just a lot of questions. I feel that you could help me in understanding yourself a little better if you would tell a little more of your feelings and so forth, than you have. Just yes and no doesn't seem to get anything. I'm more interested in how you feel toward your classwork and your school than I am, more or less, in just the factual data.

★ Here the counselor attempts to restructure the situation again. The client seems to be willing to co-operate but appears not to understand very well just what the counselor wants him to do. This late structuring is indicative of lack of satisfactory progress in counseling.

S135—Well, I like my course work quite a bit. I don't do too much on the quizzes.

C135—Mm-huh. If you didn't have the quizzes then you feel that you probably would do a little better in the courses?

S136—Yes. It wouldn't show up as much, anyway.

C136—Mm-huh. Do you feel that other students have learned as much as you have in spite of the fact that you do poorly on the tests? Do you feel that the other students really learn more or do you think that it is just because you don't do well on the tests?

S137—Well, they know quite a bit. It looks like when it comes to a test, it seems like they don't have any trouble. It works out easy for them. When I get a test, I guess it doesn't,—even, if I did have the work before.

C137—Mm-huh. (*pause*) Well, now, if those tests continue to bother you like they have up to now, and you find that for one reason or another you are not likely to do any better on the tests in the future, what sort of plans would you make for yourself?

S138—You mean if I quit the University?

C138—Yes.

S139—Well, I'd go back to farming.

C139—Mm-huh. Would you be satisfied?

S140—I think so. (*pause*)

C140—Well, if you feel that you would be satisfied doing farm work, why do you feel it would be desirable for you to spend six years or so in college to become a veterinarian?

S141—Well, it's a lot the same type of work.

C141—Mm-huh.

S142—I probably would be better at it. I'd know stock better.

C142—Mm-huh.

S143—It would take a lot more effort.

C143—Mm-huh.

S144—You can learn a lot by just meetin' people and so forth.

C144—Mm-huh. (*pause*) Well, if you could, when you got through with your veterinary course, would you plan to do farming then?

S145—Well, if I stayed and work on it and got stuck in a rural community, I would give that full time. And then maybe go back to farming, most for raisin' stock. Takin' care of stock.

C145—Mm-huh. You feel that veterinary work would be good preparation for future farm work?

S146—Yes, sir. (*very long pause*)

C146—Well, what do you think I should know about you that we perhaps haven't covered so far that would help me to help you a little better? Do you feel that I know you very well?

S147—Well, I don't know about that.

C147—Mm-huh. (*pause*) Do you feel that you know me very well?

S148—Not too well.

C148—Yes, that's right.

S149—I know you try to take all the facts out of a person.

C149—Mm-huh.

S150—Well, like putting all the details together in history, just like diagnosin', diagnosin' a disease. When you come to the answer or cure.

★ The client perceives his role in the counseling process as essentially a passive one now. The counselor has held the "lead" for so long now that the client apparently feels that his role is to answer questions, then after a time the counselor *will give him the answer.*

C150—Mm-huh. (*pause*) By asking these questions do you think that perhaps you know yourself better? Or, do you feel that you know pretty much about yourself already? (*pause*)

S151—Well,—

C151—Looks as though I understood you a little better than I did, but we haven't gotten into the testing. I suppose it would be allright if we made an appointment at a little later date so we can discuss these tests. I feel that I do understand some of the things, some of your background, some of your history and so forth. So, I can understand the testing a little bit better. And, I can perhaps make it a little bit more meaningful to you. So, perhaps we could get together some time in the future, whenever would be convenient for you, then we can talk over the tests. I have someone coming in this next hour. Perhaps if you'd like, we might discuss this whole difficulty you are having with your course work over a period of time. In other words, we can see each other on some kind of a regular schedule if you like and we'll get around to the test data when we see each other again. So, why don't we see each other about a week from today about this time, will that be all right?

S152—Sure.

C152—All right. Fine. I'll write that down on the appointment book and I'll have the receptionist make out a slip for you.

S153—Okay.

COUNSELOR'S NOTES ON THE SECOND INTERVIEW

(*Dictated Immediately after the Interview*)

★ Mr. Smith returned for interpretation of the test battery but the discussion of his background took up the full hour and we did not discuss tests. Rapport was not too satisfactory because of Mr. Smith's tendency to answer leading questions in a very short manner, using "yes, sir" as a standard answer to many of the questions. Structuring and restructuring did not seem to be too helpful. It was determined, however, that Mr. Smith dropped out of grade school some time ago and had worked on the farm ever since except for two years in the service. He has completed some correspondence courses but other than that he has had no further academic work. He feels, however, that his inability to use correct English is a limiting factor in his college work and in his establishing satisfactory relations with other students on the campus. He seems to like school well enough but just claims difficulty on the tests. If he is able to make a satisfactory record (this is doubtful), he will probably return to the farm and raise livestock with veterinary practice on the side. His uncle seems to have a similar arrangement and is the local veterinarian. He plans to return at a later date.

THIRD INTERVIEW

(*7 Days after the Second Interview*)

C1—How are you?

S1—This is nice spring weather.

C2—Yes, this is fine, isn't it? Well, let's see, where were we the last time you were here?

S2—Said you were going to tell me about the tests.

C3—Yes. (*pause*) What particular one are you interested in especially first?

S3—Well, none in particular. I would like to know the score on all four of them.

C4—Hmmm. Well, was there any particular thing that you were more concerned with than any other?

S4—Well, I would kind of like to know more about that intelligence test, what part I done good on.

C5—On this test, this is the Wechsler, half of the people will score between 90 and 110, one fourth of the people below 90 and a fourth of the people above 110. This is the normal curve. (*Counselor sketches a simple curve to illustrate his point.*) I suppose you have been graded on the curve, where most of the people make average grades, a few people make high grades and a few people make low grades. Your score would be right here (*pointing*)—92 indicating as far as average intelligence is concerned you are right here in the average range. You have what we usually call average intelligence. However, there are a number of people who will, on a test such as this, score higher than you will. A number of people will score lower than you will, so you are in this general range in the middle. Now, you were wondering about the language part of the test. You actually scored higher on that than you did on the blocks and so forth.

S5—I did?

C6—Yes.

S6—I didn't think I missed anything on those blocks.

C7—Oh? Well, you may not have worked very rapidly or something like that.

S7—Oh, I see. Mm-huh.

C8—And that may have held you back on that.

S8—Mm-huh.

C9—But you did do better on the vocabulary part. You scored 96 on that and about 90 on the other part. The overall picture was 92. Now, let's see, how does that fit you as part of the general society? It would indicate that you have ability similar to most of the people in general. Of course there will be some people who will score higher and some people lower but you are in the middle range. I might indicate, however, that in college on a test such as this the average score will be somewhat higher than it will be in the general population. For instance, I suppose you might say the one average score would be a 100; in college the average score would be 115. You have a curve something like this (*Counselor draws a curve higher on the sketch to approximate the distribution for a college population*), indicating that a score of 92 would indicate that you would have to work harder in college because of your background than the average college individual would.

S9—To score 115 or above.

C10—I beg your pardon.

S10—I say, I would have to work quite a bit harder than the guy who scored 115?

C11—That's right. You would have to put in more time, more study. You'd have to restrict your activities to overcome your deficiency in background that some of the other students don't have. (*pause*) I imagine that you have found that to be somewhat true, haven't you?

S11—Yes, that's right.

C12—Yes. In other words, this would apparently agree somewhat with your own experience?

S12—Yes. That came out pretty accurate. I was surprised they could tell that well.

C13—Mm-huh. Well, if the test is a good test it shouldn't tell you anything that you didn't suspect in the first place. And this indicates to you, you do have a background somewhat less adequate than the average students when they come to college to do college work. You have to overcome it one way or another to compensate for that. (*pause*) Well, what implications does that have for you?

★ The counselor has handled the interpretation of the intelligence test results rather well to this point. He has explained the results in such a way that the client seems to understand and accept them. However, he then *assumed* that the client prefers to remain in college at whatever "price" necessary by way of longer hours of study, less social life, etc. However, this "work harder" concept is somewhat fallacious. It would have been better if the counselor had outlined several alternatives, such as dropping out of college,

continuing on for a fuller try at college work, opportunities for
training in agriculture other than collegiate. The client would
probably have chosen to remain in college but it would have been
valuable to him to have considered this choice.

S13—Well, it means that I will have to work quite a bit harder than the
average student here.

C14—Yes. (*pause*)

S14—I got such a bad start here. I haven't been used to any classes for
a long time.

C15—Mm-huh.

S15—My grades have been picking up though.

C16—Mm-huh.

S16—That is English, math I know.

C17—Good. Why do you think that they're coming up now from what
they were?

S17—Well, getting to understand the situation better. They are getting
somewhat easier. (*pause*)

C18—Do you think that the work is becoming easier because of the
type of work that it is that makes it different or because of you? Perhaps you're studying harder or something.

S18—Well, it's probably because I'm studying harder and maybe the
type has something to do with it. (*pause*) Like our English teacher
says some students are good in spelling and others aren't. He tries to
balance up the subject to equalize it and I'm pretty good on spelling.

C19—Mm-huh. (*pause*) How do you think you'll stack up with other
people, say, a year from now as far as your college work is concerned?
Think you can see that far ahead?

S19—Well, I think it'll certainly be quite a bit better than it is now.
I believe that if I can make up enough to make this semester that I can
do quite a bit better the next one.

C20—Mm-huh. Do you think that you will be repeating any work after
this semester?

S20—Well, there might be a possibility of it. (*pause*)

C21—In other words, some courses you just may have to take twice to
really get the meat out of then, is that right?

S21—Well, yes, that might be. (*pause*)

C22—Why is it you feel that you seem to be having this difficulty with your
college work? Some students don't seem to have quite this much difficulty
do they?

S22—Well, some of them don't seem to have any trouble at all, except my roommate. He does good in all of his subjects except English.

C23—Mm-huh.

S23—He's failing English, but doing good in all of his other subjects.

C24—Hmmm. Why do you think that you're not quite as well prepared as some of the other students are? (*pause*)

S24—Because, well, my roommate, he had a better background and he can pick things up quicker than I can.

C25—You think the fact that he can pick things up a little quicker than you can and his background is a little better will give him somewhat of an advantage over you all the way through.

S25—Well,—ah—yes, sir.

C26—Do you think there is any chance of your overcoming that deficiency?

S26—Well, it could be.

C27—What do you see as possibilities for overcoming this deficiency?

S27—Well, just choosing subjects that I'm good in for one thing.

C28—Mm-huh.

S28—And then don't carry too much work.

C29—Yes. (*pause*) How many hours are you carrying this time?

S29—Well, I'm carrying 12 right now. I started out with 16, but I dropped zoology and took a subject in animal husbandry in which I can only get an hour and a half credit out of.

C30—I didn't know they had courses here that would give you an hour and a half credit.

S30—Well, I got in the middle of the course.

C31—Oh. Why did you drop your zoology?

S31—Well, I wasn't doing any good on it and more or less on the advice of the instructor.

C32—Mm-huh. That was probably a smart move. It's a pretty rough course, isn't it?

S32—Yeah. Lot of microscope work. You look at things under a microscope and identify things.

C33—Mm-huh. You couldn't do that work quite as well as others?

S33—That's right.

C34—What do you think your difficulty was there in that course?

S34—Well, I wasn't quite understanding the work for one thing.

C35—Mm-huh. You didn't know what to look for?

S35—Well, yes, that was my trouble. I was talking to another student who took zoology and he said he was having the same trouble and he went to the library and looked up things in books and drawed pictures from that first to get some idea of what he was looking for, and that helped him out. (*pause*)

C36—Did you try that as a final attack?

S36—Well, no. I already had the course dropped.

C37—Oh.

S37—I believe that I can take it again and do pretty good on it. I can see what I'm studying.

C38—Mm-huh. How do you see yourself as far as ability is concerned compared with the rest of the people you meet with?

S38—Well, I should perform things, seeing as how I'm a little better than the average. But when it comes to mental work it seems like a little lower.

★ This is about as much understanding and acceptance as can be expected at this time. If the counselor were to "push" for much more precise understanding by the client of his chances of making satisfactory progress toward a degree, he might destroy what he has accomplished so far by putting the client on the defensive. Note the apparent difference in rapport in this interview and the previous one. In this interview the counselor is attending to the interest of the client which is in marked contrast with the second interview.

C39—Mm-huh. Now, tell me something about this performance work, where you are better than they are? What type of work would that be?

S39—Well, that's doing actual work in veterinary you can go right ahead and castrate, and keep an eye on chicks, a lot of them have a lot of difficulty.

C40—In other words once you learn to do a thing with your hands, why you are pretty good at it, that it?

S40—Yeah, I can remember. I can remember way back, but this memory work I can't remember too good.

C41—Mm-huh. Do you feel that there will be a lot of this work, performance work where you will have an advantage that you will be doing in Ag. school? Where you will be in somewhat better position compared with the other students? Well, there are still going to be some courses like zoology, English, and so forth, that you may have to hurdle and they may be the ones that will give you the rough time, is that right? Is that the way you feel about it?

S41—Yes, sir. (*pause*)

C42—How are you going to get over those hurdles?

S42—You mean this mental part?

C43—Mm-huh. (*pause*)

S43—Well, I don't know. (*pause*)

C44—You can't very well get out of taking some of those courses. Do you think you can?

S44—I don't know. I don't hardly think so. They have so many required subjects.

C45—That's right.

S45—I think though that if I start zoology again that I won't have much trouble. Another thing, I dropped out when they had all of that microscope work, after I dropped out they weren't having much of that anymore. I mean, they were cutting up frogs and stuff like that.

C46—Mm-huh. (*pause*) You don't think there would be as much mental work then in cutting up frogs as there would be looking through a microscope?

S46—Not for me it wouldn't.

C47—Mm-huh. Well, for what purpose are they cutting up the frogs? Do you know?

S47—Well, trying the various parts, trying to learn the various parts, the various parts of the frog.

C48—Yes. But is that mental work or not—when you have to learn the various parts of the frogs?

S48—Well, yeah. But it is quite a bit easier than trying to find something under a microscope that you don't know what you're looking for. It's invisible to the eye. (*pause*)

C49—Well, when it comes time to make a decision as to whether you are going on into vet medicine or not, how do you think this handicap of doing mental work will be affected?

S49—Well, you don't do very much mental work in a rural community. I mean, practically all actual work. That is, go out on the calls, treat the animals.

C50—Have you ever thought of being an assistant to your uncle and going out and helping him on calls without going through all of the training?

S50—Well, yes, but it would be a lot better if I had the training.

C51—Yes. (*pause*) Do you think that you'll be able to get the training?

S51—I could get the training if I could classify, that is, get good enough in my subjects.

C52—Mm-huh. Well, that's what I'm getting at. Do you think you'll be able to get good enough in your subjects to get the training?

S52—I'm not sure about that.

C53—Mm-huh.

S53—If I don't, I can change to a B.S. degree in agriculture. That's only a four year course.

C54—That's right.

S54—So, it's not like taking a medical course where you can't hardly fall back on anything.

C55—Mm-huh. (*pause*)

S55—I've talked to some fellas who couldn't make vet school, and then switched to general ag. (*pause*)

C56—Mm-huh. Did you talk to any of them about the difficulty or the ease with which they got into vet school? For instance, have you ever talked to Mr. Agard (Assistant to Dean in Agriculture) about that?

S56—Well, yes. He just, when I came here, he just recommended me to go ahead with this work. "We'll try and get you into Vet School. If you don't get in Vet School, if you don't, take another two years and get a B.S. in agriculture."

C57—Well, the competition is pretty keen when it comes to getting into Vet School. It's just a program that's flexible enough so that you can perhaps take the agriculture degree if you don't make it into Vet medicine.

S57—This fellow I know pretty well, I think he has, already has 90 hours of credit and after this semester will have over 100 and he is going to try to get in Vet School, but if he don't—he probably will,—he has a real high standard and he'll only need a few more hours to get a B.S. in agriculture. He has it made whichever way he looks at it. (*pause*)

C58—Well, how would you feel about getting a bachelor's degree in agriculture if you weren't able to get in Vet medicine, should that come up?

S58—Well, it would be all right with me.

C59—Would it?

S59—Yes, sir. (*pause*)

C60—Well, I'm not too familiar with the curriculum in agriculture at the moment. But, if you feel that you'll be able to get some of these courses, performance type courses, you're going to get through them well enough you may be able to improve your record somewhat above what it looks like it's going to be right now, you see? But, I think that what this thing tells us is that you are going to have to press pretty hard.

S60—Yes, sir.

C61—And, I think that the idea that you suggested that you plan to take a light course,—I think that is a good one. I think you'll be better satisfied if you do that.

S61—That's where I made my mistake this semester.

C62—Mm-huh. (*pause*) You'll have more time to devote to each course if you take lighter loads. (*pause*)

S62—I have another relative. He's a judge, for 20 years.

C63—Mm-huh.

S63—Never completed high school.

C64—Is that right?

S64—He had the ability when it comes to . . . (*a few words lost*).

C65—Yes. How did he get his law experience?

S65—Just from books, one thing and another.

C66—He just picked it up on the side?

S66—Mm-huh. Come election he would run way ahead. Every election he would get a few more votes.

C67—Hmmmm.

S67—He started out bad though. First election he lost just by a few votes. After that he just kept creepin' up.

C68—Mm-huh. Would you like that type of a job?

★ The counselor missed the point the client was trying to make here. Apparently he was trying to show how his uncle had "made good" without a high school education, implying that there was a chance that he could also.

S68—No. I wouldn't care for it.

C69—Mm-huh.

S69—There's too much competition on a public job like that.

C70—You have to keep the public happy, is that the idea?

S70—That's right.

C71—Mm-huh. You don't feel that you would do very well on that type of thing?

S71—Well, no, I wouldn't like it.

C72—Mm-huh. Don't you think you'll have to keep the public happy if you were able to work as a veterinarian?

S72—Well, yeah, but not, not like hunting for votes.

C73—Yes. That's very different, isn't it?

S73—Yeah. You have to get out and hunt votes. You have to run the administration right to get a large majority.

C74—Yes, mm-huh. How many uncles do you have?

S74—Oh, I have—six.

C75—Do you? Have one who is a veterinarian, one who is a judge. Do you have any other professional people in your family?

S75—Well, no. The rest of them are just farmers, something like that.

C76—Mm-huh. Farmers then aren't quite as important as veterinarians and judges?

S76—Well, no—that is, they don't do public work. They're restricted to the farm. It doesn't make much difference what the next person thinks of them.

C77—They're not known by as many people, I suppose.

S77—That's right.

C78—Mm-huh. Would you be satisfied with that type of a job or would you like to be known by a lot of people?

S78—Well, I don't care about being known by people much, like on an election job.

C79—What is it about an election job you don't like?

S79—Well, there is too much criticism, competition sometimes.

C80—How about your father, is he an important man around there?

S80—Oh, he's just a farmer.

C81—Just a farmer, huh?

S81—Mm-huh.

C82—What do other people think of him?

S82—Well, I don't know—never tell me much about him. (*pause*)

C83—Would you like to be like him?

S83—Well,—ah—no. That is, I like to keep learning and keep up to date on things. That's the way my uncle is that's a vet. He has a good foundation and just keeps learning about a lot of new things and uses them and my dad isn't that way.

C84—Mm-huh.

S84—When there's a better method for something he changes right over and uses it. He keeps right on his feet, on comparing things.

C85—Mm-huh.

S85—Of course, my dad is pretty old now. He's about seventy.

C86—Mm-huh. He was pretty old when you were born, wasn't he?

S86—Yes, sir.

C87—You never really knew him when he was a young man, did you?

S87—Huh-uh.

C88—Do you think he was a little more up-to-date when he was younger?

S88—Well, yeah. He started out up-to-date, but he never changed a thing on the farm.—Bought a new tractor, at that time it was up-to-date but he kept using that tractor year after year.

C89—Mm-huh. (*pause*) What do you see about your father other than that you wouldn't do if you were in his shoes?

S89—Well, I don't know.

C90—This keeping up-to-date then is pretty important, isn't it?

S90—Yes, sir.

C91—Mm-huh.

S91—He sort of let the world go by. The way I see it, the world keeps going on. Never did come back.

C92—Does your father have any tractor at all, now?

S92—He has one old tractor.

C93—One old one, mm-huh. Are there any other farmers in the neighborhood that use a team like he does?

S93—Well, no, there isn't. The last few years they've been selling their last teams—buying tractors. (*pause*)

C94—Takes a lot of money to run your own farm, doesn't it?

S94—Yes, sir, it does now. Seem to be pretty specialized.

C95—Have to know a lot, don't you?

S95—Yes, sir, over a lot of things.

C96—Mm-huh.

S96—When a person first comes to the farm he won't hardly know anything to do any good, but if they stay out there long enough and start studyin' they soon pick up and do as good and better than the farmers around there. If they don't do that they're no good. (*pause*) I know once there was a man in our neighborhood and the first two years he wasn't doing any good at all. He got to studyin' things and now he does better than a lot of the farmers around there.

★ This is one of several indications that the client has maturity of judgment in some areas which might not be expected from some of the record. On the other hand there are instances of rather crude concepts. The contrast is striking.

C97—Mm-huh. (*pause*) Now, your brother is on the farm with your dad, too, isn't he?

S97—Yes, sir.

C98—Does he notice that your father is sort of behind the times?

S98—Oh, yeah.

C99—Mm-huh. Does he make any effort to bring him up-to-date?

S99—Well, yeah, to a certain extent, but it's pretty hard to do.

C100—I see. He has pretty much his own ideas.

S100—Yes, sir.

C101—How much of a handicap do you think it will be to you if you go back to the farm when you get your degree in agriculture and work with him? How much of a handicap do you think it will be to you to work with him with his methods?

> ★ The client might have interpreted this response as reassurance concerning earning a bachelor's degree. However, it would be very difficult for the client to come to a "completely" realistic perception of himself and his environment at this time on the basis of counseling alone. Other cases similar to this one suggest that one of the most effective agents in producing accurate perception of self in relation to demands of the environment is *to experience the demands of the environment.*

S101—Well, it would be quite a bit.

C102—Do you think that you would be able to overcome his methods? Change his ways?

S102—It'd be pretty doubtful.

C103—He's pretty hard to handle?

S103—Well, yes, to a certain extent.

C104—Would you say that once he gets an idea that he doesn't change his mind very soon?

S104—Well, yeah, that's right. He doesn't want to put it aside. He wants it to work now.

C105—Mm-huh. Do you get sort of provoked at him when he does? When he won't change?

S105—I don't—we never argue with him over anything.

C106—Just sort of let him have his way. Do you talk it over with your brother though?

S106—Oh, yes. (*pause*)

C107—Why is it that you don't talk it over with your dad?

S107—Well, I don't think he's going to change his mind now.

C108—Is he pretty strict?

S108—Well, on certain things he is and on other things he isn't.

C109—Mm-huh. Well, is he easy to talk to?

S109—No, not very easy.

C110—Mm-huh.

S110—That is, he says if I can learn them things, he'll start tellin' me things.

C111—How do you like that?

S111—I don't.

C112—Why is it you resent his telling you things?

S112—Well, if it's a good thing in which there would be headway, I would be interested but I don't care about goin' back 30 years.

C113—Mm-huh. (*long pause*) Well, what else do you want to know about yourself?

S113—Well, what I came to see you most about was these tests.

C114—Mm-huh. What use do you think these tests will be to you?

S114—Well, I know about where I stand with a lot of guys taking the tests.

C115—Think you'll know then how you stack up and what some of your—

S115—(*Client interrupts*) What the general weak spots are and the strong points.

C116—Yes.

S116—Everybody has a weak and strong point, but on a farm I believe you're better off if you had—ah—good performances—but—ah—in your place you're better off if you had good mental qualifications.

C117—Mm-huh. You feel then that you are best qualified for farm work, is that right?

S117—Yes, sir.

C118—Mm-huh. (*pause*) Well, if you are going to do farm work do you think you could study up and do a good job of farming? By studying at home as well as you could by studying here at the University.

S118—Well, yes, sir. There's a lot that you could learn, but you wouldn't learn as quick at home.

C119—Yes.

S119—Thing is, when you're in animal husbandry, our instructor always tell us *why,* and you get more.

C120—You like to know why things are different?

S120—Yes, sir.

C121—When you ask your father why he does certain things, can he tell you why?

S121—Well, I don't know, to a certain extent he does, yes, sir. (*pause*)

C122—Why do you think it is that your father is so much behind the times?

S122—You do find quite a few of the people that-a-way but not all of them. I notice—ah—the main thing—ah—in most families is a good educational background even if it was 70 years ago. They're right up-to-date. They keep right following things up, but one that hasn't, they just drop back. I mean, most—ah—a large percentage.

C123—Mm-huh.

S123—In fact, I've noticed a lot of 60-70 year old guys that's pushin' things ahead, keepin' up-to-date and makin' progress.

C124—Mm-huh. (*pause*) Do you think that you would be able to stay up-to-date if you had a farm of your own? Do you think you would be able to stay up-to-date better with a college education or would it make any difference?

S124—Well, I figure it's a little better with a college education. 'Course a person living on a farm, there's a lot of farm magazines and ways to pick up knowledge.

C125—Mm-huh. (*pause*) Well, has the work you have taken so far this semester been helpful to you?

S125—Oh, yes, sir! I can write quite a bit faster and better.

★ Again we see a rather crude perception of college work. This faulty perception supports the suggested interpretation of the MMPI.

C126—Can you?

S126—Mm-huh.

C127—Do you have to do a lot of writing to do farm work?

S127—Well, no, not very much.

C128—Mm-huh.

S128—People are doing more writing, that is, keeping books. Like—used to, a farmer never kept a book, gettin' so now everybody keeps books.

C129—Mm-huh. (*pause*) Well, you took a reading test here, too. I was rather interested in this. It would appear that reading perhaps is not one of your strong points. Have you done much reading?

S129—Well, I have here recently. I used to not do very much. (*long pause*)

C130—You don't read very fast do you? Do you find it difficult to remember what you have read?

S130—Well,—ah—yes.

C131—That's the way that it appeared on the test. It seems as though you don't read very fast and you don't remember too much about what you read, either. (*pause*) Do you feel that this will be a handicap to you?

S131—Well, yes. I guess it would.

C132—What sort of an approach do you think you might make to overcome that particular difficulty?

S132—Well, I'm not too good at pronunciation. That is, there are a lot of words I can't pronounce.

C133—How do you overcome that?

S133—Well, I sometimes look the word up in the dictionary and—

C134—(*Counselor interrupts*) Does that help you?

S134—Yes, sir.

C135—What else can you do?

S135—Well, if somebody's around ask them the word. (*pause*) Then if I'm in a class, like in English someone reads a sentence, I learned how to pronounce it and I catch on that way.

C136—Mm-huh, good. I might mention that we have a reading and study clinic in connection with the counseling service here. That might be helpful to you if you'd like to spend a little bit of time to brush up on your reading speed and your ability to remember what you have read. (*pause*) Miss Ready is in charge of the reading clinic and she has found that many students if they can spend about two hours a week in the clinic really profit by it. Some students are able to do considerably better with their reading ability when they get through than they did before. She has materials there, stories of one kind or another to read and in doing so you make a conscious effort to read faster and to remember, and by gaining skill in reading better and faster you're able to read your class work better. If you'd like, you might make an appointment with her, she could explain it better than I could. But I might make that suggestion if you'd be interested in something like that you might like to see her.

S136—Yes, I need some improvement in this line. What are her regular office hours?

C137—She'll be here this afternoon 2:30 and she is also here on Thursday at 2:30 in the afternoon.

S137—I have a class this afternoon, but I could see her Thursday.

C138—All right. Why don't you drop back Thursday afternoon and talk with her and you might mention to her that you've taken the reading test, and she'll be interested in seeing about the level of your difficulty so that she'll know about where she will have to start, you see, in giving you assistance. You might find that to be very helpful to you in overcoming that difficulty. You'll find her very easy to talk to, I think. She is a very interesting person. That might be a way of improving your background, helping yourself out a little bit. (*pause*) Well, let's see what time it is getting to be?

S138—10:35.

C139—Oh, is that right? Do you have a 10:30 class?

S139—No, sir, not 'till 11:30.

C140—Mm-huh. Well, the hour just sort of slipped by, here. I have a couple of more here that we might chat about next time if you like. I would suggest that in the meantime you do see Miss Ready and I think she will give you some material. I don't think that you have to make an appointment here with her for that particular hour on Thursday, but you might check as you go out to see whether you do or not.

S140—I'll check.

C141—Yes. Whenever it is convenient for you, we'll chat again.

S141—Okay. I'll need to make an appointment for that?

C142—Yes, you'd better make an appointment to make sure that we can get together.

COUNSELOR'S NOTES ON THE THIRD INTERVIEW
(*Dictated Immediately after the Interview*)

★ Mr. Smith returned for discussion and interpretation of test data. The intelligence test and the Triggs Reading test were interpreted to him. Mr. Smith did not seem to accept his low ability because of his satisfaction with his ability to do "performance type work." He feels that this is to his advantage in the College of Agriculture and if he does not make grades sufficient to enter veterinary medicine he will be able to obtain a B.S. degree in agriculture. As a result of the interpretation of the Triggs test he felt that work with Miss Ready (Reading Clinician) might be helpful to him. She was contacted and given a brief description of Mr. Smith's reading ability. He plans to return for discussion of further test data.

His home life was discussed somewhat and there were no conflicts here, or he apparently did not recognize any other than the superficial discussion of his father being old-fashioned in his farming methods.

COUNSELOR'S NOTES ON FOURTH INTERVIEW
(*Four Months after the Third Interview*)

Mr. Smith was in the counseling center to re-take the H.S. G.E.D. Tests. He hopes to be admitted as a regular rather than a special student. When he had completed one test, he asked this counselor if he would interpret the personality test he had taken previously.

During the interview he explained that he had had a poor record in the Spring semester but thought his summer work was passing. He is now hoping to work out a B.S. degree in Agriculture and if he completes this, he will then make a decision as to whether or not he will attempt Veterinary School. This seems to be much more realistic. However, it seems doubtful that he will be able to complete requirements for a B.S. degree.

Mr. Smith seemed to be more sure of himself in this interview than he had been previously. He attributed this to remedial work in the speech department. Apparently, the clinicians there have been able to give him rather individualized attention. This probably has been helpful in making him more outgoing and making him less conscious of his limited vocabulary. This fall he plans to continue in the Speech Clinic and he also plans to get help in the Reading Clinic.

He said he plans to get married in the near future but must wait for the consent of his fiancee's parents as his fiancee is under legal age. She plans to work if they are married.

The MMPI was interpreted to him as indicating that he was a "withdrawn" person living "within-his-shell." He thought it amazing that the test could be so accurate. He felt, however, that work in the Speech Clinic was assisting him to "talk better" and as a result making him more expansive. The Pd indicated lack of "family closeness." This had been brought out in previous interviews. He seems to be making a reasonably satisfactory adjustment and he was invited to return to the counseling center any time he wished to do so.

COUNSELOR'S NOTES ON THE FIFTH INTERVIEW
(*8 Months after the Fourth Interview*)

The client presented the following letter when he made the appointment for this interview:

> The bearer of this note, Mr. Tom Smith, is one of my advisees and is a fourth semester preveterinary student.
> Mr. Smith is having a little trouble with his course work and at the present time is reported as being deficient in three of his classes. I have discussed this matter with Mr. Smith, and we both feel that it might be a good idea if he could take a series of tests which would give us a better idea of his aptitudes and abilities.

Mr. Smith came in and stated that he is now experiencing difficulty again, and that he had three F's at midsemester. He stated that his reading has improved after having gone to the reading clinic. However, he felt that he was still reading very slowly. He said that he has switched from veterinary medicine to general agriculture and he feels that he is very definitely getting something and he would like to stay in school. However, with this increased difficulty he is now thinking in terms of being admitted as an unclassified student (not a candidate for a degree). He indicated that he would like more information on the unclassified student status and we discussed this for some time. I checked with an assistant in the dean's office who indicated that it could be done in this particular individual's case. The client

said that he would like to get the degree, but it was really secondary as far as he was concerned because he did feel that with
what he was getting he would be a much better farmer eventually. The client indicated that he was going back to see his
adviser to find out what his chances were for passing this semester. When we terminated the interview the situation seemed to
depend on how his grades were at the end of this semester. This
would govern whether he took definite steps to become an unclassified student or whether he would try to continue working
toward a degree. There didn't seem to be any evidence on the
part of the student that not being permitted to go on for the
degree would be especially disturbing to him. He seems to realize
at this time that he doesn't have the ability that would be necessary to complete a degree in four years, and it has now come to
a point where he would like to get as much as he possibly can
in technical training and then return to general farming. No
further contacts were planned.

✽ ✽ ✽ ✽ ✽

As might have been expected, a follow-up indicated that Mr.
Smith did not fare well academically. He continued in the University for about two years registering as an unclassified student,
taking courses which would be helpful to him when he returned
to farming. He felt that his time was being well spent; that is, he
was profiting from his college experience.

ADDENDUM

★ The Case of Tom Smith exemplifies the counseling problems involved with a client who might be considered to have high aspirations and relatively low scholastic aptitude (as compared with
other college students). Actually, a high level of aspiration may
not be as much the central theme of the case as the reader may
think on first reading. The client's self-concept may revolve
around these ideas: (1) Others have gone to high school and
have an educational advantage over me; (2) My speech and
educational background handicap me in class and in my social
relationships; (3) I can do practical things better than others in
my classes, though; (4) I can get this school work if they'll only
give me time—"day by day I'm getting better and better;" (5) I
don't want to go home—I want to be an educated farmer; (6) If
I can get some schooling here, I can be a leader in my community; (7) Through education I can attain status which might
evade me at home on the farm; (8) I want to go home when I
can assert myself and not be dominated by my father; (9) This
counselor is educated and deserves respect; (10) The counselor
doesn't understand me very well.

Some of these concepts made the counselor's task doubly dif-
cult. The fact that the client's values were difficult to compre-

hend by the counselor also added to the counselor's problems. Certainly the counselor was not always able to understand a young man from a strictly rural background, sometimes misinterpreting client responses.

As the client tested his ability to do college work, he gradually adjusted his "sights" to fit the circumstances. Such action apparently caused little anxiety as long as he was permitted time to make the adjustment. Success to the client is not necessarily the concept of success held by those who have achieved well in school. The client was able to accept successive lower levels of aspiration without any drastic reorganization of his self-concept.

The Case of

RUTH BROOK

★ THE CASE consists of three interviews. The client learned of the services of the counseling center from her high school principal who had been informed that the services were available to high school juniors and seniors for help in considering posthigh school plans.

The counselor of the case had earned a doctor's degree in educational psychology and had had ten years post-doctoral experience in the counseling field, two years at the high school level and eight years at the college and university level which included counseling, administering a college counseling center, and training counselors at the graduate level.

Since the client was to be on campus for a two-consecutive day period only, certain data were obtained concerning the client prior to the first interview. The following information was known to the counselor at the time of the first interview:

Client:—Age: 16 years.
      Marital status: Single.
      Born in a metropolitan area and lived there until she was seven or eight years old.
      Educational History: She has attended several elementary schools and one high school. Just completed junior year in high school. Present home address is in a small city in the state. Extra-curricular activities include sports, dramatics, school newspaper, orchestra, art, pep club, student government. Leisure time activities; music, art, church work, dancing, sports, reading, driving a car. Has made a "straight A" scholastic record during the first three years in high school.
      Work Experience: Baby sitting, art work, summer tutoring jobs. Liked art work best and tutoring least.
      Educational and vocational plans: Plans to attend college for four years. Expressed vocational interests: architect, C.P.A. in a foreign office, commercial artist.

Family:—Father dead. It was not stated what his education and occupation were. Mother living; not remarried; occupation—teacher; education—master's degree.

STRONG VOCATIONAL INTEREST TEST - WOMEN

SEE OTHER SIDE FOR EXPLANATION

OCCUPATION	C	C +	B -	B	B +	A
STANDARD SCALE	0 10 20	30		40	50 60 70

ARTIST	-200 -150 -100 -50	0 50 100 150 200 250
AUTHOR	-200 -150 -100 -50	0 50 100 150 200 250 300
LIBRARIAN	-50	50 100 150 200
ENGLISH TEACHER	0	50 100 150
SOCIAL WORKER	-50	0 50 100 150
PSYCHOLOGIST	0	50 100 150 200
LAWYER	-50	0 50 100 150
SOCIAL SCIENCE TEACHER	-50 0	50 100 150
Y.W.C.A. SECRETARY	0 50	100 150 200 250
LIFE INSUR. SALESWOMAN	-50 0	50 100 150
BUYER	-50 0	50 100 150
HOUSEWIFE	-100 -50 0	50 100 150
ELEMENTARY TEACHER	-50 0	50 100 150
OFFICE WORKER	-150 -100 -50 0	50 100 150
STENOG.-SECY.	-100 -50 0	50 100 150
BUSINESS ED. TEACHER	-100 -50 0	50 100 150
HOME ECON. TEACHER	-50 0 50	100 150 200
DIETITIAN	-50 0	50 100 150
PHYSICAL ED. TEACHER	-50 0 50	100 150 200
OCCUP. THERAPIST	-50 0	50 100
NURSE	-50 0	50 100
MATH.-SCIENCE TEACHER	-50	50 100 150
DENTIST	-100 -50 0	50 100
LABORATORY TECHNICIAN	-50 0	50 100 150
PHYSICIAN	-50 0	50 100 150 200

STANDARD SCALE	75	70	65	60	55	50	45	40	35	30	25
FEMININITY-MASCULINITY	-100					-50				0	M

BROOK, Ruth

Reprinted with the permission of the author, E. K. Strong, Jr., the publisher, Stanford University Press, and E. J. Hankes of Engineers Northwest.

NAME   AGENCY OR SCHOOL   AGE 16   DATE   NUMBER

No siblings.

Client lives with the mother. No other persons in the household.

A report from one of the client's high school teachers indicates that the client does unusually well in all subject matter areas and has considerable artistic ability. She has a driving ambition to rate high in all activities. Her home is one of the more privileged ones socio-economically speaking.

The Strong Vocational Interest Blank, Form W, was mailed to the client who then answered it and returned it to the counselor. It was scored and the results were available at the time of the first interview. See profile.

FIRST INTERVIEW

C1—Well, you had to get up a little early this morning, didn't you?

S1—Oh, yes!

C2—Sit here. (*pause*) You were in the eleventh grade, weren't you?

S2—Yes, I'll be a senior next year.

C3—You don't have any immediate worries then about your future plans.

S3—No, but we want to choose my college and we're thinking in terms of scholarships. Oh, I don't know, I don't believe that you should wait until the last minute (*laughs*).

> ★ The counselor knew that he was dealing with a student who was still in high school and not making immediate plans to go to work or enter college. The first statement of the client included the word "we"; thereafter she shifted to the use of "I." This probably had no significance—anyway the counselor made no issue of it. It is usually an error for the counselor to pounce upon such minute points this early in the interview. Such practice may lead to guarded speech by the client—certainly the antithesis of "good" counseling.

C4—What kinds of things are you interested in that we can do for you here? What did you have in mind when you came in?

S4—Do you mean questions to be answered? Well, I have other problems, I guess, that come up. I like mathematics very much, and I am very interested in art. I have considered a lot of possibilities and things to do with my mathematics, and you meet the recurring problem all the time that there are no openings for women—in the mathematical field, and I'd like to find out more about what openings there would be and what possible combinations, such as architecture.

C5—Mm-huh.

S5—You could combine art and math in some way. (*pause*)

C6—Well, have you had some other ideas, perhaps, what you'd like to do? That's one. (*pause*)

S6—Well, at one time I had considered law and politics, but I don't want quite that much of a career. (*laughs*)

C7—You mean, you're interested in an objective someday. Have you set it up in your thinking—career, or marriage, or can it be both, or just how do you feel about it?

S7—Well, I always figured, perhaps, I'd finish college and go into my career and spend a year or so in that; and after marriage, I'd drop the career. I don't think I'd want to try to be a housewife and carry on a career. Marriage would definitely be a possibility, and that's not all out. I'm afraid that's one reason why I discarded law in my thinking—because that would mean a career.

C8—Yes, that'd mean 6 or 7 years in preparation for it. (*pause*)

★ This response might have been improved by the counselor's re-sponding to the client's rather ambiguous statement regarding marriage. So far the problem has been designated as one of edu-cational and vocational planning and that has been delimited to a significant extent by the client's statement that she is ultimately interested in marriage rather than a career. Essentially she is asking how can she combine her interest in mathematics and art into a career (short term) which does not require extensive prep-aration and which does not require her to deviate very far from the usual feminine pattern of behavior. That is, she is looking for a plan which will allow self-expression of interests and abilities which at the same time will not interfere with marriage or preparation for marriage.

S8—I'd—at one time considered going four years. I do not want to go to an *art* school.

C9—I see.

S9—I suppose, I could get a scholarship, probably in art, because I've had some luck at winning things on my work and I like to do it, enjoy it a lot; but I didn't want to go to, say, an art institute or some such thing because I have other interests, too.

C10—Yes, you say you've had success wih this art. Would you tell me a little bit about it?

S10—Well, last year I sent some art work to a contest and I got an award on that and sent it on to a national contest and I got first place award in the national contest on that. This year I sent some more to the contest and won a first place there and went on to national and got a first again. For a junior in high school, I figure that it shows that there is some hope there.

C11—Sure. I expect that you have had many things exhibited in high school.

S11—Oh, yes.

C12—Have you done anything commercially?

S12—I do sign painting some. Of course, my jobs are mostly for church and organizations. (*laughs*) I can't compete with the men at home who do that. I do earn quite a bit of money, though, on the side, with art. I do hand lettering and anything that requires stylus work for the mimeoscope. I do just little odd jobs that come along.

C13—What have you done in high school—for your groups in high school?

S13—Oh, I've served as chairman of the decorating committees; and I make posters for everything that comes along. (*laughs*)

C14—I guess, they would keep you busy on that.

S14—During student elections I worked for several candidates. (*laughs*) It's just that there's always a need for it in school; and as much time as you can make, you can always use it. (*laughs*)

C15—You've done well scholastically, too, your record shows that.

★ The counselor is dealing with a high school student whose experience in art has been exceptional. Her ability has been established to some extent through her achievement.

S15—Oh, I've had a lot of luck.

C16—What do you mean by that?

S16—Some place along the line, I guess, I learned to use my time in class because I had to run an awfully close schedule on extracurricular activities.

C17—You just about had to get your lessons in class, is that it? It came pretty easy for you, I mean.

S17—Yes, I would say so because, I know, I don't work as hard as some of my friends do that make pretty good grades. I don't know, I work— I study—you have to.

★ This is an example of how one develops a realistic self-concept through experience or reality-testing. The client already has developed a fairly good concept of how she compares with her peers in mental ability or at least in "ability to get grades."

C18—Sure, what I was getting at was that you work. You didn't just sit around and get the grades that you do. You'd have to do something, but you didn't have to put in hours of drudgery.

S18—No, it's no drudgery, it's all pleasure. (*laughs*)

C19—Art and math are the two things you mentioned. How are the other subjects in terms of your thinking? (*pause*) Do you like them?

S19—Yes, I like everything. That's my big problem.

> ★ This is sometimes a difficult client response for the counselor to handle. The counselor, of course, can repeat the statement of the client. He can respond to the feeling of discouragement, futility, elation, indifference, and so on, as the case may be. This particular counselor used simple acceptance and permitted the client to continue.

C20—Mm-huh.

S20—I don't know, English is perhaps the worst of my subjects; however, I like to read, and I do a lot of reading. I don't write well.

C21—I see.

S21—It is one of my difficulties.

C22—You have more difficulty expressing an idea in writing than you have in drawing or painting.

S22—Mm-huh. However, in our high school, set up as we are, there's very little chance for competition. Perhaps I do more than a passable job at it, I don't know. My mother teaches.

C23—Mm-huh.

S23—I don't know, it's always funny, my English teachers are always getting, you know, irritated at me a little. However, I have managed to get my grades all right.

C24—Well, has your mother been critical of that?

S24—Probably so. Mm-huh.

C25—Sometimes they are that way.

S25—I like to cook, and I like to sew. I just like to do everything.

C26—You just like everything.

S26—Mm-huh.

C27—What other activities do you like?

S27—Just everything.

C28—It makes it difficult to choose between two activities, doesn't it?

S28—It certainly does.

> ★ The counselor at this point in the interview felt that the client was not too certain about the counseling process. She seemed rather willing to discuss some of her interests and achievements but somewhat restrained when discussing her mother (**S24**). She changed the topic of discussion in **S25** and added little there-

after. The counselor in **C29** tried structuring the counseling relationship, emphasizing (1) the value of verbalizing about herself, and (2) the personal nature of the counseling relationship. In the discussion concerning parents, the counselor was attempting to reassure her that everything discussed in the interview would not be reported back to her parents. This is sometimes a "touchy" subject with some adolescents. Later developments indicated that this was unnecessary because the client and her mother evidently confided in each other. Whether the structuring or some other factor caused it, the client began in **S30** to verbalize about her activities.

C29—Well, now let's see, there're some ideas here. Understand, we don't have any gadgets whereby we can tell you, "You ought to be this or that or the other thing." It involves mainly talking over what your plans might be and how these fit in with some other ideas we can piece together from tests or some other information that we have. And the materials discussed in here are between us. We don't even discuss it with parents unless they request it, and then we don't tell them everything. (*client laughs*). By putting together some of the bits of information, sometimes we give you a little better understanding of perhaps some goals that might be better than others.

S29—Mm-huh.

C30—Now, you say you've been very active in terms of your extracurricular activities in high school. What about out of school? I mean, do you have a lot of activities in the community that you—

S30—Well, I've been very interested in church work, and I have served in various things I won't go through. I served in state and national offices. This year I was delegate to the national convention. I had a lot of fun, and that involved running back and forth on weekends and meetings; and I'm an officer of our state right now. Well, I do that, and I'm a Girl Scout; however, I haven't been too active in that. I'm counselor at camp in the summer time—but, oh, I went to Girls' State this year and I make talks, of course, about that. (*laughs*)—What else am I interested in? I play in the symphony.

C31—You're a musician, too.

S31—(*Laughs*) Well, we'll put it this way. I play a little.

C32—Oh yes, well, that's musical ability to me!

S32—I like music very much, but my musical ability is rather nil. And what I learn is rote. Music, I don't have any particular gift for it. I play the piano a little, the clarinet a little, and the string bass. I've played for a long time and get a lot of kick out of it, and that's just why I play it.

C33—Well, you seem to discount music entirely. (*pause*) You say, your mother teaches. I expect she's a graduate of a college.

S33—She went to college and later got a Master's Degree.

C34—Uh-huh, and your dad?

S34—He died.

C35—Oh, I see.

S35—Mother and he were separated—and then he died recently.

C36—Oh, yes. Did you have any association with him before he died? I mean did you stay with him at all or—

S36—No, I hadn't, I stayed with mother. He had an operation, and I went out there at that time. He wanted to see me, and I went out to see him at that time.

C37—Then you never had much association with him.

S37—Not very much.

C38—And how old were you when—

S38—Hmmm, six, and I went to the second grade while mother was getting her Master's.

C39—Uh-huh. (*pause*) Well, now as far as your other activities, social activities and so on—you've been pretty active, in terms of dating?

S39—Oh, I'd say average or a little below. I don't date too much. I know why I don't because I'm too masculine as a woman. Why, everything the boys can do, I can do, too. There's not, however, much dating in my home town. There's not much done. Our student body is 700; and 25 school couples and 25 alumni couples go to most of the dances, so it's kind of narrowed down, so—. However, I have my share of dates and activities and the like.

C40—You say, you're quite masculine.

S40—I guess, I am. I don't know.

C41—Well, I was just wondering, that's your own observation? Has somebody told you that?

S41—No, it's not an observation.

C42—Well, just what makes you believe that?

S42—Oh, I don't know. I like to play cards, and just a couple of things that have cropped up lately have occurred to me that I am. I can beat boys. If they teach me a card game, I can beat them at their own card game. I have found myself consciously slowing down out at the swimming pool so that I won't outswim them. I can dive, and it gives you a rather weird feeling,—"Well, can you do a one and a half?" and I go up and do it. "Can you?" and the boy says, "No, I don't have the nerve to do it," you know, and things like that. I just know, it crops up along the line.

C43—How about other sports, have you been active in them?

S43—As active as my home town will permit. Matter of fact, in high school they have no interest in school sports for girls, just gym class. I bowl, I play ping pong, play at tennis, and swim and play golf. (*laughs*)

C44—You're right, there isn't much that you haven't tried. How is your golf?

S44—Not so hot! (*laughs*) Anybody can beat me in golf. I'm not very good at it, but I'm one of the few girls around town that even plays golf. That's just my observation.

C45—That may be the sport you have to play with the boys.

S45—I think so. I don't mean that I excel in sports, or anything, I'm just trying to get at what made me believe—(*laughs*)—just a couple things that crop up and you make an observation on yourself.

C46—Does your mother keep pretty close tab on you in terms of getting out, dating, and that kind of thing?

S46—No.

C47—Then she hasn't tried to hold you down and you—

S447—No, not at all.

C48—(*Continues*) . . . get along well with your mother.

S48—Yes, very well.

C49—Uh-huh. She has some of the same interests that you have?

S49—Yes, we are close. We get along fine, I should say, in most cases. Mother and I have always been very close, we've always gotten along *very well*, we travel well together—and things like that.

C50—Will it be sort of a hard break when you have to get away from home? Will it be a new experience?

S50—Well, that is something that I have thought about more. Mother and I are living in our house by ourselves, and I've given it a lot of thought. The only difference it will make,—it will, of course, be a break for me; but I have done a lot of traveling, and I have been on my own a lot. Mother pretty well recognizes my self-proficiency in a lot things. The only thing is, that I think she will want me to go close to school, close to my home town, the first two years anyway, fairly close that's the only thing. I don't think you could term it a particularly hard break. Most of them always are breaks to make.

C51—You're going to have to, I mean, you're not home for breakfast, dinner, and supper like you were, and so on. It is an adjustment every family has to make.

★ The counselor was attempting to see if the client felt the full impact of the "break" in light of the previous statement and that of **S50**. It is interesting to note that the client in **S51** stresses the mother's adjustment rather than her own.

S51—I expect it will be harder for mother to make the adjustment than it will for me. Because it will mean—perhaps she will get someone to live in the house with her and matters like that. (*pause*)

C52—Will some of your other friends be going to go away to school, too?

S52—Yes, all the girls I run with, I think, are going to college. Two of them, I think, will enter nursing and rest of them will enter college. The three of them with me today talk that way. They are the main ones I run around with. Mother encouraged all my gang to come down to this (*counseling service*).

C53—Part of our job, of course, is talking about these things. We find that examining the past records, you might say, and experiences people have had plus some things we may be able to pick up from some interest inventories, and things like that, may be of some help in charting the course. We can't pinpoint things usually to the point where you can say, "well, this is the thing I'm going to do without fail." Life's a little bit too uncertain to try doing that kind of thing. Sometimes you don't gain much out of sitting down chatting with somebody because you find out your plans are pretty well formulated. Now, where you have this wide range of interests, we can at least introduce you to some new ideas perhaps; and then we can chat about them a little bit. It might be of some help to discuss architecture. A little more discussion of it, what it would mean in terms of training and what kinds of people architects may be, would be part of this whole picture.

S53—Mm-huh.

C54—Now we have several tests that might be possibilities. We have one interest inventory that you took and mailed to us. We have that scored. We'd like to give you another one. It's a different kind, just a check.

S54—Um-huh.

C55—And then in terms of ability, I don't know, you've given me indications that you have rather high ability in book work, that is, your studies. We might give you something that isn't too long as a check up with entering freshmen, for example.

S55—Um-huh.

C56—Something on personality might be worth while. This "masculine" thing you were talking about (*client laughs*) might or might not show up on that, and you might be fooled a little bit in terms of what you think you are there; but it sometimes is very helpful in terms of trying to narrow where you'll probably go and where you will like it a little better. I don't know if there is any other kind of question you might have. If there is anything about yourself that you'd like to find out, that we might be able to test for, I don't know. That's the interest, ability and personality part of it, is there anything else? (*pause*)

S56—Well, I guess that about covers it.

C57—We might have an art aptitude test, but you've already indicated an aptitude. Our tests are certainly not half as good as what you've shown through these contests and other things that you do; so that would be a waste of time.

S57—Um-huh.

C58—Then, of course, we have occupational information about some of these different kinds of things that you might like to look over. You can also look at the university catalogues in terms of what they have to say about some of these things.

S58—Um-huh.

C59—Would that—meet your interests a bit?

S59—I think so.

C60—Well, then, we might as well get you started on some of these.

★ There followed at this point a discussion with the client of the arrangements for transportation back to her home town.

C61—You may have a little time when you and one of the other girls may have time to go out and look over the campus or something of that kind.

S61—I'd like to look at the art department if there is anything going on up there.

C62—I don't know—during the late summer, of course, activities slow down around here terrifically and you never know, but I'll make a note of that.

S62—One other observation on this masculine deal. There's a family at home, several boys, one my age, one a year older. The one a year older, we've been thrown together an awful lot in youth work on a brotherly and sisterly basis.

★ The client's return to the "masculine" discussion is an interesting turn of events. She may have been cut off too quickly by the counselor in their previous discussion; she may have at last felt sufficiently secure to discuss the topic further; or it may have taken her several minutes to marshall her evidence to the counselor's question in C42. Later events probably indicate that C42 was a challenge to her; and she was not going to let the question go unanswered or permit the counselor to feel that her judgment in the matter was immature or unwarranted.

C63—Um-huh.

S63—It's been awfully nice. He intends to enter the ministry, I think; but anyway, we have always made it a practice of being open with each other—criticising. We talk about college a lot, and he's going this year.

He got a $4,000 scholarship (*laughs*) to College D. But anyway he made the observation the other day—I was saying that I didn't know whether I wanted to go to a girls' school or not, that I just couldn't exactly see myself in a girls' school, and he said, "No, I can't either, you like to compete with men too much." That would be just another observation there on—that.

C64—Tell me how you feel about his observation.

S64—(*laughs*) It's always been my observation in class that the boys are my—that the boys are the people that I compete with, with my good grades, that it's a boy always that has a political view that I'd like to challenge, and there is a boy that's got this, or says this that I don't agree or something, you know how it goes.

C65—How do you account for it?

S65—I don't know. (*pause*) It may just be purely happenstance.

C66—Uh-huh.

S66—And then again it may not. I have, in my lifetime, had a chance to be associated with some very brilliant boys.

C67—Uh-huh.

S67—And I just always found them just stimulating experiences. I play bridge, I'm learning to play bridge, and this boy that I play cards with—

C68—Uh-huh.

S68—(*continues*). . . and so on like that. And I think that what's behind it all is the fact that I have so many interests and that my particular girl friends, in fact, all of the girls, are apt—in fact they disturb me at times. I always manage to conceal it, but it disturbs me that they just sit around.

C69—Yes.

S69—And so, I have gone out and done other things. And in my doing other things, I have picked up some masculine companionships.

C70—Uh-huh.

S70—That's why I hesitate—oh, I have had dates on purely a social basis.

C71—Yes.

S71—But I hate to say that—I can't ever—I mean, you can't draw a line between your friends and your dates, you know.

C72—Well, let's start from here tomorrow.

S72—Okay.

COUNSELOR'S NOTES ON THE FIRST INTERVIEW
(*Dictated Immediately after the Interview*)

★ The client came to the counseling center to participate in our high school counseling service upon the recommendation of her mother. Her mother seems to influence all of the girls who came to the center this date. The client is a junior in high school and is leading her class in scholarship. In telling about her experiences, she related a wide range of interests. Basically she seems to have an interest in art and mathematics. The art interest has been expressed by entering several art contests. She has won national contests. In addition she has won several other prizes in art work. The client has done some free lance art work, poster work and so on for some of the organizations in her home town. Other experiences have included playing in the symphony orchestra in her home town and in various musical organizations in high school. She feels that she has only mediocre musical ability but nevertheless has been able to do many activities. She seems to have been the center of many of the high school activities. Perhaps art has been the entree to these groups. She has been very active in church work and traveled a great deal as a result of it to various conferences about the country. She has been very active in social activities with her own sex and with boys, going to dances and parties and athletic events of various kinds. She likes to be with people and seems to have tremendous drive for activities.

She expressed her vocational interests as something which might combine both art and mathematics. For example, she has thought very seriously about architecture, and wants more information on this subject. She has also thought about some type of foreign service but has more or less discarded that. Something in strictly art work would of course be also appropriate. She is considering both career and marriage, and does not plan to use her training as strictly career with marriage only a possibility. She hopes to be married within a few years after graduation from college.

A very interesting part of the first interview was comments she made about being masculine. It seems that one close boy friend had observed the fact that she was quite masculine in many of her characteristics. She went on to emphasize the fact that she has always been competing with boys. Girls evidently have not been much competition; but, on what she thinks of as a friendly basis, she has competed with boys in her classes, in athletics, and various other things. She finds that in many instances she has to hold back so that she doesn't always beat the boys. An illustration of that was in swimming, where she holds up just a little so that the boys are not too far outdistanced in swimming, and she went on to explain about in diving, that they'll ask her if she can do a particular dive and she goes up and does it. She asks them if they can, and they say no. There may be something in this particular area that may be worth discussing. She said that her mother has not made it difficult for her to adjust to the opposite sex. Her mother is a high school teacher and separated from her husband when the client was about six years of age. The client has had very little contact with her father. He died recently. The client did go to see her father before he passed away. The client has already thought about the problem and evidently has begun to face the fact that there will be a day when she will have to break the ties at home.

We discussed various tests. I suggested a Kuder Preference Record, a Minnesota Multiphasic, and the A.C.E. I am not too sure that any information on these tests will be significant. I believe that some occupational information plus further discussion about some of her activities may be most helpful.

TEST DATA

In addition to the test data available at the beginning of the first interview the following tests were administered between the first and second interviews with the following results:

(1) American Council on Education Psychological Examination for College Freshmen, 1942 Edition—

	Raw Score	*Percentile Rank***
Q-score	51	86
L-score	85	95
Total score	136	94

* (the norm group was local university freshmen)

(2) Kuder Preference Record, Vocational, Form CM, see profile.

(3) Minnesota Multiphasic Personality Inventory, Booklet Form, see profile.

(4) Rotter Incomplete Sentences Blank, College Form, see protocol.

SECOND INTERVIEW

(One Day after the First Interview)

C1—Well, what did you think of the tests?

S1—Oh, what'd I think of the tests? Well, one made me feel awfully slow. I don't know whether I was just in a slow day, but I just couldn't get any place at all—speed on the time test.

C2—Oh, yes. That was the college aptitude test that we give to the freshmen.

S2—Uh-huh.

C3—What made you think you didn't do so well on that?

S3—Oh—I don't know, I just thought, I didn't even get half done with some of it. It was the speed. I think, what I got, I got right, mostly.

C4—Is that a disturbing feeling—that you can't finish things?

First Revision, February 1951

SELF-INTERPRETING

PROFILE SHEET

for the

KUDER PREFERENCE RECORD
VOCATIONAL

Form C

MEN and WOMEN

DIRECTIONS FOR PROFILING

1. Copy the V-Score from the back page of your answer pad in the box at the right.

   [36]

   If your V-Score is 37 or less, there is some reason for doubting the value of your answers, and your other scores may not be very accurate. If your V-Score is 45 or more, you may not have understood the directions, since 44 is the highest possible score. If your score is not between 38 and 44, inclusive, you should see your adviser. He will probably recommend that you read the directions again, and then that you fill out the blank a second time, being careful to follow the directions exactly and to give sincere replies.

   If your V-Score is between 38 and 44, inclusive, go ahead with the following directions.

2. Copy the scores 0 through 9 in the spaces at the top of the profile chart. Under "OUTDOOR" find the number which is the same as the score at the top. Use the numbers under M if you are a man and the numbers under F if you are a woman. Draw a line through this number from one side to the other of the entire column under OUTDOOR. Do the same thing for the scores at the top of each of the other columns. If a score is larger than any number in the column, draw a line across the top of the column: if it is smaller, draw a line across the bottom.

3. With your pencil blacken the entire space between the lines you have drawn and the bottom of the chart. The result is your profile for the *Kuder Preference Record—Vocational.*

Published by SCIENCE RESEARCH ASSOCIATES
228 South Wabash Avenue, Chicago 4, Illinois
Copyright 1951, by G. Frederic Kuder. Copyright under International Copyright Union. All rights reserved under Fourth International American Convention (1910). Printed in the U.S.A. Copyright 1951 in Canada.

Please use code number 7-299 when reordering this profile.

T-21-X

The Minnesota Multiphasic Personality Inventory
Starke R. Hathaway and J. Charnley M...nley

F Female

Name ___ K, Ruth ___

Address ___

Occupation ___ Student ___ Date Tested ___

Education ___ high school senior ___ Age ___ 16 ___

Marital Status ___ Single ___ Referred by ___

NOTES

The experimental scales — Re, St, and
Do — were not available to the
counselor at the time of this case.
They are reported here for the interest
of the reader.

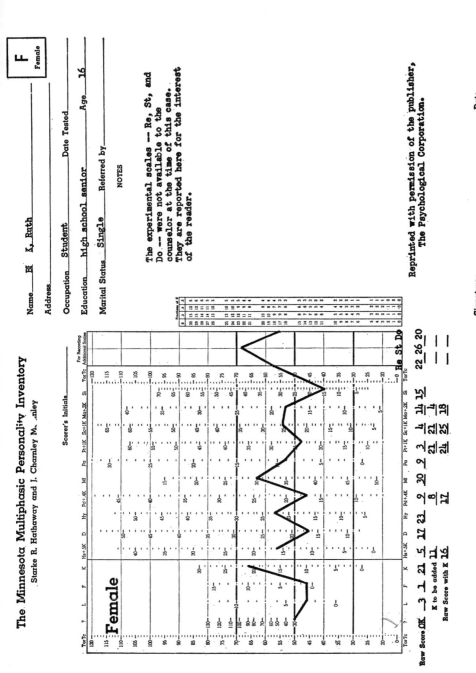

Female

Raw Score	?K	L	F	K	Hs+.5K	D	Hy	Pd+.4K	Mf	Pa	Pt+1K	Sc+1K	Ma+.2K	Si	Re	St	Do
	3	1	21	5	17	23	9	30	9	3	4	11	15		22	26	20
K to be added				11			8		21	21	4						
Raw Score with K				16			17		24	25	18						

Signature ___ Date ___

INCOMPLETE SENTENCES BLANK — COLLEGE FORM

Name Brook, Ruth   Sex F   Age 16   Marital Status Single

School _____ Class Senior   Date _____

Complete these sentences to express <u>your real feelings</u>. Try to do every one.
Be sure to make a complete sentence.

1. I like all types of art, including abstract and cubism.

2. The happiest time I have are when I am with other people.

3. I want to know more about mathematics.

4. Back home my mother is waiting for me.

5. I regret some of my "spur of the moment" activities.

6. At bedtime I like to think over my day's activities.

7. Boys are better companions than girls.

8. The best art is usually simple.

9. What annoys me are persons who are always slow.

10. People are always fascinating.

11. A mother is a girl's best friend.

12. I feel good and am happy most of the time.

13. My greatest fear is of snakes.

14. In high school you make many lasting friends.

15. I can't ever remember being dreadfully unhappy.

(TURN PAGE OVER AND CONTINUE)

Copyright 1950
The Psychological Corporation
522 Fifth Avenue
New York 18, N. Y.

Printed in U. S. A. 50-111 AS

JULIAN B. ROTTER, AUTHOR

16. Sports are a fine means of getting to know people.

17. When I was a child I liked to play hide-and-go-seek.

18. My nerves are fairly steady, but my hand sometimes shakes.

19. Other people are fun to be with.

20. I suffer only when I am forced into solitude.

21. I failed to evaluate other people's ability.

22. Reading is an instructive and pleasurable pastime.

23. My mind is not made up concerning future vocation.

24. The future is some indefinite quantity to look forward to.

25. I need to do more self-criticizing. blech

26. Marriage is the best career for most women.

27. I am best when I can successfully lead a group.

28. Sometimes I wish I had more money.

29. What pains me is a "catty" girl.

30. I hate to bo caught without an answer.

31. This school is particular attractive in all ways.

32. I am very glad that I am growing up.

33. The only trouble is that you always leave something behind.

34. I wish that I could find the right path for the future.

35. My father died last spring.

36. I secretly admire intelligent people.

37. I would like to know a lot more than I do.

38. Dancing is lots of fun, and a real art.

39 My greatest worry is that other people don't like me.

40. Most girls are attractive in some way.

S4—Um-huh, it is. Very disturbing. (*pause*)

C5—Umm. Let me get the results. Now, on the total test, for people that enter the university as a freshmen, your score was equal to or above the score of 94 per cent of them. (*pause*) Depending on what your standards are, it's not bad.

> ★ The counselor might have discussed the client's attitude toward tasks which she can't finish. The reassurance given in **C5** may be questioned as not too essential. The client already had some insight into her level of ability, so this type of information was not crucial in the case. The client's standards for her own achievement or her striving for perfection would have been appropriate topics for discussion.

S5—Um-huh.

C6—Because of the fact you are still in high school. You're not—

S6—I know that the word-definitions.—I had time on that section which I could not use because I wasn't familiar with the words. I know that in junior English we had extensive word study; and I know that we will cover a lot of the words next year that I didn't know.

C7—Well, the derivation doesn't mean very—

S7—Um-huh. Some of my Latin helped on some of them but there were some of them that were so far—

C8—Well, those tests were devised so that it would be a very unusual person that would ever finish—

S8—any section.

C9—Uh-huh. They're devised for that purpose.

S9—Um-huh, devised for a genius. (*laughing*)

C10—Yes, that might be.

S10—Um-huh.

C11—You still have a year to go, and sometimes that year of experience is important—sometimes it isn't. It might be in your case where you're in so many activities and so many varied experiences. (*pause*)

S11—It'll be good experience, I think, to be subjected to a test like that, I mean, now—

C12—Well, yes, you'll get so you can take them easily —

S12—You'll know a little more.

C13—Yes, that's right.

S13—I speeded up considerably. By the end of the test I was able to work more rapidly than I was a first. I—

C14—I think that's typical. Even the freshmen, when they take it, start out in a rather leisurely fashion and find out that time's up. They didn't get very far, and so with the next one—

S14—Kinda schooled on it, so you can get it faster as you go along.

C15—That ties in pretty well with your record of marks—this striving for perfection and all that—

S15—Um-huh.

C16—in terms of school marks. (*pause*) Well, in addition to that, of course, we have some other things that might be of interest. Now, here are two interest tests. Maybe you can explain some of their differences. This is an interest inventory that compares your interests with women who have worked—oh—for at least three years, I would say, in these various occupations. Usually, we figure, that where there's a high similarity of your interests with theirs, your score will fall in the B+ to A on this printed form.

> ★ The counselor was asking the client for assistance in the interpretation of any inconsistencies between the interest tests and the clinical data. By playing somewhat confused, the counselor sometimes is able to elicit client discussion and prevent sterile, technical test interpretations.

S16—Huh-mm. (*laughs*) Office worker.

C17—Now, don't get excited, I'll explain that.

> ★ This type of response may seem out of place and could have been improved, but the manner in which it was said, and the tendency of the client to jump to conclusions probably caused the counselor to bring any unwarranted conclusions to an abrupt halt. The fact that the client seemed to accept the response indicated substantial rapport between client and counselor.

S17—Okay.

C18—Now, in the next group would be the B and B— area. We know that there is a slight similarity of interests when it's in that area and when it is down here, it's more dissimilarity than anything, in terms that it is a "might be and it might not be."

S18—Umm.

C19—Now, in that area you see down here there isn't—

S19—There isn't particularly a strong interest in—

C20—There isn't much to pin down on any one of them. This is what is characteristic of most women. It will show up on this one. (*pointing to office worker*)

S20—Huh-mmm.

C21—Take what we call a housewife pattern, those who think in terms of marriage, typically would come up on housewife and elementary teacher, office worker, stenographer, secretary, on these four right in here. Yours are very interesting.

   ★ The counselor comment, "Yours are very interesting," can be easily misinterpreted. Actually it was an attempt to draw out the client and might have worked had the counselor paused for client reaction. Such a response is rather ambiguous and requires more time for answering than a direct question.

S21—Um-huh.

C22—Maybe that masculine idea that we—

S22—What is this?

C23—Well, that is in terms of interest. Your interests tend toward the masculine—

S23—Would this be—this would be—

C24—This would be the women's end of it.

S24—Oh, uh-huh.

C25—and this would be the men's. This is in terms of interests—the activities that —

S25—the things you seem to like.

C26—The things you seem to like would tend a little bit toward the masculine type of activities, which you pointed out, I think, a little bit in your conversation yesterday.

S26—Mm-huh.

C27—You might recall it, I don't know. But it is in the middle somewhere.

S27—(*laughing*) I guess, everything I preferred was in the middle.

C28—Now, on this one, this is a little different. This may be influenced by everyday events, immediate things, like you have "words" with your English teacher, and you take this right afterwards. Chances are it will have some effect on this inventory.

S28—Um-huh.

C29—If you've had a very pleasant experience out-of-doors, for example, recently, it might tend to fluctuate. It's not quite as reliable a test as this one, but it's something to give you some information. Now, computational activities, your interest in mathematics shows up.

   ★ The use of the word reliable here may be questioned by "test experts." Test reliability to the test expert may mean one thing, to the client another. The counselor was using the word "reliable" in the sense that the test expert uses validity. It raises the question, "Should the counselor use his professional terms with clients or try to express ideas in words with which the client is familiar?"

S29—Um-huh.

C30—Your interest in art activities shows up a little bit, there's some here in music as indicated by your everyday activities.

S30—Um-huh.

C31—Then there's the mechanical.

S31—Well, an observation I might make that I was conscious of it as I took the test. Of course, I've lost most of the tests, though. I've lost which one is which exactly—

C32—Well, that is where you had the three activities.

S32—This is the three activities.

C33—to paint pictures, to row a boat, to repair an automobile.

S33—Well, all through the test, on this one where you had three choices, I thought that I was contradicting myself because one time I'd take one thing, you know, and another time I'd pick another.

C34—How do you account for that?

S34—I don't know. There'd be three things, and I'd pick—one time I even picked the one I'd like to be best to be a buyer out of those three; and yet in all the others I'd voted that's what I'd like to be least. There were different contradictions there.

C35—Well, that is brought out by this score over here. (*Points to verification score*) There was some inconsistency involved—

★ The verification score of 36 falls below the verification range suggested by Kuder and, therefore, is in the "doubtful" category. The counselor felt that the client had taken the test properly and conscientiously. The other alternative suggested by Kuder is that preferences are so atypical that she (the client) actually does not prefer activities ordinarily chosen by the overwhelming majority of people. This seemed like the logical conclusion for the client in this case. Her interests and achievements were extraordinary; consequently, she might have easily chosen activities which were not in line with typical adolescent preferences. Because of his hypothesis, the counselor made no issue of the verification score and used the scale scores to open interest areas for discussion. In a later response, S53, the client again raises the issue, and the counselor implemented the original responses concerning the verification score. This time the client in S55 and S56 indicated some concern over her wide range of interests and activities.

S35—Um-huh.

C36—Would you explain it in terms of your many interests?

S36—Uh-huh.

C37—Perhaps your inability to, what would you say, make a decisive decision on anything.

S37—Uh-huh.

C38—I mean, you like everything.

S38—Uh-huh.

C39—It might be pretty hard to choose between three things when you like them all.

S39—Um-huh. I think that's just about it.

C40—One time you went one way and another time you went another way.

S40—Um-huh. I think that, when I voted, when the choice had something to do with art, then I usually voted for that; but you notice that I chose music quite a bit, too. When the choice didn't include art, well, it would sometimes be music.

C41—Uh-huh. Well, the three things that you mentioned yesterday show up—as being the main areas—

S41—Uh-huh.

C42—Math, art, music on this one.

S42—What do these negatives mean?

C43—Well, now that is social service. Those are activities, such as helping people—

S43—(*laughs*)

C44—Occupations that might typify it would be teaching, nursing, and that sort of thing.

S44—I compared notes with some of the others. We were talking, of course, last night about our tests; and they said there were several questions—oh—"Would you like to visit slums?" "Would you like to help with the deaf people?" and things like that. And mainly they voted "yes" pretty consistently, and I know that I had voted "no" consistently.

C45—A difference in make-up, in personality, and so on, may be involved here.

S45—I don't like sick people at all.

C46—How do you account for that?

S46—I don't know. There's nothing—they just—(*pause*)

C47—How do you feel about helping people?

★ The counselor was in error here in his attempt to clarify **S45**. He should have waited for the client to finish **S46**. The client never had an opportunity to respond to **C46** which was potentially an adequate response.

S47—Helping people?

C48—Um-huh.

S48—I like to help people. I particularly like to help little children. I like —I've done a little tutoring in my life; and I like to teach them games; and I like teaching them to dive and swim and things like that.

> ★ Sometimes when a person indicates that he likes to work with children better than his contemporaries, he is meaning that he doesn't get along very well with his peers and is using working with children as a substitute.

C49—Are you patient with them?

S49—Yes, I like to baby sit, and—I like children very much, and that doesn't seem to show up.

C50—Well, (*pause*)

S50—I voted teaching down all along.

C51—Of course, many of the activities in this area would involve activities, such as working with people in slums, and—

S51—Mm-huh.

C52—(*continues*) the kind of activities, such as a social worker would have.—

S52—That doesn't intrigue me in the least.

C53—(*continues*) and the kind of activities that a teacher would have to perform in a regular school setting, and right from this at least it would just indicate a rejection of it. Most of your other activities (*pointing to remaining scales*) are in areas that we just simply say, "Well, you have some, and they're not the most outstanding—"

S53—It says if your score is not between 38 and 44 you should see your adviser. (*laughs*) Well, that came easy. (*pause*)

C54—Well, that gets at the inconsistency with which the thing is taken.

S54—Um huh.

C55—and that's—ah—I'm not too surprised. (*pause*) You took it and tried to do the best you could with the decisions that were just beyond you. They had to be made but were difficult because of your many activities.

S55—I always worried about my interests. People have always told me that, but it's awfully hard to stay out of things. (*pause*) I often have sat there and wondered what it would be like if I just dropped all my other subjects and concentrated entirely on art, whether I'd become a really great artist. (*laughs*)

C56—Uh-huh.

S56—(*laughing*) You know you just sit there and wonder what would happen. (*pause*) More recently I have.

C57—Well, that would tie in pretty well with this social service. Let's just consider this right here.

S57—Um-huh.

C58—For example, now take artist, these are women artists. Their interests tend toward that. Now what would men artists be like—with more masculine interests? This doesn't compare you with men. This just compares you with women.

S58—Yes.

C59—As you mentioned before, you have—you like to compete against men and it might tie in there, I don't know. (*pause*) This certainly would not be an architect, a technical artist.

S59—No.

C60—It would be more of the painting, sculpturing, and that type of thing.

S60—That probably shows up there.

C61—Well, see these scales. I mentioned, we typically think of as masculine type of interests.

> ★ The counselor was drawing this conclusion on the basis of the research reported by Kuder in one edition of his manual. On the basis of research, masculinity-femininity scores were derived from the scales. The scales to the left side of the profile were loaded in the direction of masculine interests, while those on the right side tended toward feminine interests. The counselor was trying to relate the Kuder to the discussion concerning masculinity in the first interview.

S61—Umm.

C62—Outdoor, mechanical, computational, and scientific.

S62—Literary and mechanical show up about the same.

C63—We think of them as more feminine types of activities. (*pointing to right side of profile sheet*)

S63—(*laughing*) Clerical?

C64—Now some of them you go along with, some you reject.

S64—Um-huh.

C65—Now none of the men's activities do you reject entirely.

S65—Scientific.

C66—Well, that is, usually, when it's down here, (*pointing to 10th percentile rank and below*) we think of rejection mainly.

S66—Um-huh.

C67—There's a tendency to prefer some of these others, but you can't be high in everything.

S67—No, we have to reject something—

C68—Uh-huh.

S68—say something that we like the least.

C69—And so you would expect some of these things to be down. (*pause*)

S69—What do the two marks indicate on there? (*client points to Strong Vocational Interest Blank*)

C70—Oh, I was just looking it over, and I just put marks on the zero point here in each case. You'll notice yours follows pretty well that neutral point in every instance. Once in a while you're a little above it, and once in a while you're a little below it. (*pause*)

S70—Well, what do you mean by that now?

C71—Well, it's in terms of setting up the test itself.

S71—Oh.

C72—And as far as interpreting is concerned, it wouldn't probably mean too much—

S72—Um-huh.

C73—to give you the exact interpretation of it, except to say that in the standardization of this thing, that's the breaking point between—

S73—Um-huh.

C74— —likes and dislikes for women—and, for women, you're just about average in most respects. In all these things, there is nothing that stands out—

> ★ This is not a literal interpretation, but it probably served the purpose for which it was intended, i.e., to indicate that the client's likes and dislikes canceled each other out resulting in raw scores near "0" for each occupational comparison.

S74—Um-huh.

C75—and there are a few instances where you rejected something— not rejected necessarily, but where your interests are definitely quite dissimilar, such as nursing. (*pause*)

S75—Buyer.

C76—There's some with the buyer. (*pause*)

S76—Well, is that it?

C77—Yes. Well, where does that leave us?

> ★ The counselor used this rather ambiguous response to see what conclusions the client may have drawn thus far from the test

interpretation. The counselor realized that nothing startling had been discovered and wondered whether the client misinterpreted any of the counselor's responses or whether any erroneous conclusions had been drawn from the test data. Other responses might have been, "What do you make of this?" or "How do these results impress you?"

S77—What?

C78—Where does that leave us?

S78—(*laughs*) Just where we started.

C79—We have the results of this personality test you might like to look over to see if we can tie that in with these interest inventories. This scale here is one that indicates the extent to which you try to put your best foot forward.

S79—Which now? This?

C80—Yes, and you have a tendency to want to present yourself as best you can—I mean in the best light in order to put your best foot forward with everbody. That is typical of many college students. (*Counselor is referring to the K-scale of the MMPI*).

S80—Um-huh.

C81—It is very atypical if your college person comes down on that. He does not present himself in the worst light and belittle himself in order to obtain satisfaction, if you want to use that expression. And the majority of our college people will have this kind of a thing here so that—

S81—Is this the one that you answered as "true" or "mostly true" or "false" or "mostly false"?

★ The counselor has "lost" the client momentarily. He might have avoided this by first asking the client if she remembered the personality test or what she thought of the personality test in order to establish its identity before proceeding with an interpretation.

C82—"True," "false," and then "can't say" were the categories. Now some of these other things, for example, here would bear out somewhat the discussion that we had yesterday. A woman who scored that way might have a tendency to get along with others. (*Counselor is referring to Si scale.*) There are indications in other ways that you get along with others. This competition idea that you brought out yesterday, wanting to compete with boys, would be a part of that (*pointing to Mf scale.*) This sort of person, for example, might find it difficult to get away from competition with boys, though, and establish what you might call an affectionate relationship with a boy. Now I don't know whether you have any problems or whether that statement pertains to you.

★ The counselor was trying to draw together many clues from the first interview and the MMPI for this interpretation. Refer to the following responses in the first interview: S63, S70 and S71. Especially significant is S71 where the client says, ". . . I can't ever —I mean, you can't draw a line between your friends and your dates, you know."

S82—Mmmm.

C83—But they sometimes find it a little difficult to (*pause*) drop this competition idea. Marriage isn't a competition.

S83—No, I see what you're driving at but, of course, I wouldn't know— now, I mean I'm too young to know. I've gotten along well on the subject, I think—as well as most of my friends; but, of course, I'm not mature enough or old enough to know.

C84—How do you account for the fact that you don't compete with the girls?

S84—Never have had any to compete with. (*laughs*)

C85—Does that mean you don't want to?—How do you mean that?

S85—Well, I mean they don't swim and they don't—

C86—You mean none of the girls swim?

S86—No, well, not very many of them. At least I—ah—ah I guess, I'm way ahead of them. I mean, I can always—ah—they always fall behind in some way.

C87—Your main interest has been to find someone to compete with, then?

S87—Well, not particularly, yet I don't know. I wouldn't say that cause I don't go around, "Well, I want to beat somebody," you know.

C88—Oh.

S88—But, I mean, you have a whole lot more fun if you, well, play ping pong with somebody that's better than you are than to play with somebody you can beat with your left hand. You see what I mean, in games.

C89—Uh-huh.

S80—Now, I did all my bowling with girls, and I competed with girls in that, and I never had so much fun in my life. But there were girls who bowled, and girls who bowled better than I did, and we just had a lot of fun, and I didn't do particularly well, and I never—I'm not out—I'm not ever out to win. I mean, that's not—it makes no difference to me who wins.

C90—What are you trying to seek from this competition? (*pause*)

S90—Pleasure.

C91—What are you trying to seek? I mean, you said that you're not out to win. You're out to find some competition, to find somebody that can beat you perhaps or at least that can come close.

S91—It's more fun.

C92—Why? What is there that is satisfying about that? (*pause*)

S92—Oh, I don't know other than it is a stimulating experience. (*pause*)

C93—Who's your main center of interest when you feel that way?

S93—What do you mean?

C94—Well, who are you concerned with more, when your feelings are that way? (*pause*) The other fellow or yourself?

S94—The other fellow or myself? (*pause*) Stop to consider these things, you don't really know. (*laughs*)

C95—I'm just throwing in some questions here for you to think about. Ah—it would seem to me, just as an observation, that where you had a person who was always looking for competition, it didn't make any difference whether it was a boy or a girl, but he wanted somebody that was a little bit better than he, that his main interest would be in himself—because he is trying to improve himself.

S95—Yes, I believe that's right.

C96—He's not interested in this other fellow that he can beat, that he may be able to help improve his skills—by playing with him. How did this person get better? Playing with some duffers?

S96—(*short pause*) That's the truth, however, I don't think I ever turn anybody down. Many a night I've spent down at our teen-age club and played ping pong with my girl friend.

★ The client seemed to go along with the counselor in his interpretation without entirely accepting or rejecting the point.

C97—Um-huh.

S97—I mean, if they want to.

C98—Yes.

S98—But most of the time they just say they don't want to.

C99—Uh-huh.

S99—So I—a boy comes up to me, wants to play ping pong, and I play with him. Nine times out of ten he'll beat me, but I have a darn good time.

C100—(*short pause*) Like to get beat by the boys?

S100—I like to get beat by anybody. I don't care, I really do.

C101—Well, is that cricket with everybody, I mean, wanting to be beaten by them?

S101—Oh, I don't know, I don't—Oh, gosh, this is getting twisted.

C102—Is it this striving for perfection, and you feel that by getting beat enough that you will improve enough so that you can surpass everybody? Is that your goal or is it the satisfaction you get out of getting beat, having somebody beat you?

★ Because the client did not entirely accept the self-centered interpretation, the counselor was trying to attack the competitive drive from another angle, from that of a striving for absolute perfection. In **S102** the client expresses interest in the conversation without committing herself.

S102—Oh, I say, this is kind of interesting. (*laughs*) I'm thinking about things in a way that I never thought of them before.

C103—Well, I'm not trying to probe into your affairs or anything other than to get you to think about yourself a little bit—

S103—Ummm-huh.

C104— . . . in some of these things. You still have a year left in high school.

S104—Uh-huh.

C105—And you have the opportunity certainly and the advantages at home to practice some things maybe that you haven't practiced previously.

S105—Um-huh.

C106—And if we can get you to think about yourself a little bit maybe in terms of some areas where maybe they're neglected, maybe they would be covered anyway, but—ah—there are always some areas . . .

S106—Um-huh.

C107— . . . that maybe in terms of your inter-personal relations with others can be improved and that's all I'm trying—

S107—Um-huh.

C108—to get at here. I'm not trying to confuse you or mix you up.

★ The counselor, having gotten at cross purposes with the client in few responses preceding this, has now restructured the situation so that they are on common ground again.

S108—Oh, no. It's quite interesting to see things. I mean, I never even thought about that before why—what—why I did like to always have somebody there that—

C109—Well, now take marriage as an illustration. If that is your goal someday, it means that marriage has to be looked upon as a cooperative type of thing and competition isn't going to work.

S109—You can't compete with your husband.

C110—Well, it's not always good to do so; however, if it is done in the right fashion, I think a certain amount of it is all right; but it can break them, too.

S110—Uh-huh.

C111—And it would be something to think of in terms of, well, am I going to get enough satisfaction out of marriage to meet the needs that I've set up. Well, I don't know if this idea that—if you've always got to find somebody who is a little better than you are in some of these things. You're apt to get a husband who can't swim worth a rock.

★ The counselor is trying to help the client project her attitude toward competition into future marriage relationships. In one sense, this is an exploratory process; and, in another way, this is a form of practicing the application of attitudes, an important part of learning.

S111—Uh-huh.

C112—What would you do then? (*pause*)

S112—That would be hard. I mean, I—

C113—Would you look for your equivalent, for a man who could beat you at everything, that could excel you at every activity you're in?

S113—Well, that would be practically impossible because, I mean, your interests—he probably would stand out in things I can't do at all.

C114—Would you be willing to accept a boy—who couldn't surpass you in some of your activities?

S114—Oh yes. The only trouble is, would he accept me if I could out-swim him? That's the deal. Now I know it makes a—it makes a—if you have a date with a boy and you go down to the lake or something and you want to swim and you know that you can swim faster and that he gets awfully tired and that you want to swim out to that raft and he can't make it, you've just got to sit there because there's nothing that burns him up more than to find they have a date with somebody that makes them feel low and embarrassed because they can't do it; so you just sit there.

C115—Does that burn you up?

S115—No, ah—not particularly—

C116—Describe some of these boy friends that you've mentioned to me a little bit. Can you do it?

★ The counselor was using this technique to permit the client to bring out her own attitudes through her description of her relationship with one of the boy friends. Through such descriptions the counselor can discover sources of irritations which in turn can yield insight into the client's frame of reference.

S116—Well—ah—there're a lot of different types and—I like people. There are very few people that I meet that I don't like. There is something about them anyway; and I cannot approve of a person so far as morals and things like that and yet I manage to like the person though. Now as a general observation on that point, on the boys, I admire manners. I think, it irritates me very much to go with boys who do not have nice manners.

C117—Uh-huh.

(*A few responses are missing*).

S117— . . . do a nice job of it. I mean, you know—

C118—Yes, that's right.

S118—(*continues*) . . . just have a certain amount of finesse there that I like for them. I don't like boys that just, well, don't have any interests or activities at all. There are some that don't that I meet. I went with one boy for a long time. We tried to make a go of going steady, and I finally just got—irritated—

C119—Um-huh.

S119— . . . because he was an athlete in the school; but he couldn't dance. I tried to teach him—and, well we could stumble around the floor, but he didn't enjoy it and neither did I. Well, we maybe sat at the side line at the dances. He couldn't play ping pong; well, he didn't play ping pong. He didn't like to swim, and he didn't swim; and it narrowed down until there just wasn't much common interest there to get along.

C120—You have found some other boys with a wider range of interests to fit into your scheme of thinking?

S120—Um-huh.

C121—Can you describe one for me?

S121—Well, I was mentioning this boy of mine—boy of mine (*laughs*)— friend of mine, that is, I mentioned him yesterday, that got this large scholarship to go to College D.

C122—Yes.

S122—He far surpasses me in many fields. He—he is not artistic at all. He just guffaws at things that are artistic, and yet he realizes that he needs to absorb a little of it; but he is a great mathematician and surpasses me so far in history, in knowledge of historical things. He fascinates me, I just sit and listen to him. I've had several opportunities as a speech student to listen to him—and—it just fascinates me. He is a marvelous athlete all the way around and he's a very stimulating person to be with. I have just—oh—a wonderful time; I date quite a bit at the young people's meetings Sunday and then maybe go to a show after that.

C123—Is he quite popular with the other men?

> ★ The counselor was interested in the kind of man to which she was attracted. The counselor might have responded to the idea that the client admires perfection in her boy friends or some attitude expressed in S122.

S123—Yes.

C124—Um-huh.

S124—He gets along very well with them. See I—there's—I am rather sympathetic to people who are not well liked by other people. I always feel a little sorry for them and, I wonder, can I see something that I like in them. Then I think, "Well, they really had a rough time with these kids at school that rebuffed them and made fun of them," you know. (*pause*)

C125—Does anybody in this group that came down with you fall in that category?

S125—No, the group that came down are girls that I run around with—I had in mind one particular boy that I've had some dates with and I've been kinda—oh—"What do you see in him." I always manage to have a good time. We do things like play croquet. We'll just sit around and play croquet by the hour, and it's lots of fun and—

C126—And does this idea of good manners and social graces—what if you ran into a boy that had a wide range of interests but was a little crude? Ah—how would you react to him?

S126—You pick out one in my imagination. (*laughing*) Oh, I react fairly well to him.

C127—What I'm wondering about is this—

S127—If you'd ask me, it'd have to be one or the other—that they'd either have to have manners or they'd have to have a wide range of interests.

C128—Many boys just don't have—

S128—either one and they just—they wouldn't appeal to me at all.

C129—Well, many boys later on will develop social graces as they realize their importance; but when they are in high school at least they're crude in some of these.

S129—Um-huh.

C130—I was just interested in your reaction there.

S130—I—ah—have had some dates with boys that—lacked background and maybe some that had quit or were planning to quit school, you know the type; and I often wonder why they ever asked me for a date in the first place cause we don't have any fun, you know, there's just nothing there—that—(*pause*)

C131—You don't feel then that your goal in terms of companionship with boys is so high that you can't attain it?

S131—No. (*pause*)

C132—Or that your interest in masculine activities will in any way interfere with your finding somebody eventually to marry. What I'm getting at is that many men like their women feminine.

S132—I know that. Mother keeps telling me that. I come home and complain or something, you know; and she'll always say that. I expect that it'll probably give me trouble unless I can, so to say, turn over a new leaf on the subject.

C133—Well, or resolve some of the—

S133—Pipe dreams—

C134—high aspirations.

S134—Uh-huh—pipe dreams, athletics, and things, that are there all the time. I do it some. I mentioned swimming down at the lake. I just sit there. (*laughs*)

C135—Well, you certainly ought to find some swimmers somewhere.

★ This remark of the counselor was unnecessary, but he probably became tired of the client's repeated references to swimming for illustrations.

S135—Um-huh.

C136—I'm wondering about some of the other—

S136—activities—

C137—Uh-huh.

S137—Uh-huh—let me see (*pause*). Mother and I were talking about the same thing not very long ago, (*pause*) I suppose, everybody has the pull that, when you like to make good grades and have a good reputation in the community and everything, you look at the kids that don't make good grades and aren't too high morally, drink and things like that; and you think, well, gee, they look like they're having a wonderful time, and you had this pull on yourself; and I managed in the past year to get over that a little bit and decided, well, that the grass on this side of the fence was a lot greener anyway. So—but—we—Mother and I talk a great deal and —about this business of mine- -of not being feminine enough. That's probably what originally gave me the idea, this idea about myself was from her. (*pause*)

C138—Yes. (*pause*)

S138—That isn't—as bad, I guess, as it could be. (*Pointing to M-F scale of Strong Vocational Interest Blank*).

C139—No, it indicates that there's a slight tendency on it, that's all.

S139—Uh-huh.

C140—Towards that end of the scale. Under each there—there are many interests probably.

S140—Oh, I like to keep house, and I like to cook, and I like to sew and purely the mechanical things of being a housewife. (*pause*)

C141—It seems to me a slight tendency, though, to a career, a career drive, I guess, . . .

S141—Um-huh.

C142—that you want to go out and make your own life and then maybe get married along the way somewhere, but (*pause*).

S142—Well, I never, along that line, I would never consider—at least now I don't think that I could probably fall in love enough that I would want to quit before I finished four years of college anyway. I mean that would be my opinion of it right now that it all—that at all costs I want to have my four years of school and that would, I think, parallel that that you were driving at.

> ★ Also, this may reflect the mother's attitudes. Since the mother's marriage did not last very long and she found it necessary to use her college education for gainful employment, she may feel that her daughter should have the economic protection of a college education also.

C143—Your relationship with boys then has been mainly one that was friendly—to play games with and to be around and so on; but as far as affection is concerned, it's been somewhat lacking.

S143—Yes, there have only been—oh—most of the boys—the one boy that I have gone with several years, he doesn't live in town, but his family does, and he comes home a lot on weekends; and, I mean, if I had—if we together had followed the course that a lot of people think, we might have been talking and thinking about eventual marriage; but, of course, there is nothing—just that we have a wonderful time together, but we're not very affectionate at all and—

C144—You're not afraid to make attempts at it?

S144—Well, it would depend entirely on the boy whether I did or not.

C145—You think you're capable of it, though?

S145—Yes, oh yes. (*laughs*)

C146—Well, when I say that. I'm not thinking in terms of carousing around and that type of thing; but, I mean, you can show affection in other ways than petting parties—

S146—Um-huh.

C147—and activities of that kind.

S147—I know what you mean.

C148—There're many other ways, little kindnesses and little considerations that show affection that do not have to lead to the other forms of behavior.

S148—Well, I—ah—I—ah I have liked some boys, I mean, that way, I mean you know, getting real affectionate and—(*pause*)

★ The counselor has been trying to have the client evaluate her relationships with boys. The client responded well (S143, S144, S145, S148). Apparently she is capable of affection, yet she finds only a limited number of boys who are attractive to her.

C149—Well, there is this part of this whole thing that ties into the picture vocationally—and that is this, that the line of work right now that would seem to fit into your interests and personality make-up might be something that would tend towards what is considered to be a masculine activity.

S149—I noticed that.

C150—Now architect, the one that you brought out, for example, . . .

S150—Uh-huh.

C151— . . . might well be an outlet for that very thing, in the sense that typically the majority of architects are going to be men.

S151—Um-huh.

C152—Perhaps a job where you could go out and compete with men on an equal footing would be the most satisfying to you right at this moment.

S152—What about the rest of this?

C153—Why, there isn't too much right in here that you can see (referring to MMPI profile). Actually, when it gets right in close here all you can say is that the person seems to have made adjustment to the various areas of living to the point where there's nothing—of—much consideration. For example, this one is based on the activities that people get into —ah—college activities. For example, it would indicate that you are quite an activity fiend. Well, you know that—

S153—That's right.

C154—and it bears out what you've already said about that type of thing. These are so close that you can't make an interpretation of them. These here are the same way.

S154—Uh-huh.

C155—But—there seems to be an indication that so far as your home is concerned that you've learned how to be affectionate—you've experienced it in your home; and that, of course, augurs well for your future in the sense of knowing, having experienced it in your home.

S155—Um-huh.

C156—You should be able to utilize that a little better, a little bit better outside the home; but there isn't too much there other than perhaps this masculine thing that we discussed; and it might well be a part of your consideration in picking an area of work. Would you be satisfied to go in and work with feminine women—in a job exclusively?

S156—If I went into commercial art, there again I would be—

C157—Is that basically a men's or a women's—

S157—It depends entirely. If you go into advertising layout, it's men's. If you go into fabrics which I would have considered doing—in fabric design—oh—display, something like that, you go into a feminine job. Well, now there I could take it all out on creating and, I think, I'd be all right because I, well, when you're doing art work you don't compete with anybody but your own emotion in getting it across.

C158—Well, art may be a good way of sublimating this drive of competition.

S158—Well, you're right on this self-betterment thing. I like to learn, and I like to improve myself; and, I don't know, I just don't drive to make myself a better person, but I just like everything that—

C159—Of course, you may give other people the appearance of being a driver.

S159—Um-huh. I hope not. I don't think I do, though, just from comments people make on my good grades and things. "Well, gee, you don't study more than we do."

C160—It just comes naturally.

S160—They say. "You don't work," "You just learn stuff naturally," I mean, well, you know things like that. They don't—I know how to do league bowling. I can fit in with almost any kind of a crowd of people, I can get along with them.

C161—Um-huh.

S161—I like to sit around in drug stores, like to go to shows and lots of things most kids like and, you know—

C162—You don't feel that too many kids have it in for you then.

S162—Oh, no, (*laughs*) I know, but there were so many questions on that personality deal, "Do you think people are following you?" "Do you think the world is against you?" "Do you think this and that?" I guess, I got a big kick out of it.

C163—Well, there are indications here that probably you don't have tendencies along that line;—

S163—Uh-huh.

C164— . . . don't worry about that kind of thing; and ah—but you do I have sort of—ah—an outgoing kind of personality where you mix in with groups.

S164—I have been very active in church work, but I always know people; and I have not been, well, say, I've been a class officer only once since I've been in school. I mean, I haven't been what you'd call extra popular with kids. And I was interested when I went to Girl's State to see, since I didn't know anyone there, how I would—how we would react, how I would get along.

C165—Um-huh.

S165—I was very interested in it to see what other girls of college entrance material, most of them, would—how I would get along with them, and I got along just beautifully. I, oh, I won a state office; and so I was encouraged that maybe I could get out and get along with people when I was on my own.

C166—I wasn't worried particularly about that in terms of things you've said before. That would be one of the problems that a person has with a lot of interests and ability and so on, the fact that he sometimes may be accused of using others for his own purposes. He sees the way things can be done, not by shoving people around but by nudging them gently. That sometimes creates irritation on the part of students, whether founded or unfounded, whatever their feelings may be; and that's why I was interested in the group, the gang that you've been going around with. What role do you play in that group?

S166—Just a cog in the wheel.

C167—Are you the leader?

S167—No.

C168—Well, who's the leader? Or don't you have one?

S168—We don't exactly have one. One person will set the pattern for a while, and then another; but I'm just another cog in the wheel. I don't particularly make suggestions or anything on what to do. (*pause*)

C169—You recognize yourself pretty well for what you are.

S169—I've always tried to, I don't know. (*pause*) This business of making good grades in school is something that has to be handled with a soft touch, you know, and this business of not trying to let anybody know that you're making good grades, you know. And I have always watched and waited for the day in school when I'd have repercussions on this business that mother is a teacher; but so far—this boy I went with got teased quite a bit because he had a mother in school—but otherwise that's about the only thing. People don't—I have never heard anyone make the crack, "Well, she makes good grades because her mother teaches," and things like that.

C171—Would that hurt you?

S171—No, because I feel like I've earned them—earned them on my own. But I hate for people—other people to get that chip on their shoulder.

C172—Umm-huh.

S172—All my friends like to come to our house. I've been interested in that too very much whether mother would so-call frighten them away, particularly now since she will have all the boys and girls who have been my friends in class. She has them all. I've been interested, but the kids have always seemed to like to come over to my house; and I like it, and mother likes it, and so—it's fun to—the kids always know that they're welcome when they come over.

★ The counselor felt that the client had established social relationships with her peer group; perhaps she might have certain adjustments to make in her affectional relationships. On the other hand, there were few indications that she couldn't make a satisfying adjustment. The counselor might have summarized the discussion thus far and added to the counseling effectiveness. Because of the fact that the client had indicated an interest in architecture, the counselor probably felt compelled to discuss this objective.

C173—It's nice to feel that your friends are welcome in your home. (*pause*) Well, what about this deal on architecture? What's your thinking on that subject since you had a chance to look it over? (*The counselor had given the student a pamphlet to look over between the first and second contacts*)

S173—Well, I don't know how you do it, how would you get into it, after you graduated, after you became a licensed architect. Before you did that, would you be an apprentice, would you be a draftsman for a firm?

C174—That would be one way of getting in. You wouldn't be quite a draftsman, but you'd be a junior partner, like a law firm. You'd probably do some of the dirty work for the senior partners; but that would be one of the ways, of course. That would mean that you'd have to go to a large city or a large community because in the smaller community the architect would be a "lone wolf" type of job.

S174—We have a man, in our town, who is quite a good architect; and I have been intending to have a talk with him because I thought—

C175—Yes, that might be an idea to go and talk with him and see what he's doing and what his activities are—

S175—and see how he got his start.

C176—Certainly, in terms of a community that isn't a large city, to see what a smaller-community person would do.

S176—This might be something to throw in as a sideline. If I ever made a good enough name for myself, I mean, became a good enough architect, I would like to do foreign work. (*pause*).

C177—Any special reason?

S177—I don't know. Foreign; maybe that's just a stage I'm going through. I don't know, I've done a lot of traveling, and I spent three weeks abroad last year; and that's where, I think, I first got the idea. This lady, some foreign woman, came to a women's conference and was assigned to this state as a place to go and visit; and I talked to her. She, of course, is a successful importer. She's married, and her husband does something, I don't know, anyway he has a good job and she was talking about building and the opportunities for rapid advancement and wonderful living conditions and everything in some of these foreign countries.

C178—Well, that of course is certainly part of the picture. You probably wouldn't go to some of your more advanced communities.

S178—No, ah—

C179—There are certain nations, such as England and France.

S179—No, they've got their own.

C180—You'd probably go there to learn.

S180—Um-huh.

C181—You'd have to go to some of the more undeveloped areas. (*pause*) Architecture would have the creative aspect to it that you're interested in. There's enough creativeness there for you. You realize that architecture—that some of it is traditional and some has broken away from tradition.

S181—All that I know is that, I think, the fine detail would appeal to me. It would also appeal to me to learn about engineering and electrical things that you have to know to be an architect—cost of production, keeping it in a price range.

C182—That's right. Your mechanical interests here, that might fit in. The engineering courses would not be too hard for you to take.

S182—Um-huh. (*short pause*) There's always this about art, the kind of creative art I would like to do, it is always a fascinating hobby and you can always have it as an avocation rather than vocation; and in commercial art you can fall back on teaching.

C183—Um-huh. That's a possibility.

S183—The thing is this—with this wide range of interests of mine, I don't want to do what would make me a successful artist, that is to go to an art school.

C184—Have you ever thought of interior decorating?

S184—Uh, yes. I wondered perhaps whether my liking for interior decorating and things like that wouldn't stand me in good stead, if I ever get to be a good enough architect that I would be creating things. Some of the boys at school—they offer a course in architectural drawing which I'm not going to be able to take, you have to take one year of mechanical drawing and then one of architectural. The boys plan their houses, and from engineering principles I expect they're pretty good houses, but from the standpoint of how on earth you'd ever decorate them to make them look attractive they're just absolutely flat!

C185—Well, why do you have to take the mechanical drawing before you get into that?

S185—Oh, I don't know.

C186—Did you ever talk to them?

S186—Um-huh.

C187—And they wouldn't let you?

S187—Oh, I expect they really would if I pried into it. Mother wants me to take typing next year; and I think I should. I've been working with a secretarial agency, and I have enjoyed doing it this year.

C188—Um-huh.

S188—And I've only been doing part-time work because I'm not a very good typist. I do my own typing. I taught myself, and it's not hunt and peck.

C189—Yes.

S189—It's a fairly good system, but it still isn't theirs so I think it will be a very good idea because I'm going to have to earn money—along with college—someday.

C190—Well, are you able to settle for a B or C if you have to?

★ The counselor was trying to find out the client's reaction to school marks and how much the grade point average meant to her. Actually she had a mature viewpoint (**S190**) and recognized marks as only symbols and not the ultimate in her striving for perfection.

S190—Oh, yes. I always try to make good grades, but it wouldn't hurt me if I didn't.

(*a few remarks missing*)

S191—She's going to get a splendid scholarship and everything; and she's that kind of a person. Mother gave her a B one time. She went into tears, you know, and that wouldn't affect me like that at all.

C192—The reason I asked that mainly was so many times where you teach yourself typing you get into difficulty.

S192—Oh, I am expecting to. I'm fully prepared to because I know good and well that I have many, many habits that I'm going to have to be breaking. I think it would be better to break them now than not at all. (*pause*) I'm also taking solid geometry and trigonometry next year and I don't expect to be able to make as good grades in there.

C193—Uh-huh.

S193—The teacher is very sparse with his grades. The highest one that he gave last year was a B but it doesn't matter. I don't work for grades.

C194—You work to learn.

S194—I work to learn (*pause*) 'cause I figure that a grade doesn't tell me very much anyway because there are not very many people in school that— if I make an A in a subject, well, that's no guage of what, I think, somebody will do in another school who is really good in that subject. They might make an A, too, and yet I'd fall way way below them.

C195—Yes. Well, I have another person that I have to see—

S195—Yes, I know it.

C196— . . . this morning. Now what I was wondering was if you wanted to go over some of this occupational information. We haven't gone into that very much. We have this one on architecture, and I can find some on interior decoration and some of these other things, if you'd like. I'd be glad to sit down with you and go over some more of this occupational information if you like. I leave it up to you.

★ This is a typical approach to the introduction of occupational information into counseling. The client's reaction in S197 is also very typical. The information *per se* is not as important as client reaction to various facets of the information obtained. This counselor response did not make this point clear and, as a result, fell flat. Fortunately, the client gave the counselor another opening in S198.

S196—(*pause*) This would seem to be it on architecture then.

C196—Yes, I think probably it is just about the only thing we have on architecture that's worth looking at.

S197—Well, I pretty well combed it out looking at engineering. I mean that doesn't appeal to me. I don't want to go that far (*laughs*) but I believe that, on this interior decoration and different things, there's ah— enough at home in our library and in our school library on those subjects.

C197—Let me add this—that, if at anytime you'd like to come back—discuss other things, other occupations, or anything else, why, you just feel perfectly free.

S198—Um-huh. What would this school, now we didn't get to that, offer on architecture. I looked through your bulletins and I—

> ★ The client had a question which the counselor could have answered by a simple "no." Instead the counselor was convinced that she could profit from the use of occupational and educational information and postponed an answer until a third interview. In the meantime, the counselor had an opportunity to organize some materials which might be useful for the client.

C198—Are you going to be around here at one this afternoon?

S199—Yes, three of us were planning to go down town for a while, but I could plan to be back here.

C199—Why don't you do that? This afternoon I'll see that I have whatever information we have on file.

S200—Um-huh. I might make this observation. I might tell you this, that the school that I've considered going to is a small college or girls' school, the first two years; and then I had thought that I would go to University M, it's privately endowed; but it's an awfully long way from home!

C200—Well, of course, that's something that you're going to have to face one of these days.

S201—Well, it's not so much that as the expense. School teachers don't make enough money (*laughs*).

C201—I have an appreciation for that. Well, I'll see you. I'll have some information for you.

S202—All right and thank you very much.

COUNSELOR'S NOTES ON THE SECOND INTERVIEW
(*Dictated Immediately after the Interview*)

> ★ The client came in to obtain an interpretation of the test results. We started with the interpretation of the A.C.E. in terms of her ranking in the upper 10 per cent of entering college freshmen. She indicated that she was a little disappointed that she couldn't finish all of the items on the tests. Her marks in high school substantiate the results of the test. It must be remembered that the client has just completed the eleventh grade. She gave indications at least of being quite confident of her ability to do college work. We then shifted our discussion to the interest inventories—first discussing the Strong Vocational Interest Blank. The Strong Vocational Interest Blank indicated no areas that

were particularly significant. This, I think, came as sort of a disappointment to her, but after discussing it at some length, she seemed to go along with it. It is interesting to note that the artist scale on the Strong Vocational Interest Blank was not significantly high. The subject of the housewife pattern was also brought up but the client did not react to it. We then discussed the meaning of the Kuder Preference Record which has areas in computational, artistic, and music, as the three peaks. All three substantiate her leisure-time activities and her expressed interests. Her rejection of the social service scale was also discussed and she could go along quite well with the interpretation. She evidently does not have many interests where she is vitally concerned in the welfare of others and helping others, although she did indicate that she had upon numerous occasions worked with children and tried to help them learn. I believe that the younger children she might help but I am not so sure that she could help anyone of her own age and that she would become quite dissatisfied with the slower learners particularly. We also discussed the MMPI. It is interesting to note that the bulk of the interview seemed to center around the interpretation of the Mf scales and her experiences with boys and girls.

We discussed the client's striving for perfection and this competitive idea that has run through the first interview. Some very interesting information concerning her idea of herself in relationship to others came out at this point. She may not have accepted fully the interpretation given to some of the material; nevertheless she did seem to accept the idea that perhaps her strong striving for competition and for someone who could beat her at games and was a little better than she may be due to a certain amount of self-interest. She seemed to go along with this idea. It ties in with the low social service scale on the Kuder.

We discussed also the role that she would play if she wanted to become an architect and discussed the individuals with whom she would be competing. She brought out for the second or third time the idea that she did not want to attend a regular art school. Near the end of the interview she raised the question of schools of architecture. Since it was time to end the interview this question was held over for another interview.

THIRD INTERVIEW

(The Afternoon of the Same Day as the Second Interview)

C1—Come on in.

S1—Hello.

C2—I've been looking around here, trying to find something. The university doesn't offer anything in architecture.

S2—I thought that was so. I was pretty sure because I had never seen anything—

C3—I tried to pick one, though, that was as close by as you could find. Now there are others. Are you interested in which schools do offer architecture?

S3—Um-huh.

C4—I think I can give that information to you if you'd like it.

S4—I'd like that. I'd like very much to have that.

C5—We'll look around—

S5—May I jot that here?

C6—Here's some paper and here's a pencil.

S6—Thank you. (*pause*)

C7—Maybe you'd want them—fairly close, wouldn't you?

S7—Uh-huh. I don't care anything about going east.

★ (For several responses the counselor read the list of accredited schools of architecture.)

S8—Is university G listed?

C8—University G isn't listed here. Now they may have added recently such a school.

S9—They had offered courses in it, I know. I had their catalog.

C9—These, of course, are mostly the accredited colleges in architecture; but, of course, they can always add to the list. It isn't something, you know, that is set for all time. There's University H and University J. Now those are the—

S10—accredited ones.

C10—They are about the only ones that we have data on now.

S11—Um-huh.

C11—Now you might write to University G and obtain information as to whether they're accredited or whether they're just offering some courses in it.

S12—Um-huh.

C12—Now this school—I thought, you might be interested in the curriculum that they offer in architecture. I imagine that they're rather similar as you go from one school to another.

S13—Yes, I would be very interested.

C13—It says that they're accredited by the national organization and, as a result, I imagine they have to follow pretty much the same pattern. Now this is the one in general architecture and then there's a structural option of architecture where they offer you a five year program.

S14—Yes, I mentioned that—that I knew it was five years.

C14—Now I don't know what the option is here, I guess, it's more of an interior option. Here's physics. You haven't had any?

S15—No. It was either solid and trig or physics—one or the other that I could take. I took the solid geometry.

C15—It was more math here. (*pause*) Statics and calculus—statics is really math. Strength of materials would have mathematics. Here is a little archaeology, I notice, down here.

S16—Oh, I notice the watercolor drawing, life drawing, modeling— There's quite a lot of art in it.

C16—Concrete construction? I think that is more in large building, city planning, and—

S17—I doubt that—that would probably not be what I am interested in.

C17—Um-huh, it would be a little rough going, I imagine, for a woman and I doubt that many go—in that area.

S18—That would probably be true. (*pause*) I don't know, though.

C18—And then you have four semesters of interior design, arts and crafts, accoustics—(*pause*)

S19—Pretty much solid, isn't it—a solid schedule to get it all in.

C19—Um-huh. You have an elective (*laughs*) I notice, here are four semesters with six electives.

S20—Well, what do you do if you go into architecture? You don't ever get any degree—or receive a diploma—fifth year.

C20—Well, now let's just see. (*reading index of the catalog*)—admissions, courses of study for degrees (*reads from catalog that a graduate receives a Bachelor of Architecture*).

★ Throughout the interview client and counselor examined many kinds of materials. Pertinent passages were read out loud and the client given a chance to react to them. This method of using information seems far superior to the "hand out" method whereby the client is given materials for reading with few further checks on the actual outcomes of such reading. It seems to be a dangerous assumption that clients can assimilate all of the information and relate it to their own self-concepts. Furthermore, the personal interest of the counselor in such occupational and educational materials may provide the stimulus necessary to motivate the client. The counselor is striving to aid the client in an understanding of the role played by a worker in a given occupation. The purpose of occupational information is not simply one of "disseminating information." In reality occupational information provides a splendid nonemotional stimulus for the client to examine his own drives, needs and values (*15, 55, 57*).

S21—That would be what I'd be wanting. I'm certain—I rather imagine that what, ah—the way University D offers it, that they have no school of architecture there, that there'd be some sort of courses there.

C21—Many professional organizations have been insisting more and more that the people have a five-year training program to become qualified.

S22—Um-huh. (*pause*) Well, if I went into art, I'd almost have to take five years, four years to finish some college and then a year in an art school, if I went into any type of display work or designing or—

C22—if you want a college degree.

S23—Um-huh—huh-mm. This is all the school of architecture!

C23—Now let us take a look at entrance requirements. (*reading of high school credits necessary for entrance*)—physics or chemistry, etc.

S24—Um-huh. I think, from reading over everything, I think, I could even enter the engineering. I have enough math credits.

C24—Well, typically, if you have enough math credits, you can.

S25—Um-huh. And you have to get your science some way to graduate from high school. I haven't taken too much science. I don't know whether I'd like it or not.

C25—Let's see what you have here. There is one year of physics.

S26—Um-huh. (*pause*) That would really hit my math if I could make it. Analytic geometry and calculus—statistics, statics, (*laughs*) I'm a little afraid.

C26—Well, that's the study of stresses and strains on materials. Ah—you'd use your math for that.

S27—That'd be study of Gothic arches and things too, wouldn't it? I mean the weight of stones and—ah—

C27—Well, it may get into that; but I think that it's more in terms of just learning how to compute stresses and strains on any part of a structure.

S28—Mechanical design, (*pause*) archaeology, and surveying—(*laughs*) That tickles me. (*pause*)

C28—You might be called in to design a city park—your work there would certainly have surveying involved in the thing.

S29—Um-huh. To tell you the truth, I don't think that as far as big buildings—

C29—Then this interior architecture might be to your liking.

S30—Well, perhaps that's what I'd go into because this looks pretty much like ah—definitely a man's field—(*pause*) building bridges, (*laughs*) buildings, and stuff like that.

C30—That's right. There's no doubt about that. There's some overlap undoubtedly between these—it's just probably a little bit, not too much, as you get into air-conditioning there—stresses and strains of structures, and a few courses of that kind. There is much design work in interior architecture.

S31—Um-huh. Really a surprise. (*both count the number of design courses*)

C31—You can have more if you want it.

S32—Sure, well, for electives can you take foreign language?

C32—Well, let's see. I imagine you can go outside the area here for that.

S33—English?—French?—

C33—Maybe Spanish. See, University H offers a great many courses in other areas.

S34—Um-huh.

C34—These are the courses, I imagine, that are taught specifically in the school of architecture.

S35—Um-huh.

C35—And certainly you wouldn't—you wouldn't have too much trouble. Now, here, let's see for electives. (*reads from catalog*) Here you have languages, French, German, Spanish. Here, you can pick some of them.

S36—That would not—(*pause*) well, that looks pretty good to me. Looks like an awful lot of hard work. Looks like you'd have to be pretty smart to make good grades. (*laughs*) Wonder how much the elimination is on it?

C36—I don't know. You want some competition.

S37—I don't know whether I want it out in the open, though. (*laughs*)

C37—You're worried about that part of it, are you?

S38—No, uh-uh. I just wonder what it will be like really.

C38—Oh, yes, you'll find that every school has a certain number of eliminations.

S39—(*laughs*) Yes.

C39—There are usually several reasons for this. One is lack of interest. Some people go into architecture because, "Oh, that sounds nice." They enroll there and find it's entirely different from what they figured it would be. And then you find some who went in but who never were able to do school work. Well, you find some in there who just don't feel at home with the other students.

S40—Um-huh.

C40—I'm not so sure but what you wouldn't feel right at home, though, in the sense that you have a little confidence in yourself in terms of what you can do artistically, you're not afraid of them, and ah—that would be the group you'd be competing with.

S41—Um-huh. The figures—I had to laugh at—engineering 277,000 men and 740 women (*laughs*) according to the census or something.

C41—Well, there is hardly an occupation in this country but what there aren't some women working in it. And that goes for everything from driving mules to climbing telephone and light poles.

S42—Um-huh. Well, I'm glad I came back then to see this.

C42—You can take it, if you want; and the few minutes while you're waiting, just look from beginning to end if you want to and see, for example, what some of the courses are about.

S43—Um-huh.

C43—While the description is never too good, you can at least look over them.

S44—Could I write to all of these schools?

C44—Yes, you could write for all of—

S45—Um-huh.

C45—. . . those if you wanted to, and all you'd have to do is send them a post card.

S46—Um-huh.

C46—If you want to write a formal letter, just simply state what you're interested in, that you're interested in architecture, and that you'd like to have anything they have concerning that area.

S47—Mother will be able to tell me a little bit. I don't understand it just exactly. Now if I went into something like this university that has a school of architecture, I'd get my degree in architecture and I'd never go through the general education; and if I, probably, I think at University G I don't know what I'd get my degree in, but I thought maybe it would be something other than architecture with a major probably in architecture.

C47—Well, now it depends. Maybe the problem varies in terms of how strongly you want a career and when you finish your schooling, if you want to have a license at the end of your senior year. Or is it that you'd just like to have something in that area that you could tinker around with and maybe work in an architect's office, or that he would be the licensed one. See, they license all architects.

S48—I was reading in the little book and ah—I, of course, didn't realize that.

C48—Because, of course, in many cases they are involved with health and safety. For that reason, if you're going to be a practicing architect, you will have to be licensed. Of course, now if you went to work under somebody who is licensed, would you be satisfied with a flunky's job in an architect's office?

S49—Uh-uh. I probably wouldn't be satisfied with it unless there was some chance. I would be willing to start with that, but I probably would want to go beyond that—

C49—You'll never be able to go beyond unless you have the training—because of the national organization. They've set up these things; and you must have these types of courses.

S50—(*pause*) Um-huh. (*pause*) One thing that this shows me is that, if I want to go on with that program, I can't go to a girls' school or a very small college my first year because I wouldn't have the right credits.

> ★ This is an example of the importance of crucial occupational or educational information in the choice of colleges. If the client is seriously interested in architecture, the number of colleges which she might consider entering will be quite limited.

C50—It might. Yes, it might mean the sixth year.

S51—The way it looks, it undoubtedly would, looking over this.

C51—Of course, there may be variations between schools and that would be the advantage of writing to practically every one of these to get their material; and then run comparisons between the various schools to see. There may be one, that by crowding the courses a little bit in various ways, you can have a year or two somewhere else.

S52—Um-huh.

C52—Then if you go to University G, you can pick your courses carefully.

S53—If I didn't want to go to one school all along, I'd have to make up my mind exactly what I was going to do and plan my courses so that my credits would come out right.

C53—That's right.

S54—'Cause I've seen it done time and again people changing schools lose their credits or don't have the right ones, one or the other. The way this plan looks—there won't be any of this business of, when you're thinking about college and don't know what you're going to do, you can go away and your first two years you can make up your mind what you want to do. Well, with something like this, you couldn't do that.

C54—That is true if you don't go into engineering, architecture or—

S55—If you go into English or History, or something like the fine arts—

C55—Journalism, Law and things of that kind, you can take liberal arts two years, and then switch very nicely. But when you go into some of these where the national organization has set up the prerequisites and everything else, then you have trouble.

S56—What about, say, accounting or something like that in math? You may meet the same situation—couldn't you on being licensed?

C56—Well, being licensed, yes, but you can recover—in business courses —if you wait for a year or two, you can skip back (*client laughs*) and not lose too much in the end. Now there is another possibility that we haven't discussed at all here and one that I'd like to throw in the "hopper." That is statistician. Have you ever thought of going into that?

S57—I was just going to ask you about accounting or something like that. We hadn't touched on something that was purely math.

C57—Um-huh.

S58—The only thing that ever worries me about something like that was would it drive me nuts just to work with numbers.

C58—Well, here's the thing, I think, you might consider whenever you go into statistics, you'll usually have to have something to go with it— business, economics, science; in other words, your statistics in and of itself is just a tool—unless you want to teach it. That way, you may teach it away from economics or something; but if you go out on a job, you're going to be hired as a statistician in economics, or a statistician in business, or something of that kind, and perhaps it'd be best to couple statistics with something else. What would work best with you, I don't know. You have a wide range of interests to pick from.

S59—Um-huh.

C59—Maybe you could possibly pick one that would fit in quite well, statistics and sociology. There are many combinations that you could work out.

S60—If you went into something like that then, would you go into a liberal course the first two years? Or would you—?

C60—Now, let me take a look for information and see if we have materials to work with.

S61—Do you have time?

C61—Oh, yes. I will not have another appointment this afternoon. (*Counselor leaves office for materials*) Here's a pamphlet they put out, the mathematics people put it out, I don't know if you've ever seen this.

S62—No, I haven't.

C62—It points out the applications of mathematics to many kinds of work. (*pause*) Now this university does train statisticians. (*pause*) I was looking for *Women in Mathematics and Statistics*. It is similar to the material which you looked at in architecture. You can see it a lot easier this way.

S63—Um-huh.

C63—Now there is a rather important idea that we haven't touched upon. That is the idea that if you go into mathematics and statistics, a bachelor's degree is just about going to amount to—

S64—a hill of beans.

C64—Well, no, not quite. (*Both laugh*) It isn't going to give you quite the same power that a bachelor's degree in architecture, for example, would give you. In terms of employment, you might have to spend a great deal of time out on the job working up.

S65—Um-huh.

C65—I imagine it would be clerical, routine kind of thing that might not be as intriguing.

S66—I wouldn't mind, of course, going on in school work. Although I am not particularly pressed financially, four years will certainly eat (*laughs*) desperately into any—

C66—There is this, though, that you ought to take into account—and that is an attempt for scholarships.

S67—Yes, I'm planning to.

C67—And when you see a school that you say, "now here's a school that I think I would be very much interested in," if you would write to the school—to the dean of the school of applied arts or whatever it is and ask him to describe available scholarships.

S68—Well, that is why I'm doing this this summer. On scholarships you have to get started in the fall. That's my reason for going into this now. If I was just going to go, I would wait till a little bit later. If I go around to any of these schools, most schools around here close, I'd get some sort of a scholarship. Unless something drastic happens, I've been expecting it to happen every year but it never has, unless something drastic happens, I imagine I'll be valedictorian of my class; and that offers some type of scholarship. Here at the university I think I could probably get those small scholarships.

C68—There'll be that and then, of course, and if you come and make good, there'd be other opportunities for other scholarships too.

S69—It'd be nice to get a really good one, you know what I mean.

C69—That's right. If you need any help and you don't seem to be making any progress, if you'll write, I'll see whether we can help you in some way. (*a few words missing*) Which means that you can find the jobs with bachelor's degrees. The question is, are they going to be the kind of jobs that are going to prove stimulating?

S70—There is one thing that I know about. This lady that I know that was a friend of mother's graduated from college with a degree in mathematics; and she entered a firm in the actuarial department and tried to become an actuary. From the attitude of the men in the office and the men on the examining board, after she'd worked at it 2 years, she knew it was useless to work at it any longer because they would never let her pass the board examination anyway.

C70—Uh-huh.

S71—So she's secretary-treasurer of College M now.

C71—Yes.

S72—That is what I wonder about when you go into something like that.

C72—Well, there is always that difficulty although typically there has been a change in attitude toward women working in the last 10 years.

S73—There is another woman from my home town who knows mother and she has a degree in mathematics and she gave up on actuarial work too (*laughs*).

C73—I'm not sure but what you would find the architectural type of thing a little more to your liking from that angle, especially going into interior work. However, you might meet up with some other women who would say that architecture was also rough. (*pause*)

S74—There's a lot of work in government for mathematicians.

C74—The government uses some in architecture, too. (*pause*)

S75—Mother is almost no help to me at all in this because after she took one year in math in college, (*laughing*) she couldn't get by. She never liked it at all. What I wonder now, this always comes into my mind too, you know. They say that many boys that go into engineering, after the second year, they go into business because of mathematics. Is it terribly hard?

C75—Well, it is if math isn't easy for you.

S76—I wonder what would happen then if—well, I'll know more after next year, I expect, after I get into a little bit higher mathematics.

C76—Well, have you had any struggle?

S77—No. (*pause*) The only things that I've had to struggle against are the little careless traits.

C77—Mathematics, once you go into engineering, is the same thing that I was driving at before. Some go in, they think they have interest, they don't know what it's all about, and they find that they do not like the field. Some think they have some ability, they were given a C once in a math course and figure they were geniuses, (*client laughs*) they go in, they find out that math is a rougher proposition on the college level, they just can't make it, they don't have any aptitude for mathematics, and they don't have any interest in it. Many go into engineering because they think it's like tinkering with cars and machinery. Actually, engineering is a lot of theory.

S78—Um-huh.

C78—Engineers do the planning, and much of the actual dirty work is done by others; and some of them, I guess, figure that they're going to work with their hands rather than their head and they just aren't suited for it. And some of them are these outgoing individuals who want to sell.

They don't want to put up with going through all the theory in order to sell. They want to sell shirts. They don't want to get a bachelor's degree in engineering to sell shirts—many who drop out of school, drop out because of lack of ability, lack of interest, lack of motivation, or they just don't seem to fit very well with the people that they're working with.

S79—This boy that I mentioned that I'd gone with for a long time, he is going to graduate from high school in three years instead of four and— he is going to a small college, and he has an appointment to West Point if he can get past another test. That's what he's taking. He hurried up and went to summer school this summer to finish high school so he can have a year of prep school.

C79—Oh, I see.

S80—But he wants to be an engineer, and he's a whole lot better mathematician than I am.

C80—In what way?

S81—Well, he's quicker. He sees things in algebra, particularly, quicker than I do—and I just wondered, knowing him, I don't know whether rapidity helps any or not. I'm slow, a little bit inclined to be. I never get too much on mental arithmetic. I haven't schooled myself that way enough, I don't think. I'm a little too reliant on thinking it through. I guess, though, that I probably have as good a chance in math as I would in anything else.

C81—We have your marks. (*pause*)

S82—Did you send to school for them?

C82—Yes, Uh-huh. We have your marks, and we have this scholastic aptitude test that we give to college freshmen which puts you in the upper 10 per cent, as a matter of fact, it's pretty close to the upper 5 per cent of the entering freshmen, and you're still a junior in high school.

S83—Um-huh. Strangely enough, with my desire to create I am a neat person. My handwriting is not very neat, you notice. I like neat things. I think that's partly art; and I don't mind doing, and I get a certain pleasure out of doing, I've been assisting in a secretarial agency, just doing dirty work; but I get a certain amount of pleasure out of seeing how quickly I can do it, a slow job and things like that.

C83—Well, do you think in the work you've had to do there you've had to revise the goal that people ordinarily have in order to be satisfied? Have you put your goal right now to see how quickly you can do it and how easy it can be—to get over the routine aspect of it?

S84—Um-huh.

C84—Well, here's this (*reading from pamphlet*) "required training for a statistician"—You can see what they are—quite a bit of mathematics there.

S85—I think I'd like the analytical geometry. I'd like to take that. Graphs have always fascinated me.

C85—Mmm.

S86—(*pause*) There is more mathematics in this—a whole lot more than in architecture.

C86—Um-huh.

S87—Boy whew. (*laughs*) I can't even pronounce the words.

C87—(*pause*) Now see here are the branches. Now notice that this ties in with what I told you. Now here are the branches you can go in and specialize in actuarial, biological, economical, educational, financial, industrial, psychological research, social and vital statistics. These are more or less specializations.

S88—I expect that financial or economics or industrial perhaps would be my pick there. (*pause*) And I doubt that industry would be the place exactly, I don't know. What would this be?

C88—Vital statistics would have to do with the state, federal governments in populations.

S89—I don't believe that I'd like to get into anything like income tax. Now what would lead into that?

C89—Ah—accounting. There would be some statistics involved. Accounting is higher mathematics, a great deal of it.

S90—Uh—(*pause*)—how about this CPA?

C90—Oh yes. Well, let's see what they have to say about various things. Let's take a look at these things and see. Mathematics for trades, mathematics for professional workers, workers in pure mathematics, workers in applied (*pause*)—

S91—It might be in applied.

C91—Probably. "Pure" would be more the mathematician type of thing.

S92—Teaching?

C92—(*pause*) Yes, much of it might be in that area. (*reading from pamphlet*)—"and then there are many problems in business, industry, government, insurance, hotel, etc. and banking," and it goes on to say here, "In brief the practical mathematician helps work out the theory and often operates under the name of physicist, chemist, economist," and so on—and then it goes on to tell about teachers of mathematics.

S93—What would the economist do? I mean, what would that be?

C93—It has to do with the state of—well, you might say the economic conditions in this country and matters of that kind, trying to work out laws or ways of predicting matters of that kind (*client laughs*) and trying to prove that his theories are good and proper. Business, of course, is very eager to know what's going to happen during the next year or 5 years from now; and the economist is the one that helps them try to predict economic trends.

S94—The worst part of it is to pronounce the word. (*laughs*) I wouldn't be surprised but what business would probably be the way to do it. (*pause*)

C94—There is this quality control. They use statisticians in industry. In assembly lines where they are making, say, telephone receivers, and they can't test every one. It would be just too expensive to go through and test every telephone receiver the normal way that they should; so what they do is they take thirty of them and the statistician then tests them and the statistician sits down and tries to give them some idea of how many telephone receivers have been defective in the whole lot. Now then if too many have been defective, they'll probably take the whole works back to redo them; but if the probability is very low that there are many defective ones in the whole group, why they just ship them out. But they're used for what they call quality control.

S95—Now who hires statisticians?

C95—Government, industry—

S96—How do you get there? I mean, do you get just a good job and get out? (*pause*)

C96—There's one for government. Here's another one. (*pause*)

S97—Marketing specialist. I wouldn't want that. (*laughs*) (*pause*) Sounds awfully complicated. (*pause*)

C97—Well, let's put it this way. Say you're going to be a dentist. When you're a dentist, you're a specialist in something. You go out and set up an office. A statistician can hardly work for himself unless he's good enough to come up with some new theories and make a go of it alone.

S98—I don't believe that research would appeal to me. (*pause*) And I've met a few civil service workers. (*pause*) I was just reading, (*reading in pamphlet*) "Are there only a few girls in your solid and trig class, don't be fooled into thinking there isn't a chance for girls in the field of mathematics." I'll be the only girl. Now there, I'll be the only girl in my class next year taking senior math. There it is again coming back. What about CPA? (*pause*) That doesn't require as much math as something like this does—statistician.

C98—No, not quite, but it's not far from it. (*pause*)

S99—That would be even more, though, pretty routine, wouldn't it?

C99—Not necessarily. You might work for yourself. A bank or some firm wants not one of their own accountants to certify to the accuracy of the books. They want a third party. The bank would be required by law to have somebody from the outside do it. So he will go in, and they have to check all the records, and they have to check all the books—and ferret out any discrepancies that might show up, and try to find out how it occurred, or he might be called in to set up an accounting system.

S100—Um-huh.

C100—He might be called on to do all sorts of services of that kind, which means that it has a great deal of variety to it.

S101—You're in business for yourself and are not working for a firm.

C101—I think most of them are. Now, the work as a senior accountant or a junior accountant is for a firm.

S102—Um-huh.

C102—Then you're the one that has to account for the expenditure of funds.

S103—It's a higher class of bookkeeping, huh? (*laughs*)

C103—Well, with bookkeeping you always think of it in terms of just arithmetic.

S104—Um-huh.

C104—Accounting involves higher mathematics, and then it involves an understanding of business administration. That is an important part of your education.

S105—I know a man who is a CPA and worked with a company in New York as head of their office. Wonderful job—he flies back home and passes out things to all the neighbors; (*laughs*) and sends his parents each five hundred dollar checks for their birthdays, Christmas, and anniversaries. He, of course, is very high in the field.

C105—Yes.

S106—I mean, he has an extra good job.

C106—It seems to me that with these many interests that you're going to have to say, "Well, just what is it that I want out of life?" Take, for example, take a new attack. If you're going into statistics, you're going to be restricted as to where you can work. You're going to have to go where the job is.

S107—Um-huh.

C107—If you go into architecture, you can go into practically any community and practice—

★ This response may seem to be a tendency for the counselor to push one objective. This was not the intent. The counselor was attempting to have the client react to another difference between the areas of work.

S108—Um-huh.

C108—. . . even if you are married.

S109—Um-huh.

C109—Or if you are going to teach mathematics somewhere, at least you can go most anywhere and locate something. If you want to go into accounting, you can go to most communities—at least in bookkeeping.

S110—If you want to go into teaching, though, you have to take education courses?

C110—That's right.

S111—And if you had, say, gotten your degree in mathematics, in some type of mathematics and then decided that you wanted to go into teaching, you'd have to go back and gather up your education courses?

C111—Unless you wanted to go into college teaching.

S112—You mean, you don't have to for college teaching?

C112—Uh-huh. The competition is rougher, though.

S113—You'd have to gamble, though. Almost like, say, you want to be a musician. (*pause*) I don't think that teaching high school mathematics— I can't think of anything worse than trying to pound mathematics into the heads of kids in high school, not that I don't like kids, not that. My mother thinks I ought to be a school teacher. I mean, she just thinks that's what I'm cut out for because I like kids and I go along with them. And everyone has tried to convince me for a long time that I ought to plan just to teach art.

C113—(*pause*) What do you think about it?

S114—(*pause*) Well—to tell you the truth, I have a little more ambition than that.

C114—Um-mm.

S115—You just can't help but say that there is not much competition in teaching. You can get a job. I mean, if I go into education, into art, I would graduate from college, I could go get a good job some place and settle down; and that'd be it.

C115—Uh-huh. You don't feel that you could get at the creative aspect of the thing that you would like; and there wouldn't be enough of your spare time to meet that need. You'd rather be creative while you're working—is that it?

★ The counselor missed the point of the client's response, but the client went on to clarify her own statement. It is not unusual for a student with some special talent to reject teaching as a career because he perceives teaching as lacking in prestige and opportunity for advancement. Teaching to him is acceptable only after many other occupational possibilities have been exhausted.

The prestige values of any occupation can be an important factor in vocational choice.

S116—No. (*pause*) I suspect that I have—maybe I am a little prejudiced against teaching to begin with because mother is a teacher. I hear some of her gripes, you know.

C116—Um-huh.

S117—There is always the salary gripe and—(*pause*)

C117—Are you at all concerned about having to get out of school and going out and work, build your own clientele. Or would you rather work with someone else?

S118—I believe I'd rather work for someone else, first—

C118—Well, I was just wondering, for example, school teaching is nice in the sense that, once you find a job, you let the other fellow worry about it, where the money is coming from—

S119—Um-huh.

C119—. . . that there will be enough children to teach, and things of that kind.

S120—I'm afraid of what would happen to me, though. I don't think that I have the right temperament to go into school teaching. Mother is a good deal the same way except she's in teaching; and she just comes home and takes it out on me. She gets so disgusted with the way things are going, and she sees how they could be made better. She wants to tell somebody to do something about it, and I feel that undoubtedly I'd be the same way. With anything else, if you start at the bottom and believe you have ideas that are good, you can work up; but with school teaching, you're there. Your salary may increase as you stay there longer and longer, but—

C120—That's about the only way that you can make progress. (*pause*)

S121—Well, we've just about covered the situation, have we?

C121—Well, we've gone into many different things. I don't know that we've covered everything.

S122—It's given me some ideas to work on. I really think that if it could be worked out, statistics would be my pick.

C122—Um-huh.

S123—But, I guess, you can change your mind; however, I'm not in the habit of changing my mind.

★ Throughout this interview there has been extensive use made of occupational and educational information materials. Many times the client asked a question, the counselor and client found the answer, and then the client reacted to that information. Examine, for example, S26 through S31; S67 through S68; S82 through S87;

and S115 through C119. This practice is the use of information in its best sense. There is no reason why occupational information, in a manner similar to test data, cannot also be made to provide the stimulus necessary for developing self-understandings.

C123—Well, you have time to mull it over and start working on it and thinking about it. You're not quite in the same position as if you were a senior last year.

S124—Well, thank you very much.

C124—Perfectly all right. Happy to help you out in any way we can.

S125—Well, now you keep that file on me.

C125—This will be here and any time you want to talk with us further about it or write us for an appointment, we'll be happy to do what we can. (*pause*)

S126—Okay. I'm going to write particularly to some of these schools.

C126—It will be interesting to get their information and make some comparisons.

S127—To tell the truth, I wouldn't mind going into a liberal arts course for the first two years, but if it's a question of between two choices, I would have to weigh the two things there and see how it would end up; but I think this is it. I'm glad that I came over because I have a lot of new ideas on it. I'll have this year, especially this summer, to find out. I'd like to have my mind made up pretty much by Christmas for this scholarship.

C127—Well, if later on you'd like to take off and drive over, if there are some materials which you'd like to have me look up and go over with you, and if you need help in any way possible, you just drop me a line and I'll try to make an appointment.

S128—Okay. (*pause*) Would there be any reason why any college would ever want to know what's in your file? Or would they finally find it out for themselves?

C128—Our practice generally is that we will send the materials to anyone we feel is competent to handle them.

S129—Um-huh.

C129—We're not going to just send that material out helter-skelter, and it would have to be over your signature.

S130—Um-huh.

C130—We wouldn't release it unless you gave it in writing, and we were satisfied that we were sending it to somebody who knew what it was all about.

★ The client was interested in the possible use of the data collected by tests; probably she was concerned over future scholarships.

She raised a question of ethics which the counselor answered in **C128, C129,** and **C130.** Ethics for counselors are still in a process of evolution, but several contributions have been developed within recent years (*8, 9, 440*).

S131—Um-huh. I just thought I'd ask about that and find out. (*pause*) Well, thank you again very much. I think I have gained a lot from this, at least in the matter of thinking.

C131—Well, we're very happy to help you out in any way.

COUNSELOR'S NOTES

(*Dictated Immediately after the Interview*)

★ The interview opened with a discussion of different schools offering work in architecture. Of course, the university does not have such a school and so the attention was shifted to schools within a 300 mile radius. We spent the early part of the interview going over the names of schools and locations so that the client could make a copy of the schools. She wants to contact some of them to find out the pertinent information concerning them. We then discussed the school at University H—not so much for the sake of the school as in terms of the courses, the pattern of courses in architecture curriculum. We discussed the new curricula they have, the general curriculum in architecture, and also the interior curriculum. We discussed entrance requirements and the licensing of architects—all the time trying to see how she would fit into architecture—what she would have to do to become an architect. She was quite eager to explore this phase of the problem and, I would say, came out with a rather thorough picture in terms of architecture.

I then introduced the idea of statistician and discussed it at some length in terms of what it would mean. We discussed the fact she would have to consider statistics in combination with some other area such as economics, science, education, etc. Then we discussed the various places where statisticians are employed.

We then went into the teaching of mathematics and a very interesting discussion centered around the experiences of her mother as a teacher. The client felt that perhaps she had been influenced unduly by experiences of her mother. We then went into a discussion of financial problems that may arise if she wanted to go to a school of architecture or some other school. We discussed loans and scholarships—a little bit about the cost of education. The client left the office giving the impression that she might want to check back later to see how her interests had changed.

ADDENDUM

The case of Ruth Brook illustrates counseling with the well-adjusted adolescent girl. She was invited to attend a two-day summer counseling service on a university campus. As a result of limitations imposed by time, Ruth Brook did not have the opportunity to work through her questions to any final conclusions. Adolescence is a period of exploration; sometimes decisions are reached precipitously and more often they are postponed until the very moment that action is required by circumstances. She was utilizing the counseling experiences for exploratory and informational purposes, postponing final decisions until later.

The client had completed the eleventh grade and had exhibited a high level of scholarship. In addition, she had won many honors because of her artistic talents. She was able to achieve success in most any activity attempted, including contacts with her peer group. Her interests were so wide and diverse that she found difficulty in evaluating them. Mathematics and art seem to have taken over at the time of counseling. Ruth had been able to maintain rather high standards of personal conduct and seems to have resolved any conflicts in this area. Her vocational objectives, architecture, statistician, etc., were not fantasy choices. Her final objective may be the result more of circumstances (a school offering a substantial scholarship) rather than picking a vocational objective and seeking out appropriate training.

Coming from a home of above average socio-economic status, Ruth Brook lives in an adult world. She exhibited many adult mannerisms, still maintaining sufficient contact with adolescence to cause uncertainties and normal apprehensions concerning the future. Her more satisfying associations have been with older individuals and also those who have some unique and outstanding talent. She exhibits an adult type of introspection, analyzing her strengths and weaknesses with insight. Her discussion of masculine interests indicates a type of introspection not always verbalized by the typical adolescent.

In summary, the case of Ruth Brook exemplifies counseling with a client who is progressing normally (for her level of ability and special talents) through adolescence. Although her desire for making plans and for self analysis are not always present in the typical adolescent, she is a very intelligent girl and consequently does not follow the pattern of less talented girls. Successive counseling interviews with her school counselor might assist Ruth in formulating her plans, but there is evidence in the three interviews which indicates she has maturity sufficient to plan wisely on her own.

CHAPTER 6

The Case of

JOHN BATTLE

★ THE CASE consists of eleven interviews; the first ten were phonographically recorded. Only about two-thirds of the originally recorded material is presented here. The first four interviews have been preserved essentially as they occurred. Extraneous and nonessential portions of interviews six through ten have been omitted. All of interview nine was omitted. Material is presented here on the basis of how much it contributed to the understanding of the case.

In the four cases presented so far, the authors have inserted comments at appropriate places to call the reader's attention to certain ideas pertaining to counseling which were suggested by the protocols. The comments were intended to be of use to the counselor-in-training. It was felt that there should be one case in the book in which few, if any, comments were inserted so that the reader might make his own interpretation and evaluation of the interviews and the critical points therein. Experiences in using these cases in the instructional program have indicated that the student is now ready to analyze a case without aid of interpretive comments. The *Case of John Battle* lends itself well to such a purpose. It is of sufficient complexity and length to serve as a challenge to most students. For these reasons, the case is presented with only a few minor comments.

The counselor in this case had completed most of the requirements for the doctor's degree in counseling and educational psychology and had had three years post-master's experience in counseling, teaching and administering a college counseling center.

The client was referred by Dr. Crew, a counselor in White University which the client had previously attended. Mr. Battle had consulted Dr. Crew on several occasions prior to the time of referral. The referral was well made and was well received by the client. Dr. Crew telephoned prior to the client's arrival on campus. Dr. Crew was personally acquainted with the director of the counseling service.

The following letter containing test results was received after the first interview had taken place. It is presented first, however, since its contents had been summarized in the telephone conversation.

❀ ❀ ❀ ❀ ❀

Counseling Services
WHITE UNIVERSITY

Director of Counseling   Re: John Battle
Green University
Dear Sir:

Mr. Battle has been in and around this city for quite awhile. He has several times attempted to go to school in the East and has several times attempted White University. His father is a retired civil service employee.

This student was in the Navy for several months and worked as a machinist mate. He has only about one semester of G.I. Bill left.

In addition to White University he has attended at least two different times, Blue College and Maroon College. Among the jobs which he has personally held are shipping clerk, service station attendant, checker in a grocery store.

At times this student seemed very listless. He used to like going to school but lately has found it hard to become interested. Again and again counselors have worked with this boy when he has come back to break off with a particular girl. Recently he has felt that this problem might be solved because he took the girl out again and had very little residue of the feelings.

This last semester he went to Blue College, became depressed, and quit. He loafed around and finally came back home at the Christmas holiday. He stayed in the fraternity house and "just spent his time around." This boy is not willing to give up school and he is really apparently not willing to go to school. He has been responsive to counseling and is rather "warm." It is felt that if he can have regular counseling in your counseling center, he may overcome some of his inability to organize his work and to integrate his personality around things which he plans to do.

Now this is a very brief extract of the materials we have on this student. If more is desired please feel free to write me.

With warmest personal regards,
Marvin Crew
Director of Counseling

MC/rb
Encls.: Psychological test reports.

TEST DATA

(1) Minnesota Multiphasic Personality Inventory—See Profile.

(2) Kuder Preference Record, Vocational, Form C.—See Profile.

(3) Strong Vocational Interest Blank, Men (Partial scoring)—See Profile.

The Minnesota Multiphasic Personality Inventory

Starke R. Hathaway and J. Charnley McKinley

Name BATTLE, John

Address Suburbia

Occupation Student Date Tested _____

Education College junior Age 24

Marital Status Single Referred by Dr. Crew, White Univ.

NOTES

Test administered at White University.

Signature _____ Date _____

M
Male

Male

Scorer's Initials. _____

	?	L	F	K	Hs+.5K	D	Hy	Pd+.4K	Mf	Pa	Pt+1K	Sc+1K	Ma+.2K	Si	TorTc
Raw Score	2	3	6	8	5	26	20	25	24	14	28	31	24		
K to be added					4			3			8	8	2		
Raw Score with K					9			28			36	39	26		

Copyright 1948
THE PSYCHOLOGICAL CORPORATION
522 Fifth Avenue
New York 18, New York

Printed in U.S.A.   51-125S

NAME __BATTLE,____John_____ AGE 24 SEX M Code 84·72—90·13 _____DATE OF TEST _____
　　　Print　　　Last　　　　　First　　　　　Initial　　　　　　　　　　M or F

First Revision, February 1951

SELF-INTERPRETING

PROFILE SHEET

for the
KUDER PREFERENCE RECORD
VOCATIONAL

Form C

MEN and WOMEN

DIRECTIONS FOR PROFILING

1. Copy the V-Score from the back page of your answer pad in the box at the right. [?]

   If your V-Score is 37 or less, there is some reason for doubting the value of your answers, and your other scores may not be very accurate. *If your V-Score is 45 or more*, you may not have understood the directions, since 44 is the highest possible score. *If your score is not between 38 and 44*, inclusive, you should see your adviser. He will probably recommend that you read the directions again, and then that you fill out the blank a second time, being careful to follow the directions exactly and to give sincere replies.

   If your V-Score is between 38 and 44, inclusive, go ahead with the following directions.

2. Copy the scores 0 through 9 in the spaces at the top of the profile chart. Under "OUTDOOR" find the number which is the same as the score at the top. Use the numbers under M if you are a man and the numbers under F if you are a woman. Draw a line through this number from one side to the other of the entire column under OUTDOOR. Do the same thing for the scores at the top of each of the other columns. If a score is larger than any number in the column, draw a line across the top of the column; if it is smaller, draw a line across the bottom.

3. With your pencil blacken the entire space between the lines you have drawn and the bottom of the chart. The result is your profile for the *Kuder Preference Record—Vocational*.

Published by SCIENCE RESEARCH ASSOCIATES
228 South Wabash Avenue, Chicago 4, Illinois
Copyright 1951, by G. Frederic Kuder. Copyright under International Copyright Union. All rights reserved under Fourth International American Convention (1910). Printed in the U.S.A. Copyright 1951 in Canada.

Please use code number 7-299 when reordering this profile.

T-21-X

Profile chart header (scores): 0 27 | 1 36 | 2 32 | 3 33 | 4 58 | 5 20 | 6 19 | 7 15 | 8 60 | 9 28

| OUTDOOR | MECHANICAL | COMPUTATIONAL | SCIENTIFIC | PERSUASIVE | ARTISTIC | LITERARY | MUSICAL | SOCIAL SERVICE | CLERICAL |
| M F | M F | M F | M F | M F | M F | M F | M F | M F | M F |

STRONG VOCATIONAL INTEREST TEST—MEN

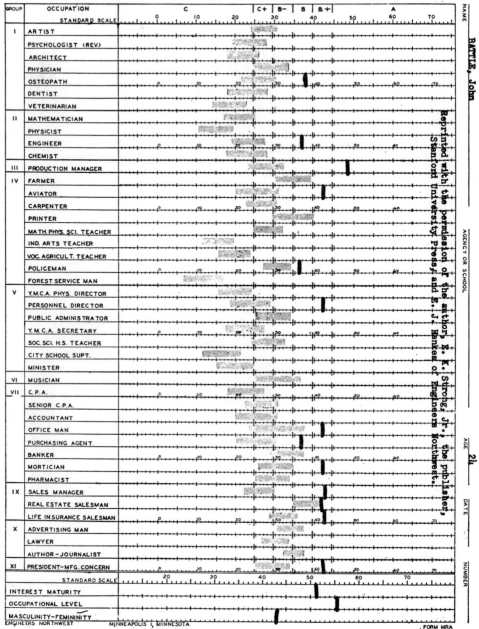

(4) Engineering & Physical Science Aptitude
(Norm group: engineering freshmen)

			Raw Score	Rank Percentile
Part I	—	Mathematics	21	77
Part II	—	Formulation	7	62
Part III	—	Physical Science Comprehension	10	20
Part IV	—	Arithmetic Reasoning	4	41
Part V	—	Verbal Comprehension	27	61
Part VI	—	Mechanical Comprehension	9	13
Total			78	38

(5.) Revised Minnesota Paper Form Board,
Form AA   41   40
(Norm group: engineering freshmen)

(6.) Wechsler-Bellevue Intelligence Scale,
Form II — Adolescents & Adults

	Weighted Score	I.Q.
Verbal Scale	59	114
Performance Scale	64	118
Full Scale	125	119

FIRST INTERVIEW

C1—I'll need a little briefing on this situation.

S1—Best place is the beginning, I suppose. I spent, well, my first two years I spent at Maroon College. So, then after I spent two years there—well, I guess something—it would be a good idea to bring in here—well, my first year was very good as far as teachers and everything.

C2—You mean you enjoyed the teachers that you had?

S2—Yes. Well, I don't know if you know very much about Maroon College, but—

C3—Not very much.

S3—It's not too well known and on top of that anyone can say anything about it. They don't have much faith in the thing. My first year I had very good instructors, both in chemistry and math. In my second year it sort of tapered off.

C4—Mm-huh

S4—They weren't too good. And then I went up to Blue College. I continued on and took engineering. So I had a little trouble—there was a girl back here and I was up there. I didn't take too much interest in the school, so my first semester I went on probation. The second semester I picked up a lot of my business courses and I came off probation, made my average for the fraternity. So, then when I came back here, the intent was to go to White University and finish up out there, so that the two of us can go together.

C5—So, the third year you spent at Blue College and it ended up to be a successful year?

S5—Well, it wasn't exactly successful. I just went ahead and I made no progress whatsoever, as far as I was concerned, because I couldn't keep my mind on my studies. I didn't do my best. I passed and that's about all.

C6—I see.

S6—In fact, I took 15 hours—and out of 15 hours, I made three D's, an A and a C, which in the courses that I was taking, I didn't consider as doing very well for myself. I came back here when we had it out during the summer.

C7—You and the young lady?

S7—Yes. Then I decided to start into White University. Well, then I found out there was a lot of trouble because I was under the strain, more or less—the idea of breaking up.

C8—Um-huh.

S8—So, I made no progress whatsoever. I was making half decent grades, but I didn't feel that I was doing anything so I just got up to the point where it was such a strain, and I kept worrying about things. So, I just went ahead and quit school about two weeks before finals. So, then I moped around until spring and then I went to work and I worked until September. Saved every dime and nickel I could. I went back up to Blue College this last fall. And, when I got back up there I thought things would go pretty well. When I was at White University I had taken tests, when I had this trouble. So, I figured after a while things would straighten out. I started to work and things seemed to straighten out— everything would go ahead and take care of themselves. So, I saved up my money and went back up to Blue College. I was up there 'till about, well, second week in October it started. I got a little behind in my studies —not enough to make much difference. Then I got a phone call from my family, said something about the Navy calling. So I was in the reserves, but I was unaware—under the impression, rather, that I was discharged from the reserves last summer. So the minute I heard that, I was so disgusted anyway, that I went ahead and quit school again. When I came back here, I found that there wasn't anything to it. So, then right away I figure, well, I mean, this is where I put all my basis. I keep saving money and scrounged on different things I'd like to have, but can't have if I want to save money; but if I keep saving money and going to school for some reason, I keep wasting it; but I always keep going back. That's why, I think, there is something there. That's what I've been trying to find out. I talked with Dr. Crew, I don't know if you know him—in White University.

C9—I know him slightly.

S9—So, I put a lot of faith in him and that's one thing I didn't do when I had these troubles. When I had trouble the first time, why ah, I didn't know Dr. Crew.

C10—Um-hm.

S10—I had taken the tests. He and I were supposed to have little conferences which after a while I thought I didn't need. But I found out that I was entirely wrong. So, then when I came home this last time, he was the first person I contacted. The reason, well, I quit school at Blue College and I messed around before I came home. I met a nice little girl up there and she and I hit it off pretty well and I began to think.

C11—This was up at Blue College?

S11—No. She went to Buff College nearby. Then I began to realize that being in the condition I am, I couldn't do anything as far as plans were concerned. So I figured, she and I both figured, the best thing to do would be to come back and get this straightened out. So, being down to about the lowest minimum of money that you could possibly get to, and on top of that, not having too much of a desire to go back to Blue College because of the troubles associated with it, I figured I'd put in application down here. So I made application in Arts College as an unclassified student, more or less, to take half a semester to try and work things out and decide whether I should stay in engineering or try something else. But I got back and I talked to Dr. Crew and he told me that he thought it would be a good idea to come up here. But, now that I've definitely decided to come up here, he said that he would send my record (*referring to report of counseling contacts with Dr. Crew*).

C12—So, here you are.

S12—Here I am. (*laughter*) My record should have been sent up. I came up last week, the early part of the week, to try to figure out things as far as a schedule was concerned, and I got over as far as the Arts and Science department. Miss Blick (Academic Adviser in office of Dean of Arts and Science) sort of figured I was fouled up. So, she said that she didn't think it was a good idea to continue the way I had been. Well, at the time my idea on the thing was that I'd go ahead and on a week end that I got in, I'd talk things over with Dr. Crew. But, she said that it would be a good idea to talk to someone up here and I think it's the best now because in case things come up, it would be better to have them settled right here than to go back to Dr. Crew. He said he'd send up all my material. But when I came over the tests weren't here. But I thought that perhaps they might be tied up in the mails. So, I don't know, I can't—I think my main interest I mean because I'm so far in engineering that's what I think I'd like to continue with. Dr. Smith was telling me this morning that they're thinking of starting an industrial engineering curriculum up here.

C13—That's right.

S13—And what I like about that very much is that if I did get settled I might go back to Blue College. But if I could get enough credit, it would be to my advantage to stay up here. Because if I did once finish up in engineering, my desire all the time was to get my degree in industrial engineering, and then come here and take up law.

C14—Um-huh.

S14—So I think the way it looks to me is that it would be very beneficial. If they are going to have industrial engineering, I could probably finish up. I would be one of the first students to graduate with a degree in industrial engineering. What I'd like to do is take up a teaching job up here and work on my law degree.

C15—I see.

S15—So that's why it sounds pretty good to me. And, perhaps some day I'd better go and talk to this Mr. Jonel (Prof. of Engineering).

C16—Yes.

S16—For, I mean, they'd probably be looking for someone like that. And that's what I would like to do. I would like to go ahead on that and do some teaching while I'm working on my law degree if it's at all possible.

C17—Your plans are a little long range, aren't they?

S17—Yes.

C18—What did you and Dr. Crew talk about in terms of your interest in engineering? Did you have any—

S18—(*interrupting*) We never did have any talks, as far as (*pause*) I never stopped to realize about two words. I knew they were there, but I never stopped to realize it—how important they are and how much they mean together—interest and ability—the two of them together—how important they are. I mean, the tests I took—I took all the tests. Of course, the main thing I was worried about, I mean, I'm not trying to say that the tests are incorrect, or that I have more ability than the tests show, but I don't know if it's taken into consideration—but I was under a strain when I took those tests. That was right at the center of the time of the emotional strain.

C19—Um-huh.

S19—I mean, if they actually show something else, that's okay with me, as far as trying something else. But we never did talk too much about it.

C20—I see. You mean you talked mostly about your human relationships rather that your vocational ideas there.

S20—Yes. Um-huh. In fact, the only thing that I can really remember talking about was, ah, let's see, he decided on some talks and going at points, different words about the things that are wrong with me. The only thing we ever did get to was "rationalization." I rationalize—I never did too much before. I'd see some sort of a job that had to be done and I'd go ahead and do it. That's all there was to it. I usually got through with it. If I decided on something, I undertook it and finished it.

C21—Um-huh.

S21—But towards the end there, when I was having all this trouble, well, there'd be some sort of a job out there (*pointing*) that I'd try to get to and I couldn't. I'd go this way and I'd go that way and first thing I'd know I'd be going around in circles.

C22—Um-huh.

S22—I'd be about 50 feet away from it. I'd never reach it. And, there-fore, I came to the point where I did rationalize too much. I'd ration-alize things that were actually of no concern at all to what the problem was. They'd be altogether off on some other line someplace. But that's about the only thing that we did ever discuss as far as the tests were concerned.

C23—I see. (*pause*) I was just wondering about the nature of your association with Dr. Crew.

S23—Well, we never did get too many things hashed out. Any time I'd have any trouble I'd go out and see him. I put quite a bit of faith in him. I don't know if you know very much about him personally, but he is a brilliant man. He's very well noted for things like this. It's not just at school, but all over town. Anybody who is anybody down there knows him and knows what he's done. So, any time that I'd have any trouble, I'd always go out to see him.

C24—Um-huh.

S24—And we never would talk too much about the trouble, it'd be more or less briefing before the trouble. He figured, I guess, that was probably the best way instead of going right into it—to kind of work into it grad-ually. So, the things we'd talk about would never be too important. Then, if it didn't always satisfy me so much, I'd figure, well, that's the end of that. So, he used this process of briefings instead of going into it. So I went to him whenever I had trouble.

C25—Gives you an opportunity to reorient yourself in that respect and that probably is about the nature of it. Everybody operates a little bit differently, but in general that may be the purpose of what we may want to do here. That is, if you get to feeling that you are having some dif-ficulty with some things around here—

S25—(*interrupts*) That's right. I've got that feeling right now—it's sort of a funny thing the way the problems were before. In some ways I felt that they weren't important, weren't worth telling, in other ways I felt that they were important, but who to confide in? As far as confiding in your fraternity brothers and things like that, I have the feeling from the counseling center right here that there is a definite gain to coming over here. So, I'm glad I found it, for it's something that I need very badly. And it's going to be an advantage to me, I realize that now.

C26—Well, the process of counseling is the talking out of various things that are bothering you or that you are thinking about. And, in so doing, you can view them in a way in which you can't see when you just mull them over in your mind by yourself. In order to explain it to me, for instance, you have to put it in such phraseology and organize it in such a way so that I can understand it. Well, in so doing you organize it for yourself and you are able to see it in a different light. When you are merely thinking about it, all these things impress themselves upon you in different ways—emotional attitudes. You can't evaluate those things just in a mental wrangle, but when you tell me about them, you have to organize them, you have to say, well, this is important and this isn't and in talking it over with me, it becomes a little more clear, because you have to organize it in such a way that I can understand it and, in so doing, it helps you to understand it. Then I can more or less take these things and re-evaluate them, and hold them up so that you can consider them. Not that I believe that my particular evaluation is more correct than yours, but I want to give you several alternatives to look at, and in that way, we can put it more in the light of a problem that you can attack than something that is entirely overwhelming and is entirely in the emotional area. (*pause*)

S26—I just happened to think of one thing. All the time I was up at Blue College I mean, up until the time of this last trouble I had, I, more or less, blamed this girl for it, see?

C27—Mm-hm.

S27—And, I thought that there was actually something there so the one thing I decided on—It happened over Thanksgiving. I didn't come home. I stayed up there. Went to a friend's home. We went out one night and he knew this girl and she had this other girl friend of hers who was up. And, I never met a girl in my life like this one as far as being brilliant is concerned. And she was very well read. And, I mean, she was the type of person—well—well—how she went at it at first was that she tried to psychoanalyze everyone in the crowd.

C28—I see.

S28—I mean, I like to be more or less the center of attraction, at times, and she annoyed me quite a bit. There were only four people, but she really did annoy me. I actually disliked the girl until—I mean, unless

I actually think it's important, I usually don't listen to people. Something like this I consider important, I take quite a bit of interest in. And, if someone is talking, I'd say, well, he's so-and-so and so-and-so and to heck with it. But then after an hour, we went to the show and went back to this girl's house and we stayed there when we got back at 12:30 and after about half an hour, I didn't say anything. I just sat back and listened to her. I didn't realize how many brains she had in her head and how well she understood things in people and so I just sat there and talked to that girl until four o'clock in the morning. And, I mean, we had a very nice conversation. I think, I certainly even astonished myself that I could carry on a conversation with someone like that.

C29—Um-hm.

S29—And she told me that she thought one of the things that I should do— after I had told her all my troubles—she told me that she thought one of the things I should do was to go back and see this girl, this girl in nurse's training at the hospital at home. So, I went back at Christmastime and came home and I took this girl out, just for an evening to talk. I was very glad I did this for this was the first time in my life that I could actually shake hands with the girl. I mean that. I realized that I was completely over it. It hit me so hard at first I thought I'd never get over it. But, I'm glad I did it. It was an advantage in that I actually found out there wasn't anything there any more. That it was strictly on a friendship basis. So I was very happy about that, very relieved.

C30—Uh-hm.

S30—I think that might be an advantage from now on also.

C31—I think you have a point there. Dr. Crew thought that was an advantage, too, didn't he? (*client nods.*) Well, now your immediate situation here is that you must decide what you are going to do this coming semester?

S31—That's right. I kinda wish the tests were here. (*pause*) Well, there are two courses that I've sort of decided on. I think there would be an advantage in taking—the way the situation is today with the world. I always did want to take Russian, so, I mean, the way things are, being a veteran, though only about 18 months, I thought there was a very good chance of going back. I think there is something there that would be an advantage. So I intended to sign up for that. And, then I was thinking about taking Psych. 1, because regardless of what I go into—engineering or anything, I would need psychology. So, I figured a psych. course would be to my advantage. The main thing that Miss Blick wants is that—she said I should definitely decide on what I intend to do or else come over to the counseling center and have you as sort of a guardian angel over here so that, I mean, she wouldn't have to worry about me. (*Counselor laughs.*) because they'd be there to help me, you know.

C32—Yes, I see that. Well, you may not want to make a definite decision as to exactly what you want to do. I think this unclassified student status is an advantage and could be well used as an exploratory type of thing. But, how many hours did you plan on carrying?

S32—Well, the maximum is 16, isn't it? (*Counselor nods.*) Well, the way things are set up now, as far as studying is concerned, I have an advantage there. I have a room over a business establishment and, well, I had a similar set-up for nine months when I was up at Maroon College. I had a nice room and that's an advantage to me for I find myself in a place where it's quiet and I can really concentrate and study.

C33—What kind of work do you do?

S33—Well, I more or less help out in the business and pick-ups, things like that. And maybe help out if I have the time. I'll have to live pretty skimpy, until summer—until I get a job. I'll have to work this summer in order to come back to school this fall. I can always get a job in my home town. And, I can make good money there. So, the money situation isn't too bad and it's not too good. I mean as far as my meals are concerned, I don't have to worry about that, I can take care of that. If I get too short I'll probably get some sort of a job. But, as far as devoting time to my studies, I should have plenty this semester.

C34—Now, you've pretty well decided then, that you want to take this language course in Russian and a basic course in psych.

S34—I think there are two things there. This Russian, I mean, if things stay the way they are I don't expect to stay in school. I mean, I might even be called back in before the end of this semester. In the reserves—you see, the way it was explained to me, I was supposed to have been discharged in July. However, I was in a sort of a specialized rating. They're dying for the guys right now. So, I never did hear too much about it other than that call I got. I received a letter last week at home and it said they were calling up reserves. Well, that, more or less, is a scare anyway, to get out and join a squadron, and fly on week ends and things like that.

C35—(*interrupting*) I did see something—a little notice in the paper yesterday, very briefly, and it said all naval reservists will be recalled. Kind of a broad statement, but that's the way the paper phrased it.

S35—Yes. Well, I don't even mind going back in so much and getting out of school for a while, but I think a lot differently than when I went in the last time when I was 18. So, if I can settle most of this, I think, as far as leaving school, it doesn't matter too much to me for I've always thought a lot of school and I intend to go through with it. So that if I didn't get bumped off in the process, why I'd be back in school. So, while I would be in the service, it would be an advantage to save money because I could look at it from two angles. I'd realize that I was going back to school so that I could devote a lot of time to my own research, working on my own—instead of going into town and running around every night. I'd be saving money and I'd be giving myself some sort of a foundation for coming back to school. So, it doesn't make too much difference to me, the idea of going back into the service. But, if I could go back in with this straightened out, it'd be an advantage to me for then I could be ahead instead of wasting time.

C36—Now, you say—"get this straightened out." I'd like to find out about this a little more clearly. Are you talking about your attitudes toward school? Or some of the other attitudes which may have caused this trouble in school?

S36—Well, I think, more or less, both of them. I mean, I think I'm the type of fellow that—maybe after this is straightened out I won't find it that way—but, I think I'm the type of fellow that has to have an interest in things. I mean, like when this came up, I could have gone to work, but I wouldn't have been satisfied. But in school especially if there's something I think I'm making progress in, that I can take an interest in, it's mine and I work at it, and work at it very hard. So, that's what I think. I mean, as far as straightening this out, if I can actually find out where I'm going and know that I'm going at in in the right way, then I think everything would be settled. I think the main thing is, if I can produce in school and actually be interested in it, and, I think that if I'm actually producing, I will be interested in it. (*pause*) I'd say even after—oh, almost a year after I used to think about it quite a bit, but towards the end I didn't have any idea at all. (*referring to relationship with girl-friend*).

C37—Uh-hm.

S37—And, I think things have been settled. I mean, I don't know. The night we were out—why, after the night was over and I figured, more or less, if there was still something there, why—I'd be thinking about it, maybe for a short time afterwards. Well, I thought about it as soon as I left her and two or three hours after that there wasn't too much to think about. I didn't even concentrate on it.

C38—You feel that that situation is solved but that the overall picture is not, because certain things are still there that may produce a similar situation.

S38—That's right. I mean, as far as the effects of it. I mean, my reasons for quitting school and for being the way I am and not having interests and thinking of those interests, that's the thing that's flubbed up. I think that that's about the only thing that remains of it.

C39—Well, we may want to get at that later on in the semester, as things progress. Some of the things which we might term as causal factors, or basic things, which are really external to the situation itself, still may be present. And that may reinforce, may act as a carry-over to another situation even though this as an individual thing has been solved satisfactorily. Maybe we can investigate here and find out what particular factors were involved and instead of treating the individual thing take the broad point of view and see if we can't build this thing to the point where you feel capable of handling not only that, but any situation. You see what I mean? (*client nods.*) And so, therefore, we want to find what surrounded the whole thing because they may still be there even though the situation itself is already solved. See what I mean?

S39—Yes.

C40—This has now disappeared, but the forces may still be there by themselves and still operating.

S40—Well, that's the prospect that worries me a little bit. I'm always a little cautious about women. (*laughs*) I always say, boy, you understand women. And then, afterwards I say, well, maybe you don't. So, I've always been a little cautious about it. And, this girl that I met up at school up there, she's very sincere, but (*laughter*) there's still this little idea, you know, that maybe you're going to get another fast shuffle. So, well, it's sort of a funny situation, but we were pinned. And, it was sort of a friendly pin, I mean, being unsettled like I was with the idea of getting pinned and then trying to see if things would work out. So she went—she seemed hog wild on the deal.

C41—Um-hm.

S41—So it never bothered me too much, because I realized that there might be another downfall and I didn't want to get too close to it. So, we've been writing pretty regular, and finally she came to the point where she realized that 'til things were settled it was kind of silly for her to continue. She was very sincere about it as far as being pinned. She was really serious. She said that she felt pretty bad about it as far as going out and things like that. I more or less started it off. I said that I didn't think it was fair either. So, she said that she thought the best thing to do would be to send the pin back so that sort of hit me. I mean, I asked for it but when it came back it sort of knocked me off my feet.

C42—Um-huh.

S42—So, then I stopped to think about it. I realized that it was probably the best thing. I don't know, if this thing actually blew up—how much of an effect it would have on me. But that is about the only worry I have right now—that it might have some effect on me. So, if it does blow up and you hear a pounding on (*laughs*) on your door (*laughter*)—

C43—Well, you brought up the idea originally, because it seems intelligent to you when you reason it out, a perfectly logical thing. But because of this other situation you kind of hoped that it wouldn't happen.

S43—Yes.

C44—You see, one is an emotional feeling and the other is an intelligent action and if you get those two things tied together we act one way and hope another—and tend to get the two twisted.

S44—I think probably that if she's messed up about the deal as I am, why—when I get back up there, and, if there is still something there it'll probably get serious then. It'll be something to plan on. It's something just like schooling. I mean, you plan on finishing up and getting a job. Well, it's the same thing with a girl. Plan on finishing up school and marrying the girl and settling down and having a family.

C45—Yes.

S45—But right now I don't think it would bother too much, whether or not it would be a long drawn out affair after it'd happened. I mean, if it'd bother me for a while after it had happened or not. That's what I'm wondering about. I mean, if I could stop and think about it after it did happen, I mean, I couldn't definitely blame her or anything. I mean, it's more than too much to ask of somebody like that, you know, you walk around and you don't know exactly what's going to happen. You know, what plans you have—. I mean, if I could stop to look at it, instead of emotionally, look at it intelligently, I think it'd be all right, if it did happen.

C46—You think you might be making a transfer here. That is, you have an external situation which seems to be very similar, and that similarity might be causing some of your thoughts along this line. That is, when you went to Blue College, you left the situation and it kind of drifted away from you while you were gone. And, now you may be afraid the same thing might be taking place, and on the surface it's the same kind of an idea. You have that feeling about it.

S46—Something like that.

C47—Well, happily that's an external similarity on the surface and you must view it as that because every time someone leaves somebody else it has a similarity to other things that have happened in that same regard —we must realize the things may be entirely different—and you sometimes attach too much importance to these surface similarities. We want to get things out in the open so you can't attach incomplete similarity to something that is fairly serious.

S47—Yes.

C48—Well, we'll look into these things a little bit more definitely and try to think them out more clearly, a bit more atomistic approach. But we want to return here for a little bit to your immediate problem. Do you have an adviser or has Miss Blick said that we would work with you?

S48—That's more or less it.

C49—Uh-huh. She'll have to sign the program, though, and that sort of thing. Well, let's get down to some of these mundane matters. (*laughter*) How many hours of credit do you have approximately? I mean, I think we might have that as a point because we want to find out how much time you can put in as an unclassified student.

S49—Well, do you mean as far as the time that I have, or the time that the university has given me credit for?

C50—I mean how much you have been given credit for.

S50—Well, that is something I don't know. As far as what sort of a curriculum they put me in Arts College and how they accredit me and everything. I don't know exactly how they work it when I'm an unclassified student, whether they—(*Counselor interrupts*).

C51—Well, for an unclassified student, they don't prescribe anything that you take. That's one of the beauties of it. But, if you are going to work eventually towards a degree, then you are going to have to consider requirements for that degree. Things that you want that might help in an exploratory way and yet, things that are not too far from the things that will help you in terms of getting requirements for a degree. In industrial engineering, we don't want to limit you to that, but, to more or less consider it. The full curriculum has not been worked out. It's still in a nebulous stage. It's, ah—(*Client interrupts*).

S51—Do you have any idea when they'd be starting that?

C52—Mr. Jonel can tell you a whole lot about that. I had the idea that they were going to put it in its initial stages in September, but I'm not sure about that. That might be wrong, but I got that impression from him.

S52—I was wondering—probably while this is going on—my idea on the situation was that they'll probably, if they have the chance, put it into effect, because of the shortage of students. What I understand is that they'll be pretty short of students next semester.

C53—Yes.

S53—Well, as a drawing card, they may originate it before next September.

C54—Well, certainly in industrial engineering the basic background in psych. is not going to do you any harm and you may take a few courses there. I think one thing we can do, just for the fun of it, is look at a university that has such a course and see if there is a curriculum outlined for industrial engineering.

S54—I have a Blue College catalogue here.

C55—All right, what do they have?

(*Counselor gets a university catalogue and client looks at both catalogues and schedule of courses. They discuss various courses which the client may be interested in taking. Then they arrange for an appointment for a later date.*)

SECOND INTERVIEW
(25 Days after the First Interview)

S1—Did you get back from your trip okay?

C1—Oh, yes.

S2—We had a little trouble over the week end. I hadn't heard from this girl so I, it hit me between the eyes, so I had to call her up; I tried to get in touch with her.

C2—That girl from home, you mean?

S3—No, this is the girl up at Blue College.

C3—Oh, I see.

S4—So, I tried to get in touch with her but she was gone for the weekend and I finally got in touch with her yesterday.

C4—Um-huh.

S5—I don't know what brought it on. I don't know exactly. I mean, it was more the idea of not hearing from her. I guess I began to think and wonder a lot of different things so I had a pretty good heart-to-heart talk with her on the phone last night. So she wrote a letter last night,—well, I don't exactly know what the score is—which way I want the letter to be exactly. But I explained to her that I didn't think—I mean, as far as things are going right now, they're going pretty good. And, as far as things coming up to interfere with what's going good, I explained to her and I said it would benefit both of us and I said I was trying to keep it at a minimum. So, I said let's be perfectly honest about this and said if there's nothing there let's face it. I said I didn't know exactly as far as I knew whether there was something there. But from the way I acted, I presumed there was. I want to try to get up there over spring vacation. I don't know whether I'll be able to or not.

C5—In other words, you feel that you want to get this thing settled. Is that right?

S6—Yes, because, I mean, that's the way I explained it. I don't know—a lot of times you more or less stick your chin out. Well, I keep looking at it in this way—that I am sticking my chin out again, the way I did the last time. But, up to this point, she has been very honest with me. I mean, she really has. When she saw—I mean—that it was this circumstance when we became pinned up there. It was sort of forced and I didn't think anything would grow out of it and I was surprised that it had gone that far.

C6—Um-huh.

S7—And at the time I was up there, she was very serious and I wasn't and I said that I was wondering if she had more or less changed her opinion as of lately. But she was very honest. A lot of gals in my estimation would have said, what the heck, I might as well keep the pin. But she was very honest in that respect. And so, she sent the pin back and explained how things were. Of course, there was sort of a funny proposition that led up to this. She had final exams the last part of the month. She had played around a lot last semester, especially when I was up there. We went out every night, so she didn't do much studying. So when it came the end of the semester, why, she had a lot of catching up to do, so when she did try to catch up, it took quite a bit of time. She didn't get much chance to write. Well, I had all that free time before I came up to school here so I used to write quite often. Then after I got up to school here I began to think—well, letters will probably start coming in. Well, the first part of the month they didn't. I got sort of childish about the thing and said, well, I'll just sit back and wait until she writes some letters. So then, she said she didn't receive any letters from me there for a while so she felt the same way. So, I wrote a letter to her last night and I explained it, and said, it was more or less childish on both our parts and that I realized my foolish mistake by acting that way instead of saying, I'm not going to write. I should have written a letter and said, well, exactly why aren't you writing? I mean, if you are busy or have an excuse, what do you think about it? So I put everything I had to say, that I didn't say over the phone—I think I put about the same thing in the letter. But—I mean—it sort of hit me over the weekend. I felt about the same way that I did up at Blue College when I had that trouble. Of course, I didn't have anything to base it on then—but—I don't know, I guess it isn't right. When it did happen, I got sort of worried about it and then just sort of—sort of suspicious nature—about exactly just what is going on up there, see?

C7—Um-huh.

S8—I mean, that probably is the normal tendency. When you get a little worried like that, to more or less accept that suspicious nature, so I explained everything pretty fully to her last night but—

C8—(*Counselor interrupts*). What did she say to you?

S9—She didn't have too much to say. I guess I did most of the talking. She did say that she had gone on probation, I think, because she didn't study too much last time, and consequently she had been studying quite a bit. So that may be ʹtrue. Of course, I explained it to her that I didn't expect her to sit around, but I told her that I'd come down here and I was working hard and I said I'm trying to accomplish something. I said that about the only thing that I would actually like to do is to write letters once in a while, enough that would keep me going. I said that was about the only thing that would cause me any trouble. You know, when I wouldn't receive any letters, then I'd begin to worry. Either receive letters, or if I'm not going to receive letters, know the reason why, and if there's going to be some reason why. If it is because she doesn't particularly care about writing or something like that, why let's cut it off here while it's at the minimum before it gets to be to the point where it really gives me some trouble. So, she said that she had been studying pretty hard. Well, before I talked to her I talked to this girl from home. She said that she wished that I'd drop out to see her. So, of course, we talked quite a bit about Jane while I was back here, you know, it became more or less a buddy-buddy routine. So, I called her up. I called Mary up and I said, well, what do you think? And she more or less told me to call her up—Well, I said in more or less selected words—I said, am I getting a runaround on this deal. And she said, no, I don't think you are. She said Jane had been going out quite a bit, you know that. And I said I knew that, but I was just wondering why she didn't write. I said it gave me a little trouble over the weekend and it started out as something not very great and then it finally built up to where I just couldn't control myself. I just had the idea that I just had to call up and get in touch with her. I mean, it's more or less that gnawing inside that I had when I was up at Blue College. I mean, though it wasn't exactly that, I wouldn't be satisfied until I'd called her up and found out what the score was. I got away from it partly Sunday. Went off to study. I mean, this is about the way it started off last time—when I quit Blue College, I mean. When something like this started, I got this more or less depressive attitude.

C9—Mm-huh.

S10—And then it just started and it continues and there wasn't any stopping. If there was any stopping it, it was because I did something that took my mind off it. I mean, like going to a show or going with the boys or something like that. But as far as sitting down with the books and studying—I mean, you try to concentrate on the books and you can't concentrate. My mind keeps drifting off that way because the subject's there and you want to think about it. So, Sunday afternoon I got away from it more or less and then it came back. Yes, it came back Sunday night. So, after I called up Mary and talked it over with her, why, then I decided I wouldn't call Jane for she would probably find out about it. So then Monday, yesterday, I decided it would be best to call. I went ahead and called, and as I said before I did do most of the talking. About the only thing, she said was that she had been pretty busy as far as studying went, that she was on probation, that she did have a little trouble—I don't know, she came in late one night from a date or something. She was supposed to get three weeks campused for it. But, the thing that gets me is—I don't know why—I shouldn't be that way—but when I hadn't heard from her for a long time, then I received this letter that she wrote from home. She said something about that she had gotten into trouble up at school and she was going to be campused for three weeks. So, when I didn't get any letters after that, I began, the idea of being campused got into my mind and I began to form all kinds of conclusions around why she had been campused. I came to a lot of wrong conclusions, I hope! Before, I didn't even take anything like that into consideration and that's what really got me. The idea that when something like that comes up, it gets you down so much that you are just liable to think almost anything about something like that.

C10—Tends to build up.

S11—Yes.

C11—Well, now—

S12—(*Client interrupts*). So, I think it's pretty well straightened out now as far as—I mean—if I do get a ride up there at Easter, that might give me some trouble there as far as—it's more or less one of those things that I try. It's more or less a must, it should be done, so—. . .

C12—(*Counselor interrupts*). Well, let's go back and look at this thing just a little bit. First of all, the pin has been returned, is that right?

S13—Yes. She returned the pin. That's right.

C13—When you left Blue College?

S14—No when I was up at Blue College we became pinned under funny circumstances. Then we talked it over and I was supposed to go down to X city at Christmas and then suddenly we began to realize that all I was doing was just playing around and having a lot of fun and trying to forget about all this stuff behind me by having this fun, see? So, I finally realized that if this was the real one and I actually wanted to make something of it—in the condition I was, I couldn't do anything about it.

C14—Mm-huh.

S15—So, we never talked too much about it—the idea of my going back. So, this particular weekend we had this party at the fraternity house, and she came up that weekend. Well, having so much fun and being about the last big social event of that particular school year before we went home for Christmas, I began to think about it, so when we got back over to school I told her—previously during the weekend I had told her that I was going down and stay at her house over Christmas. So she was real happy about that so then I began to think it over later in the afternoon and Sunday night when we got back over there. I hit her right between the eyes with the idea. I said, I'm leaving Wednesday. So she got pretty upset about this. So I said, okay, I'll come back over Monday night. Well, this was on Sunday night, so I went back over the following Monday night and we went out and it was about the first time that we had really settled down and talked seriously. She said that she thought it over after I had startled the heck out of her and she said that she had realized that maybe it was a good thing because the sooner I got this thing settled the better it would be for both of us. She said that she thought she would keep the fraternity pin. I came home and I received a lot of letters up until about the middle of January and I wrote a letter and said something about it, that I didn't actually think it was fair for her to be pinned. I wrote this letter and she said something, evidently she got the wrong idea that—wait a minute, how did it go? (*pause*) I wrote her a letter and I said that I didn't think it was right for her to be as serious as she was, or something to that nature and I guess I wanted it. I thought it was only fair so I wrote her this letter and so she sent back something to the same effect. I mean, she said she was thinking about it and she had felt rather bad about going out and having the pin. So then, when she wrote this letter back—I mean—I had originally started this discussion, but when it came back to me, I sort of—I don't know—maybe I was trying to check on her or something like that. But anyway, when it came back to me, I wasn't particularly happy about it. I mean, I had more or less started it but I wasn't particularly happy about it when it came back to me. So when she said something about sending the pin back, instead of taking into consideration exactly what the score was, why, I wrote her back. She'd given me this ring of hers, this class ring. So I wrote her back and said that since she was sending me something back, I should send the thing back that she had given me. So, I wrote back that I should send the ring back. So when she got this letter that said I should send the ring back, because she had sent the fraternity pin back, she became very upset. She sort of thought that I was more or less trying to discontinue it right there and said that wasn't exactly what she wanted. She wanted to keep up the correspondence with me and try and see if we could work something out to get together, but as far as her having my fraternity pin and wearing the fraternity pin, she didn't feel right about it, as far as going out was concerned.

C15—Um-huh.

S16—I mean, that's what I'm trying to drive at—the honest effect that I'm trying to bring in there, the way she was actually honest there.

C16—Um-huh.

S17—And when she received this letter that said I was sending the ring back because she was sending the pin back, why, she thought I was trying to cut it off. I don't know exactly what I had in mind. It just upset me when I received the letter, as a counter letter to my one letter stating about the pin, you see. I don't know exactly what I was thinking when I wrote this letter about sending her ring back. She stated that she didn't think it was a good idea to call it quits and everything like that, that she just sent it back because she didn't feel right keeping it. So then, I wised up to a certain extent after I had read the letter. I mean, after I had a day or two to think it over. I wrote her this letter back and explained what my feelings were exactly on the situation, that I would have liked to have kept her ring and hoped that in the very near future I could get up and more or less straighten things out. And this girl from home that is going up to school up there, that I talked with over the Christmas holiday, she told me that she thought that if I possibly got up there that things could be verified and cleared out and that things could be pretty well established. She thought it was the idea of the two of us getting together again and seeing one another that something could be determined. I didn't know exactly what she based her claims on. I mean, she's been around Jane up at school and she must have some reasons for basing her claims but that is the condition under which the ring was sent back.

C17—Now, how would you define your relationship at that time?

S18—Well,—(*pause*) I think it was reaching a point that I was beginning to be a little bit serious—more serious than I thought I'd been, of course.

C18—Um-huh.

S19—This is my nature—being the way it is now because it's a fouled up thing. I see one thing one way and then I decide that, well—maybe it's the other way.

C19—Um-huh.

S20—So what I wanted to try and figure out was—see, when I came here I didn't know a soul. And as far as dates around here and things like that are concerned, why, I'm very gregarious and I like to be around people and as far as not knowing anyone, and not knowing any girls around town, I wondered if it was because of that lonesomeness that I was feeling that way, see?

C20—Um-huh.

S21—I mean—things just don't happen like that. When you come into a town, it takes time to make connections and meet people and things like that. Now, I have met some people. There is a girl who teaches over at Orange College who lives next door and she and I were out Saturday night. We had a very nice time. We just sat around and talked the entire evening. I mean, it was more or less—an educational—. We were talking about different things, about high school and things like that. I mean, just two people getting together. She was very lonesome Saturday night and I was too. I didn't know her from Adam—so I just happened to call her up. I mean—the people where I'm staying knew her from living next door.

C21—Um-huh.

S22—But, that's what I was wondering—the idea that not knowing people around and being lonesome, and wanting to know people—if that could have some effect on me.

C22—Well, that's possible. I'm not trying to steer away from the things you've just said—but to get this thing into a state where we can analyze it and reorganize it to a point where it has a position in your thinking, would you say that when you started to school here that your relationship with the girl at Blue College had any stability to it? Was it a nebulous sort of an agreement in which there was not real agreement?

S23—Well—

C23—In other words, I just want to find out if you had any kind of an agreement or concreteness to your relationship or whether the two of you had purposely left the thing pretty much up in the air?

S24—Well, exactly what was going to happen, we weren't sure. I mean—when I left to come down here, I didn't have the least idea in the world—I mean (*pause*) I tried something that I had been told is the way to go to school and that is to try to put it into brief form, in as few words as few words as possible—a paragraph you read on factory management or personnel management, or something like that. You take a book and you go through and you more or less outline it. You have something that contains 12 parts and you can write those 12 parts down with a little notation as to what each part stands for. So if you read an ornate type of book where they talk about one type of topic, you put it in one type of paragraph. Well, the ideal way to study is to read that paragraph and after you read the paragraph, try to put the paragraph in as few words as you possibly can. In other words, put in your own words. So, when you go back to review you can read that paragraph and you know exactly about what you meant by what you wrote down there and that more or less brings back what the paragraph contains. So, I've been doing that. It was a job at first to get used to doing that. To sitting down and reading a book like that. Of course, whether it has had any advantage for me, I don't know. That's because I haven't had any opportunity to produce from it, as far as taking tests or quizzes or anything like that.

C24—Um-huh.

S25—And whether it has an advantage, whether I'm getting something out of it or whether I haven't. But, I've been studying at that pretty hard and when I first came down here, from Blue College, something like that seemed the farthest thing possible away from me—as far as actually getting down to studying and figuring out things. However, since I've been here, I've found out that doing that, and making myself do that, has helped me out more. I've gotten more out of the last few weeks of college this year than I have out of school in a long time. Even the driest course has some connection now. I don't care how dry it is, I actually pick something out. Then when the instructor says something about it, I actually recall reading something about it. So that more or less creates an interest in it and that's something that I didn't have before. I mean, I couldn't more or less put my mind down to studying because of the trouble I was having. So consequently I was just drifting around; therefore, I didn't know exactly where the heck I was going.

C25—Um-huh.

S26—I was going in one big circle. So, I think that I'm far enough advanced now that I can say that such-and-such a thing is going to happen. Number one—and there are probably ten little steps from here on. I don't know what two, three, four, five, six, seven, eight and nine and ten are, but I have some idea about one. So that I think that if I could get up there, I think we could more or less decide on something.

C26—Well, now, that's what you want to gain by going there, to come to some definite conclusion?

S27—I think so.

C27—Um-huh.

S28—I mean, ah—

C28—You feel the need, then, to come to some definite conclusion?

S29—I think so, because I think if I don't it might cause me some trouble. Such as this right here.

C29—In other words, when things are left open it has a disturbing effect.

S30—Yes, it does. Quite a bit. I think that I can tell pretty much from the letters. She said that she was going to write last night and I think that I can more or less figure out pretty well from the first letter that I receive quite a bit about the relationship. I was very upset by the—I mean—I more or less gave her the idea. I think that I know somewhat about where I am going now. Previously, as far as trying to figure out things and trying to talk about different things—if there was something bothering me— to say something about it to her—I mean—I didn't do it. I think, for that reason that I didn't know exactly where I was going. But now that I have some idea of exactly where I'm going I also have with it the idea of saying my convictions, of why I think they're that way and telling her things —saying things to her—you know what I mean. Before, whenever I was in that state of going around in circles, why, I just let these things go around in circles. So, I've more or less given her the idea that there is actually something happening there. There's something building up— something solid. I've more or less been able to say things that I probably wouldn't have been able to say before because I wasn't set in my ways. I was in the vicious circle there.

C30—So you feel that you can come to some definite conclusion by going up there?

S31—Well, (*pause*) I don't know exactly if we'll arrive at a very definite conclusion, but I think we will probably be able to, I mean, if we get together up there, the idea of seeing one another again is going to have some effect. As far as my attitude—I mean, as far as more or less explaining myself and trying to straighten things out, I think that will probably have some effect. However, what conclusions we will arrive at, I don't have any idea. I mean—whether we'll both decide that that is enough to build something on, or whether it's something that we can look forward to. I mean, it has definite advantages to look forward to and think about.

C31—In other words, you want to go up to get some reassurance, find out what your status is.

S32—That's probably about it. Yes. Of course, I might find out in the letter—I don't know. As far as going home—well—the family lives out·side the city and after really, truly considering myself as actually working very hard up here, I consider the seven days more or less as quite a big rest period. Well, there isn't particularly anything at home that I care too much for. I mean, as far as seeing my family I go down on weekends and things like that occasionally. But as far as spending seven days, I don't particularly care to spend them out some place where there isn't anything doing. I mean, I feel that after studying pretty hard that these seven days I deserve. This friend of mine at home—he'll be working, so there wouldn't be too much doing down there during the seven days. I have quite a few friends at Blue College. Besides Jane there's this one very good friend of mine and then there's about three or four of my fraternity brothers. So I think that that also has something to do with it, as far as going up there. I mean, it's the idea that you have a certain amount of time, you'd like to spend it where you think you'll have the best time. And I think that I could spend my seven days up there to a greater advantage than I could any place around here. And there's something else, I don't know what bearing it has here, but I was thinking about it. If a letter did come through, stating that there was nothing there anymore, I'd figure, well, there's no reason particularly to go. I received a letter from this one fraternity brother of mine. He lives up there. I was thinking that if I did —if she wrote last night and mailed it today, it would take at least three days to get up here, so I wouldn't probably receive it until Monday or sometime Saturday maybe. If before then, I received some communication from these notices that I've put up, as far as a ride up for the holidays is concerned, I'd probably take it and go on up and stay at a fraternity brother's house. I mean, I'd like to go up to see Jane but—I mean—I'd probably still go up there—whether I'd go see her—whether in the back of my mind the reason for going up would be to be up there where she is and to maybe see her—but—I mean—I was more or less thinking along these circles and I was all fouled up there as far as going up there was concerned. Even if she wrote me a letter and said that there wasn't any- thing to it, I'd still probably go up there if I got a ride because I think that it's a place where I could spend a few days and have myself a lot of fun.

C32—But you'd still try to see her?

S33—(*laughs*) That's what I don't know. I mean—I'd try—I guess—. . .

C33—Um-huh.

S34—I guess, I keep looking. I mean—I don't know whether I'm trying to tell myself there's actually something that—. . . (*pause*)

C34—Well, look at it this way then. You went through this experience with the girl at home. For some reason or other, that didn't work out and, am I correct in assuming that it was rather a strong blow to your pride and upset you pretty much?

S35—Yes, it did.

C35—Okay.—

S36—(*Client interrupts*). Here's the question that is something that has been bothering me. It might be—might be classified as being conceited, but I don't know why I have the feeling at times when I walk down the street that people look at me. I don't know exactly what kind of a— especially females.

C36—Um-huh.

S37—I have some relatives and all I used to hear about when I used to go out to their home to see them was what a fine looking boy I was and they used to introduce me around to all their friends and all that kind of stuff. I was wondering if that had any effect on me as far as—I mean—I feel that females are watching me when I walk down the street. Of course, they're actually not probably. I mean, it's conceit or something, I think.

C37—Then perhaps this rejection and other circumstances are a kind of blow to your pride.

S38—I think very definitely.

C38—And, when we consider the girl at Blue College, is it because of her as an individual, or are you trying to reassure yourself of a position, and trying to say, well, this can't happen to me again. In other words, are you interpreting this in the light of the other? And, just trying to make sure you're not going to go through the same process which is in effect not considering the girl as an individual at all.

S39—That's true.

C39—We all have a certain desire for prestige, recognition, achievement, but when you get too intense along a particular line and get the idea that these things are always going to happen to you, then you can start doing some funny thinking about it. Now, what you want, if possible, is to try to reason out—and I will try to help you with that—is what can you do at Blue College which is going to help the total situation. Do you want at this time to come to a definite conclusion or do you want reassurance merely—that I still have some status here? In other words, is it your own status that you are thinking of, or is it something for the real future? Is it your own status you're afraid of? And that's all. Your own status as concerns the relationship with individual girls. Now you feel, perhaps—

S40—That's a very good point right there.

C40—Let me carry it a little bit further. Am I correct in that you feel that as long as you go out with girls and don't get into any particular kind of attachment that everything is going along fine? You feel secure as long as you don't put out any particular strong attachment, but the minute you do that, you feel that you are putting yourself on the defensive.

S41—Here's a funny thing. This is showing conceit, but it is actually true. The girl that I went with at home—I've always been more or less backward, I suppose, but she actually—did take the first step. I think she actually did and this situation with Jane is about the same thing. I mean, because at the time of the beginning, there wasn't much to it. I mean, as far as I was concerned. And she took more or less the same attitude. But here's something else that I happened to think of. When Mary and I talked over the Christmas holidays, she told me that Jane struck her as being a very simple girl and I said well, what relationship does she want with me and she said that she thought she was quite serious with me. Of course, that was a female talking for a female. But I do put quite a bit of faith in what she says for she's a straight shooter and she's a nice girl. She's the kind of a girl that you'd like for a friend—I mean, to fall back on. She told me that most of the time, whenever Jane came in on a date or something like that she sometimes said that the guy was nice, but Mary said that she thought it was different between Jane and me. However, there didn't seem to be too much. I mean, it was that way. We used to go out. I'd go over and pick her up from her school and we'd go out to this place where all the college kids went out and we'd have to leave there in time to get back before 11:00 o'clock. So, we just went out and she thought I was crazy and I thought she was crazy and we had a lot of fun together. We never did talk serious. So, when I was having a lot of fun it was something that was taking my mind off what exactly had happened previously. I don't know if I've said this—but it is very important. So I'd better say it again. Some fraternity brothers of mine said something about it—that they thought it might be getting serious, my going over there every night. Well, it wasn't getting too serious I thought—for I was more or less taking that attitude to go over there and be in a crowd where I could be out with —be gregarious—be around people. So, it was every night and every time I could get a chance to get over there. (*pause*) And there was one time that came up, this is something else I just happened to think of. During this phase, before things went supposedly serious, when I was going over there every night—why, I wanted to go over and this friend of mine had said he'd loan me his car and he went down town and he didn't come back. So, I had no way of getting over there. So, I was very upset about this. I made my mind up, it was one of those times that I'd made my mind up to do something and I was going to do it. So, I

rented a car off of one of my fraternity brothers. So I got over there. But
up to this point I had been pushing off the idea of going home and trying to straighten this out instead of having a good time. So, I went down,
I had a couple of dates with Jane before Thanksgiving. By the time this
Thanksgiving weekend was over I decided I was going home. So, I had
been telling my fraternity brothers that all the way up to this time and
they said, you'll be here until after the Christmas dance. So I said the
only thing that would keep me here is that if I get pinned tonight! So—
ah—I went over—and up to this point things didn't seem very serious,
but I went over there Wednesday night and I gave her the pin. After
I had given her the pin and tried to explain and everything else, there
wasn't much I could do. I mean, I couldn't explain my actions. I tried
more or less—but I told her it was more or less something to try to—in
other words—build a foundation on it and in the same place use it on
the foundation. Do you get me there?

C41—No.

S42—I mean, something to more or less steady me and settle down and
then use it in turn up here again to build on and continue the base of
the thing. So, ah—

C42—(*Counselor interrupts*) Just a minute! Look—you're talking about
foundations—things on which to build. In other words, you were using
this even at the very beginning, seemingly out of a desire for a certain
sense of security, rather than anything in particular with this girl as
such. I mean, from the beginning that was it.

S43—Right.

C43—From a basic need to assert yourself you felt that need and you
were using that need in trying to find something on which you could
depend.

S44—Yes.

C44—Let's remember that as a motivation.

S45—Um-huh.

C45—You see, we can go back to a statement of fundamentals—desire
for something on which you can stand solidly. You felt from the deal at
home that the props had been knocked out from under you. I want to
get you to think about your motivation in this. The girl seemed to be
secondary.

S46—True—I mean—there is still the idea—I mean—since I have used
her for this purpose is there more there? That's what I'm trying to find
out.

C46—Your basic desire again is going up there for reassurance. And the
point is, can you ever do that without coming to a very hard and fast
set of conclusions? Will you ever have a foundation until some hard and

fast decision is reached? Can you, if it remains as vague as it is now?

S47—Well, here's the thing. If the foundation were built on this—what I'm doing now is all centered around this. If it is kicked out from underneath what's going to happen then? You see, that's something I'll feel. (*pause*)

C47—You mean, your decision to go to school is based on your relationship with the girl?

S48—Quite a bit.

C48—Well, let's see if we can think this thing out. Your decision to go to school—whenever I'm wrong, I want you to correct me because I want to get a complete understanding of this—your decision to go to school has been based somewhat on your relationship with the girl at Blue College.

S49—Uh-huh. Because up to that point I had nothing to base it on. That was the first thing that came along that gave me a chance to base it on. So, consequently, it had to base on that.

C49—But, the relationship was nothing definite and is a rather difficult feeling to explain. There was certainly nothing concrete there with the pins and rings going back and forth. In other words, you're trying to go to school to try to get a degree based on the relationship you can't explain yourself. (*pause*) Reaching out in a desire to build back up a self-esteem which you felt was knocked out from under you. Maybe there's something more behind that, too. In other words, we all have a certain amount of that, but some of us can take quite a beating and still be unaffected. We then ask the question, why in a situation like this should it affect one person more than another? Well, is there something else which increases the desire for security on your part more than other people? (*pause*) I've turned away from the specific to the general—to a more general situation. Now, is there something else you may investigate which makes you more inclined to grab and need a constant reassurance more than someone else? Even further back, behind the thing perhaps something in the home or perhaps not. We all have this very same thing except that you're building it up into an extreme situation. You're going—and again, I'm not putting this out as law—

S50—That's okay.

C50—This is the impression I have from you, that you are going to Blue College to gain reassurance. This reassurance then gives you enough confidence to come back until something else happens when you will need reassurance again.

S51—That's true.

C51—As long as the situation remains undefined, you're always going to be needing it because you can't decide anything in a relationship such as you have, because you have an indefinite relationship. Now then, the other alternative is, to reach a definite relationship. Are you ready to do that? Or have you been building this thing, as we saw before, for a foundation that has little to do with the girl herself?

S52—I think it started out that way.

C52—Now, is there a change? Has it changed only because she has become identified with this situation, not because of something in the girl herself? Or is she representative of the thing you need?

S53—In other words, has she become established here because I realize that I might be losing her? Is that about what you mean?

C53—Um-huh.

S54—There, that's it! That's everything that we've mentioned.

C54—Well.—

S55—Here's what it would be if—I mean—I think it is the way I would explain it to her. The way I feel now in school, I have accomplished quite a bit. However, if my grades are up to what I think they should be, and I decide to stay in engineering, I'd probably go back to Blue College. Because I think I could accomplish something up there then. I mean, if I continue studying the way I am, when I reach the end and actually see that I've accomplished something, I could go back to Blue College and finish up there. This would be okay then, because I would have been up there recently and would know if there was something to it. And, that's about the way I would explain it to her. However, I would tell her that because I'm not sure—I think they're going to come out this way, but then again it might not come out that way. I mean—maybe after studying all this time, I won't make the grades that I think because I'll get excited and quit or something like that from nervousness. I mean, maybe I won't get the grades that I think I'm going to get, but that's about the way I intend to explain it to her. Maybe after this semester, even though I make good grades, I'll decide that I'm not going to return to Blue College. Maybe I'll stay here and go into another field or something like that. I can see the advantages and I'm doing very well so far in school, and getting everything out of it. But as to what I'm going to decide to do through the semester with the counseling and going over the tests and talking like this, I mean, I don't know exactly what it's going to be here.

C55—In other words, what you want is reassurance without giving out anything in return.

S56—That's about it. Ah—it's a heck of a thing to ask.

C56—We're still getting back to the point of whether or not this thing is involved in something more basic than what appears on the surface. That is, the desire for establishing yourself. Something knocked it out from under you, and now you've built this thing up to a point where it's important. And everything that takes place either has an action for or against it, whether it has anything to do with her or not. You have a constant need of reassurance in emotional situations. You should understand that when you go up to Blue College, you want to find out what exactly you can accomplish up there.

S57—That's true.

C57—If you can accomplish a definite decision which will free you of all of these things which are causing you a disturbance and allow you to concentrate and to devote your entire energies towards working in school, that is a desirable thing. You must find out whether or not you want to make that decision in and of itself and not make a decision as a secondary thing merely to bolster up a situation.

S58—In other words, not to be going up there with the idea of getting this reassurance and coming back and then having to go back to be reassured again.

C58—More than that. If you do come to a definite decision, are you ready at this time to come to any decision at all? Is it a desirable situation, that is, are you ready to come to a decision to marry the girl when you are not sure that the total situation took place because of her as an individual in the first place? Now—

S59—(*Client interrupts*) What do you exactly think? If I were to go up there and find out that there is actually nothing there—do you think it would help me to some extent to continue with this foundation even though I have already felt that she's been part of the construction as far as actually going on from there, do you think that there's any advantage to be derived from my trip up there?

C59—Well, that's the thing I've been trying to talk through with you, whether there is any advantage to going up there at all. If there is an advantage, you must try to define it. What can you accomplish?

S60—In other words, what am I going up there for? I'd just be—

C60—What can you do which is going to help *you*, or help you and Jane? What can you do together? Is it possible for you to do *anything*?

(*An additional five minutes of the interview took place during which the client rendered no definite decision regarding his trip. Another appointment was made.*)

THIRD INTERVIEW

(*7 Days after Second Interview*)

C1—How are you today?

S1—Oh, pretty good.

C2—I certainly hope this weather keeps up.

S2—It is nice.

C3—Have you made up your mind about going to Blue College?

S3—Well, Friday evening, I received a call from a girl on campus here. She and her fiancé were thinking about driving up. I never did hear from this girl up at Blue College. But, like I was saying before, regardless of whether anything comes up or not, as far as my going up there—if I get the chance—I still think I'll go up just for the vacation. And, as far as I can see, I could probably have just as much fun up there as I could anywhere else. I could have just as much fun there if not more as I could have at home or any place else as long as my friends are there. As far as traveling, I get quite a kick out of that.

C4—You think it'll be well worth the expense then ?

S4—I do. As far as spending much money up there—I wouldn't spend very much. I'd either be staying at this girl's house or else I'd be staying at one of my fraternity brother's. So as far as the overhead is concerned, there won't be much overhead. So, I don't know, she said she was going to write last, last Monday, after I'd called her and since I've talked to you. She claimed she was going to write a letter Sunday night, so I've been waiting around for the letter. The last letter I received from her had an error in the address. So I keep telling myself that she had probably put down the wrong address. Yesterday I walked back to the house after my 9:30 class—the mail comes in about quarter to ten to ten-thirty, something around there, so I figured I'd walk back out to the house.

C5—You felt the letter would be fairly important.

S5—Yes. When I got out there—why—the idea of receiving a letter— that's what caused a lot of the trouble. I mean, putting a lot of faith in these letters, you know, and I'd think, well, a letter will probably come today and thinking how great the letter is going to be and all that sort of stuff and taking that big trip out here, all the way, and having these high hopes, and then when you get out there there's no letter. It just gets to bothering me.

C6—Mm-huh.

S6—I noticed that until this came up, I hadn't been having any trouble as far as this depressive feeling, but here lately, for no particular reason at all—it's like hot and cold running water which you keep turning off and on. I mean—something comes up and it might be a nice day out and I'll step outside and sag. (*pause*) Of course, everyone has depressive feelings, but—I mean—it's just like taking two faucets and turning one on and then the other one on. First you turn the hot on and it feels real warm and then bingo!—all of a sudden the cold comes on. It just cuts it all off.

C7—For no apparent reason!

S7—For no apparent reason. It feels like it. I could be thinking about something and well, it doesn't seem to have too much to do with anything in particular, just in general, and then something will come up. Just sort of tears down this principle here. I mean—it doesn't, I mean—I guess it's sort of a rationalization, more or less. Something might come up that doesn't seem very important—seems all right—seems to be working perfectly—in good working condition and then all of a sudden—rationalize something out here and bring it into it and it starts to tear it down. Five minutes later it's all right and then something else will come in and then —I mean—I've been trying to put my finger on it, but I can't. I haven't had this trouble until this little episode started and it doesn't seem like the things that happen have anything to do with it. I mean, as far as sitting down and studying, why, sometimes it just doesn't go too well and previous to this I didn't have very much trouble.

C8—Mm-huh.

S8—So, I don't know. I've been thinking quite a bit about what you said the last time—as far as whether she is actually part of it or not. And, I think that probably she isn't. I think that if I were to go up there—I could find out by being up there whether she is some part of it or not. I think that while I was up there that I could settle this as far as—I mean —the idea is like you said before—as far as going up there, getting satisfaction, establishing myself, coming back at the least little thing that happens is silly. Well, I think that I should probably go up there. The way my intentions are now, I could, more or less, cut it off—stop it. If I found out when I got up there that I could, I'd be pretty sure of myself then. Then, as far as this joking around and kidding about it, I mean, not willing to think about it or take it into too much consideration, I realize that that's not very good because if it does come up from time to time, it's going to cause trouble. So that if I do go up here it's going to be cut and dried—period! I mean, I'll have to arrive at some decision, satisfactory to both of us.

C9—Well, can you?

S9—I think I can. I mean, the way I look at it now is in its more or less true light as far as actually the way it was. And, after an explanation— I mean, some talking about it—so far there's nothing tangible there to put your hand on. Therefore, if because it is this reassurance, and because this reassurance can cause so much trouble, to go up there and find out if I can actually say, more or less, because of this reassurance that's why we shouldn't place anything on it. And, I think if I do decide on that, I mean—it's in my mind that that's about the way the situation is. Now, if I get up there it might change, and I think if it changed it would be for the better.

C10—Well, let's try to identify "for the better." What would be a situation that you would consider to be for the better?

S10—Well, (*sigh*) that would have to take into consideration quite a few things. (*pause*) My intention right now, as I was saying before, is that probably the best thing for me to do would be to cut it off. If I do get up there and find out that I can't cut it off and I realize that it isn't just some sort of infatuation, and that when I do make a decision, I'd have some basis for a decision, as far as the specifics of the thing goes. How exactly it would be worked out is—that's going to be quite a job. I mean, what I'll try to do, is have a real honest-to-goodness talk about it and try to arrive at some conclusion as to how to work this out. It's like we were saying the last time, it's more or less upon the girl. (*pause*)

C11—Let's see. Now at this time does *she* feel the need to work it out? You see, people have to have a reason or a need to do things and *you* have a reason and a need, but does *she?* I mean, is she in a situation where working it out isn't particularly important to her one way of the other?

S11—Well, that's what I don't know.

C12—Now, is this a pattern that is typical of a girl of her age? She'd react no differently than any other girl of her age would react, in all probability.

S12—Yes, that's true.

C13—Now, I'm not predicting on this, one way or the other. But you feel a need at this time for coming to something rather definite because that gives you a feeling of security, and without the security you seem to have some difficulties in continuing in any straight line of action. Now, the thing we want to try to consider is, why is this need in you any more than it is in other fellows your age? Well, on the surface we can turn it back to this other situation that took place with the nurse. Maybe we can find out something there that will show up something more basic. What was it that took place then beneath the surface that seemed to build this thing up? You said, I believe, that prior to that time nothing of this nature had ever occurred to you.

S13—Well, there's one thing about that thing with the nurse. I even told her this the last time that I saw her. She is about—well—she is the sweetest girl I've ever met. I mean, she is well-liked by everyone. She has a wonderful personality and that was what was so hard. I mean, the complete change-over from when everything was fine and was sweet to when things started to tear it down, I mean, Dr. Jekyll and Mr. Hyde routine, more or less.

C14—Mm-huh.

S14—She has that—that split personality.

C15—You feel that she actually made a complete shift.

S15—That's right. When she has no particular use for anybody—it's that complete shift from one side to the other. And, that was what was really hard to take—more than anything else—outside of the—I mean —I knew it was there—more or less—but the idea of it actually coming up—

C16—Mm-huh.

S16—That was the part that was really hard to take.

C17—How did this actually occur, then?

S17—Well, let's see, when I was up at Blue College she came up for the fall house party and things, and that was about the first time that I realized there was anything serious there.

C18—Um-huh.

S18—Up until that point she had been very serious and I hadn't been serious. But I had been very truthful and told her that I wasn't serious. Well, after the house party, she went back home. And, I had one heck of a good time—that is when the trouble first started—right there—when she left. I couldn't study. I used to just sit around and look out of the window and things like that.

C19—Mm-huh.

S19—I was going fairly well in my studies up to that time and after that I just wasn't worth a thing. In fact, out of six courses, I withdrew from two, I flunked two and I passed two. Let's see, I passed one with a D and one with a C. But I just shot the entire semester. Well, that's when the trouble really started.

C20—When she came to Blue College?

S20—Yes, I mean, then I really got the word. I found out—

C21—Let's see if I understand this. What do you mean by "getting the word?" I want to be sure I understand it all.

S21—In other words, that's when I found out that I was actually in love with the girl.

C22—I see.

S22—I mean, I had never had that feeling before.

C23—You never had this feeling before?

S23—No.

C24—Was there anything said during that period that would give you an indication that she did not feel that way while she was at Blue College?

S24—No. Things were very nice. We had a very swell time that weekend. We had a lot of fun. We hadn't seen one another since the middle of September. So, she had been very serious up to that time and I had, as I said before, not been very serious and I have been very truthful about it, which I had never done before! She left on a Sunday afternoon, and, we had a really swell time. I didn't stop to take into consideration exactly what was going on. After she left, I began to realize that I felt awfully lonely and I thought it was just perhaps the idea of having a good time that weekend—kind of a let down after it's all over. So, I began to think about it. Maybe it could be and maybe it couldn't. We'll wait and see. She was flying back and the weather got pretty bad and she was forced down. She had to stay overnight.

C25—Mm-huh.

S25—She called about three o'clock and she told me she had been forced down and—I mean—that mutual attraction was there. You could feel it on both ends. It was on both ends of the phone. I didn't know what exactly to do. I was thinking about borrowing this buddy's car of mine and going up there. If I had, I'd probably be married and have six kids today. But I didn't go up. Then when she got back home, all the rest of the week, it started to hit me hard. I just couldn't take any more, so I walked into the Dean's office and talked about withdrawing from school. Well, something like this had never happened to me before. When it hit, it really hit hard. So I figured, well, I'm going back home. We had a few talks and he finally convinced me that I should stay and I talked to her on the phone a few times. My phone bill for one month was over $25.00. When I look back on all of that stuff now—(*laughs*) So he talked me into staying. A relative of mine was getting married over a holiday and he had written me about coming home and being best man. So I took money out of my bank account and bought myself an airplane ticket. I figured I'd leave early. I didn't have much of an interest in school at that time, so I decided I'd get out as soon as I could. The main reason I went home was to see this girl. I mean, the wedding was more or less secondary, but it was a good excuse to go home, as far as I was concerned.

C26—At that time, did you look upon it as an excuse?

S26—I considered it an excuse at that time. As I explain here, you'll see that the wedding didn't have too much bearing on it. I got in on a Saturday afternoon, and she met me at the airport. Well, she lived in one town and I lived in another, but I'd gone to school up there and I knew a lot of fellows up there so we went up to her home. We went out that night. I stayed up at one of the lodges. I stayed for about three days— and I didn't even tell my family or anything. They didn't particularly care for that. I finally came home about Wednesday or Thursday. They finally got wind that I'd been around that long and hadn't called or anything and they were pretty mad about it. It started Betty off on a bad foot with the family, I guess.

C27—Um.

S27—They didn't particularly care for her. Of course, my father is— well, he's a very, very—not *too* strict—but he pays quite a bit of attention to his religion. And, Betty's mother has been divorced. He doesn't particularly care for it and it wasn't her fault. I mean, two people if they're serious—it's their life to lead and plan out and not anybody else's. I didn't worry about that too much—but then we got in there on Thursday, and they were supposed to have a party for me at this one girl's house, Friday night. And my relative was getting married Saturday morning and he told me if I wanted to be the best man, please be down here on Saturday morning. Have a good time, but do me a favor, and be at the wedding on time. So, I said, okay. And we went up to the party Friday night. We had a pretty good time at the party, all the kids I knew from school were out there. We stayed till about three o'clock and ate and got ready to go back for the wedding. So, I got down there on time, but I wasn't ready to go to the wedding. I was tired from the party, not getting much sleep. He helped me get ready to go to the wedding. (*laughs*) I was supposed to be the best man and he helped me to get ready for the wedding. Took a few years to forget about it, but finally forgot it. But, he wasn't too happy about it. I realize how stupid I was *now*—the way I acted, but that just goes to show you how things were then. I mean the importance of the wedding as far as I was concerned.

C28—Mm-huh.

S28—So, it was at that point that I told her how I felt. I mean—she had known exactly from the phone conversation and the way I was acting, how I felt. We decided that I'd go back up to Blue College and finish out this semester and maybe next semester. See how things worked out. So, I went back after the weekend—the Thanksgiving vacation. I stayed up there until Christmas and I came home Christmas and—I pulled a similar deal over Christmas. I don't think I came in early, but I spent most of the time up at her home and I didn't let my family know when I came in. That went over like a lead balloon. I spent almost all of my time with her over Christmas time. We had a good time. We didn't ever talk too seriously about things. We let everything take its own natural course. We figured we'd wait and see. So, I finished out the semester and I didn't do too well. So the next semester I was on probation. Next semester I devoted quite a bit of time to study, but I couldn't seem to get any place at all. But, I was taking this beating all the time and Betty is a funny sort of a girl, she—

C29—Now, wait a minute. Let me identify this again. At that time you had some idea that things were not going too well?

S29—Well, up until Christmas time, everything was fine.

C30—Mm-huh.

S30—I went back and finished out the semester and I had intended to go home between semesters but, I changed my mind and I thought—well, the best thing to do is not to go home. I didn't have too much time and

I figured it would cost too much money, so I thought I would stay up there. But things were all right as far as the correspondence—there were plenty of letters. Things seemed to be going okay. There wasn't any indication of things—a lot of letters written and everything else up until Easter. Well, at Easter time I found this fellow who was thinking of driving home over Easter.

C31—Mm-huh.

S31—Betty was supposed to meet me.

C32—Mm-huh.

S32—She has her own car and she drove out to pick me up. Well, things were still peachy then, it was at Easter time and there were no indications that anything was wrong. We had a good time over Easter. So, I went on back up and, I don't know just exactly how long after that, things didn't seem to do too well. Letters sort of dropped off and—the spring house party was coming up. I decided rather than try to get her to come up—she didn't have a heck of a lotta money. So, she didn't come up and I tried to call her one night. I remembered this one night in particular. I couldn't get in touch with her. What I was trying to do—there were two fellows and Betty had her own car so I thought if I could work a deal where I could get maybe two other fellows that had girls from home and wanted them to come up to the house party—since Betty had her own car, maybe they could make some sort of a deal. So, I called her about it. This one particular night that I called, she wasn't home. She was out with somebody. I wasn't too happy about it, but I thought there was no real reason why she should sit at home. But, when I did finally get in touch with her she told me she didn't think it would work out— as far as coming up. That's when I began to think. The letters started getting behind, and, oh, it started giving me quite a bit of trouble. I got through the semester and made poor grades. As soon as I got through with school, I packed up and I got back home as fast as I could. When we first got together I could tell something was wrong.

C33—Mm-huh.

S33—It was just that there wasn't any particular interest any more as far as she was concerned. At first—I mean—to me she seemed that way. She has a wonderful personality and she's very well liked. She isn't attractive, she's very homely, but she can get almost any man she wants. I've seen it happen since we broke up. I've been around town there and I've *seen* it happen. I mean—everyone considers himself fairly great. I consider myself fairly great. She got me—so she got somebody great. I could see it coming on and it had never happened before. So—I thought well, this *can't* be. So I fought like a silly fool to hold on. And that's what made it worse. I kept on trying to hold her and I just couldn't do it. And, I tried to hold on to her and that's when I recall I had trouble. I just kept coming back for more. And, as I was saying before on this Dr. Jekyll and Mr. Hyde routine—well, I started to get Mr. Hyde.

C34—Mm-huh.

S34—I started to fight to hold on to her. I kept getting the bad side and it kept getting worse. *Boy,* I really led a dog's life. I remember one time in particular. I've never been so worked up in all my life. I let everything go and at that time she had been doing nothing as far as work and everything was concerned. She had gone to a girl's school for a year I think. Then she had transferred to Maroon College.

C35—That's where you met her?

S35—Yes. Well, we went together, then about—oh—I'd say not too long after— I'd—well—I'd had a bad crush on this other girl. This goes even further back. She was a really beautiful blonde and her father was in charge of some company. So we had corresponded all through the remainder of high school and, they had moved back East and I'd never been able to see this girl.

C36—Mm-huh.

S36—So that was what made me look for a school in some part of the country where I could see this girl. And that was partly the reason that I went East to Blue College because of this girl. I mean, Betty knew about it, she wasn't too particularly happy but I told her. I had been up to see this girl even before I met Betty. This was a love-life—sort of in a series like. You end up with one and you pick up with another one. Whether it's serious or not, it doesn't make much difference. I mean, it just runs along more or less in a string. So, I had been East over Thanksgiving, the fall before I had met Betty. So things didn't go too well up there. I realized that there wasn't anything there, but I still intended to go up to Blue College. Well, I went up there knowing that there wasn't anything doing as far as that goes.

C37—And you felt that way, too?

S37—Yes.

C38—Mm-huh.

S38—Let's see now—then, when I came back Betty hadn't done anything —she'd gone to school for a year and a half—but as far as any other plans, why she hadn't made any. Her mother and her father both worked. And her mother gave Betty anything she wanted. I mean, she had a lot of clothes, and wore them well, too.

C39—Mm-huh.

S39—Her mother gave her spending money. She didn't work, until finally she did get a job. So that fall that I went up to Blue College she had taken this job and she was really nuts about the job. But, I mean, as far as any plans in her life—she hadn't made any serious plans. So she went ahead—and—I don't know—something happened. I don't think it was her fault. I never really found out about it. But something happened and they laid her off. I don't think they needed her or something like that. She was pretty broken up about it. That happened later in the spring sometime and whether that had any effect on our relationship, I don't know. But then she began to decide that she was going into nurse's training. Her family decided to take a trip at that time. They decided to go West and visit some friends. Well, we had a big argument just before she left and I told her, well, you decide while you're out there. And I thought at the time that it wouldn't affect me—as far as her being gone. Well, as soon as I got home I found out that it did.

C40—Well, we've got several things here. Let's take the last one of this series you mentioned here. One, the Dr. Jekyll and Mr. Hyde business, could you trace that possibly to her decision to go into nurse's training. In other words, she had an interest here which was over and beyond you. Prior to this time she'd been doing very little of anything that had any particular purpose, and then she began to see something that she really liked as far as work was concerned, starting when she began working in the office. She made a decision to go into nurse's training and that seemed to consume a good portion of her time. That in itself left little, in terms of her immediate plans, for you.

S40—Well, see, here's the thing on that. At the time—there was this friend that she knew, a fellow she knew from school. We used to double date with him all the time.

C41—Mm-huh.

S41—They were always crazy about boating and we used to go up to the lake and he took out this girl friend of Betty's and they were always good buddies. And, Bill evidently caught some of this sweetness from Betty. I mean, he began to think—well, maybe there is something there as far as I'm concerned.

C42—Mm-huh.

S42—Maybe I'm interested. So he began to take her out quite a bit. When she began, she wasn't under too much of an impression that there was anything there.

C43—Mm-huh.

S43—But there was just something that she thought, well, I'll just toy around with him a little bit and see if there is something. I don't think that she ever really was under the impression that there was anything there, but they went out quite a bit and he gave her his fraternity pin and she wore it for a while. Well, that was my competition. I mean, the thing was—when I looked at it afterwards—I had really stooped to a complete low.

C44—Mm-huh.

S44—Because I was willing to share her with somebody else, just in order to hold on to her, see?

C45—Was it in order to hold on to her, or was it to keep your status as a "ladies' man," as you had always thought of yourself?

S45—Yeah, that's what I always tried to chalk it up to. I've never been sure. But a lot of people told me that—I have a sister-in-law that's a pretty smart old chick. She always did tell me, well, you like Betty, but you also like yourself quite a bit. She always told me, "the only thing wrong with you is your pride's hurt."

C46—Mm-huh.

S46—Well, it was really here, then, and I can realize that. I don't *like* to look at it that way, but I can realize that because I can see. I mean, it wasn't so bad, the idea of losing out.

C47—Mm-huh.

S47—But the idea of losing out and then turning around and losing again. It was my own fault because I tried to hold on, and I turned around and lost out umteen times. That was the idea that took me so long to finally wise up. But when I did come back, I had intended to go to school in my hometown and I thought that with the two of us in school we wouldn't probably have much time.

C48—Mm-huh.

S48—And that way we could both be serious about things. I sort of took things seriously. I got to the point where I intended to finish up school just a little bit before she did, see?

C49—Mm-huh.

S49—I'd go to White University to graduate from there. Get my degree in industrial engineering from there. So, I really began to plan quite a few things. But all this time I was just getting further and further away. I wasn't making any progress. I wasn't even staying in one position. At the end of it, I was just shifting back further in the negative direction.

C50—Well, let's go back and look at this a little bit. When you first started going with her, you mentioned that she seemed to be a little more serious than you were. That you were just having a lot of fun. The minute you began to put yourself in a serious position, then things started to change somewhat. The same thing seems to have happened to the other girl right now. It's all in the same line. As long as things are going well you're not too serious, but as soon as things start to drift away from you a little bit, then it starts to bother you, even though you yourself have structured it, or outlined or organized it, in a not too serious sense. You, up to this time, had been successful with girls as far as the relationship would go. And you probably got recognition for this, but the minute that reputation is going to be challenged, you want to protect yourself and your own reputation. Now, is it possible that everything you've been doing has been to preserve that reputation?

S50—Yes. Well, the only thing is that (*pause*) with Betty it was, was a lot different than it is with—I mean—I see it, as you say. I mean—I can see it very clearly—as I also can see other things when I walk out of this office.

C51—Mm-huh.

S51—I know about what the feeling is, and I believe that I can differentiate now between that feeling.

C52—Mm-huh.

S52—Just a feeling of wanting to still establish myself.

C53—Mm-huh.

S53—It does seem that that is the way. But the thing that is going to be hard for me to do, if I do go up to Blue College, is to get this idea out of my mind— the worrying about trying to establish myself as a male.

C54—Mm-huh.

S54—Unless I can definitely establish something there and know that there is some feeling, I'll try to hesitate from doing that, because I realize that even if I do find out that there is some feeling there, I'm still inconveniencing myself because if I come back here and I do have that feeling, I know what it's like because I went through it before.

C55—Mm-huh.

S55—I mean, she's up there and I'm down here and even if I find out that I think quite a bit of her and all, it's still an inconvenience to be so far away from someone you like. So, that's why I think that if I do go up there I have enough sense now and I realize what the situation is. I'm not going to fool around and—I mean—I don't *think* I will. There's always that idea in the back of my mind that I might, but I actually can see it now.

C56—Mm-huh.

S56—And, as far as my going up there, I'll try my hardest to stay away from it, as far as trying to establish myself, get into position again and put myself up on a little pedestal.

C57—Mm-huh.

S57—Assure myself that I'm up there and come on back. I mean, someone's liable to bump that pedestal and I'll fall off. But that's the one thing —that I'm going to try to stay away from if I do go up there.

C58—But if you come back with some feeling of having established a degree of security, then you may feel that something has to be done.

C58—Yes.

C59—Let's look at the pattern that has gone on and try to get its possible significance. I'd like to investigate this matter further and perhaps we can take it up again next week, that is, if I see you before you leave.

S59—Mm-huh.

C60—People have very basic needs. One basic need is the need for security. Now, we've talked about that, but I'm going to approach it from a slightly different angle. Let's look at the pattern. Now, you have been trying to manipulate yourself for some time to gain security. Now, what we want to find out is, why do you feel the need to do that? You left one school to go to Blue College in order to try to bring to a head something that was very nebulous that took place when you were 18. You then manipulated yourself back home to find out about something. You then went back to Blue College and received another set-back and then you came all the way back here again and now you want to go back there again. You are constantly manipulating yourself in order to gain a sense of security. Now, is there something, perhaps, in your basic environment which did not satisfy that need for security and you're trying to make up for it in other ways? I'm referring, perhaps, to something within your own home environment.

S60—Well, here's a very important point. My entire college career has been on my own. I mean, the G. I. Bill has helped out and, I had never, never in my life been around in circles. I mean—really not wealthy circles—but semiwealthy circles, until I met this friend of mine up at school. I mean it's a position I like *very* much.

★ The client brings up a very crucial point. His difficulty with interpersonal relationships have a deeper base and more significant meaning than is ordinarily the case. Here the client is indicating what his real motivation is in terms of going about with the various girls. This is of major concern to the client and is a major point in the whole case. A few responses later the client begins to see that even with Betty his general motivation was the same as with the other girls.

C61—Mm-huh.

S61—Jane is in such a position. She lives in a well-to-do section.

C62—Mm-huh.

S62—The wealthiest people live out around that section. Now, I like to place myself—I can talk to people like that and I get a bigger kick—I mean— I'm very gregarious to begin with—I enjoy something like that much more because I've never had the opportunity for that.

C63—Mm-huh. Your family has never been able to give you that?

S63—That's right. I mean, as far as my plane, I live in such and such a plane. I live in a nice neighborhood and things like that. I've always had plenty to eat and things like that, but as far as getting out of your social status, getting up into another social status and meeting people and knowing how important people are and how wealthy people are— I mean—I do look at it at times, from the crude angle as far as the dollar and cents value there. But the reason I try to win or hold on to the plane, I guess, when I've thought about it, is that even if there is nothing doing there, she still is the medium there for me to meet people.

C64—Mm-huh.

S64—It's a crude way of looking at it. I don't consider it too bad in a way, because as long as I'm truthful about it, I think that is something that is very important because I have a gift of gab.

C65—Mm-huh.

S65—I can talk to people and I like to go to parties like that—cocktail parties—where important people are and talk to them. That is quite a bit the reason that I'm going up there. That's why I also look at not so much importance as far as she is concerned in my opinion, if there is nothing up there as far as she is concerned.

C66—Mm-huh.

S66—But this friend of mine comes from a very wealthy family and there's another fellow that—he's in a different fraternity, but he and I are great buddies. He comes from a very wealthy family and most of the people I know up there are in this plane that I like so much.

C67—Mm-huh. And you're trying to get out of the general level of social environment that is represented by your family.

S67—That's right.

C68—Mm-huh. And that's where you feel insecure as far as your total goals are concerned, just within your own circle.

S68—Betty—I mean—I didn't—I looked at Betty from a different angle. I actually was in love with the girl. What I would derive from that relationship was altogether different, see?

C69—But it was still something that went towards security even though it was of a different sort?

S69—That's right to a certain extent. She knew some fairly wealthy people. But, it might be directly because of that. I mean—because she had a such a wonderful personality, she was so well liked that she could gain entrance to those circles, see?

C70—Mm-huh.

S70—So, far as that is concerned, she was a definite asset. It could be that there, too.

C71—Well, I think we're getting down to something that may be a little more basic now and perhaps give you an opportunity to view it in this rational plane rather than on some emotional plane and—

S71—(*Client interrupts*) I can think of quite a few good points at this stage. I mean I've tried to keep away from this feeling, but—you're supposed to have a lot of respect for your mother and father. Well being in this plane—being with these people—I wonder what effect it would have on me. I try to say, I don't have the opportunity, but it could happen I don't think the opportunity will present itself, but it might some day. But as far as that social plane, that higher social plane being up there and me being down here, it appeals to me more.

C72—Mm-huh.

S72—And those people up there don't know anything about it. Well, my family's in that social plane.

C73—Mm-huh.

S73—And there is still some idea of, do I want people to meet my family? I mean—they don't—there's nothing *wrong* with them.

C74—Mm-huh.

S74—But, what reaction do people have towards my family? If I sat down to think it out, I'd probably arrive at some conclusion. If things ever did get serious enough to me, I'd probably go ahead with it, with Jane—I probably look at the bad end of things. I look for what her reaction would be if she met my family. Of course, I don't know anything about her family, other than that they're fairly wealthy. I mean, I know very little about her. That's why I'd like to go up and find out things about her family. I might find that we have things in common—I don't know—you see?

C75—That feeling of not knowing again, is a thing that doesn't contribute to any stability.

S75—Mm-huh.

C76—Let's start off on that particular point next time, that is, the relationship of the way you feel toward your family and towards your environment prior to even entering college and see what relationship we can see there and what has been going on during this time. Maybe we can—

S76—I think that—yeah—I think we can.

C77—Well, I think that perhaps until Easter my office will be just the way it has been.

S77—I'll make the appointment for—how much time do you have Tuesday? I mean—that would probably be the last time—Tuesday and Thursday afternoon of next week.

C78—That's right.

S78—And then the following week I'd be leaving, see?

C79—Yes.

S79—You want to make both those times or do you think once would be enough?

C80—Well, that's entirely up to you. Let's make it for this Thursday, because I want to get in a pattern of having these sessions on Thursday.

S80—Okay.

C81—Then, if you want to come in on Tuesday, that will be perfectly all right, and up to you.

S81—Okay, I'll do that, then. I'll make the appointment, and then if there's anything before this Thursday, why, I'll—

C82—Yes, feel perfectly free to call me.

FOURTH INTERVIEW

(9 *Days after the Third Interview*)

C1—How're you this morning?

S1—Oh, pretty good, if I didn't have this quiz at 4:00 o'clock.

C2—You have a 4:00 o'clock quiz, have you?

S2—Yeah. (*laughs*)

C3—What's that in?

S3—Industrial Management. Took one the other day. Made me so mad when I got it back. I made—well, the class average was about 70, and I made an 80 on it. I had all the theory right, made a few arithmetical errors, really gets you down. (*laughs*) Especially in a course like that where you have the theory right and then make some—

C4—You still got a good grade on it though, didn't you?

S4—Mm-huh, 80. So, I guess it's not too bad.

C5—Well, how have things been going otherwise?

S5—Well, pretty good. I have had no correspondence.

C6—Mm-huh.

S6—I wrote this buddy of mine that I told you about staying at his place. But I never did hear from him so it's hanging in the wind. I've got a ride definitely, this one fellow's wife is up there and he'd like to get up to see her, so he put up a notice. He has quite a few fellows that want to go.

C7—Mm-huh.

S7—So the trip would be pretty reasonable.

S8—But, I don't know, I don't think I'll go unless I have some place to stay up there and he might be doing something or going some place else. So, it might be on the verge of falling out, as far as going up there, I mean. I don't know for sure. I should receive a letter by Monday. I think I'll just tell this fellow to forget about it and go home over the holidays—

take off and go some place. I don't know where—but—if it's good weather we're liable to end up in California or some place. (*laughs*)

C9—You don't particularly care about going back home?

S9—Well, there's nothing to do, as far as I'm concerned. The family lives outside the city and it's right out in God's country. There isn't a thing to do out there.

C10—Um-huh.

S10—Of course, there'll be plenty to do through the day, little odds and ends around the house. But the only thing I have against that is that at night you're out there stranded and you can't do anything about it. No place to go around there unless you go down to the local pub and not too much life. I can't see going down there.

C11—Mm-huh.

S11—There's a lot of stuff to do around the house as far as helping my father. I'll probably spend a couple days in town unless something comes up. And then I take off and go some place. I don't know where. So— generally things seem to be coming along pretty good.

C12—How do you feel about the situation of not having heard from the girl?

S12—Quieted down—quite a bit.

C13—Mm-huh.

S13—Certain days I tell myself, well, today there's going to be a letter. And, I didn't get a letter so I—finally resolved myself that there's nothing there.

C14—Mm-huh.

S14—But even being nothing there, I hate to have loose ends hanging— without having any decision of any kind. Not hearing from her, I imagine she put two and two together and ended it up and got four, see?

C15—Mm-huh.

S15—I imagine that's what it is. She figures, well, what difference does it make, there's nothing doing here. Let's just forget about it. She probably gets a big kick out of these letters I write. I sit down and I tell myself, okay, let's really pour it out. And I put down a lot of nothing and that's about all it consists of.

C16—Mm-huh.

S16—But, she's treated me pretty square, so if I go up, there's only one thing that I'd like to do. She started to knit a pair of socks for me—and I had this happen once before—I was supposed to get a pair of socks from this girl and she was kind of a slow knitter, but, before the socks were completed we broke up. 'Course I didn't have anything to hold over her head. Now, this gal, I've got her ring, I'm going to get those pair of socks, if it's the last thing I do. (*laughs*)

C17—Socks are becoming a symbol for this, are they?

S17—Yes, I guess so. I asked her to knit a pair of socks before Christmas. I talked to this one girl friend of hers and evidently she had trouble with socks. Socks were similar to pins being exchanged as gifts. Pins stick friendship and pearls bring tears—and there was some reaction there with socks that she was afraid of, see?

C18—(*laughs*)

S18—She didn't want to knit socks after that so after Christmas she told me the reason she wouldn't knit me socks was because at the time I asked it was pretty close to Christmas and she thought that she'd like to give them to me for Christmas, but she didn't have enough time to knit them by Christmas.

C19—Mm-huh.

S19—But the other girl, when we were going together—let's see, I even paid for the packs that contained the wool, if I'm not mistaken. I *know* I paid. We were down town one day and I had a few bucks in my pocket that was burning a hole, so she saw this nice little knitting bag. So I thought, well, things look like they're going to last for a long time here and we'll just put these socks into mass production.

C20—(*laughs*)

S20—So, I thought, well, that's not bad. Just think, boy, you got yourself two pair of socks, why you gain another time as much as you put in it. I figure a good pair of argyle socks worth about three bucks, so I figured, well, I'll put three and a half in this little knitting case, you know, and it'll pay dividends some time later on. I never did get the socks, see? Well—

C21—Lost your investment.

S21—Yes sir! Three and a half down the drain—period! So, I figured that I have an investment. Well, I don't exactly have an investment, but I have collateral on this other deal here. I have collateral commonly known as a ring, so, I'd like a pair of socks. Of course I would like very much to see the girl and get this thing definitely straightened out—

C22—Mm-huh.

S22—But she'd probably tell me to take the ring and keep it, if I wrote her a letter and said, well, when you send the socks I'll send the ring. (*laughs*) That wouldn't be too nice when you get right down to it, I guess. I mean, generally speaking, I think it would be a good idea if I get a chance to go up there because, as I was saying before, unless I could decide on something other than just this wishy-washy deal. I mean, if I went up there and found that there was actually something there to base it on why, then okay. But, I realize that there isn't anything there so, I think if I went up there and I found out that there wasn't anything concrete, I wouldn't say, well, let's carry it out a little further here. I mean, I think I'd just say, well, let's forget about it.

C23—Mm-huh.

S23—And from her general action, I think that's about the idea that she has. So, I don't think I'd be getting myself in any dutch by going up there.

C24—Let's get on to this point of basing your school work and your plans for your own career on something. Do you feel that that is necessary?

S24—Mm-huh. (*pause*) It doesn't seem to have too much of an interest any other way. I guess it all goes back to the idea of being in a little world of my own and thinking that I'm a little tin god up on a pedestal. So everything I've thought about was consequently around me. My education was me and everything else, but since I've realized that somebody kicked that pedestal and I fell off the pedestal—it's just not me any more. Before, when I tried to base this all upon myself I had some reason for it, I thought, and then I found out that I didn't have that reason because of what happened, so I have to look around for something else. And, ah, I think that, that is to be derived from some relationship. I mean, a showing of mutual interests and the planning of something that you choose for—

C25—Mm-huh.

S25—Getting out of school and things like that—that's about the way I look at it.

C26—Mm-huh. Well, you don't feel then, that you can base this on something in the future without a particular individual in mind? In other words, to base it just on your own future knowing that some other individual who is unknown at this time will enter into it in the future?

S26—Well, I don't know, to be truthful about that. I *might* be able to, but I'm not really positive.

C27—Mm-huh.

S27—That's one thing—one of the few places where I'm not positive. I'm not *really* positive. It might be possible—ah—I think it would be possible if I could find something that I could really put my heart and soul into.

C28—Mm-huh.

S28—I mean really take an interest in. I think then, if I could be so interested in it, it wouldn't be—I mean—if I go along with this idea that there has to be someone else, then, it's going to be still a little forcing on my part. If things are to be derived from it and everything else, there's still going to be some forcing on my part.

C29—Mm-huh.

S29—But, I think that if I did find something that I really took an interest in and had some definite goal in mind which would be success in that particular thing because of this interest, I think I could do it, because of my own interest. I mean—because I had such an interest in it and it was so appealing to me that I wouldn't have to have any outside help as far as reaching the ultimate end—the ultimate goal of it.

C30—Mm-huh.

S30—I think if I could find something like that, why, I could do it very much on my own, then.

C31—Well, let's look at it in this way then. Instead of saying that the interest must be—intrinsically within the school work itself, it will be in the ultimate goal of establishing yourself as a successful individual so that you can then make some of these contacts.

S31—Mm-huh.

C32—And get into the—well—let's say, social environment that you were speaking of last time. That is, you can still keep that as a social goal without having it at the time.

S32—Mm-huh.

C33—And that can be the goal. It is possible, then, for you to base what you are doing now upon that thing rather than on something real at this time. It still is a real thing and that is probably the way most of us go along. We have these visualizations that in the future we will be successful individuals and that, therefore, being established as such, we can then proceed to fulfill these other things which are part and parcel of that goal. They aren't secondary, they're really a part of it, but one is a step toward the other.

S33—That is about the general idea of what I had in mind in a sort of round-about way, when I was up on a little pedestal.

C34—Mm-huh.

S34—I mean—that is about the basis of everything at that time, see? And it's *normal.* It seems average and everything else and that is about what it was. I mean, after things happened and I went around in a big mess, I tried to establish that the general consensus of the idea was that I was concerned more with myself, but that is about the idea I had at the time. Graduating from school and being a big success and working at it very hard. But when the bottom was kicked out from beneath me, it all came down and it was a jar. It gave me the impression—it gave me the idea in myself that because it happened, I couldn't be a success and then

I started to fight trying to get back up there and I kept falling back down, see?

C35—Then actually this thing had nothing to do with your ultimate success, only as success as you viewed it at that time within that environment.

S35—Yes.

C36—Let me make a statement here and see what you think about it. Some of us go along and build, over a period of years, a certain reputation. You've indicated that that reputation was being rather successful in your contacts with girls. All right. You felt that you had that reputation and you were in a situation where other fellows were looking at you all the time. You enjoyed that type of thing. To you, it meant a certain type of respect from these other fellows. When you were jolted once or twice by a girl, you felt that you lost your status within the eyes of the other fellows—fraternity brothers—the other fellows with whom you were going to school. That bothered you, perhaps as much as anything that happened to you individually, the fact that you lost your status as that type of individual within your own friends.

S36—Well, yes.

C37—Do you think that is a possibility?

S37—That is very true. I mean—it's not—not outright—but it has some bearing back some place. Evidently it can't be brought to the front, but I can realize it and actually something like that *does* exist.

> ★ Here the client may have been able to give some other instances of the interpretation previously suggested by the counselor, had he been given an opportunity. Instead of this the counselor interrupts him. Also, in the following remarks, the client uses devious methods of evading a point. Here we find the counselor trying to bring him back always to the point rather than following the evasion.

C38—All right. Let's carry it a step further. When this happens to someone else are you inclined to laugh at him? Or, do you take it pretty much as, well, that's just a situation that happens to everyone?

S38—Well, exactly what do you mean?

C39—Let's suppose that a fraternity brother of yours has a little bit of difficulty with a girl. How do you feel about him? Do you lose respect for him?

S39—Well, no. I had a particular instance of something like that. This girl that I was talking about that goes to school up there who is from home—ah—this fraternity brother of mine is a kind of rowdy. He goes out about every weekend and this girl is—well—she doesn't, she doesn't drink. She drinks very little, she doesn't smoke, and she's a good—you can have a lot of fun with her at a party or something like that, but she is just strictly—she comes from a very well-to-do family, and she is—I don't know exactly how to say it—but she is more or less the ideal type.

C40—Mm-huh.

S40—That is the kind of a girl I would like to marry.

C41—Mm-huh.

S41—Joe met her at a party over Thanksgiving and he decided he was going to take her out. So he raises holy heck at parties all the time—whether he has a date or not. And he was sort of on the verge of quieting down a little bit with this girl. And, he asked me about it and he knew that I'd be home at Christmas time and he thought it would be a good idea perhaps if I'd talk to her. So, I went out and I talked to her and—ah—this didn't bother me in any particular way as to what her decision was. But I do have the idea of a helping tendency.

C42—Mm-huh.

S42—And, I tried to help along there and say things for him and, still be truthful to her. And, I told her in common words that I thought she'd be very good for the fellow because she could probably quiet him down. He has "beaucoup" brains and if he'd ever put his mind down to studying in school he would really have gotten some place.

C43—Mm-huh.

S43—But, he just messed around a lot, and he had a wonderful opportunity. His father owns a large company. It's a very good company. He had a very good chance to set himself up there when he got out of school. When I look at this social angle I know that consists in a social group of high standing and I know what it's like. I look at some of these fellows that I know that are in deals like that and how they take no advantage of it whatsoever. It's so much easier to start out in a plane like that than first starting out in another plane and working up to that plane and working in that plane until you get as far ahead as you possibly can and then maybe getting up into another plane.

C44—Mm-huh.

S44—And, I mean, I took that consideration about this fellow. And, I tried to see if there was any particular interest between this girl and the fella and I tried to help out in every respect I could because she would be a very definite asset to this fellow. But, he was just a little too rowdy and she's got the right idea—I guess. There are a lot of things in life she wants to do yet.

C45—Mm-huh.

S45—She wasn't like most of the girls—who were set in their ways or worried about getting married. (*laughs*) She's a very smart girl—she has the idea that there are quite a few things she wants to do yet in life besides just getting married and settling down and raising a big family.

C46—Mm-huh.

S46—That's why she told me she didn't feel too much like getting serious with him.

C47—All right, but you haven't lost any particular respect for this individual?

S47—No.

C48—Because of this girl's attitude, here?

S48—No.

C49—Well, is there any reason then, to suppose that your fraternity brothers or your friends have lost any respect for you because of this other situation?

S49—No.

C50—Then, actually, then, there isn't anything to worry about as far as your status within your own group is concerned.

S50—That's true. (*pause*) But—it has some—some effect. Now what it is, I don't know. It's getting more minor and minor every day, but it does have some effect. (*pause*) Ah, an example—I was going to try an experiment on my own. This girl who lives next door, she teaches at Orange College.

C51—I remember you told me you went out with her one Saturday night.

S51—Yes. We've been hitting it off pretty well. I was wondering if I wasn't getting some interest there. I just wanted to see what her reaction was, so I told her—of course, I realized I was probably getting myself right back, jumping out of the frying pan into the fire, see?

C52—Mm-huh.

S52—But, I told her, well, I think there might be some mutual attraction growing here. She is kind of a different girl. She has quite a few brains and she doesn't immediately pick up something like that and say, (*falsetto*) "Oh, I'm so happy"—and all that kind of stuff.

C53—(*laughs*)

S53—She looks at it from a very wise angle. She's just that type of girl that thinks like that, and not knowing a person for very long, why, they don't have very much effect on her. She has to have time to think about it. So, I thought, well, fellow, you're just trying to see if you can get this girl to where you think you want to be with her and then just drop it to satisfy yourself. So, I went over the other night and talked to her. I was perfectly truthful about what I'd said the night before about mutual attraction and I said, I don't know, I guess it was a kind of spur of the moment but there probably isn't too much doing there. I said, well, I guess you'd better forget about it. So, she said, well, okay, that's up to you. So, I said, yes, I think that's the best idea. We haven't known each other too long. We've had a lot of fun together and let it go at that. So she gave me the idea that when something like this did come up it took quite some time for her to find out whether she did actually have interest in somebody or not. So I've been kidding her about it now because of being the way she is, as far as not knowing whether anything is really serious or not and, I'm glad I told her exactly the way it added up because now I can joke about it and I don't actually mean anything by it.

C54—It's the same way the other thing started out.

S54—(*laughs*) That's what I was thinking about. So—

C55—(*laughs*) In other words, you're trying to stay on the safe side for a while.

S55—(*laughs*) Yes. I was thinking about that and I don't think anything would come of it, unless she actually showed that she had some interest.

C56—Mm-huh.

S56—And the chances of her showing some interest are about one out of a million, between now and June. Because when June comes around I won't be around where she is. So, the chances of the two of us being together as far as any time through the summer is probably practically zero. But, there wouldn't be anything to get me bothered unless she showed some interest. I mean, as long as I can look at it as a joke—

C57—Mm-huh.

S57—But, I don't think that anything could develop out of it. I really don't. I'm very serious about that. I don't know exactly how I've looked at it. I suppose because of the way she is, looks at things for quite some time before she says something about them.

C58—Mm-huh.

S58—I don't know, it's more fun that way. As long as there's nothing doing there—the joking about it. I think it's—it's better and easier on me.

C59—How long is it going to remain a joking situation?

S59—Well, (*laughs*)—ah—I think probably forever.

C60—Mm-huh.

S60—I really do.

C61—The thing that intrigues me is why you think there is a *necessity* for you to become involved to some extent or other. You always seem to be leaving the way open for this thing to happen.

S61—Yep.

C62—Now, can you think of any reason for that?

S62—Well, let's see.

C63—Is this a pattern for other people to follow? Is this a pattern that most fellows you know follow?

S63—Yes, I guess that is about it. I may be wrong, but, I imagine that is about the way that most guys go at something like that. Maybe it's to satisfy yourself, if you like someone to show that they think quite a bit of you in return.

C64—Mm-huh.

S64—And, you might look at it from the angle that quite a few males look at it. If I say I like this girl and we get real serious about things, I might be playing her for a clown and maybe I'm actually serious about it. Maybe I can derive something from this. Maybe I can get some sex out of this or something like that—I mean—whether I'm looking at it in that respect, I don't know. I don't think so, because—

C65—Well, in either case it's almost purely a selfish activity.

S65—Yes, true. The one thing that I undertook this for—this idea with this girl—is because I wanted to see if I could actually get someone interested in me and just drop it.

C66—Mm-huh.

S66—But, after I thought it over I realized that that isn't too nice. It was more or less to satisfy myself as far as the idea that could I actually get someone interested in me again.

C67—In other words, you want to prove to yourself that you're still the same fellow you used to be?

S67—Yes, I did want that, but I told her the next day, let's just forget about this.

C68—Mm-huh.

S68—But, I don't think I could do it. I had never been hurt before up to the time that this little thing happened, and, it didn't worry me about how people were or how they reacted to the thing—the strong survive and that's about all. Then when I got beaten up once I looked at it from a different angle, I thought well, that hurts quite a bit when someone drops you like that.

C69—In other words, it can happen to everyone.

S69—That's right. So, I started this proposition here with the idea that I'd see what it'd feel like to be back as my own self again. Build this gal's hopes up and then, whish!—pull the bottom out of it. But I thought it over one day and I thought, uh-uh, that's no good. So, I told her, well, let's forget about it.

C70—Mm-huh. (*pause*) Well, you remember last time we discussed the possibility of looking further back into this situation? Let me make a statement and see what you think of it. It's been said that the male role in this society is a very difficult one. You have to strike a happy medium between being too dependent or too independent. If you're too independent, you are someone who has no moral sense of right and wrong and is completely on his own and everything is bent to that one thing. Too dependent is on the other extreme. So, the male role is to find something in between them. He has to be an independent individual but he can't be so independent that he becomes an egocentric burden on society. He can't be so dependent that he goes completely to the other side. Well, that makes family relationships rather difficult, because you have to assume certain relationships with your father and with your mother and yet not go overboard on either of them. And overprotection or complete rejection within a family group will bend you one way or another. Now, if you feel for some reason or another that you are not completely happy with or accepted by your family, then you have a tendency to go toward this independence sort of thing. But, if you don't completely accept your independency, then you want to go back to something else in which you want security or dependency. Now, does that strike anything as far as your situation is concerned?

S70—Yes—I mean—it's the idea of the social aspect—I think—more than anything else.

C71—Mm-huh.

S71—Because of my family and most of the things that I associate with my early life, I have been bouncing over to this side and then wanting to bounce back into something. It's more or less on two planes. Here's the lower plane that I was in and I bounce across to this side and then I want to bounce back up to this same category but a higher plane. (*Illustrates two planes with hands.*)

C72—Mm-huh.

S72—And, that is about where I would like to place myself, see?

C73—Then the original thing on this is that you are not, and never were, completely satisfied with your early home environment?

S73—Well, it's—it's not so much that. It's these particular aspects of it that weren't there.

C74—What particular aspects?

S74—I mean—ah—well—I place quite a bit of value on money.

C75—Mm-huh.

S75—I come from a large family and, we always had plenty to eat and plenty of clothes to wear, but I gained a sense of responsibility when I was about 13 as far as money was concerned. And, from the time I've been 13 up until now I have paid for all my clothes and all my spending money.

C76—Mm-huh.

S76—And, I've paid my way through college with the help of the G.I. Bill, I went to a parochial high school, the tuition was about thirty dollars. Well, I paid all that.

C77—Mm-huh.

S77—Of course, I had my room and board and stuff like that at home when I was in high school. But, when I see friends of mine—fellows that I've been to school with from wealthy families—exactly what they have, I look back upon my previous environment and I think about it—and I think, boy, how I would like to have had that when I was young.

C78—Mm-huh.

S78—And, that is my sort of rebelling stage there—in other words, I didn't have it.

C79—Yes.

S79—And other people did have it, *see?* So, I think, let's see—you're here at this age now, and you'd like to place yourself in that plane so that you can have those things that you didn't have previously.

C80—Mm-huh. In other words, you were independent, at least in one sense of the term, from about the age of 13.

S80—That's right.

C81—You looked at these other fellows—you didn't get any security in the same way that they did, and now you want to place yourself in that plane and get security in a different way. That's still the same desire.

S81—That's right.

C82—The form that the thing seems to have taken, then, is getting yourself accepted in a way which will in itself command respect and still give you a sense of security.

S82—And, that is one of the factors that goes right back to this situation that we have here. Any girl that I look at, homely or beautiful, I always look at the social plane she's in.

C83—Mm-huh.

S83—Now this girl up in the East, Jane, was in the social plane that I particularly cared for.

C84—Mm-huh.

S84—And that did have some effect on me in that respect, in that I was trying to get in that social plane and I was pfttt . . . Out, see? And it did have quite a bit of effect on me. I was trying hard—the trip to the East —the reason it doesn't bother me so much now is because I'm not getting into the social plane, the particular one that she's in. But, if I do go to this friend's house I am getting into one similar to it.

C85—Mm-huh.

S85—Very similar, maybe the same. It might be the same—friends and everything like that. You said something about home, and where would I go down there and things like that. Well, there isn't anything down there as far as—I don't care to get into a social plane where you go to parties and just raise ned and drink and drink and drink.

C86—Mm-huh.

S86—I like people on a higher plane.

C87—With whom you can identify yourself.

S87—That's right—associate—talk and through my actions, give them the idea that, well—I'm just about equal to you as far as—this plane is concerned because I can carry on a conversation with you and talk about different interests, and things like that—and meeting people and talking to them, see?

C88—Mm-huh.

S88—There isn't anything—I sort of recognize that as being very important at the present time.

C89—You want to show them that you're as good as they are.

S89—Well, yes. Not so much the idea of being as good as they are, as the idea of saying that in a way I *belong* in this plane just as much as you do.

C90—Yes.

S90—So that's why there isn't anything in my hometown.

C91—Mm-huh.

S91—And there's nothing to do. I can work a little bit and putter around and watch television and things like that. It's not the idea of having some definite place to go, it's just the idea that where I am is the complete *opposite* of what I want.

C92—Yes.

S92—Therefore, there isn't any particular interest for me in where I am. That is about the idea of the family life. That is about the basis of it. It's because, there isn't any particular thing—I mean—I love my family—I have a lot of respect for them—but—ah—as far as just being there, there isn't anything there that particularly interests me.

C93—You want to get on this other social plane in order to compensate for what you felt you missed.

S93—That's about it.

C94—And, this girl business is a form of that very same feeling.

S94—Yes, that is about it. Ah—when I was talking to this girl the other night, I was kidding her and she's going home over the holidays and I thought, well, I'll go down. I said, if I don't go East I'll come down and spend my vacation down there. You know, the minute I said that it was this idea of the social plane, I was thinking about it indirectly.

C95—Mm-huh.

S95—I mean its a place to meet people. Evidently, it's on a higher plane than I've been used to—and—my interest in her, it didn't seem too much, it was just the idea of this plane. Of course I thought it over and looked at it from the intelligent angle, other than I had been doing, previously. I stopped and looked at it and said, well, the chances of going to her home over the holidays are pretty slim.

C96—Mm-huh.

S96—So, let's not get all worked up about it. Let's just drop it right here. When I did look at it from that angle—as far as the social plane, I placed her mother and father in a definite plane. Well, I thought her father's in business—he's got bucks—they live in a nice house—they associate with very nice people—it ought to be pretty good. I looked at it right away from that angle. I just stamped it with a certain name on it—title, and everything and just let it go at that.

C97—Well, if I understand you correctly, you still feel the same way, except now instead of being very emotional about it, you've got the thing a little bit more in mind and you can now plan for it a little more intelligently and rationally, rather than emotionally.

S97—That's right.

C98—Mm-huh. (*pause*) Well, we're almost at the end of the hour. Now, let's try to summarize a little bit. We seem to have established that you want to put yourself on another social level and to compensate for what you felt was a lack of financial security. You feel that you want to do this by identifying and putting yourself in the company of those people who are on that particular level. You have tried to do this by means of your associations with girls who themselves operate in this particular plane. It has fallen through on at least one and perhaps two occasions. Now, what can we possibly do, or you possibly do, in terms of what you are doing right now in the long range situation to go toward that goal of what you might call "bettering yourself?" That is, is it possible for you to get your degree, work, and achieve success wherein that success itself will bring you into the company where this same situation can take place, instead of trying to do it through identification with another, you can then do it yourself? Not by making so much money, necessarily, that you are going to immediately raise your financial status, but by working and being in a social plane as an engineer or whatever else you may happen to pick, that your position itself will command respect within that particular group. That is, we may have gone a little bit fast here and I hope that you haven't lost sight—

S98—No—ah—

C99—Of what we—I mean—you've followed it all the way through?

S99—I think we've really hashed quite a bit today. I mean, you've gotten through quite a bit. We've progressed faster today, than we have any other day, and it seemed more sensible to me than the other days.

C100—Mm-huh.

S100—It seems as if it makes more sense than it has previously.

C101—Well, it's always a little bit rough to go too fast and it's best for us to understand each other rather completely than to go along half-cocked on incomplete information. Well, there's something for you to consider and think about, you can't come to any definite conclusions now, you can't resolve the whole thing while sitting in that chair.

S101—No, I know.

C102—It may give you some ideas.

S102—Yes.

C103—'Til next week.

S103—Previously—well—like after the first interview—what was said— what I said before—it didn't add up as well as what we said today added up.

C104—Mm-huh.

S104—It didn't add up as well as what we said the previous discussion added up, so consequently it didn't have as much effect on me as thinking about it later on.

C105—Mm-huh.

S105—Well, like the last interview we had—I thought about it through the entire week from time to time. It would come up and I would just happen to think about it, add two and two and get four, this will probably follow right through with it as far as, it seems even more clear and so consequently there will be more thinking about it.

C106—In other words, after you leave, you seem to get more ideas and clarification from it than immediately while you're sitting here.

S106—That's right. I think of what is said, and I say, well, yes, that's right. I say it's right because of one, and as I leave, I say, you know, that was right because of one, two, three, four, five, six and seven.

C107—Mm-huh.

S107—And, I mean, it just enlarges upon itself and helps me to understand it better.

C108—Mm-huh.

S108—But—I think that as time goes on—it has seemed that way in the past—it just keeps developing more and more.

C109—Mm-huh.

S109—Which is good.

C110—Well, now let's look at the schedule. (*pause*) How about Saturday?

S110—Yes, I could see you Saturday.

C111—Saturday—Let's see that puts us in the first week after vacation.

S111—Well, I'll tell you, I—I won't be going in this weekend and if—if I go East I won't see the family, see?

C112—Mm-huh.

S112—So, what I'll probably do is, if I have something definite, why—ah —what I'd like to do, if it's possible, I'll probably go in and see the family that weekend, see?

C113—Mm-huh.

S113—Because I haven't seen them in about three weeks now, and I won't see them over vacation or this weekend. But I would like to go in and see them that week. However, if there is something that I have—I'll make an appointment and come in and see you Saturday morning.

C114—All right.

S114—If anything comes up between now and before I leave, why, I'll come in and see you Tuesday. I'll call in.

C115—Well, we'll more or less leave it at that fluid state and—

S115—See how things develop, I mean, something might happen, over the holidays, I don't know. If I go up there something might happen. Even if I don't go something might happen. So, I'll leave it go at that and if I don't go, why, I'll come in and see you for sure on the Saturday. Because I'll be home over the holidays and there won't be any reason to come in the following week, see? If I do go up there, why I'll probably go in that weekend. (*pause*) If anything comes up, I'll see you about Tuesday. Thank you.

C116—Bye.

FIFTH INTERVIEW

(*22 Days after the Fourth Interview*)

★ The client spent the first 82 responses discussing a quiz that he had taken.

C1—What'd you do over Easter?

S1—Oh, not too much. I did a lot of work around the house. I'm glad I didn't go up now because it's getting nice out and there's a lot of work to do around, put out strawberry plants, sawed down a couple of trees.

C2—Mm-huh.

S2—This one girl, she came home.

C3—The girl from the East?

S3—Yes. She came home. So, I was supposed to go out and see her. I didn't get a chance. I talked to her on the phone and—she explained a little bit about it. She said that Jane had—I think she'd got caught breaking a rule or something. She owned up to it—she didn't have to, but she owned up to it and, well, there were about three or four girls that did.

C4—Mm-huh.

S4—They got suspended for two weeks. So—that was on her mind. And she didn't write, but Mary told me she said, if I were you, I'd just forget about the whole deal, and I said, yes, I'd think about it. I think that's probably about the best thing. So I just decided that'd be best to forget about the whole thing.

C5—Mm-huh.

S5—Of course, I told Mary to tell her if she wants her ring back she had to finish the socks and send them.

C6—Well, this doesn't seem particularly painful to you now

S6—No, it doesn't. There doesn't seem to be any outcome of it as far as, oh,—I think about it once in a while and wonder how things would have turned out, but—as I look back on it now I realize it's—I know very little about the girl, her family or anything, see?

C7—Mm-huh.

S7—I can see quite a few things now that I couldn't see before that are wrong with the deal and I can understand a few of the points just from little bits of information I picked up. I can understand a few of the things about this girl I didn't understand previously.

C8—They weren't clear before, but you have a better idea of them now.

S8—Yes. I think the best thing is just to forget about the whole deal. As far as my going up there, I realize now—she was out of school at that time.

C9—Mm-huh.

S9—That is, she wasn't even in town. She was probably down in Florida for two weeks, or some place else.

C10—I see.

S10—So there wouldn't have been too much doing up there and I think about all the stuff that has to be done around home and I'm glad I stayed there now because there were a lot of things that my dad needed me to help him with.

C11—The folks were glad to have you home then?

S11—Yes. I saw how much there was to do around there, so I think I'm going to be going in every weekend from now on since I can get out of here on Friday afternoon. So, I think I'll go in every weekend.

C12—You'll be going home every weekend?

S12—Because it's nice now and there's a lot to be done around outside and I can help my dad on that.

C13—Mm-huh.

S13—So, I think probably that's what I'll be doing. I'll be going in every weekend.

C14—Mm-huh. (*pause*) They like the idea of your coming home every weekend?

S14—Oh, yes, think so, but it's a meager existence out there. That's the bad part about it. (*laughs*) There isn't anything to do.

C15—Mm-huh.

S15—So, I think that's what I'll be doing. The main thing that interests me now is the idea—ah—my dad wants me to work down there this summer because I can get this job back if I want to, but I don't think I will, I think I'm going to take off. I have to write this one friend of mine up at school and—most of the guys are worried about this draft situation but—

C16—Mm-huh.

S16—Well, if any of the fellows do get deferred, I want to try and talk—sell them into going some place and working for the summer. And this fellow usually, well, what he usually does is he usually goes down South or some place. His dad runs a large company.

C17—Yes, you mentioned it to me one day.

S17—His father runs the company and he has quite a bit to do with other companies around—

C18—Mm-huh.

S18—Through the country. So, Joe worked last summer in the company.

C19—You think you could make more by going away from home or would you just enjoy it more?

S19—I think—the way the situation is set up, if I did stay at home, I'd have two alternatives: one is that I'd have to find a place to live in town—the other is, I'd have to get myself some transportation and live out at the house. Well, my dad told me, he said he'd loan me a couple hundred bucks and I could buy a car. And then after the summer was over I could sell it. Well, that'd give me my transportation backwards and forwards to work and I could live at home which would cost me very little. But I don't particularly care for that because it would be a heckuvan inconvenience for me because I'd have to come in those miles all of the time and then on top of that working shift work, why it'd be an inconvenience as far as breaking up my sleep and stuff like that coming in and out all the time and as far as being around the house that much I don't have that much desire to be there.

C20—Mm-huh.

S20—And there's just a little too much time for thinking and that is where a lot of my trouble is. That's where a lot of my trouble lies, because when this thing first started I was working at the plant.

C21—Mm-huh.

S21—This was the summer that the break-up started between this girl and myself.

C22—I see.

S22—She was gone out West on a trip with her family for about three or four weeks. I mean—actually you didn't have to think while you were doing the job.

C23—You had a lot of free mental time on your hands.

S23—Yes, I did. And it was right in that time that things started to get rough, see?

C24—The more time you had the more you thought about it?

S24—Boy, I used to hate that job. I'd like, well, there's one thing I didn't say that I started to think of when I was talking of this job. I haven't done any really hard work in a heckuva long time, see? I think it would probably do me a lot of good to get out and really get myself a hard job, not to kill myself, but something more than just sitting around.

C25—Think the exertion of it might do some good.

S25—Yes. I think it might. It probably would do me some good—really. So that's why I'd like to take off and go some place. If I work at home, I'd be silly to take any other job than that because it pays pretty good money and if I could get this overtime job, why, I'd probably be able to put myself a nice pile of money away.

C26—Mm. Well, that's something to consider.

S26—And I really would like to get a hard job just to see if I could take it and see if I'd like it and I think I would. So, that's why I'd really like to get some place and get out and get away because if I worked down there, it's going to be the same old thing.

C27—(*laughs*) Well, I think you can mull over this a little bit. You've got some time to make that decision. Next time we'd like to talk just a little more about this thing. And perhaps we can work into a little more about where your education is taking you.

S27—Yes, there are a few points about that that I've been thinking about and they're starting to clear up, but they're a little hazy right now. The only thing that worries me is—ah—according to my tests and other things like that, am I capable to go on or if I do go on and the challenge is so great that I can't overcome it, will it give me trouble? So, that's one thing I've been thinking about and I figured we could talk about it pretty soon.

C28—That's a good idea.

S28—Okay, then, I'll make an appointment for next Thursday.

C29—Bye.

S29—Thanks a lot.

★ The client is now beginning to make a transition from interpersonal relationships to thinking about his future in terms of more specific things. That is, what will I do this summer and shall I continue on in my present goal in industrial engineering, or is that going to be something a little too difficult for me? This interview is more or less a transition interview between the affective aspects of the case to the more cognitive material involved.

SIXTH INTERVIEW

(*6 Days after the Fifth Interview*)

★The first 9 responses were spent in discussing client's grades at mid-semester.

C1—Well, so the academic situation seems to be in pretty good shape.

S1—Either I have a brain I didn't know I had or this is an easy school, one of the two.

★ Here the client begins to make a comparison between his former institution and the one he is attending at this time. He is a little confused as to whether or not his increased interest in school and his increased achievement record is because he himself has made some progress or is due to the difference between schools. He is also using this as a means to try to get at whether or not he wants to stay in industrial engineering curriculum. Expressed in theory terminology, he is testing his self-concept against the realities of the environment and is about to make a readjustment in his concept of himself.

C2—Well, maybe your environment is a little more conducive to study or a little less conducive to play.

S2—That might be it.

C3—You think on the whole living in close proximity to friends, as you did in a fraternity house, may have affected some of your academic work? That is, in addition to the female angle?

S3—Well, I don't think so. Probably before I never tried to take into consideration too much the idea of studying along with the playing.

C4—Mm-huh.

S4—I can see a definite disadvantage to living there because I can just take so much of this stuff of not being able to talk to anybody—then I just—close up the book and take off or go next door and talk to this girl I've been taking out over there. That's about the general outlet of it.

C5—Mm-huh.

S5—But, I mean, whereas I figure if I lived with somebody, I mean, maybe wasting five or ten minutes every so often or just meeting someone in the hall, you know, and batting the breeze, or just talking to them or saying "hi" or something like that, I think it would have quite a bit of an advantage.

C6—Feel a little lonely up there.

S6—Yes. So this next semester, why, I think I'll probably get some place to live where I'm around with a bunch of fellas.

C7—You plan on coming back here in September, then?

S7—Well, now, that's one thing I'm not quite sure about yet. I mean, I probably will come back because even if I decide to stay in engineering, why I think I could pick up another full semester of courses. I could use everything that I've taken this semester and, if I still wasn't too decided after this semester is over, there are still courses that I can take that I could transfer up there. And if I went ahead in engineering here and got my industrial option, why, it would take at least two years.

C8—Two years past the end of this semester?

S8—Yes. Well, that may be just a little less.

C9—That's something you're going to have to decide here.

S9—Yes—the only thing that worries me is the idea of staying in engineering.

C10—Mm-huh.

S10—I took this one electrical engineering course, and I didn't seem to do worth a damn in it.

C11—In other words, you're not too confident of your ability in engineering.

S11—True, I think my interest lies there but there still is the idea of doubting whether I have the ability, for the course, you see.

C12—Mm-huh.

S12—I mean—I'm not sure that I haven't and I'm not sure that I have—simply because at the time that I took these courses I was all mixed up. So I might have the ability, but I'm not sure.

C13—You feel then that you may have failed any course under the conditions that you were working.

S13—Mm-huh. That is the trouble right now as far as the approach to the problem. The thing I don't quite understand is exactly what approach to use on the problem.

C14—Mm-huh. Well, how about engineering and allied courses that you took under conditions that were not so emotionally loaded. Do you feel that you did all right during those times?

S14—Well—ah—(*pause*)—there're two situations that sort of govern that. The first situation is my second year at college. I got a good grade out of them but it was a small school and everybody just goofed off. So, I mean, that is another thing that makes me wonder about this ability. I mean, the ability is probably there but the background in the course might not be too good. And, being away from it for some time might even make it worse.

C15—Mm-huh.

S15—And the second thing that comes to mind is when I first went up to Blue College, it was somewhat of a change because the school I had gone to was a small school. The first part of the semester I took this course in thermodynamics and even before the things started to come up I didn't do too well in thermodynamics. I mean, I didn't quite grasp the full knowledge of the fact that it was a hard school, I was starting to get the idea that it was a hard school—it was a lot different than the school I had gone to.

C16—Mm-huh.

S16—But before I had the chance to grasp that full knowledge, why things began to go wrong. It was right after the end of October when this girl came up to school and then went back, then things really started to get bad as far as—she was back here and I was up there. And then everything went on the "kafritz" because I didn't do any more studying from then on. I mean—I just tried to apply myself, but I couldn't. See?

C17—So, you're not sure then whether you lack the ability, or whether you have the ability, but haven't been able to use it?

S17—That was one of the reasons that I took those tests at White University.

C18—Mm-huh.

S18—That is the big issue. I think after that, after that issue is hurdled, there will not be many more big ones, in fact, there aren't any more big ones as far as I'm concerned.

C19—That is the main issue now.

S19—The main issue right now is that. I mean, as soon as that is settled, I can go on from there. As far as the outcome, I'm not worried about it.

C20—Well, did Dr. Crew (*counselor at White University*) ever go over the test results with you?

S20—No, he never did.

C21—Mm-huh. Would you like to take a look at some of them?

S21—Do you think—I mean—I imagine that they can help out probably —I mean—that's about the only thing that I can say even—even a test— ah—although they can help out some way—ah—I think that there's still —there's just a little doubt in my mind because of this poor background, see?

★ Note the change in the client's speaking tempo when he is considering an idea of major importance to him. From a rather smooth, fluent delivery his speech changed to a halting fumbling for words.

C22—Mm-huh.

S22—That second year those are important courses. Now—how to combat that—why—ah—I don't know.

C23—Yes. In other words, even if you had the interest and had the ability, you're in doubt as to how to go about going on because you lack some of the fundamentals which—you missed. Well—(*pause*)—how about the other angle of it? Do you feel now that you can return to Blue College without any repercussions of the other difficulty arising? That is, you now feel that you can go back with the idea of purely going to school?

S23—Yes. It would be a lot different because—before I didn't take too much into consideration, the value of studying, I mean. I never did place full value on it until here recently as far as really going at it and getting something out of the courses I'm taking. I did it my first year in college but I haven't done it since.

C24—Mm-huh.

S24—So—ah—now I realize that it has to be done. Therefore, I go ahead and do it. So I don't think I'd have any trouble in that respect. I could study like a fool all week long, and when the weekend comes—party and play. Before when I went to school up there, I didn't have any particular reason for running around as much as I did. I just did it without taking it into consideration. I wouldn't do it now, because I'm a lot smarter. I've become used to it. Things flash in my mind and say you got a lecture tomorrow in industrial management, you should have read this over. Whereas up at Blue College I didn't take that into consideration. It just didn't come to mind. And, I just wasted time, just wasted it completely just doing nothing.

C25—You think the attitude you've built up down here will transfer up there?

S25—I do. Really, I mean it. (*sigh*) It scares me a little bit, the idea of going back up there because of the situation that has happened every time that I've been up there. I think that it will be a lot different this time, I really do.

C26—You think you can look at it a lot more maturely now.

S26—I really do.

C27—Mm-huh. Well, will you be able to take the gaff financially?

S27—What I would like to do would be to probably go to my home town and get a job and work from January until September and go to night school. That would give me a chance to save money in between there and still continue with my schooling, see?

C28—Now, when do you want to do this?

S28—The only time I'd be able to make it, if I do go to school next fall would be to make it this summer.

C29—Um-huh.

S29—Well, it's going to be—it's going to cost me money to live next fall.

C30—Yes.

S30—So, that I would have enough money—ah—the following January to go up to Blue College. I might have enough to last me through until —until June.

C31—Mm-huh.

S31—Perhaps I might have enough, I don't know—with a very economical semester here next fall.

C32—You're not considering the possibility then of going to Blue College in the fall?

S32—No—ah—I don't think so. I hadn't looked at it too much mainly because I thought that I could pick up, as I said before, some 15 hours here which would be quite a bit cheaper than taking them up there.

C33—Mm-huh. Well, then you mentioned something about going to evening college?

S33—Mm-huh. What I thought I'd do is—would be to go here next semester up until January and then I could probably take some courses at night school in my home town, see?

C34—Then you would have enough money to fill one full year at Blue College? Is that the idea?

S34—I'd probably go up there in the fall and go through but I might— I hadn't looked at—since you mentioned it I've been thinking about it now and I'll probably think more about it and might be able to work something out. I would like to go up to Blue College. I've thought about it, but I never did dwell too much on the situation, but I would like to go up there next January, see?

C35—Mm-huh.

S35—Because if I did have enough money to last me through until June, why, I could probably go ahead and work that summer and go on back.

C36—Yes.

S36—That way I might be able to finish it up in two semesters, see? I'd be able to graduate—be able to graduate in January then, instead of waiting until the following June.

C37—Well, most of that will depend on how much money you make this summer and how much you're able to save. One of the things you want to get clear in your own thinking is your motivation in going back. If you're going back because you feel that the degree offered there is more of what you're looking for than what you can get here, that is one thing. If you're going back primarily for the reassociation with old friends then it is another thing, although it may be a desirable thing. It depends on which is really your central point in your own motivation. You must be honest with yourself on that because if you're going back for that reason and that's your primary motivation, then I think it's going to show up in terms of where your real interest lies after you get up there. In other words, if you go on up in order to get back with the "gang," then when you do get back with the "gang" that's going to be the central point of your activity. However, if you're going up for a combination of reasons, you might be able to continue the results and gains that you've made here.

S37—Mm-huh.

C38—But you want to be honest with yourself as to why you really want to go back because any attempt to deceive yourself on that point is only going to result in so much deception in terms of your ultimate goal.

S38—Mm-huh. (*pause*) Well, it has to be considered more, but I think the reason is because—the idea of getting a degree from up there and the association with those fraternity brothers because—(*pause*)—I haven't found anything to compare with that. When I got tied up with this gal, and I got pretty serious, I didn't spend too much time with the boys. It's natural to like a female, to want to be with females, but having trouble with females, and also having that idea of wanting to be around fellows like that, a group of guys in a fraternity house—

C39—Mm-huh.

S39—And all that's connected with it—there isn't anything that causes any more trouble there, see?

C40—Mm-huh.

S40—It's just a bunch of guys and you just have a good time and you study and you work, and when you work, you work, and when you study, you study.

C41—Mm-huh.

S41—I haven't found anything like that since I had this trouble, any other place than Blue College.

C42—Mm-huh.

S42—I mean, down around home, I never did care too much for the guys in high school I bummed around with.

C43—Mm-huh. Well that's a point of consideration, this business of trying to think through your own motivation, that might be something to mull over.

S43—And, I think that—as we were talking before about this jump between social planes—

C44—Mm-huh.

S44—I think that's some place back there that's in with the fraternity life because it's not a meager existence. I mean, regardless of whether you're, whether you're as poor as a churchmouse, if you have some initiative and you want to work, why, you can live under those conditions. It's not very easy but you can do it. I'd be working up there for my meals, but it wouldn't bother me as far as the rest of the fellows are concerned, and I'd have opportunities when the time presented itself—I'd be able to step into these social planes, because of being in that surrounding.

C45—Mm-huh.

S45—But, I still think and I'm almost positive that if my interest does lie in engineering and I can make a showing in it that I will continue to study and to work like I have done here. But the thing is, I don't want to get in the situation if it might go "ka-flooey" on me because I've gotten to this point now and if I went up there and I stayed in engineering and had trouble, it'd put me right back where I was before, see?

C46—Mm-huh.

S46—And, I've finally—I've managed—and I might even be willing to concede that I wasn't cut out to be an engineer.

C47—Mm-huh—that's why it is increasingly important that you be honest with yourself as to your real reason for going back. Now, I don't think that we should ignore the advantages of living a little more normal existence nor should we ignore your motivation of trying to have contact with what you term the "upper social plane." That is a point of consideration, too, and it's part of your motivation. You must think through this thing rather clearly in terms of the goals that you have.

S47—Yes.

C48—So that you know pretty well in your own mind what you're really going back for.

S48—Well, I keep looking back and thinking about the association of studying and everything else and I think that it can be carried through. I'm almost positive.

C49—Well, that's something that we might discuss next time if you have the opportunity to give much thought to it. Our hour is just about up. I think it would be a good point at which to start next time.

S49—Mm-huh.

C50—And I'd like to have some of your ideas on it next time.

S50—Well, I'll think it over. I'll bat it around a little between now and next Thursday.

C51—Okay.

S51—Bye, thanks a lot.

SEVENTH INTERVIEW

(*7 Days after the Sixth Interview*)

C1—How're you doing?

S1—Pretty good. I want to get my tobacco. I forgot it. (*pause*) I haven't been, I don't know, I've been thinking about what I was supposed to think about and as far as this deciding about this going back to Blue College—I haven't been able to get too far. I mean—I'd like to go back, but yet there's—I can't seem to (*pause*) be too sure about the idea of going back. I mean—as far as too sure about the idea of staying in engineering.

C2—Well, what are some of the pros and cons?

S2—Well,—ah—(*pause*) the main thing for it is (*pause*) just that continual idea and urge that (*pause*) that there is an interest there because I'm thinking so much of it, you know.

C3—You mean in engineering?

S3—Yes. (*pause*) The background is just a little bit too fuzzy.

C4—Well. (*pause*) You don't have any doubts about—about whether or not you're interested in it, eh?

S4—No. I don't think so. (*pause*) I found out something that made me very happy. Of course, I haven't decided anything definite about it. It's this Extension Service they have over here—correspondence courses.

C5—Mm-huh. All right, but one thing always to be careful of in correspondence or extension courses is whether or not the course is of such a nature that various questions will arise as to procedure or as to content itself. So that you will have no one to go to. Now, if that comes up, it makes things pretty difficult and has a discouraging effect on you and you have the idea, well, I can't do it because I don't know this one particular small part. If I knew that, I'd be able to go ahead. So, you have a tendency to pitch it aside. Ah—now if your courses are not of that nature, then you have a better possibility of getting through. I mean it's something to look at.

S5—Yes, I know, and—

C6—If your courses require library facilities and extensive reading it's a lot easier to drift across the campus and go into the university library than it is to run down and try to get a book.

S6—Yes, I see what you mean. That would make it very bad if, if the course that, if I found myself in such, such a location some little burg about 800 population, something like that, where I wouldn't be able to get the reference material.

C7—Well, it's also true—

S7—Well, I mean that's, that's a good point, I mean, as far as looking into—ah—undoubtedly before I decide to take the course, and if I would need such a thing as this, as continual reference and if I knew I'd be located in some small burg, why, it wouldn't hardly pay me to take it.

C8—Well, even if you were at home, not all of your small branch libraries would have the kind of material you're looking for.

S8—No, no, I'd have to go downtown.

C9—And—ah—during your working hours that might run into some difficulty too. I'm not trying to discourage you. Ah—but I do want you to go into this thing with your eyes open.

S9—Well, yes, I realize that it's pretty rough. I mean, it's not all peaches and cream. And another thing is whereas it doesn't seem like a lot of money—ah—four dollars per credit hour and three credit hours—well, that's twelve bucks. I mean if (*pause*) there's any idea I have that it's just twelve bucks shot down the drain, why, we're going to think about it twice before—I mean, such as these little problems arising as far as, well, I can't understand this particular problem here and—let's just forget about the whole thing, well, there's the idea of looking back and saying, well, this course cost you twelve bucks.

C10—Well, then the crux of the situation does not seem to be your interest, but (*pause*) your concern over whether or not you have the ability to complete the course.

S10—That's about it.

C11—Well, can you identify that a little bit more? Is it a general idea, or is it in some particular area of work, or is it after you get out of school? (*pause*) By the area of work, I'm referring to subject matter, but is it over and beyond the educational material itself into the work idea?

S11—It doesn't seem to revolve too much around the actual school work itself as it does—ah—after the school work, as far as being out in the business world.

S12—Mm-huh.

S12—Ah—(*pause*)—I guess it's more or less—it's not inborn—but to a certain extent it's inborn in that in the last—ah—well, ever since I got out of the service, and this idea of going to school and being an engineer, that's just been inborn from that time on.

C13—It's something you've stayed with.

S13—And, it's kind of hard to shift away from the field.

C14—You're concerned then over whether or not you will actually do well in the field after you leave school.

S14—Well, the only thing that worries me in that respect is—ah— (*pause*) the idea of placement because of—ah—this continual hopping around on my record.

C15—Mm-huh.

S15—But, I think, the way I look at it is that if I can do as well, that would give me a chance, by doing well, to explain this part previous to that being bad, I mean, as far as placement or anything else. That's why I hate to go into it because—it—it just enlarges this bad part or this bad period, I mean—

C16—Yes.

S16—This bad period is in there and there's nothing you can do about it, and if you keep enlarging it, why—ah—it's not going to do you any good, I'm okay as far as placement and going to work some place.

C17—Mm-huh.

S17—But if I don't do well, it's going to have quite a bit of effect on me because I realize that that period just keeps expanding.

C18—Yes.

S18—And it just doesn't look good. Because it's a definite record. It's like they tell you when you go in the Navy, better be good because people are going to look at this the rest of your life. Every time you go to apply for a job, why, they're going to open it up and say, "Oh! He was a bad little boy." That's about the same way that you think about this stuff.

C19—Mm-huh.

S19—But, that is one of the biggest worries I have. As I said before, is the idea that—it would be kind of bad if, I just started stepping lower and lower.

C20—Well—

S20—That's the part that worries me.

C21—Let's try to evaluate frankly and openly, what your possibilities are of getting into more difficulty. Do you feel that you're a little more aware of what the situation usually is that leads up to these things? Ah— by realizing what your goals are and what the hindrances are going to be if you get into difficulty or do you feel if the situation arises you won't be able to cope with it again?

S21—Well, it's a funny thing. Ah—(*pause*) after things have happened, it's kinda hard to look back on them and explain them.

C22—Mm-huh.

S22—So,—ah—(*pause*)—this general attitude that I had, I think about it at times as far as—ah—attitude that I had when I was up at Blue College. I just didn't give a hoot about anything. The entire studying procedure up there seemed to be just the opposite of down here. I felt like I just wasn't getting any place.

C23—Well, what was it in the *environment* or in *you* that would create that difference? Is there a difference in the schools or difference in your attitude, or is the difference in the fact that you don't have these emotional situations that—prevent you from it? Is it an emotional thing? Is it the difference in just the atmosphere? Or have you now—ah—taken more cognizance of your goals as such? Can you identify it in that way at all?

S23—That's the one—the one bad thing about it. I can't identify it and, it worries me to a certain extent, but it doesn't worry me enough to cause any sort of relapse at the present time.

C24—Mm-huh.

S24—But that is one of the big things as far as going back up there. Of course, it all revolved around this idea of ability. Ability in a particular field. Now, if there is something in that environment to cause that—ah—trying to put your finger on it is a hard thing. I realize the complete difference between the situation up there and down here. Yet I can't put any definite reason why it should be that way.

C25—You mean, you don't know why they're different.

S25—I mean—(*pause*)—there's a very good chance that they won't be different any more because the situation—without taking into consideration what the causes are, the situation could have been exactly the same down here. Yet, it wasn't.

C26—You're not quite sure of what the difference is between the atmosphere you find yourself in here and the atmosphere up there. Is that it?

S26—Well—ah—I mean, the difference might be in the idea that I have never talked about this to anybody and since I've talked about it to somebody and sorta straightened out that has tended to change this from being a situation similar to that up there.

C27—You think it might be just the counseling has done it.

S27—That's right. I mean, it's—ah—that's why, I think probably if I do go back up there and have counseling, if I need it, that the situation up there can be okay. But there's still the idea that there might, as you said before, there might be some emotional tie-up or some sort of tie-up with the situation up there that I can't put my finger on. That might come up when I get back. It's like looking for the invisible man.

C28—Well—

S28—So that's the one thing I wonder and worry about the situation up there. If the schools, evidently—ah—there isn't that much difference in them—I don't think.

C29—Well, let me throw this out and see what you think about it. Down here you are living pretty well alone. You don't have a chapter of your fraternity here. That has its limitations, but has a possible advantage. (*pause*) When you are in a fraternity house or a rooming house, I'm not limiting this to fraternities, but when you're living with a group of fellows, you have certain standards to protect, standards within the group as to going out and having a good time and standards as to your ability to handle a social situation that involves girls. Ah—standards of being a good guy, and with your particular ideas on these social points, you have that as a motivation. You have an idea—well, I want to participate in activities with these fellows because they represent a way of life which I like. And in order to—do this thing ultimately, I have to get in with these people. Consequently, you're devoting a great deal of your time and your motivation to that end. Your motivation, your ambition, your drive, is somewhat split. Whether it's split enough that it will keep you from studying is another question. But it may have a tendency to confuse you as to which is the more important thing and which is the best and the quickest way to these goals. A part of your goal, at least, as I understand it, is to elevate your particular social level. Now, I've put this in a round-about way, but boiling it down, it involves this: that having a status to protect in a group, you go along with the line of taking care of that situation because it looks like a shortcut to a particular goal and you necessarily devote some of your time, in fact, at times a great deal of it, to that end. Maybe this girl situation came up in that line. You not only had the past experience which was a sore point, and you were trying to prove something to yourself, but you also had this elevation of social plane involved. Now, if you can go up there with the idea of knowing yourself and knowing what you're going to do and be able to handle it, not by avoiding it, but by being aware of it, and knowing what you're doing, that is one thing. But if you go up there and still enter into this confusing thing where you bounce back and forth and have a relatively confused idea of which way you're going and how you're going to get there, then you are going to enter into another situation. (*pause*) Now, I only threw that out. It's not meant to be an absolute diagnosis.

S29—Even as you started to say it, I mean, prior to even the first few words, I was thinking about the same idea. The idea—ah—with all these things such as that, can I go ahead and—ah—transfer all these concepts and ideas of study from here up there.

C30—Well, this may be involved in an idea or maybe it's a matter of maturity. (*pause*) And maturity comes somewhat through experience. Now, do you feel that the experience you have had in seeing the differences and that you have gained here has been enough to enable you to be able to cope with these things?

S30—I think so. That's—this here's just—I mean—this little talk that you've given right now has given me an idea that perhaps, one of the best things for me to do, having this urge to stay in engineering—but still not quite being sure, but being settled, quite a bit—it's just an idea that hit me, but, it needs some more thought.

C31—Mm-huh.

S31—But the idea of returning to Blue College this fall—if I'm still not sure about staying in engineering—if I were to return up there and take engineering courses under the conditions that I'm taking courses out here, having the idea that I understand the situation—ah—having the idea that it more or less is a trial to see whether I have the ability or not—returning up there next semester, in the fall, for that sole purpose of finding out whether I have the ability and the desire to stay in engineering. In other words, the, the situation up there is pretty serious to a certain extent, I can't be definite about it until I get into it.

C32—Could you clarify that? I'm not sure what you mean.

S32—Well, in other words, I think and I wonder about—can I transfer over the study conditions from here up there? Will the social activities be different now that I realize the conditions of study, how they should be worked? It's a 50-50 proposition. You devote your time to your studies and see that they get done, and your time to your social affairs.

C33—Mm-huh.

S33—And, I think I can do it, but I can't be definitely sure until I place myself in that position.

C34—Mm-huh.

S34—I think with this general understanding and this complete knowledge of the situation, I think I might be quite a bit better off in going up, getting that out of my system. That way if I actually decided that I wasn't cut out for engineering courses and if I did find out, I think it wouldn't bother me so much, that I couldn't come back here for the following semester and start into business school.

C35—Mm-huh.

S35—In other words, the more I think about the situation it's more than just the idea of getting a college degree, because that is one of the things that—ah—is quite a big problem. The idea of—can I get into the situation that involves work and play and devote as much time to work as I do to play.

C36—Mm-huh.

S36—In other words, situations are going to arise throughout your life where you're going to have something like that—you're going to have to work and play and you're going to devote as much time to either one. That is about the only thing at the present time that is giving me trouble.

C37—In other words, this thing isn't a thing that's limited to school. It's a general thing that you're going to have to settle.

S37—That's true. I never looked at it before, but I realize now that everything else seems to be pretty clear except that. It's the idea of always drifting back to the question, do I have the ability?

C38—Mm-huh.

S38—And the only thing that tends to take me away from the ability is the idea that—ah—probably too much playing around.

C39—Mm-huh. All right, now, let's try to settle on that just a little bit. The thing that's bothering you to some extent is whether or not you have the ability to do engineering work. All right. Now try to identify why you don't know whether or not you have the ability. You're not sure as to whether or not it's basic intelligence or ability or whether or not it is—has been due to the fact of this emotional stress and the social activities. You're not sure which one it is.

S39—Well, I am worried more about the basic ability than anything else, but there still has to be taken into consideration the other one, because I never did give the basic ability idea a chance to come to the front.

C40—Mm-huh.

S40—I mean, I never did really devote myself fully where I could have shown myself that I did have the basic ability.

C41—Mm-huh.

S41—I mean, it was always the idea that I just played when I should have been working, so that this playing concept came in and not the working concept. I mean, I've done it here and if I could do it there, it would be to a definite advantage to me because I think probably that before I can go I have to knock out this playing attitude because when I was playing up there, I didn't have any definite reason for playing.

C42—You feel that you have solved it here.

S42—I think so.

C43—And you think that if you can solve it up there, you will have solved it for all time.

S43—I think I will.

C44—Mm-huh.

S44—And then I can go ahead and go to work on this ability proposition.

C45—Well, now you mentioned once before that you thought your test results were affected by the fact that you were in some sort of emotional stress during the time you took the tests. Do you feel that it would help you in your thinking ability to take an individual test now which would be taken under relatively stable conditions?

S45—Well, it all goes back to the idea that if I take—if I take a test now—perhaps you can explain this to me, but I think that if I take a test now, I'm going to think about, I don't have the ability. Of course, whether that just is an excuse for not taking a test, or whether that is an excuse for the idea that I think I might make a bad grade on the test, what I mean is, it all goes back to the idea that—I get to this point now where I'm taking a test and I tell myself, well, do you have the ability? And, I know I'll think about that when I'm taking the test.

C46—Mm-huh.

S46—I can't help it. It's one of my main ideas. It's something that's been worrying me and it just worries me and I just can't do anything about it.

C47—Well, that's why I mentioned an individual test rather than some paper and pencil thing. Now, that is entirely up to you.

S47—Well—

C48—If you think it's going to help you—fine. If it's going to confuse you—we'll let it go.

S48—Well, what type of a test do you mean by an individual test?

C49—Well, where someone talks to you and asks you the question, you don't have any pressure of time on you, to any great extent.

S49—In other words, they ask you questions, and you more or less explain yourself.

C50--That's right.

S50—Well now, a test like that, that sounds quite a bit better than the regular intelligence test, where you're working under strain and you have a problem to complete or so many problems to complete, or something like that. I mean, that sounds like it would be a definite advantage to me.

C51—Well, that's the type of thing I was thinking of. I thought you may want to take it just to clarify your thinking. If you do, okay.

S51—I think I'll probably go ahead and take it.

C52—All right, I'll see if they can arrange a time for you.

S52—Do you give the test, or does someone else give the test?

C53—Well, I can give it, but I prefer someone else to give it.

WECHSLER-BELLEVUE INTELLIGENCE SCALE
FOR ADOLESCENTS AND ADULTS

RECORD FORM **I**

NAME **BATTLE, John** AGE **24-4** EDUC. **Jr.** DATE OF EXAM. NO.
OCCUP. **Student** NAT. **Am.** BIRTHDATE COLOR **W**
PLACE OF EXAM. **Counseling Center** EXAM. BY PREVIOUS EXAM. **Form II**

TABLE OF WEIGHTED SCORES†											
Equivalent Weighted Score	RAW SCORE										Equivalent Weighted Score
	Information	Comprehension	Digit Span	Arithmetic	Similarities	Vocabulary	Picture Arrangement	Picture Completion	Block Design	Object Assembly	Digit Symbol	
18	25	20		14	23-24	41-42	20+		38+			18
17	24	19	17	13	21-22	39-40	20		38	26		17
16	23	18	16	12	20	37-38	19		35-37	25	66-67	16
15	21-22	17		11	19	35-36	18	15	33-34	24	62-65	15
14	20		15			32-34	16-17			23	57-61	14
13		15		10	16		15	13	28-29	22		13
12	17	14		9	15	27-28			25-27	20-21	49-52	12
11	15-16	12-13	13		13-14	25-26	12-13		23-24	19	45-48	11
10	13-14	11	12	8	12	22-24	11	11	20-22	18	41-44	10
9	12	10	11		11	20-21	10	10	18-19	17	37-40	9
8	10-11	9			9-10	17-19	9	9	16-17	16	33-36	8
7	9	8	10	6	8	15-16	7-8	8	13-15		29-32	7
6	7-8	7	9	5	7	12-14	6	7	11-12	13	24-28	6
5	6	5-6			5-6	10-11	5		8-10	12	20-23	5
4	4-5	4	8	4	4	7-9	4	6	6-7	10-11	16-19	4
3	2-3	3	7	3	3	5-6	2-3	5	3-5	9	12-15	3
2	1	2	6			1-2	3-4	1	1-2	8	8-11	2
1	0	1		2	0	1-2	0	4	0	7	4-7	1
0		0	5			0		2		5-6	0-3	0

SUMMARY		
TEST	R.S.	WT.S.
INFORMATION	18	13
COMPREHENSION	16	14
DIGIT SPAN	14	13
ARITHMETIC	7	9
SIMILARITIES	18	14
(VOCABULARY)	(29.5)	(13)
VERBAL SCORE*		63
P. ARRANGEMENT	14	12
P. COMPLETION	14	14
BLOCK DESIGN	30	14
OBJECT ASSEMBLY	14	7
DIGIT SYMBOL	53.5	13
PERFORMANCE SCORE*		60
TOTAL SCORE		123

*Proration is necessary if four or six Verbal tests are given or four Performance tests.

VERBAL SCALE	63	I.Q.	119
PERFORM. SCALE	60	I.Q.	113
FULL SCALE	123	I.Q.	118

†Clinicians who wish to draw a "psychograph" on the above table may do so by connecting the appropriate raw scores; however, one must recognize the relative unreliability of these subtest scores when they are thus treated.

Norms: 20—24 yrs.

TEST ANALYSIS AND OBSERVATIONS Rapport seemed good. Nothing unusual noted in the test situation.

Reprinted with permission of the publisher,
The Psychological Corporation.

S53—That's what I thought, and that's why I was saying that I could take it any time between now and Thursday.

(*They make arrangements for client to take the Wechsler-Bellevue Intelligence Scale.*)

EIGHTH INTERVIEW

(*7 Days after the Seventh Interview*)

C1—How're you doing?

S1—Oh, pretty good. Did you get the test yet?

C2—Yes.

S2—Well, mm-huh, I know a lot of things that I didn't do too good on.

C3—Well, actually—you had almost the same score that you had when you took the same test at White University. You took Form II there, and this was Form I. In other words, it was an equivalent form of the same test.

S3—Yeah, I thought it was similar because I remembered blocks, that test has blocks in it, too, and forming different kinds and combinations.

C4—Yes.

S4—I could catch—ah—I say to myself—I mean the idea that—I realized —ah—took into mind that the most important part, was the arithmetic. (*laughs*) And there was one if you buy seven pounds of sugar for a quarter, how many pounds do you get for a dollar and a quarter. And I was so intent upon answering that, that I said six pounds, and just the minute after I said that (*laughs self-consciously*) I knew I had made a mistake, and from then on it was strictly guess, because of being upset like that.

C5—Mm-huh. You think you have a tendency that way.

S5—Well, now that is something—previously to coming here—I had quite a bit of trouble with exams, but here I haven't had any trouble.

C6—Mm-huh.

S6—Mm-huh, but I've noticed taking these exams, before I'd go into an exam, that I'd just be all tied up in knots. I couldn't do a thing.

C7—Mm-huh.

S7—But here it hasn't—it hasn't struck me that way. Of course, I knew yesterday that I was being tested, you know, and—ah—

C8—Mm-huh.

S8—That had some effect on it, just the one section there, that one on arithmetic.

C9—But as a whole, you aren't being bothered nearly as much as you were before.

S9—No, I'm not. Generally speaking, I'm not being bothered at all. As far as taking tests are concerned, and any kind of test used to scare me before.

C10—Well, do you think that you have a little more confidence in the studying which you've done on it? Do you think you know the material better?

S10—That's right. I mean, there's more preparation. In the past I took tests, why—ah—I'd read the material over and some place back in my mind I'd know that I hadn't read enough. Just the idea of reading it over wasn't enough. I knew that, but I'd tell myself, well, it'll come to you.

C11—Mm-huh.

S11—There wasn't as much preparation. And that's one thing that I've done here. Therefore, it's given me confidence so far as going into quizzes are concerned.

C12—Yes.

S12—It's helped out quite a bit.

C13—Mm-huh. (*pause*) Well, that—ah—should work as a little indication for you in the future.

S13—Yeah. (*pause*) I know now.

C14—Mm-huh.

S14—There's no excuse for it happening in the future. Of course, there might be times, just one of those bad days, when you go in there and all of a sudden, bingo! Can't help yourself. But, generally speaking, they shouldn't occur very often.

C15—Mm-huh. Well, what do you think the test means as far as your educational plans are concerned? I mean, that was the reason you took it.

S15—(*pause*) Well, (*pause*) you've got me.

C16—Well, maybe I can give you an interpretation that might indicate something to you. It's certainly not going to supply any real answer because it's not so high that you can go in with the greatest of confidence. And it's not so low that you could say, well, I don't have a chance. Your score was about average for college students, but slightly below average for engineers. They have a tendency to be slightly above the average for the rest of the school population. So that when we say slightly above or slightly below, you're still in that range.

S16—The middle range for me.

C17—So that a great deal of it still bounces right back on your own shoulders. In other words, motivation, study habits—which, of course, are bound up in all of these other ways you feel about things, are going to be the determining factors. (*long pause*) It doesn't indicate, in other words, that you can loll around and take things real easy and still get by. You're going to have to work to a certain degree to achieve because you're competing against people who are at least as good and at least 50 per cent of them have a little bit more to work with than you do. But you have a little bit more than the people who are below average. So, in order to make any superior grades, you're going to have to put forth the effort.

S17—Yes. That's about the idea that I got out of it. Things won't come very easy a lot of times, I realize that from being around a fraternity house where we had quite a few fellows that were really brainy.

C18—Mm-huh.

S18—You could see the difference, I've noticed a difference already. A lot of times a fellow will be doing the same problem you are and he has more insight, I guess. He can look at a problem and where it may take you fifteen minutes, he can snap it in five.

C19—Mm-huh.

S19—Because of that, higher mentality as far as engineering courses are concerned, engineering subjects, why he can visualize things. He's just cut out better to be an engineer than I am.

C20—Mm-huh.

S20—But whereas it takes me more time, if I want to devote the time to it, I can attain the same thing he does.

C21—Mm-huh, I think that's a reasonable statement.

S21—I sorta surmised that. (*pause*) Maybe that is the idea that sorta scares me. My own idea that since I'm inferior to some fellows as far as engineering courses are concerned. That does help out quite a bit. I mean, as far as knowing that. (*pause*) Well, there's something that's been bothering me. I've been trying to compare this school because I'm doing well here—I've been trying to compare this school to Blue College.

C22—Mm-huh.

S22—If I could ever establish that comparison, I think that I'd probably be a little better off than I am right now.

C23—Mm-huh.

S23—Trying to compare the instructors between the two schools and things like that.

C24—Mm-huh.

S24—I haven't had much of an opportunity. I don't have anything to really base my claims on. It all goes back to the idea that trying to find out what the particular reason was for my making low grades up there. If, if I do that, I could compare the instructors between the two schools.

C25—Well, instead of trying to compare instructors, let's for a moment try to compare you. And suppose, just for an hypothesis, that the schools are about equal. Then we get back to the difference in you. If, however, you feel that your particular work was about equal in both places, then you'd have a different slant on things. So you have a point of reference from which you must operate. One thing—it seems that you're taking, this semester, which is your first semester here, a different type of curriculum than you had at Blue College.

S25—Well, not too much, because I was trying to figure out what I took last semester. Now, I took this statics course that I'm taking now.

C26—Mm-huh. Well, now there's a direct comparison. Let's take it from there, because I think you've hit on something which is relatively important since it's going to have some bearing on your decision as to whether or not you stay here or go back. Ah—not that it should be any major consideration, but it's something for you to think about. You've taken the same course in both places. Now, just take that one course—how do you think in terms of the way you've applied yourself, the manner in which you've studied and your whole general attitude and emotional condition? Do you think that there is a difference within you?

S26—I think the courses are about equal as far as the two schools are concerned.

C27—Then the difference must lie in you. And if it lies in there in one case, where the two courses are about equal, the possibility exists that it may be the same thing with the other course. Although you don't have nearly as good a comparison. And admittedly the courses are different, not only in schools, but in departments in the same school.

S27—Well, you see the thing that I keep going back to, is the idea of comparing my application up there with my application down here.

C28—Mm-huh.

S28—That's where I can't grab hold of it. I can't—I can't evaluate my application up there.

C29—Mm-huh.

S29—Simply because the situation seems so far away at the present time.

C30—Mm-huh. You'll have to look at it as much removed from the school as you can. Get the line of thinking along how you felt about things up there, what your opportunities for study were. If you can recall what you did on various nights of the week and compare it with down here.

S30—Well, when I went up to Blue College, I had this real serious idea. I had worked real hard down home, and I had put quite a bit of money in the bank, and it was starting to burn a hole in my pocket. So, I just wanted to drift back to the same thing of more or less having a good time, I guess. And I kept telling myself, "This is all right, go ahead and have a few good days and you'll be okay." I think the main thing wrong was that I just had too few good days and they finally caught up with me.

C31—Mm-huh.

S31—And it was the idea that I'd planned so much on it that when they did catch up with me, bang! Just like that. I'd built up so much hope on it. I had worked in saving money and I'd really been very interested in it—I thought—and when I saw that it was getting right back to where I had been before, why, instead of drifting back to it, I just—whoosh—like a curve that goes up and then it sorta goes back down bell-shaped in normal distribution.

C32—Mm-huh.

S32—Well, I came up, my hopes were building up and up and up, and finally I got to this point where I began to look around and I saw that things weren't too good, and how they were going and it was just about the same way they were before and all of a sudden she just took a nose-dive.

C33—(*laughs*)

S33—And, had I been able to look at it and reason it out with someone, I think probably I'd still be up at Blue College and probably be doing pretty good.

C34—Mm-huh.

S34—But I didn't. I kept it to myself and that's what happened. I don't know if I ever told you the story, but I saw it coming and I was behind in my work, so I just went down and I took the quiz on a Saturday morning and I thought I'd done pretty poorly on the quiz. Mainly because I didn't outline the work as I've been doing up here. I didn't apply myself. I read it over; in comparison to my success up here, the way I've gone at things, I didn't go at it the same way there and so consequently, I wouldn't expect the same success, looking back on the situation.

C35—This is an evaluation then.

S35—Yes. (*pause*) I was behind a little bit up until then, then Hell Week came and after Hell Week, on a Friday night before initiation I got an illness and that laid me up the entire next week.

C36—Mm-huh.

S36—The illness gave me so much trouble that I couldn't go to class, and I was really behind then. I'll tell you what happened, and we'll talk about it some more probably next time. I came out and I started to go up to this class, and it just hit me right between the eyes and I realized how far I was behind and so, I was looking for a way out—so I decided that I'd just forget about the school and if anybody asked me what the reason was, I'd tell 'em the reserve had called me up.

C37—Mm-huh.

S37—And the funny part about it was that I let myself—I mean—this little idea, just a small idea in my mind just started this whole "kaflooey." I gave myself the impression that the reserve might call me, so the heck with it. I just built everything up around that from then on. The guys at the house asked me, is that true? Oh, yes, it's true, the reserves may call me and I'll have to go back in the service. Once I started on that slope— boy, she just went. And, I didn't go to class any more and finally—

C38—(*Counselor interrupts*) But even at the time you knew that there wasn't anything basic about this reserve business.

S38—It was just an excuse because I wasn't doing good, and I wanted to get the heck away from the situation. So, I just used that—I hated to lower myself and look like a fool in the eyes of other people, so I had to find an excuse. Once I found an excuse, a small idea in my mind—bingo! Just like that!

C39—Well, now next time let's continue this idea of using various excuses.

S39—Okay.

NINTH INTERVIEW

(*7 Days after the Eighth Interview*)

★ The ninth interview was spent in discussing various job possibilities that the client might have for the summer months. This point had been covered before and the interview in itself was rather unproductive.

TENTH INTERVIEW

(*7 Days after the Ninth Interview*)

C1—Well, now if you go to the neighboring state this summer and get some work over there—ah—do you think there's any possibility of anything arising between you and the girl that you—that was the original thing—

S1—Well, (*laughs*) there's a funny situation there. While we were talking last weekend, I asked her how—she's going around with the pre-med student down at the hospital.

C2—Mm-huh.

S2—She's in nurses' training there, as I told you before. And I asked her how she was doing with this pre-med student. Well, I never give hopes for any of her romances because they seem to last—I mean, it's the real thing—and they seem to last for a period, and then, boom. See? So I asked her how the situation was and she told me that they had fallen out. And I laughed because I had more or less figured it out that things would happen that way.

C3—Mm-huh.

S3—And so, I mean, it didn't bother me in the least to talk to her. It was strictly on a friendly basis. And so I told her, I said, well, how about fixing me up some weekend when I come in? She said, what's wrong with taking me out? I said, noooo, I don't want to get fouled up in that situation again. Heaven help anybody that's had that happen to them twice. (*laughs*) She said, I don't think you're that dumb, are you? I said, well, I don't know. I said, I don't think so. I said, but I'd rather not tempt fate and I said, well, maybe we'll take you out some weekend but—ah— I'm just a little leery about that situation. I think probably the way I'd arrange it if I did decide to call her up for a date is that—ah—I wouldn't call her up until I got in town. I mean—I probably would like to take her out because we have just a lot of laughs and everything over the phone. We could probably have a good time and all that, but—ah—I intended, if I ever did call her up for any kind of arrangements, that I would call her up the last minute I got into town because chances are that she would have a date by then and so I wouldn't have a chance to take her out anyway. But—ah—there would be the possibility of her fixing me up with someone.

C4—Yes.

S4—But as far as her being around all this summer I doubt it very much because this is her second year in nurses' training and—ah—the further you get along in nurses' training, the more time you get free in the summer, but it really doesn't amount to anything until your last year.

C5—Well—

S5—Because they have, they have pretty much a straight through period —summer, winter, fall, autumn and everything else.

C6—The thing I'm trying to get at here is—not as to whether or not she is going to be available, but what your confidence in the situation is and what you want to do—if she is available. See what I mean?

S6—Yes, I see what you mean. And I don't know. I mean, I've wondered about it a little bit—not much. I took into consideration her availability and as I said, I looked at it from the respect that she wouldn't be around much.

C7—Mm-huh.

S7—But—ah—I don't know, I'm pretty confident that—of course this goes back to the conceited male attitude—ah—I'm pretty confident that I wouldn't be involved, but I would like to think of the idea of her getting involved.

C8—Mm-huh. A little idea of revenge there?

S8—(*laughs*) You might say that.

C9—Mm-huh.

S9—Not half as much as I did previously at one time. But, I mean, there's still the idea that the general male attitude, I guess, the idea of revenge, the idea of someone having a particular interest in you, but, I mean, it would be—it would be kind of nice. I might get my fingers burned by trying to fulfill the process.

C10—Mm-huh. Well, you're not going to get them burned so badly that you won't be able to page through a book, are you?

S10—That's the thing. I don't think so.

C11—Mm-huh.

S11—I mean—if I saw myself drifting into a situation. I mean, I could tell, having been in the situation once before, if I caught myself just starting downhill in the situation, I think I could sort of kick her in reverse and back up out of it without too much trouble.

C12—In other words, you feel a lot more confident in these interpersonal relationships than you did when you first came in here?

S12—Yes—you mean, as far as this girl's concerned?

C13—Well—ah—all of them.

S13—Yes. Ah—more so in respect to this girl because there's a lot of things that I never did see about the situation 'till I backed away from it to take a good look at it and—

C14—Well, how about the girl at Blue College?

S14—Not too much there—no.

C15—How about the Orange College gal?

S15—No.

C16—Okay.

S16—She's pretty ser—well, she's not pretty. She's a—she's a smart little cookie, this gal from Orange College. She has a good head on her shoulders. I mean, she is not about to get into any situation she can't get out of.

C17—How about you?

S17—Yes, I think so.

C18—See, now the reason I'm trying to pin this down to some extent—

S18—I mean—go ahead—

C19—Ah—this is going to be the last time that I am going to be able to see you. So, I'm trying to pull these things all together—summarize what we've done during all this time.

S19—Mm-huh. (*pause*) Oh, I don't think there is any worry as far as getting involved is concerned—ah—this little gal out at Orange College, why, there's—ah—sort of conflict in circumstances.

C20—What do you mean?

S20—Well, (*pause*) religion can be a funny thing.

C21—I see.

S21—And—ah, I'm not of her faith.

C22—Mm-huh.

S22—And she is quitting teaching at Orange College to take a job as religious instructor in her church.

C23—Mm-huh.

S23—There isn't anything serious there. I mean, we have a good time and all that. But, I mean, I mean, we may go out occasionally this summer. However, she'll be so busy down there at that church that she's going to work at, that she wouldn't have much time anyway.

C24—Well—ah—I don't know whether this particular is completely settled, but—ah—at least you've indicated that you feel a lot better about it. Now the thing that we haven't worked very hard at is your actual vocational decision and choice. I don't know what we can do about that in this time. We've talked some about it and we've gone over a little bit of testing as far as ability is concerned. Now, we have this occupational information library, and if you want to go through that and if it will be of any help to you, I'll be glad to show it to you. You can come in and look it over. (*pause*) Now, the point is whether you think you can do that on your own, whether you think it's clear enough at this time, if you've reached a position where you can carry it through yourself or whether you think you'd like to work with someone on it.

S24—Well, this, this particular test that we were talking about, is that —what kind of a test—

C25—Oh, that. You remember the Wechsler-Bellevue?

S25—Yes.

C26—General mental ability test.

S26—You mean, in other words, review of that, going over the test itself. Is that what you were talking about?

C27—Yes. I was hoping that you had gotten enough out of there to give you some idea of what your ability was. If I remember correctly you didn't turn out to be a genius, but you did indicate that you had enough ability to get through if you worked at it.

S27—Well, the, the—ah—as I said before—I mean—ah—I noticed in a particular section of the test—I mean—when I felt that I was under observation—

C28—Mm-huh.

S28—And I knew what the test was prior to going in and taking it.

C29—Mm-huh.

S29—And as I was telling you before about coming to this particular section in the test and knowing that I was making mistakes and not being able to do a thing about it because knowing, you know, that I was under observation at that particular point.

C30—Even under the circumstances, your test results were sufficient to indicate that if your motivation, your study habits and all those things were up to what they should be, you should still get through school. It is these other factors that are going to play the most important role. (*pause*)

S30—Well—ah—as far as making a decision, I mean as far as the vocational end of the situation, why, we have found quite a few other things that need to be straightened out. We've had time to spend and we spent the time on it which was advantageous, which had to be done, prior to deciding on a vocation. Ah—the idea now, you know, of shifting the responsibility to my shoulders, to a certain extent, I think it's good, but—ah—I don't know—I mean, there's still enough question marks in the situation to sort of—ah—to sort of bluff me a little bit. I mean—

C31—Mm-huh.

S31—there's still quite a bit to be understood.

C32—Mm-huh. Well, now, here's this point. If you come back here, I'll be here next fall again. That is, I'm going to teach full-time this summer so I won't be available this summer. But I'll be back in this job next fall. Ah—if you come back, we can continue, but I want to get an idea, if possible, carry through for this summer on your own.

S32—Oh, I think so. It's going to be up to me. There's a lot that has to be done. And if I can carry over the scheduling and the seriousness and the idea of understanding quite a bit about things that I have had this semester, if I can carry that over into this summer and utilize it, utilize my time, why—ah—it's going to be very advantageous to me. But if I tend to just waste my time and work in the day and just go out and run around at night, it's going to tear down everything because I'll be wasting money that I should be saving.

C33—Mm-huh.

S33—I mean, things of that nature. I mean—it's reached the point where it has to be shifted off on me because nothing else can be done.

C34—Mm-huh.

S34—Ah—this summer is mine. It's mine to use in a way I think is right, that's going to benefit me the most. So that if I don't take advantage of it, why, I'm only harming myself and I think that under those conditions—ah—with a sort of periodic check through the summer to see exactly what advancement I'm making.

C35—Mm-huh.

S35—I think it will have some definite advantage.

C36—In that way you will keep your ultimate goals in mind.

S36—That's right. And whereas I haven't had much of a chance for deciding about the particular field to go into and things like that, I've always considered it rather hard to decide things like that, when you're under the conditions, such as attending school at the present time.

C37—Mm-huh.

S37—And I've always said, well, when the summer comes, why it's quite a bit easier to decide because you tend to be away from it. It gives you time to relax.

C38—You need more time to retrospect, is that the idea?

S38—Yes. You're away from the situation, it gives you a tendency, it has the idea that you can go ahead and look at it. Of course the only thing about that is that I've always said that. I mean, well, the summer is the time to decide and I've never—I've just wasted the time and never taken advantage of it, but I think that it may be different this summer.

C39—Mm-huh.

S39—Well, you've been just much help, you really have. Well, if I get the chance—I mean, if there's anything comes up—ah—that I decide on any big factors, why, if I can't get up to see you, why, I'll drop you a letter and tell you about the situation.

C40—Well, swell, I'll be glad to hear from you.

S40—Thank you.

C41—Bye.

S41—Bye.

COUNSELOR'S NOTES
(*Dictated after the Tenth Interview*)

★ The following will be a summary of ten interviews with the above-named client. These interviews, except for intervals during vacations, stretched from February until May. Mr. Battle came to the counseling center as a referral from Dr. Crew of White University, with the suggestion that continuing counseling interviews should take place with this client.

During the first interview the client had a tendency to ramble throughout many phases of his problem situation. He indicated that he had begun his college career at Maroon College. He spent approximately two years at Maroon College and then transferred to Blue College, where he began a curriculum in engineering. He finally dropped out of Blue College and came to White University and tried to finish up there. Again he dropped out of school before the end of the semester and is now entering this university. The client indicates that his difficulties scholastically have been because of his relationship with a girl who is at the present time in nurses' training. He indicates that when he left to go to Blue College he was very much in love with the girl, and that his difficulties with her have caused him much stress and worry, and that at the present time she is no longer interested in him nor he in her. But at the time that he was attempting to do his school work at Blue College he was unable to concentrate or to care about his academic activities because of his concern over his relationships with this girl.

In the first interview we also discussed a possible curriculum and vocational objective. The client indicated that although he was not positive that he was still interested in the general field of engineering, he would like to take courses that would either qualify him for such a degree in this school or those courses which would transfer satisfactorily so that he could complete his training at Blue College. Miss Blick (Academic Adviser in office of Dean of Arts and Science) indicated that he is not eligible to enter the College of Engineering but will be accepted in the College of Arts and Science. A curriculum was worked out with him so that the courses which he would take here would transfer to Blue College.

The client indicated that while he was at White University he had a counseling relationsip with Dr. Crew at that school. During this time he indicated that they did not discuss vocational choice but spent most of their time working with his personal problems.

During the latter part of the interview the client indicated that he was again confused over his relationship with another young lady, this one being a student at a girls' college located near Blue College.

The client began the second interview by indicating that he was extremely worried over his relationships with his girl friend in the East. He indicates that he has not heard from her for some time and called her on the telephone. He indicated that although they had a good talk he was still uncertain as to what his status was as regards her affections. The client indicated that when he did not hear from this girl he had a tendency to become extremely worried and to run off and ask other people what to do, especially people who knew this girl at Blue College. The client indicated that there had been an exchange of rings and pins and that he was in a little deeper than he thought he was going to get into at the beginning of their relationship. It is the counselor's opinion that this whole relationship indicates an immature emotional attitude on the part of the client and that his actions at this time are an attempt to preserve this rather nebulous relationship with his girl friend which is in turn an attempt on his part to gain some degree of security within a particular social group. During the course of the interview I attempted to work with him to gain some insight as to what his motivations were in becoming involved so seriously when he was not in a position to do so. In general, it seems to be a combination of hurt pride, emotional immaturity, and a desire to gain status in a social plane which his family and general home environment could not give him. Toward the end of the second interview the client indicated that he was going to try to go to see his girl friend during the Easter holidays. Although the counselor felt this was a rather useless and childish reaction on his part, he made no attempt definitely to dissuade the client from so doing. The counselor attempted to point out the pros and cons of such an action and help the client remove his thoughts from the emotional to the rational side of this particular question.

During the third interview the client again discussed his plans to go to see his girl friend. I then attempted to draw a relationship for the client between his difficulty with the girl from the hospital and the girl who attends school near Blue College. I tried to bring this out on the basis of a need for security without too much success at this time, I felt. The client then went off into a discussion of his previous relationships with the first girl friend. The entire interview was spent in this type of discussion and several interesting things were learned regarding the client's thoughts and reactions.

In general I feel that it is possible to say the client has a tendency to ramble and is definitely what the counselor considers to be immature in his emotional reactions toward his status in a group. He refuses to face issues and during the counseling relationship it is difficult to bring him face-to-face with any particular point, since when he gets to a point which is painful to him he merely retreats and begins a long verbal discussion about some side issue.

During the fourth interview I felt that we reached the high point of our relationship. It was here that I stopped allowing him to wander away from issues and forced him back always to face the point at question. I also made attempts to interpret his feelings to him and his environment to him. I had the feeling that he rejected some of the information but accepted the greater part of it. It was during this interview that the client indicated that one of the reasons he attempts to get involved seriously with these girls is that they represent a different way of life and social plane to him. He indicates that although his family has sufficient money to live in an average middle-class manner, this does not satisfy him—and that after he joined a fraternity and began to go with college boys who had more income he began to feel that he had missed something and he visualized their particular way of life as one which he would like to follow. He feels that going with girls whose families have money will identify him in this type of social plane. I attempted to interpret his drives and motivations to him and indicate that there were other ways to achieve this

particular goal. At the close of the interview I had the feeling
that we had gone much further than we had ever gone before
and that we had achieved a great deal more. I think that during
this time he began to get some insight into his own emotional
immaturity.

Although there were six more interviews I felt that the fourth
was the high point in our relationship. After this time we discussed
various topics including a rehash during several of the interviews
of his emotional relationships and social drives. During some portions of the interview we discussed such matters as study habits,
vocational choice, summer jobs, whether or not the client should
go back to Blue College or remain here, and his relationship with
his parents. Throughout the whole of the ten interviews the client
gave every indication of wanting someone to lean on and to make
this weakness a sort of strength, that is, he wanted always to
control the counselor and to come in whether or not he had a
regular appointment. It took some time to break him of this and
in the process I feel that the client gained some degree of independence and maturity. At the time we broke off our relationships
I felt that he was much better able to make his own decisions
than he was at the time he came in. However, this may be only
a surface consideration and it is possible that when he again
meets some sort of crisis he will slip back into his old behavior
patterns. We made some tentative arrangements to continue the
relationship next September if the client returns to this school.
His tentative decision also was to return here rather than to
continue at Blue College.

COUNSELOR'S NOTES ON THE ELEVENTH INTERVIEW

(*4 Months after the Tenth Interview*)

(*Dictated Immediately after the Interview*)

★ Mr. Battle returned to the center today for a brief visit with the
counselor. We had a pleasant chat which could not be described
in the main as a counseling interview. I am merely including this
in the notes as a follow-up type of information. Mr. Battle indicated that he had returned home after school ended last semester
and had taken a job as a track laborer for a railroad. He stated
that after the flood conditions had existed in another part of the
state, he had gone with the track crew had been engaged in the
cleaning up of this area. He stated that on two occasions, at least,
he had quit his job but had finally relented and asked the boss to
take him back. He states that he felt that this was an indication
of strength on his part. He really disliked the job intensely because
of the nature of the work which was that of shoveling mud and
debris which was rather odious and disagreeable to him. He
seemed to be rather proud of the fact that he was able to stick
out the job until the end and save enough money to return to

school. He seemed to be in a very elated state because he now has made a definite decision to take a degree in business and public administration here and has discussed this with the dean and should be able to graduate in June of this school year. He seemed to be very happy over this fact and indicates that he has matured a great deal over the past year. I am not quite as sure of this point as he is, as he still exhibits some of the behavior patterns which were present when he first came to us. He mentioned that he· was handling his relationship with members of the opposite sex satisfactorily now but was not tied down emotionally to any one of them. At the end of the conversation, the client mentioned that he again would like to have access to the counseling center "if trouble should come up again." He was assured that he would always be welcome here and was invited back for a chat even if he did not feel himself to be in any particular difficulty.

❃   ❃   ❃   ❃   ❃

In a follow-up contact with Mr. Battle about a year after he received his B.S. degree in business administration from the university, he indicated that he was working as an industrial engineer for a large, nationally known industrial concern located in the East. He was quite pleased with his work.

CHAPTER 7

Discussion of

METHODOLOGY,
TECHNIQUES AND ETHICS

MANY IDEAS concerning counseling methodology have been mentioned editorially in the cases just presented. An attempt is made in this chapter to summarize in some sort of organized fashion the comments made in connection with the cases and to relate them to some theoretical formulations. No attempt is made to present a concerted or consistent theory of counseling. Only those points which appear to need further clarification are discussed.

ORIENTATION TO COUNSELING METHODOLOGY IN THE CASES

A persistent and perennial question in counseling concerns diagnosis. Many controversies have raged around such problems as—to diagnose or not to diagnose; what is the nature of diagnosis; what is the role of diagnosis in counseling; what are the theoretical bases for diagnosis?

If diagnosis is defined broadly as development of understandings about the client, it can be said with a high degree of confidence that a large majority of counselors attempts diagnosis in some degree. It may not be formal, it may not be rigid and static, it may not be formulated in good theoretical terminology, yet it is diagnosis in the sense that the counselor attempts to develop understandings about his client.

Why does a counselor feel he needs to understand his client? Also, what does the counselor mean when he says "understand the client?" In some fashion "understanding the client" fosters a feeling of security in the counselor. On the other hand, for a counselor to feel that he does not understand his client probably creates *feelings in the counselor* which reduce his effectiveness. "To understand the client" means different things to different counselors. To one it might mean thorough understanding of the client's personality structure in the language of some generally accepted theory. To another it might mean understanding the feelings expressed by the client from moment to moment. In either event the effect on the counselor of "not understanding" may be identical.

Furthermore, it is quite evident from reading typescripts of interviews, counselors' case notes, and from listening to counselors discuss a case, that counselors do *different* things, each of which is intended to be therapeutic or problem-solving in effect. Why, then, does a counselor behave differently in different situations, with different clients? The most logical and parsimonious explanation is that the counselor chooses to employ a particular therapeutic technique from those available because of differential understandings.

If the counselor's understandings are of the moment-to-moment feelings of the client, he is apt to use techniques such as reflection, clarification, and simple acceptance of feelings. If the counselor's understandings are in terms of personality-structure concepts, he is apt to use techniques of interpretation and the giving of information in their various forms.

Certain opinions are prevalent to the effect that a counselor who uses nondirective technique to a large extent does not engage in diagnosis. One needs only to consult Rogers (281:76-77) to dispel this erroneous concept. Rogers sets forth eight criteria which must be met in order for nondirective technique to be appropriate for a particular client. Some of these criteria are: (1) the client is under a degree of emotional tension; (2) he has some capacity to cope with life; (3) he is reasonably independent of close family control; (4) he is reasonably free from excessive instabilities; and (5) he possesses adequate intelligence (dull normal or above). To evaluate a client against these criteria is to engage in diagnostic behavior. One might say that such an evaluation is not counseling. Nevertheless, such an evaluation is most often performed by the counselor and thus may be considered a part of counselor behavior. Thus it would appear that there is no basis for controversy as to whether the counselor does engage in diagnostic behavior of some sort. However, there is considerable basis for controversy concerning the *role* of diagnosis in counseling.

Also, Porter (262) discussed various kinds of interpretation as aspects of counselor behavior. *Interpretation qua construction* as defined and described by Porter refers to those counselor activities (more precisely, his thought processes) which lead to development of understandings about the client and the counseling relationship. These understandings are not necessarily interpreted to the client but do influence and guide the counselor in his activities, particularly therapeutic activities. Thus, what Porter has called *interpretation qua construction* is, in essence, identical with much of what is referred to here as diagnostic behavior of the counselor.

It appears from a study of the cases presented here that diagnostic behavior was engaged in as a search for cause, i.e., etiology of the problem, and a search for a solution of the problem. Diagnostic efforts were continuous throughout the interviews in conjunction with continuous therapeutic or problem-solving efforts. The efforts were engaged in *both* by counselor and client. As *they* began to develop a higher level of confidence in their understandings of the problem and the possible solutions to it, *they* began to bring problem-solving or therapeutic behavior into play. Diagnosis then began to drop out, although the counselor was usually alert to the possibility that new understandings might occur which would change the "problem," the counselor's technique, and even the therapeutic goals.

A quite fundamental question to be raised here is: what conceptual frames of reference did the counselor use in formulating diagnostic constructs or understandings about his client? It is apparent that he used some higher order concepts in evaluating data gleaned from interviews, tests, etc. to formulate theories, hypotheses, or understandings about his client. It is also apparent that he used his understandings of the psychology of human behavior and his knowledge of social and environmental forces as they affect the client. Probably the most fundamental concept which the counselor used concerned the psychological needs of the client and the manner and degree to which these needs were frustrated or denied satisfaction. Some of the needs which came into play in these cases were: (1) the need for a feeling of personal worth and dignity; (2) the need for satisfactory heterosexual relations; (3) the need to emancipate oneself from parental control and develop a sense of maturity and independence; and (4) the need for self-expression (a real or anticipated outlet for abilities and interests).

The role that theory plays in the counselor's choice of counseling technique is often quite obscure. This seems to be so in the cases presented here. However, there appears to have been some sort of theoretical formulations, good, bad or indifferent, which guided the counselor's choice of techniques. Fiedler (*142*) studied the relative effect of the theoretical orientation of the counselor and the degree of his "expertness" on the counseling relationship. His sample of counselors included experts and novices from three schools of thought—psychoanalytic, Adlerian and nondirective. Fiedler drew three major conclusions from his data: "(1) Expert psychotherapists of any of the three schools create a relationship more closely approximating the Ideal Therapeutic Relationship than relationships created by nonexperts; (2) The therapeutic relationship created by experts of one school resembles more closely that created by experts of other schools than it resembles relationships created by nonexperts within the same school; (3) The most important dimension (of those measured) which differentiates experts from nonexperts is related to the therapist's ability to understand, to communicate with, and to maintain rapport with the patient." It would appear then from Fiedler's study that the degree of expertness of the counselor (presumably based on training and experience) is a more important variable in counseling than is the theoretical orientation of the counselor. The effect of training and experience of the counselor seems to be present in our cases as well as in Fiedler's. The counselors with more training and experience seem to understand the clients better, communicate with them better, and possibly achieve better results than those with less training and experience.

Thurstone's (*405:51*) comments on the role of theory in science seem appropriate to a consideration of the role of theory in the choice of counseling technique, ". . . the constructs in terms of which natural phenomena are comprehended are man-made inventions. To discover a scientific law is merely to discover that a man-made scheme serves to unify, and thereby to simplify, comprehension of a certain class of natural phenomena. A scientific law is not to be thought of as having an independent existence . . . A scientific law is not a part of nature. It is only a way of comprehending nature." Much of counseling is a search (by the client and/or the counselor) for an understanding, a theory, or a "law" which will explain a series of observations, events, feelings or attitudes which puzzle the client and create anxiety and dissatisfaction in him in varying degrees. Mowrer (*243*) and Thorne (*400*) have indicated that one of the most potent characteristics of anxiety is *not to understand* about something. Thus, any explanation that is "logical" or "makes sense" to the client may be acceptable and useful to him. This explanation must meet a further criterion in order to be therapeutic. It must stand the test of reality, i.e., it must solve the problem by reducing anxiety and promoting satisfaction of needs. In a specific instance one theory may be equally as good as another, but, of course, the better theory will be more generally useful in a wider variety of situations than a poorer theory.

It should be pointed out that the counselor has no monopoly on the development of theories about his client. Quite to the contrary, counseling may be thought of as a process wherein the client is helped to discard inadequate theories about himself, and to learn and accept (to act on) better theories about himself. A counselor may be quite proficient in developing good theories about a client, i.e., he may be a good diagnostician, but, if he is unable to help the client develop good theories, his efforts will have had little positive effect on the client. The real question concerning methodology, then, becomes: Is it necessary or desirable for the counselor to develop good theories about his client in order that he may help the client develop good theories? The question must be answered in terms of the utility of the *client's theories* rather than the counselor's theories. The counselor's theories are important only as they affect the client's theories—theories which he can put into practice and which facilitate satisfaction of needs.

In order for the client to learn new and better theories about himself (ways to solve his problems) he must be an active participant in the process; he is the one who must do the learning. The counselor's role is to facilitate learning.

The problem-solving aspect of learning theory seems to be a satisfactory explanation of the counseling process apparent in our cases. The problem is identified; various reasons the problem has developed are considered; a search for possible solutions or several alternative solutions is made; a solution for try-out is selected; and the solution is reality-tested. If the solution meets the test of reality, it is accepted; if not, some alternative solution is tried. Only if the client goes through this process is counseling effective. The counselor's role is to aid the client to take these various steps.

After the client has made certain attempts to learn new theories about himself, the counselor usually does some things to test to see what learning has occurred. The counselor may explain the results of some test and then say, "How does this agree with the way you see yourself?" "Does this make any sense to you?" or "Is this of any value to you?" In other words, he is actually testing to see what learning has occurred. He may find that incomplete or erroneous learning has occurred and he may then have to make a different approach in order to facilitate appropriate learning.

Our concept of problem-solving is rather broad. It is broad enough to include learning of affective materials, such as emotionalized attitudes and ego-involved concepts about oneself. Many of the problems presented by the clients in our cases can be reduced to one problem, namely, need for a change in or clarification of self-concepts. Concepts or attitudes about oneself by their very nature involve the affect. That is, they are emotionalized or ego-involved to varying degrees depending on the needs and defenses of the individual. Dipboye (*115*) has shown that the problems of clients similar to the ones presented here can be appropriately grouped into two rough classifications—affective and cognitive. The counselors tended to respond differently in terms of therapeutic endeavors to affective problems than they did to cognitive problems. Affective problems included those involving interpersonal relations and self-concepts or self-references. Cognitive problems included educational and vocational indecision and educational skills.

Two major techniques intended to be therapeutic used by the counselors in our cases are giving of information and psychological interpretation. Other techniques such as reflection and clarification of feeling were used but they played a minor role. Where the problem called for further understandings by the client of a nature which he could readily accept and integrate into his self-concept, giving information was the technique most often used. Considerable caution needs to be used in giving information. The counselor needs to take precautions to assure that the information is valid and appropriate to the problem. He also needs to determine if the client can accept the information as presented. He needs to be alert for indications that the client is distorting or rejecting the information and, if so, consider it a cue to shift to some other techniques, such as those described by Rogers (*281, 292*).

Giving information as a counseling technique shades into psychological interpretation. Psychological interpretation deals with more complex phenomena which involve the feelings, emotions, and attitudes of the client. There are many dangers and errors to be aware of in interpreting psychological material to the client (i.e., about himself). Thorne (*400, Chap. 30*) discusses a method of interpretation in which he points out some of the dangers and errors to be avoided. The counselor needs to be reasonably sure that the formulations which he proposes to interpret are correct or at least tenable. They should pose a minimum of threat to the client. They should be tentative and be presented in such a way that the client feels free to accept, reject, or modify them. Rogers (*281: 204-206*) also recognizes interpretation as a valuable therapeutic technique. He proposes, however, a rather mild form of interpretation which he calls "clarification": "The counselor may aid this process (development of insight and self-understanding) by reformulating insights already achieved, by clarifying the new understandings at which the client has arrived. He may be of assistance in helping the client to explore and recognize the choices, the possible courses of action, which lie before him. The counselor may, in addition, suggest relationships or patterns of reaction which seem to be evident in material which the client has freely stated." Rogers continues his discussion of interpretation and clarification and lists several precautions to be observed. These precautions are similar to the ones listed by Thorne.

The use of the technique of interpretation implies that the counselor makes a continuous diagnostic evaluation throughout the case. Some may prefer to call this series of formulations, working hypotheses or they may prefer Porter's (*262*) term, *interpretation qua construction*. It appears to be the same process no matter what it is labeled.

Another kind of interpretation is that used in psychoanalysis in its various forms. Psychoanalytic interpretation is often based on unconscious motivations of the patient. Such interpretation is rarely appropriate to counseling as it is presented here. Also we would rarely find a counselor who was competent to do psychoanalytic interpretation.

A final point concerning the counseling methodology found in our cases is one often overlooked by counselors. It is concerned with the permanence of the learnings resulting from counseling. Quite frequently clients achieve certain insights and understandings which are tentative and tenuous in nature. If the client then returns to the situation or environment which helped precipitate the problem originally, the insights and understandings may be lost in part or in full. This suggests that the counselor should explore with the client the latter's probable post-counseling experience. An example of this is found in the *Case of John Battle*. The counselor raised the question of what the client's reactions might be if he returned to Blue College or re-established contact with his girl friend. A more dramatic example comes from some mental hospitals where considerable time is spent with patients discussing "what will it be like, how will I be accepted when I return home." Mental hospital personnel report this to be one of the greatest concerns of patients who are about ready to go home. If counseling is to be of real value, the client must be able to retain and use the new insights and understandings in his post-counseling living. It is not sufficient for him to verbalize the insights and understandings in the interview; he must be able to apply them in his daily life.

ASPECTS OF AND ISSUES IN COUNSELING

In addition to variations in over-all counseling methodology, the preceding cases illustrate differences among specific techniques. Since a counselor's choice of techniques may be largely dependent upon his decisions with regard to several client-counselor responsibility variables, a discussion of this division of responsibility precedes the discussion of other aspects and issues.

Client-Counselor Responsibility Variables

Many of the controversies over counseling methodology and techniques are centered in the client-counselor responsibility variables, i.e., the degree of responsibility which the counselor assumes for whatever occurs during the counseling interview. In the present cases there are four such variables which require a counselor's decision as to the degree of responsibility he wishes to accept. They center around: (1) development of the problem; (2) selection and interpretation of tests; (3) conduct of the interview; and (4) client's goals, values, and actions.

The first variable is the development of the client's problem. A client, for example, may say, "I can't concentrate." Just the fact that he cannot concentrate may make little sense to the counselor or to the client until it can be related to some more meaningful reference point. The counselor can aid the client in the development of the problem by at least two ways. One would be that which follows nondirective theory rather closely. The client's statements are reflected and clarified to the point where the client actually takes the lead in the development of the problem. A second approach is one in which the counselor assumes the initiative in developing the problem. He may start with the stated problem and then begin to search different areas of client behavior and thought in order to develop the problem. He may say, "Well, how would you describe your family?" or "What sort of activities do you engage in in school?" or "What sort of grades are you making?" Depending upon the problem, the counselor who utilizes this approach begins to search out various areas of client behavior and thought with an idea of searching for the cause(s) of the problem.

The second division of client-counselor responsibility may be seen in the selection and interpretation of tests for diagnostic and other purposes. Again two kinds of approaches have been discussed in the editorial comments of the cases. At one extreme the counselor takes the primary responsibility for selection of tests because he is interested in coming to as full an understanding of the client as possible. At the other extreme the client takes the primary responsibility in test selection and the counselor then assumes a minor role in this diagnostic behavior.

The counselor who assigns tests feels that they will aid in his understanding of the client. Such a procedure is consistent with the point of view expressed by Thorne (*400*), Williamson (*424, 428*), Darley (*104, 105*), and others. *The Case of Bette Morgan* illustrates this approach to test selection, a procedure which is not entirely dominated by the counselor. He may assign tests and yet permit client acceptance or rejection of the tests, such as that found in the *Case of Ruth Brook* and to a certain extent in the other cases.

The counselor of *Bill Davis*, on the other hand, gave the client freedom of choice and thereby accepted the possibility that there might be gaps in his understanding of the client. This approach to test selection has been publicized by the writings of Bordin and Bixler (*53*) as well as Rogers (*284*).

The counselor in the *Case of John Battle* did not propose any further testing beyond that collected prior to the referral from another counselor. The client desired and was given an intelligence test. A formal interpretation of the results was made.

Test interpretations follow patterns similar to test selection. The counselor may use test results for his own information. Formal test interpretations to the client may be the exception and not the rule. This type of counselor behavior, which may be found in the *Case of Bette Morgan*, is quite consistent with Porter's (*262*) concept of *interpretation qua construction*. On the other hand, the results of tests may be interpreted to the client in a relatively formal manner similar to that in the *Case of Bill Davis* or the *Case of Ruth Brook*. The counselor in the *Case of Tom Smith* was evidently attempting to interpret tests using the procedure suggested by Bixler and Bixler (*42*). That is, test results were tied rather closely to materials covered previously in interviews. The results of tests were presented only as they could be verified or questioned on the basis of other data. In the *Case of Tom Smith,* however, the counselor's responses failed to stimulate the desired form of client behavior.

The third variable is the client-counselor responsibility for the general conduct of the counseling interview. Counselors from various theoretical orientations may differ considerably regarding their conceptions of this responsibility. Fundamentally the argument arises from dichotomizing responsibility for the conduct of the interview. That is, the responsibility is either the counselor's or that of the client. Even the counselor with a nondirective orientation insists upon keeping some control over the interview. He sets limits within which the counseling will take place and conducts the interview in such a manner that the client is enabled to examine his affective behavior. Robinson (278) also points out that structuring speeches whether used by nondirective counselors or those from other orientations are highly directive in that they force the interview to conform to the counselor's desired pattern.

A fourth variable is one described by Rogers (281). He has insisted that the client retain responsibility for his behavior, including his goals, values, and actions. Few counselors will take issue with that point of view, even though they do not subscribe necessarily to nondirective theory in its entirety. For example, the counselor of *Bette Morgan* took an active responsibility for conducting the interview but did not assume responsibility for Miss Morgan's goals, values, and actions. The counselor was concerned only with the process whereby Miss Morgan could examine her feeling of inadequacy in interpersonal relationships; he was not attempting to determine her goals, values, or actions for her. Any counselor worthy of the title respects the autonomy of his clients and is not interested in manipulating their lives.

The only logical conclusion seems to be that the conduct of the interview is a joint responsibility involving several variables. The only major difference between counselors of different orientations is the manner in which they exercise control over several variables in the counseling interviews. Because of the fact that the counselors in the casebook were "non-nondirective," the reader has to verify this conclusion through an examination of other cases, such as those presented by Snyder (353), and other sources, such as Rogers (281: 95-108).

Structuring

Structuring, the counselor's verbalizing or demonstrating his relationship with a client, is related to the client-counselor responsibility variables. To structure is to inform the client of the desired client-counselor relationship and of the counselor's and client's roles in the counseling interview. The nature of structuring depends in large part on what

decisions the counselor has made concerning the client-counselor responsibility variables discussed above. The counselor may wish to follow
a rigid pattern of structuring or he may wish to vary the form and timing
of structuring with each counseling case.

Ideally, perhaps, the counselor is able to demonstrate by overt behavior his relationship to the client; but anyone engaged actively in
counseling is aware of the fact that client expectations prior to counseling
may be distorted and unrealistic. In this latter instance, verbal structuring may be not only appropriate but an absolute necessity if counseling
is to proceed within the limits set by the counselor. In any case, verbal
structuring seems most appropriate at the time when the counselor and
client reach a general agreement regarding the problem which they
intend to solve. This point of view was exemplified in the *Case of Bette
Morgan*. The counselor kept structuring speeches to a minimum and used
them only after the problem had been developed to the satisfaction of
the client and himself.

The degree, amount, and nature of structuring depends upon how
closely the client's concept of what is to be done approaches the counselor's concept of what he intends to do. In other words, when the
client's expectations of the counseling process are similar to what the
counselor intends it to be, very little structuring is needed. If there is
a discrepancy between the two, structuring is usually necessary. And as
that discrepancy between expectation and fact develops, additional
structuring may be necessary throughout the case. The counselor of
Ruth Brook utilized a structuring response when he felt that his client
did not clearly understand his functions as a counselor. This conclusion
was an outgrowth of the client's behavior and the general lack of public
knowledge as to what to expect from a counselor in terms of counseling
interviews and outcomes. Somewhat the same condition prevailed with
respect to the client's expectations from tests.

According to Robinson (278: 151) late structuring speeches, i.e.,
structuring after the counselor by his overt behavior has had ample
opportunities to demonstrate his relationship to a client, usually result
from a client's confusion about the counselor's role or from the counselor's feeling that the interview is not proceeding in a desirable way.
During the second interview with *Tom Smith* the counselor was con-
fronted with a series of "Yes, sir's" and "No, sir's." A series of structuring
responses by the counselor probably indicated that the counselor did not
approve of the manner in which the interview was proceeding. However,
the counselor followed the structuring responses with leads which lent
themselves to further "Yes, sir's and "No, sir's." This type of counselor
behavior emphasizes a rather important point, that a counselor may
verbalize the relationship which he wants with the client; but unless his

overt behavior reinforces his verbalizations, the client either will become more confused regarding the relationship or revert to the behavior which stimulated the original structuring response on the part of the counselor.

Closure

Closure in a counseling case refers to the resolution of the problem which confronts the client. Obviously *absolute* closure is not feasible; therefore the present discussion refers to a tentative type of closure which rests upon the level of confidence at which the counselor and the client are willing to accept the solution.

What are the symptoms and criteria of closure? First, it is appropriate to postulate an answer in terms of the needs or the need system of the client. When the needs of an individual are being satisfied, or he has reasonable expectation of satisfying them, closure has been reached. The following methods can be used for assessing closure: (1) the counselor's estimate of closure; (2) the client's feeling of closure; and (3) some fairly concrete indices of closure in terms of observable client behavior in or outside the counseling interview.

There are many types of situations where the counselor cannot use observable behavior as an index. In the *Case of Bette Morgan* the client expressed negative and hostile feelings toward her mother. A simple suggestion by the counselor was tested by the client. She said that she followed the suggestion, it seemed to work, and she felt better about it. This is one type of material which the counselor can use to judge closure. That in itself is behavior, of course, but it is nothing that can be observed. The counselor has to take her expressions of how she felt about it. In other words, there are some situations where the counselor can directly observe client behavior, but there are other times when he has to accept the client's statement, particularly *unprompted* client statements. Unprompted statements by the client can be accepted fairly well at face value if they make some sense with other data in the case.

Furthermore, there are counseling situations where the *final* resolution of the problem awaits the passage of time and added experiences and maturity along with increasing pressure for making a choice. Nevertheless, closure at a particular stage of maturity may have been reached and further planning held in abeyance until the client sees the necessity for further counseling. Consider the *Case of Ruth Brook*. At the end of the second interview the counselor did not feel that he had reached closure. Miss Brook had come with a certain problem, and all the while the counselor had been dealing with another aspect or facet of the problem, trying to determine to what extent her masculine interests and self-centeredness were going to interfere with certain adjustments which she would have to make. Near the end of the second interview the counselor had tested the hypothesis concerning her related problems at the level of confidence which he was willing to accept. The counselor had reached closure on the problem of masculine interests, realizing that Ruth Brook was still an adolescent and that they had explored the area as far as her maturity warranted. The self-centeredness still remained in the picture, but she was unable to accept this problem, so the counselor dismissed it for the time being. He then wished to schedule a third interview in order to discuss the problem of scholarships and education. Again, though, even on the discussion of education the counselor had to settle for a type of closure which was commensurate with a developmental stage of an adolescent who did not feel any pressure toward making a final choice.

The counselor in the *Case of Tom Smith* faced a somewhat similar situation as that faced by the counselor of Ruth Brook. There were successive stages of closure which were based on Tom Smith's need for reality testing with respect to scholarship. In addition, there is some evidence to indicate that the counselor's expectations for closure in this case were far beyond anything which could be reasonably expected from the client in his stage of development and thinking.

Referrals

Referrals to a counselor take many forms and show varying degrees of goodness. Basically the techniques of referral should aid the counselor in establishing satisfactory counseling relationships with the client.

The self-referral, such as that in the *Case of Bette Morgan* or the *Case of Ruth Brook*, is highly desirable and sought-after by most counselors. On the other hand, the counselor in an educational setting usually finds that a substantial number of his counseling interviews are carried on after referrals from teachers, administrators, and others in the school or community.

A referral from an instructor is shown in the *Case of Bill Davis*. Actually the client found out about the counseling service in a class discussion and, as a result, came as a self-referral to the counseling service. There are indications that Bill Davis expected a rather specific type of service. There is no way of telling whether this was due to a limited presentation by the instructor or whether Mr. Davis placed his own limitations on the service desired. Obviously the counselor is somewhat handicapped by a referral from an instructor who gives an erroneous or one-sided picture of counseling and related services to a potential client.

It is interesting to conjecture what would have happened in the case had Bill Davis been referred by an instructor and had he resisted somewhat the suggestion but felt it his duty to comply. Typically the counselor in such a predicament finds that he has to deal with the feeling of resistance before anything positive can be done regarding other client problems.

The *Case of Tom Smith,* on the other hand, represents a referral from

another source, i.e., a psychiatrist. The counselor was not able to establish with any degree of clarity the precise reason for the referral other
than that the psychiatrist probably felt that there was some need for
realistic vocational planning on the part of the client. Effective inter-
professional referrals typically involve mutual understandings and mutual
respect. The psychiatrist, social worker, clinical psychologist, and counseling psychologist should be sufficiently familiar with each other's role
that each can make and receive effective referrals. The same condition
should prevail in referrals from one counselor to another, such as that
in the *Case of John Battle*. Ethical questions regarding such referrals
are discussed in a subsequent section.

Counselor Notes

Whatever their orientation with respect to counseling methodology,
most counselors agree that it is necessary to keep some type of record
regarding each counseling interview and related activities. The manner
in which these notes are kept, though, reflects differences of opinion. At
one extreme are the highly structured notes described by Williamson
(428), and at the other extreme a highly unstructured or narrative style
of notes. In this casebook the counselor notes tend to be of a narrative
type.

Differences in style and content usually reflect differences in the purposes to be served by the notes. If the emphasis is upon formal diagnosis, the style used by Darley and Williamson is quite necessary. If
the counselor is to use his notes to refresh his memory between interviews and to aid another counselor in taking over the case at any time, a
narrative style seems as appropriate as any other style.

Four kinds of information are essential to adequate, narrative type
notes: (1) a description of client behavior, including the stated and
developed problem; (2) a description of counselor behavior and intent;
(3) the counselor's speculations and interpretations; and (4) factual data
concerning the client and his environment. Although the counselor notes
in the casebook do not always include these four types of information, it
must be remembered that the notes have not been altered in any way to
conform to any given set of criteria and that the counselors were permitted freedom in choosing their own modes of describing interview
behavior.

Experience with counselors, their counseling activities, and their interview notes indicates the value of some type of summary statement at
the close of each case. This summary may take the form of an addendum,
such as the authors have supplied for each case. The value of such a procedure seems to come from the counselor's reviewing all his data and
putting them in some organized form, thus providing a means of evaluation which can be utilized by himself or another counselor if and when
further counseling is requested by the client. The style used to present

materials in such a summary again may vary from a highly-structured to a narrative type of addendum. The form or style of presentation is less important than the act of organizing case data into a pattern which is meaningful to the counselor.

SOME ETHICAL CONSIDERATIONS IN COUNSELING

One of the major problems in counseling involves ethical considerations. Every counselor is faced with situations which call for decisions concerning courses of action to follow regarding his client's welfare, the counselor's place within the profession, and his institution or agency. Being a professional person involves personal integrity, competence, and good judgment. But it is difficult to know what course of action to follow unless one has a system of ethical principles or a code of ethics which will point the way. However, at no time does the counselor free himself from responsibility for his actions. The mere existence of a code of ethics does not solve the problem even though it may aid in the process.

Several efforts have been made to call attention of psychologists to the matter of ethical standards. Two recent publications of the American Psychological Association (8, 9) give evidence of professional concern for ethical standards and tend to clarify issues. Wrenn (440) has related the matter of ethics in psychology specifically to ethics in counseling.

It seems that many questions that arise in the actual work of the counselor involve two main issues: (1) "invasion of privacy;" and (2) ethical considerations germane to the institutional or agency setting. Hence the following statements are made as an attempt to relate these issues to the cases presented in this book.

In the *Case of Bette Morgan* there was evidence of resistance on the client's part when the counselor tried to go beyond the client's stated problem of vocational choice to problems related to her interpersonal relations. In fact, the latter was never fully accepted by her. But what if she had refused to go along with the counselor's attempts to relate the two problems? The counselor might have felt pressure to shy away from important areas of behavior lest he invade the privacy of the client. His decision to continue with Miss Morgan, even in the face of the resistance, was a decision some counselors would not make. Instead they might have decided to confine discussions to purely vocational matters, or to the topics which Miss Morgan might choose to discuss in evading other issues in her life. If Bette Morgan had refused to continue the counseling relationship, the counselor would have recognized that she had the right to make that decision. On the other hand, the counselor felt the need for considering more than the so-called vocational aspects of Miss Morgan's plans and goals. Recognizing ego-involved attitudes and the privacy of them, the counselor had to show respect for them, yet insofar as possible relate them to the over-all issues of the case. In spite of some resistance, Bette Morgan did not feel that the counselor had exceeded his role as a counselor.

In the *Case of Bill Davis* the counselor confined himself to issues raised by the client. By working only on the basis of the presented problem, the counselor knew little about Bill Davis after the counseling relationship ceased. Closure was not so apparent as in the *Case of Bette Morgan*. The counselor, even though he had learned less about Bill Davis than he might have learned respected the client's decision that further contacts were not necessary. It seems, then, that invasion of privacy depends upon the interpretations of both counselor and client. Their interpretations are important in determining the courses of action and the direction of the counseling interviews. Perhaps the counselor felt that to urge consideration of questions other than the presented problem would constitute an invasion of privacy. On the other hand, he may have felt that further diagnostic effort was unnecessary to the welfare of his client.

The *Case of Tom Smith* involves further ethical consideration. After the client displayed some reluctance to discuss his contacts with the psychiatrist, the counselor did not choose to go into the relationships between Tom Smith and the psychiatrist who had referred Mr. Smith to the counselor. He accepted the referral at its face value. Here we see the need for greater liaison between the person making the referral and the person accepting the referral. Counseling as a profession needs greater clarification of its place in clinical work. But the ethical principle involved in the *Case of Tom Smith* is that of respecting the confidential nature of the client's relationship with another professional worker. One can only assume that the psychiatrist felt that Tom Smith needed and desired counseling and that serious emotional difficulties were not present. At any rate, the counselor did not violate the ethical principle involved. Some information from the psychiatrist might have been helpful, nevertheless.

In the *Case of Ruth Brook* we see the client's interest in sending counseling information on to school officials and agency personnel. The counselor emphasized the professional nature of his work, the importance of the client's wishes in the matter, and the need for information being given in the language and on the professional level of the recipient. The incident may have been a test of the counselor's professional ethics.

The *Case of John Battle* illustrates good handling of information which is transferred from one counselor to another. In fact, Mr. Battle was waiting anxiously for the reports to reach the counselor so that the counseling might proceed.

Ethical problems which arise in an institutional or agency setting frequently come from lack of understanding as to the roles of administrators and counselors. So long as the counselor and the administrator recognize two kinds of responsibilities, namely, administrative and professional, the chances for misunderstanding are diminished. For example, the administrator who delegates counseling to the counselor and recognizes this specialty as a *professional* function, respects the status of the counselor. At the same time, the counselor who recognizes the administrative function as being in the administrator's professional province respects the status of the administrator. Within the framework of their functions and their respective principles of ethics, the administrator and the counselor will be called upon to settle problems of ethics. Both persons must operate with due consideration for the welfare of the client.

Recognizing the importance of ethical considerations, the staff of a counseling service on the university level operates on the basis of a statement of principles. These principles concern the professional counseling relationship as it applies to the counseling service and its relations with other services within the university. The intent of these principles is not to free the counselor from deciding his professional courses of action in situations that arise. They only help him do professional work in the institutional setting.

STATEMENT OF PRINCIPLES CONCERNING THE
PROFESSIONAL COUNSELING RELATIONSHIP

1. The counselor shall act to further the welfare of his client in all of his work with and concerning his client. "Client" is used here to indicate a student or other person to whom the counselor has assumed some professional responsibility, such as counseling, or psychological evaluation. This is the most important principle and, in the event of conflict with any other principle listed, this one takes precedence over it.

2. Records of a counseling relationship, such as interview notes, test data, or correspondence, are professional information and shall not be made available for any purpose other than that for which they were compiled, unless permission of the client is obtained to do so. Reports to other persons, when made, shall be of a summary nature and in such language and concepts as the recipient is able to understand and use professionally.

3. The counselor reserves the right to consult with any other person within his own profession about a client without necessarily securing the client's permission to do so. However, the counselor must obtain the permission of the client to do so if he is to *seek* information from another person concerning the client.

4. When a counselor anticipates that his relationship with a client cannot be confidential, he should make clear to the client the nature

of his role before counseling is begun. For example, the counselor may accept referrals for diagnostic evaluations or counseling from persons who are in an authoritative relationship with the client, provided that the nature of the referral is clearly understood by counselor and client. Also, the person making the referral may request and obtain reports of diagnostic evaluation or counseling if he makes the request known to the counselor at the time of the referral.

5. The counselor must refer his client to an appropriate specialist when there is evidence of a difficulty with which the counselor is not competent to deal. In the event that the client declines the suggested referral, the counselor is not necessarily obligated to continue with the case. However, in the event that the case is of an *acute* or *emergency* nature, the counselor is obligated to report the situation to the appropriate, responsible authority even though he does not have the client's permission to do so.

6. When the counselor learns of conditions which may adversely affect other students, he is obligated to report the *condition* to appropriate responsible authority, but in such a manner as not to reveal the identity of his clients.

7. When a person, agency, or department refers a student to a counselor, the counselor should make some sort of a report to the person suggesting the referral. This report is to be of such nature as not to violate any of the principles listed above. This report might be only a telephone call stating that the student has contacted the counselor.

These principles differ in some respects from those formulated by the Committee on Ethical Standards in Psychology of the American Psychological Association. These principles give the counselor more freedom to exercise judgment and discretion than do the APA principles. Also, by setting Principle 1 as taking precedence over all other principles, the counselor has been given a principle to follow in those difficult situations of possible divided loyalty. It would be a rare university administration or professional organization which would take issue with Principle 1 as applied by a professionally competent counselor. These principles have been developed from the experiences of a staff of a counseling service and from the professional literature. It can be seen that many of them do not apply to counseling alone, but are equally important in other kinds of personnel work.

In summary, the counselor operating within an institutional setting is a professional worker whose work must be carried on under a system of values and a set of operating ethical principles. He must act as a professional person whether in private practice or in an institutional or agency setting. The problem of professional ethics in counseling is one that he cannot pass on to others to solve for him.

VOCATIONAL INTEREST
OF ENGINEERING STUDENT

HANKES REPORT FORM FOR—
STRONG VOCATIONAL INTEREST TEST - MEN

GROUP	OCCUPATION	C	C+	B-	B	B+	A
I	ARTIST						
	PSYCHOLOGIST						
	ARCHITECT						
	PHYSICIAN						
	OSTEOPATH						
	DENTIST						
II	MATHEMATICIAN						
	PHYSICIST						
	ENGINEER						
	CHEMIST						
III	PRODUCTION MANAGER						
IV	FARMER						
	AVIATOR						
	CARPENTER						
	PRINTER						
	MATH. PHYS. SCI. TEACHER						
	POLICEMAN						
	FOREST SERVICE MAN						
V	Y.M.C.A. PHYS. DIRECTOR						
	PERSONNEL DIRECTOR						
	PUBLIC ADMINISTRATOR						
	Y.M.C.A. SECRETARY						
	SOC. SCI. H.S. TEACHER						
	CITY SCHOOL SUPT.						
	MINISTER						
VI	MUSICIAN						
VII	C.P.A.						
VIII	ACCOUNTANT						
	OFFICE MAN						
	PURCHASING AGENT						
	BANKER						
	MORTICIAN						
IX	SALES MANAGER						
	REAL ESTATE SALESMAN						
	LIFE INSURANCE SALESMAN						
X	ADVERTISING MAN						
	LAWYER						
	AUTHOR-JOURNALIST						
XI	PRESIDENT-MFG. CONCERN						
	INTEREST MATURITY						
	OCCUPAT. LEVEL						
	MASCULINITY-FEMIN.						

APPENDIX A

Comparison of the Distribution of the Middle 50 Per Cent of the Scores Made by the Engineer Group and the Non-Engineer Group on The Occupational Scales of the Strong Vocational Interest Blank for Men.

Legend

Non-Engineers:

Q1 Md Q3

Engineers:

Q1 Md Q3

Reprinted with the permission of the author, E. K. Strong, Jr., and the publisher, Stanford University Press.

* Adapted from Saddler (307).

Bibliography

1. Aldrich, Margaret G. An exploratory study of social guidance at the college level. *Educ. psychol. Measmt.*, 1942, 2, 209-216.

2. Aldrich, Margaret G. A follow-up study of social guidance at the college level. *J. appl. Psychol.*, 1949, 33, 258-264.

3. Alexander, F., & French, T. M. (Eds.) *Psychoanalytic therapy: principles and application.* New York: Ronald, 1946.

4. Allport, G. W. *Personality: a psychological interpretation.* New York: Henry Holt, 1937.

5. Allport, G. W. *The use of personal documents in psychological science.* New York: Social Science Research Council, 1942.

6. American Psychological Association. Division of Counseling and Guidance, Committee on Counselor Training. Practicum training of counseling psychologists. *Amer. Psychologist*, 1952, 7, 182-188.

7. American Psychological Association. Division of Counseling and Guidance, Committee on Counselor Training. Recommended standards for training counseling psychologists at the doctorate level. *Amer. Psychologist*, 1952, 7, 175-181.

8. American Psychological Association. Committee on Ethical Standards for Psychology. *Ethical standards of psychologists.* Washington: American Psychological Association, 1953.

9. American Psychological Association. Committee on Ethical Standards for Psychology. *Ethical standards of psychologists: a summary of ethical principles.* Washington: American Psychological Association, 1953.

10. Anderson, Rose G. Reported and demonstrated values of vocational counseling. *J. appl. Psychol.*, 1949, 33, 460-473.

11. Andrews, Jean S. Directive psychotherapy, I: reassurance. *J. clin. Psychol.*, 1945, 1, 52-66.

12. Applezweig, M. H. Educational levels and Minnesota Multiphasic profiles. *J. clin. Psychol.*, 1953, 9, 340-344.

13. Assum, A. L., & Levy, S. J. Analysis of a nondirective case with followup interview. *J. abnorm. soc. Psychol.*, 1948, 43, 78-89.

14. Axline, Virginia M. Nondirective therapy for poor readers. *J. consult. Psychol.*, 1947, 11, 61-69.

15. Baer, M. F., & Roeber, E. C. *Occupational information: its nature and use.* Chicago: Science Research Associates, 1951.

16. Bailey, H. W., Gilbert, W. M., & Berg, I. A. Counseling and the use of tests in the Student Personnel Bureau at the University of Illinois. *Educ. psychol. Measmt.*, 1946, 6, 37-60.

17. Baller, W. R. Characteristics of college students who demonstrate interest in counseling services. *J. educ. Psychol.*, 1944, 35, 302-308.

18. Bancroft, Gertrude. Consistency of information from records and interviews. *Amer. statist. assn. J.*, 1940, 35, 377-381.

19. Barnett, G., Handelsman, I., Stewart, L. H., & Super, D. E. The occupational level scale as a measure of drive. *Psychol. Monogr.*, 1952, *65*, No. 10 (Whole No. 342).

20. Barnett, G. J., Stewart, L. H., & Super, D. E. Level of occupational interest: deadweight or dynamism? *Educ. psychol. Measmt.*, 1953, *13*, 193-208.

21. Barry, J. R. The relation of verbal reactions to adjustment level. *J. abnorm. soc. Psychol.*, 1950, *45*, 647-658.

22. Beier, E. G. The problem of anxiety in client-centered therapy. *J. consult. Psychol.*, 1951, *15*, 359-362.

23. Beier, E. G. Client-centered therapy and the involuntary client. *J. consult. Psychol.*, 1952, *16*, 332-337.

24. Bell, H. M. *The theory and practice of personal counseling.* Stanford: Stanford University Press, 1939.

25. Bell, H. M. Personal adjustment counseling. In W. S. Monroe (Ed.), *Encyclopedia of educational research.* (Rev. Ed.) New York: Macmillan, 1950. Pp. 1327-1330.

26. Bender, I. E. & Hastorf, A. H. On measuring generalized empathic ability (social sensitivity). *J. abnorm. soc. Psychol.*, 1953, *48*, 503-506.

27. Berdie, R. F. Factors related to vocational interests. *Psychol. Bull.*, 1944, *41*, 137-157.

28. Berdie, R. F. Judgments in counseling. *Educ. psychol. Measmt.*, 1944, *4*, 35-55.

29. Berdie, R. F. Range of interests. *J. appl. Psychol.*, 1945, *29*, 268-281.

30. Berdie, R. F. Counseling methods: diagnostics. *Annu. Rev. Psychol.*, 1950, *1*, 255-266.

31. Berdie, R. F. (Ed.) *Concepts and programs of counseling.* Minneapolis: University of Minnesota Press, 1951.

32. Berdie, R. F. Changes in self-ratings as a method of evaluating counseling. *J. counsel. Psychol.*, 1954, *1*, 49-54.

33. Berg, I. A. Measures before and after therapy. *J. clin. Psychol.*, 1952, *8*, 46-50.

34. Berg, I. A. Personality structure and occupational choice. *Personnel guid. J.*, 1953, *32*, 151-154.

35. Berger, E. M. The relations between expressed acceptance of self and expressed acceptance of others. *J. abnorm. soc. Psychol.*, 1952, *47*, 778-782.

36. Bergman, D. V. Counseling method and client responses. *J. consult. Psychol.*, 1951, *15*, 216-224.

37. Billingslea, F. Y. The implications of energetics-adjustment theory for the evaluation of psychotherapy. *Psychol. serv. center J.*, 1950, *2*, 83-95.

38. Bixler, R. H. A method of case transfer. *J. clin. Psychol.*, 1946, *2*, 274-278.

39. Bixler, R. H. Counseling: eclectic or systematic? *Educ. psychol. Measmt.*, 1948, *8*, 211-214.

40. Bixler, R. H. Limits are therapy. *J. consult. Psychol.*, 1949, *13*, 1-11.

41. Bixler, R. H., & Bixler, Virginia H. Clinical counseling in vocational guidance. *J. clin. Psychol.*, 1945, *3*, 186-192.

42. Bixler, R. H., & Bixler, Virginia H. Test interpretation in vocational counseling. *Educ. psychol. Measmt.*, 1946, *6*, 145-155.

43. Black, J. D. Common factors of the patient-therapist relationship in diverse psychotherapies. *J. clin. Psychol.*, 1952, *8*, 302-306.

44. Blake, R. R., & Ramsey, G. V. (Eds.) *Perceptions: an approach to personality.* New York: Ronald, 1951.

45. Blum, M. L., & Balinsky, B. *Counseling and psychology.* New York: Prentice-Hall, 1951.

46. Bordin, E. S. A theory of vocational interests as dynamic phenomena. *Educ. psychol. Measmt.*, 1943, *3*, 49-66.

47. Bordin, E. S. Diagnosis in counseling and psychotherapy. *Educ. psychol. Measmt.*, 1946, *6*, 169-184.

48. Bordin, E. S. Dimensions of the counseling process. *J. clin. Psychol.*, 1948, *4*, 240-244.

49. Bordin, E. S. Counseling points of view, non-directive and others. In E. G. Williamson (Ed.), *Trends in student personnel work.* Minneapolis: University of Minnesota Press, 1949. Pp. 120-129.

50. Bordin, E. S. Developments in interviewing techniques. In E. G. Williamson (Ed.), *Trends in student personnel work.* Minneapolis: University of Minnesota Press, 1949. Pp. 105-113.

51. Bordin, E. S. Counseling methods: therapy. *Annu. Rev. Psychol.*, 1950, *1*, 267-276.

52. Bordin, E. S. Four uses for tests in counseling. *Educ. psychol. Measmt.*, 1951, *11*, 779-781.

53. Bordin, E. S., & Bixler, R. H. Test selection: a process of counseling. *Educ. psychol. Measmt.*, 1946, *6*, 361-374.

54. Bordin, E. S., & Wilson, E. H. Change of interest as a function of shift in curricular orientation. *Educ. psychol. Measmt.*, 1953, *13*, 297-307.

55. Brayfield, A. H. Putting occupational information across. *Educ. psychol. Measmt.*, 1948, *8*, 485-495.

56. Brayfield, A. H. (Ed.) *Readings in modern methods of counseling.* New York: Appleton-Century-Crofts, 1950.

57. Brayfield, A. H. "Dissemination" of occupational information. *Occupations*, 1951, *29*, 411-413.

58. Brayfield, A. H., Dickson, Gwendolyn S., & Paterson, D. G. Educational and vocational counseling. In W. S. Monroe (Ed.), *Encyclopedia of educational research.* (Rev. Ed.) New York: Macmillan, 1950. Pp. 1320-1324.

59. Brayfield, A. H., & Reed, P. A. How readable are occupational information booklets? *J. appl. Psychol.*, 1950, *34*, 325-328.

60. Brody, Celia. Helping a client move into psychiatric treatment through a counseling process. *Jewish soc. serv. Quart.*, 1951, *27*, 265-277.

61. Brown, H. S. Similarities and differences in college populations on the Multiphasic. *J. appl. Psychol.*, 1948, *32*, 541-549.

62. Brown, M. N. An interest inventory as a measure of personality. *J. counsel. Psychol.*, 1954, *1*, 9-11.

63. Brownfain, J. J. Stability of the self-concept as a dimension of personality. *J. abnorm. soc. Psychol.*, 1952, *47*, 597-606.

64. Burton, A., & Harris, R. E. (Eds.) *Case histories in clinical and abnormal psychology.* New York: Harper, 1947.

65. Butler, J. M. On the role of directive and nondirective techniques in the counseling process. *Educ. psychol. Measmt.,* 1948, 8, 201-214.

66. Butler, J. M. Assessing psychotherapeutic protocols with context coefficients. *J. clin. Psychol.,* 1952, 8, 199-202.

67. Butler, J. M. The interaction of client and therapist. *J. abnorm. soc. Psychol.,* 1952, 47, 366-378.

68. Butler, J. M. Measuring effectiveness of counseling and psychotherapy. *Personnel guid. J.,* 1953, 32, 88-92.

69. Callis, R., Engram, W. C., & McGowan, J. F. Coding the Kuder: an aid to interpretation of the Kuder Preference Record—Vocational. *J. appl. Psychol.,* 1954, 38, in press.

70. Calvin, A. D., & Holtzman, W. H. Adjustment and the discrepancy between self concept and inferred self. *J. consult. Psychol.,* 1953, 17, 39-44.

71. Carnes, E. F. Counselor flexibility: its extent, and its relationship to other factors in the interview. Unpublished doctor's dissertation, Ohio State University, 1949.

72. Carnes, E. F., & Robinson, F. P. The role of client talk in the counseling interview. *Educ. psychol. Measmt.,* 1948, 8, 635-644.

73. Carr, A. C. An evaluation of nine nondirective psychotherapy cases by means of the Rorschach. *J. consult. Psychol.,* 1949, 13, 196-205.

74. Carter, H. D. The development of interest in vocations. In *Yearb. Natl. Soc. Stud. Educ.,* 1944, 43, 255-276.

75. Carter, H. D. Vocational interests and job orientation. *Appl. Psychol. Monogr.,* 1944, No. 2.

76. Challman, R. C. Clinical methods: psychodiagnostics. *Annu. Rev. Psychol.,* 1951, 2, 239-258.

77. Chappell, T. L. A validity study of the level-of-abstraction index as a measure of movement within the topical discussion unit. Unpublished doctor's dissertation. Univer. of Missouri, 1953.

78. Clark, J. H. The interpretation of the MMPI profiles of college students: a comparison by college major subject. *J. clin. Psychol.,* 1953, 9, 382-384.

79. Collier, R. M. A basis for integration rather than fragmentation in psychotherapy. *J. consult. Psychol.,* 1950, 14, 199-205.

80. Combs, A. W. Follow-up of a counseling case treated by the nondirective method. *J. clin. Psychol.,* 1945, 1, 147-154.

81. Combs, A. W. Some contributions of non-directive methods to college counseling. *J. consult. Psychol.,* 1945, 9, 218-223.

82. Combs, A. W. Non-directive techniques and vocational counseling. *Occupations,* 1947, 25, 261-267.

83. Combs, A. W. Clinical practice and personality theory: a symposium, V. a phenomenological approach to adjustment theory. *J. abnorm. soc. Psychol.,* 1949, 44, 29-35.

84. Combs, A. W. Counseling as a learning process. *J. counsel. Psychol.,* 1954, 1, 31-36.

85. Combs, A. W., & Snygg, D. Implications of the phenomenological approach for the evaluation of psychotherapy. *Psychol. serv. center J.*, 1950, 2, 96-102.

86. Conrad, Dorothy C. An empirical study of the concept of psychotherapeutic success. *J. consult. Psychol.*, 1952, *16*, 92-97.

87. Cottle, W. C. Common elements in counseling. *Personnel guid. J.*, 1953, *32*, 4-8.

88. Cottle, W. C. The MMPI: a review. *Kansas studies in education,* University of Kansas Publications, School of Education. Lawrence, Kansas: Vol. 3, No. 2, 1953.

89. Cottle, W. C. Personal characteristics of counselors. *Personnel guid. J.*, 1953, *31*, 445-450.

90. Cottle, W. C., & Lewis, W. W., Jr. Personality characteristics of counselors: II. male counselor responses to the MMPI and GZTS. *J. counsel. Psychol.*, 1954, *1*, 27-30.

91. Cottrell, L. S., Jr., & Dymond, Rosalind F. The empathic responses: a neglected field for research. *Psychiat.*, 1949, *12*, 355-359.

92. Covner, B. J. Studies in phonographic recordings of verbal material. I. The use of phonographic recordings in counseling practice and research. *J. consult. Psychol.*, 1942, *6*, 105-113.

93. Covner, B. J. Studies in phonographic recordings of verbal material. II. A device for transcribing phonographic recordings of verbal material. *J. consult. Psychol.*, 1942, *6*, 149-151.

94. Covner, B. J. Studies in phonographic recordings of verbal material. III. The completeness and accuracy of counseling interview reports. *J. gen. Psychol.*, 1944, *30*, 181-203.

95. Covner, B. J. Studies in phonographic recordings of verbal material. IV. Written reports of interviews. *J. appl. Psychol.*, 1944, *28*, 89-98.

96. Covner, B. J. Non-directive interviewing techniques in vocational counseling. *J. consult. Psychol.*, 1947, *11*, 70-73.

97. Cowen, E. L., & Combs, A. W. Followup study of 32 cases treated by non-directive psychotherapy. *J. abnorm. soc. Psychol.*, 1950, *45*, 232-258.

98. Crissy, W. J. E., & Daniel, W. J. Vocational interest factors in women. *J. appl. Psychol.*, 1939, *23*, 488-494.

99. Cronbach, L. J., & Gleser, Goldine C. Assessing similarity between profiles. *Psychol. Bull.*, 1953, *50*, 456-473.

100. Curran, C. A. Structuring the counseling relationship: a case report. *J. abnorm. soc. Psychol.*, 1944, *39*, 189-216.

101. Curran, C. A. *Personality factors in counseling.* New York: Grune & Stratton, 1945.

102. Curran, C. A. *Counseling in Catholic life and education.* New York: Macmillan, 1951.

103. Daniels, E. E., & Hunter, W. A. MMPI personality patterns for various occupations. *J. appl. Psychol.*, 1949, *33*, 559-565.

104. Darley, J. G. The structure of the systematic case study in individual diagnosis and counseling. *J. consult Psychol.*, 1940, *4*, 215-220.

105. Darley, J. G. *Clinical aspects and interpretation of the Strong Vocational Interest Blank.* New York: The Psychological Corporation, 1941.

106. Darley, J. G. Review of "counseling and psychotherapy." *J. abnorm. soc. Psychol.*, 1943, *38*, 199-201.

107. Darley, J. G. *The interview in counseling: an outline of interviewing procedure for use of community advisory centers.* Washington, D. C.: U.S. Department of Labor, 1946.

108. Darley, J. G. Interest and personality measurement. In E. G. Williamson (Ed.), *Trends in student personnel work.* Minneapolis: University of Minnesota Press, 1949, Pp. 52-62.

109. Darley, J. G., & Anderson, G. V. The functions of measurement in counseling. In E. F. Lindquist (Ed.), *Educational Measurement.* Washington: American Council on Education, 1951.

110. Darley, J. G., & Berdie, R. F. Diagnostic techniques. In W. S. Monroe (Ed.), *Encyclopedia of educational research.* (Rev. Ed.) New York: Macmillan, 1950. Pp. 1305-1312.

111. Davis, S. E., & Robinson, F. P. A study of the use of certain techniques for reducing resistance during the counseling interview. *Educ. psychol. Measmt.*, 1949, *9*, 297-306.

112. Diamond, B. L., & Weihofen, H. Privileged communications and the clinical psychologist. *J. clin. Psychol.*, 1953, *9*, 388-390.

113. Diamond, S. The interpretation of interest profiles. *J. appl. Psychol.*, 1948, *32*, 512-520.

114. DiMichael, S. G. Interest—inventory results during the counseling interview. *Occupations*, 1951, *30*, 93-97.

115. Dipboye, W. J. Analysis of counselor style by discussion units. *J. counsel. Psychol.*, 1954, *1*, 21-26.

116. Dittmann, A. T. The interpersonal process in psychotherapy: development of a research method. *J. abnorm. soc. Psychol.*, 1952, *47*, 236-244.

117. Doll, E. A. Psychometric pitfalls in clinical practice. *J. consult. Psychol.*, 1947, *11*, 12-20.

118. Dollard, J., Auld, F., Jr., & White, Alice M. *Steps in psychotherapy.* New York: Macmillan, 1953.

119. Dollard, J., & Miller, N. *Personality and psychotherapy.* New York: McGraw-Hill, 1950.

120. Dollard, J., & Mowrer, O. H. A method of measuring tension in written documents. *J. abnorm. soc. Psychol.*, 1947, *42*, 3-32.

121. Donahue, Wilma T., *et al. The measurement of student adjustment and achievement.* Ann Arbor: University of Michigan Press, 1949.

122. Dressel, P. L. Evaluation of counseling. In R. F. Berdie (Ed.), *Concepts and programs of counseling.* Minneapolis: University of Minnesota Press, 1951. Pp. 70-81.

123. Dressel, P. L., & Matteson, R. W. The effect of client participation in test interpretation. *Educ. psychol. Measmt.*, 1950, *10*, 693-706.

124. Dressel, P. L., Shoben, E. J., Jr., & Pepinsky, H. B. Research in counseling: a symposium. *Personnel and guid. J.*, 1953, *31*, 284-294.

125. DuMas, F. M. A quick method of analyzing the similarity of profiles. *J. clin. Psychol.*, 1946, *2*, 80-83.

126. DuMas, F. M. On the interpretation of personality profiles. *J. clin. Psychol.*, 1947, *3*, 57-65.

127. DuMas, F. M. The co-efficient of profile similarity. *J. clin. Psychol.*, 1949, *5*, 123-131.

128. DuMas, F. M. The objective evaluation of therapeutic proficiency. *J. Psychol.*, 1949, *28*, 181-185.

129. DuMas, F. M. Quick method for the analysis of the shape, elevation and scatter of profiles. *J. clin. Psychol.*, 1953, *9*, 345-348.

130. Dymond, Rosalind M. A preliminary investigation of the relation of insight and empathy. *J. consult. Psychol.*, 1948, *12*, 228-233.

131. Dymond, Rosalind F. A scale for the measurement of empathic ability. *J. consult. Psychol.*, 1949, *13*, 127-133.

132. Dymond, Rosalind F. Personality and empathy. *J. consult. Psychol.*, 1950, *14*, 343-350.

133. Edwards, A. L., & Cronbach, L. J. Experimental design for research in psychotherapy. *J. clin. Psychol.*, 1952, *8*, 51-59.

134. Ellis, A. The validity of personality questionnaires. *Psychol. Bull.*, 1946, *43*, 385-440.

135. Ellis, A. A critique of the theoretical contributions of non-directive therapy. *J. clin. Psychol.*, 1948, *4*, 248-255.

136. Ellis, A. Requisites for research in psychotherapy. *J. clin. Psychol.*, 1950, *6*, 152-156.

137. Ellis, A. A critique of systematic theoretical foundations in clinical psychology. *J. clin. Psychol.*, 1952, *8*, 11-15.

138. Elton, C. F. A study of client responsibility: counselor technique or interview outcome? *Educ. psychol. Measmt.*, 1950, *10*, 728-737.

139. Fein, Edith. The use of judges in psychological experiments. *J. clin. Psychol.*, 1951, *7*, 98-100.

140. Feinberg, M. R. Relation of background experience to social acceptance. *J. abnorm. soc. Psychol.*, 1953, *48*, 206-214.

141. Fensterheim, H., & Tresselt, M. E. The influence of value systems on the perception of people. *J. abnorm. soc. Psychol.*, 1953, *48*, 93-98.

142. Fiedler, F. E. A comparison of therapeutic relationships in psycho-analytic, non-directive, and Adlerian therapy. *J. consult. Psychol.*, 1950, *14*, 436-445.

143. Fiedler, F. E. The concept of an ideal therapeutic relationship. *J. consult. Psychol.*, 1950, *14*, 239-245.

144. Fiedler, F. E. A method of objective quantification of certain counter-transference attitudes. *J. clin. Psychol.*, 1951, *7*, 101-107.

145. Fiedler, F. E. Factor analyses of psychoanalytic, non-directive and Adlerian therapeutic relationships. *J. consult. Psychol.*, 1951, *15*, 32-38.

146. Fiedler, F. E., & Senior, Kate. An exploratory study of unconscious feeling reactions in fifteen patient-therapist pairs. *J. abnorm. soc. Psychol.*, 1952, *47*, 446-453.

147. Flanagan, J. C. The use of comprehensive rationales in test development. *Educ. psychol. Measmt.*, 1951, *11*, 151-155.

148. Fores, B. R. Personality factors in occupational choice. *Educ. psychol. Measmt.*, 1953, *13*, 361-366.

149. Forgy, E. W., & Black, J. D. A followup after three years of clients counseled by two methods. *J. counsel. Psychol.*, 1954, *1*, 1-7.

150. Form, A. L. Measurement of student attitudes toward counseling. *Personnel and guid. J.*, 1953, *32*, 84-87.

151. Form, A. L. Users and non-users of counseling services. *Personnel and guid. J.*, 1953, *32*, 209-213.

152. Freeman, H. J., & Jones, L. Final report of the long-time effect of counseling low percentile freshmen. *School and Soc.*, 1933, *38*, 382-384.

153. Froehlich, C. P. Toward more adequate criteria of counseling effectiveness. *Educ. psychol. Measmt.*, 1949, *9*, 255-267.

154. Fryer, D. *The measurement of interests.* New York: Henry Holt, 1931.

155. Gallagher, J. J. MMPI changes concomitant with client-centered therapy. *J. consult. Psychol.*, 1953, *17*, 334-338.

156. Garrett, Annette M. *Counseling methods for personnel workers.* New York: Family Welfare Association of America, 1945.

157. Gilbert, W. M. Counseling: therapy and diagnosis. *Annu. Rev. Psychol.*, 1952, *3*, 351-380.

158. Ginzberg, E. Toward a theory of occupational choice. *Occupations*, 1952, *30*, 491-494.

159. Ginzberg, E., Ginsburg, S. W., Axelrad, S., & Herma, J. L. *Occupational choice: an approach to a general theory.* New York: Columbia University Press, 1951.

160. Good, Jeanne E., & Robinson, F. P. Feeling as a criterion of success in different types of counseling interviews. *Educ. psychol. Measmt.*, 1951, *11*, 639-645.

161. Gordon, T., Grummon, D. L., Rogers, C. R., & Seeman, J. Studies in client-centered psychotherapy I: developing a program of research in psychotherapy. *Psychol. serv. center J.*, 1951, *3*, 3-28.

162. Grant, J. D., & Grant, Marguerite O. "Therapy readiness" as a research variable. *J. consult. Psychol.*, 1950, *14*, 156-157.

163. Grossman, D. The construction and validation of two insight inventories. *J. consult. Psychol.*, 1951, *15*, 109-114.

164. Grossman, D. An experimental investigation of a psychotherapeutic technique. *J. consult. Psychol.*, 1952, *16*, 325-331.

165. Grummon, D. L. Studies in client-centered psychotherapy II: design, procedures, and subjects for block I. *Psychol. serv. center J.*, 1951, *3*, 29-46.

166. Gulliksen, H. Intrinsic validity. *Amer. Psychologist*, 1950, *5*, 511-517.

167. Gustad, J. W. Test information and learning in the counseling process. *Educ. psychol. Measmt.*, 1951, *11*, 788-795.

168. Gustad, J. W. Academic achievement and Strong occupational level scores. *J. appl. Psychol.*, 1952, *36*, 75-78.

169. Hahn, M. E. Conceptual trends in counseling. *Personnel and guid. J.*, 1953, *31*, 231-235.

170. Hahn, M. E., & Kendall, W. E. Some comments in defense of non-nondirective counseling. *J. consult. Psychol.*, 1947, 2, 74-81.

171. Hahn, M. E. & MacLean, M. S. *General clinical counseling in educational institutions.* New York: McGraw-Hill, 1950.

172. Haigh, G. Defensive behavior in client-centered therapy. *J. consult. Psychol.*, 1949, 13, 181-189.

173. Haigh, G., & Kell, B. L. Multiple therapy as a method for training and research in psychotherapy. *J. abnorm. soc. Psychol.*, 1950, 45, 659-666.

174. Haimowitz, N. R., & Haimowitz, M. L. Personality changes in client-centered therapy. In W. Wolff & J. A. Precker (Eds.), *Success in Psychotherapy.* New York: Grune and Stratton, 1952.

175. Hamlin, R. M., & Albee, G. W. Muench's tests: a control group for his subjects. *J. consult. Psychol.*, 1948, 12, 412-416.

176. Hamrin, S. A., & Paulson, Blanche. *Counseling adolescents.* Chicago: Science Research Associates, 1950.

177. Hanes, B. Reading ease and MMPI results. *J. clin. Psychol.*, 1953, 9, 83-85.

178. Harmon, L. R., & Wiener, D. N. Use of the Minnesota Multiphasic Personality Inventory in vocational adjustment. *J. appl. Psychol.*, 1945, 29, 132-141.

179. Harris, R. E., *et al. Recent advances in diagnostic psychological testing: a critical summary.* Springfield, Ill.: C. C. Thomas, 1950.

180. Hastorf, A. H., & Bender, I. E. A caution respecting the measurement of empathic ability. *J. abnorm. soc. Psychol.*, 1952, 47, 574-576.

181. Hathaway, S. R. A coding system for MMPI profile classification. *J. consult. Psychol.*, 1947, 11, 334-337.

182. Hathaway, S. R. Some considerations relative to nondirective counseling as therapy. *J. clin. Psychol.*, 1948, 4, 226-231.

183. Hathaway, S. R. Clinical methods: psychotherapy. *Annu. Rev. Psychol.*, 1951, 2, 259-280.

184. Hilgard, E. R. Human motives and the concept of self. *Amer. Psychologist*, 1949, 4, 374-382.

185. Hoffman, A. E. A study of reported behavior changes in counseling. *J. consult. Psychol.*, 1949, 13, 190-195.

186. Hogan, R. A. A theory of threat and defense. *J. consult. Psychol.*, 1952, 16, 417-424.

187. Horrocks, J. E., & Nagy, G. The relationship between the ability to make a diagnosis and to select appropriate remedial procedures. *J. gen. Psychol.*, 1948, 38, 139-146.

188. Hunt, H. F. On goals, methods and tactics in psychotherapy. *J. consult. Psychol.*, 1948, 12, 68-75.

189. Hunt, H. F. Clinical methods: psychodiagnostics. *Annu. Rev. Psychol.*, 1950, 1, 207-220.

190. Hunt, J. McV. (Ed.) *Personality and the behavior disorders.* New York: Ronald, 1944. 2 vols.

191. Hunt, J. McV. Measuring movement in casework. *J. soc. Casewk.*, 1948, 29, 343-351.

192. Hunt, J. McV. The problem of measuring the results of psychotherapy. *Psychol. serv. center J.*, 1949, *1*, 122-135.

193. Hunt, J. McV. Psychological services in the tactics of psychological science. *Amer. Psychologist*, 1952, 7, 608-622.

194. Hunt, J. McV. Toward an integrated program of research on psychotherapy. *J. consult. Psychol.*, 1952, *16*, 237-246.

195. Hunt, J. McV., & Kogan, L. S. The need for psychological theory in evaluating the results of psychotherapy. *Psychol. serv. center J.*, 1950, 2, 77-82.

196. Hunt, W. A. Diagnosis and non-directive therapy. *J. clin. Psychol.*, 1948, *4*, 232-236.

197. Institute for Human Adjustment. *Training of psychological counselors.* Ann Arbor: University of Michigan Press, 1950.

198. Johnson, A. P. Counseling engineering freshmen. *Educ. psychol. Measmt.*, 1953, *13*, 133-144.

199. Johnson, D. G. Effect of vocational counseling on self-knowledge. *Educ. psychol. Measmt.*, 1953, *13*, 330-338.

200. Johnson, R. H., & Bond, G. L. Reading ease of commonly used tests. *J. appl. Psychol.*, 1950, *34*, 319-324.

201. Kamm, R. B., & Wrenn, C. G. Client acceptance of self-information in counseling. *Educ. psychol. Measmt.*, 1950, *10*, 32-42.

202. Kauffman, P. E., & Raimy, V. C. Two methods of assessing therapeutic progress. *J. abnorm. soc. Psychol.*, 1949, *43*, 379-385.

203. Keet, C. D. Two verbal techniques in a miniature counseling situation. *Psychol. Monogr.*, 1948, *62*, No. 294.

204. Kelly, G. A. (Ed.) *New methods in applied psychology.* College Park, Maryland: University of Maryland, 1947.

205. Kemble, R. P. Constructive use of the ending of treatment. *Amer. J. Orthopsychiat.*, 1941, *11*, 684-690.

206. Kircheimer, B. A., Axelroad, D. W., & Hickerson, G. A. An objective evaluation of counseling. *J. appl. Psychol.*, 1949, 33, 249-257.

207. Kirk, Barbara A. How counseling affects vocational goals. *Educ. psychol. Measmt.*, 1952, *12*, 692-698.

208. Kirk, Barbara A., & Headley, R. R. Factors related to voluntary discontinuance of contact during counseling. *J. consult. Psychol.*, 1950, *14*, 386-392.

209. Kirk, Barbara A., & Michels, Marjorie E. A study of counselee reading of occupational materials. *Occupations*, 1950, *28*, 446-450.

210. Klein, G. S. Clinical practice and personality theory: a symposium. VII. A clinical perspective for personality research. *J. abnorm. soc. Psychol.*, 1949, *44*, 42-49.

211. Kluckhohn, C., & Murray, H. (Eds.) *Personality in nature, society, and culture.* (2nd Ed.) New York: Knopf, 1953.

212. Kogan, L. S. An outline of the contributions. *Psychol. serv. center J.*, 1950, 2, 130-131.

213. Kogan, L. S., & Hunt, J. McV. After comments. *Psychol. serv. center J.*, 1950, 2, 132-138.

214. Kuder, G. F. Identifying the faker. *Personnel Psychol.*, 1950, *3*, 155-167.
215. Laing, Louise D. The use of reassurance in psychotherapy. *Smith Coll. Stud. soc. Wk.*, 1952, *22*, 75-90.
216. Law, S. G. *Therapy through interview.* New York: McGraw-Hill, 1948.
217. Lecky, P. *Self-consistency: a theory of personality.* New York: Island Press, 1945.
218. Levin, M. M. Status anxiety and occupational choice. *Educ. psychol. Measmt.*, 1949, *9*, 29-38.
219. Lindgren, H. C. & Robinson, Jacqueline. An evaluation of Dymond's Test of Insight and Empathy. *J. consult. Psychol.*, 1953, *17*, 172-176.
220. Lipkin, S. The client evaluates non-directive therapy. *J. consult. Psychol.*, 1948, *12*, 137-146.
221. Louttit, C. M. Training for non-directive counseling: a critique. *J. clin. Psychol.*, 1948, *4*, 236-239.
222. Luft, J. Differences in prediction based on hearing versus reading verbatim clinical interviews. *J. consult. Psychol.*, 1951, *15*, 115-119.
223. McClelland, W. A., & Sinaiko, H. W. An investigation of a counselor attitude questionnaire. *Educ. psychol. Measmt.*, 1950, *10*, 128-133.
224. McKinney, F. Four years of a college adjustment clinic: I. Organization of a clinic and problems of counselees. II. Characteristics of counselees. *J. consult. Psychol.*, 1945, *5*, 203-217.
225. MacKinnon, D. W. Clinical practice and personality theory: a symposium II. Psychodiagnosis in clinical practice and personality theory. *J. abnorm. soc. Psychol.*, 1949, *44*, 7-13.
226. MacKinnon, D. W. A topological and vector analysis of change through psychotherapy. *Psychol. serv. center J.*, 1950, *2*, 103-108.
227. Magaret, Ann. Generalization in successful psychotherapy. *J. consult. Psychol.*, 1950, *14*, 64-70.
228. Magaret, Ann. Clinical methods: psychodiagnostics. *Annu. Rev. Psychol.*, 1952, *3*, 282-320.
229. Maier, N. R. F. *Frustration: the study of behavior without a goal.* New York: McGraw-Hill, 1949.
230. Margolis, B. D. The problem of "façade" in the counseling of low scholarship students. *J. consult. Psychol.*, 1945, *9*, 138-141.
231. Maslow, A. H. A theory of human motivation. *Psychol. Rev.*, 1943, *50*, 370-396.
232. Mathewson, R. H. The role of the counselor. *Harvard Educ. Rev.*, 1947, *17*, 10-27.
233. Meadow, A., Grenblatt, M., Levine, J., & Solomon, H. C. The discomfort-relief-quotient as a measure of tension and adjustment. *J. abnorm. soc. Psychol.*, 1952, *47*, 658-661.
234. Meehl, P. E. Configural scoring. *J. consult. Psychol.*, 1950, *14*, 165-171.
235. Meehl, P. E., & McClosky, H. Ethical and political aspects of applied psychology. *J. abnorm. soc. Psychol.*, 1947, *42*, 91-98.
236. Merrill, R. M. On Keet's study, "Two verbal techniques in a miniature counseling situation." *J. abnorm. soc. Psychol.*, 1952, *47*, 722.

237. Miller, Helen E. "Acceptance" and related attitudes as demonstrated in psychotherapeutic interviews. *J. clin. Psychol.*, 1949, 5, 83-87.

238. Miller, J. G. The implications of psychoanalytic theory for the evaluation of psychotherapy. *Psychol. serv. center J.*, 1950, 2, 123-129.

239. Moreno, J. L. Discussion of Snyder's "The present status of psychotherapeutic counseling." *Psychol. Bull.*, 1947, 44, 564-567.

240. Mowrer, O. H. Learning theory and the neurotic paradox. *Amer. J. Orthopsychiat.*, 1948, 18, 571-610.

241. Mowrer, O. H. Implications of a two-factor learning theory. *Psychol. serv. center J.*, 1950, 2, 116-122.

242. Mowrer, O. H. *Learning theory and personality dynamics: selected papers.* New York: Ronald, 1950.

243. Mowrer, O. H. Anxiety theory as a basis for distinguishing between counseling and psychotherapy. In R. F. Berdie (Ed.), *Concepts and programs of counseling.* Minneapolis: University of Minnesota Press, 1951. Pp. 7-26.

244. Mowrer, O. H. (Ed.) *Psychotherapy: theory and research.* New York: Ronald, 1953.

245. Muench, G. A. An evaluation of non-directive psychotherapy. *Appl. Psychol. Monogr.*, 1947, No. 13.

246. Muench, G. A. The application of diagnostic psychological methods to counseling and psychotherapy. In R. E. Harris, *et al.* (Ed.), *Recent advances in diagnostic psychological testing: a critical summary.* Springfield, Ill.: Thomas, 1950.

247. Murphy, G. *Personality: a biosocial approach to origins and structure.* New York: Harper, 1947.

248. Muthard, J. E. The relative effectiveness of larger units used in interview analysis. *J. consult. Psychol.*, 1953, 17, 184-188.

249. Norman, R. D., & Redlo, M. MMPI personality patterns for various college major groups. *J. appl. Psychol.*, 1952, 36, 404-409.

250. Paterson, D. G. The genesis of modern guidance. *Educ. Rec.*, 1938, 1, 36-46.

251. Paterson, D. G. Developments in vocational counseling technique. In E. G. Williamson (Ed.), *Trends in student personnel work.* Minneapolis: University of Minnesota Press, 1949. Pp. 80-96.

252. Patterson, C. H. Is psychotherapy dependent upon diagnosis? *Amer. Psychologist*, 1948, 3, 155-159.

253. Pepinsky, H. B. The selection and use of diagnostic categories in clinical counseling. *Appl. Psychol. Monogr.*, 1948, No. 15.

254. Pepinsky, H. B. Counseling methods: therapy. *Annu. Rev. Psychol.*, 1951, 2, 317-344.

255. Pepinsky, H. B., Clyde, R. J., Oleson, Barbara A., & VanAtta, E. L. The criterion in counseling: I, individual personality and behavior in a social group. *Educ. psychol. Measmt.*, 1952, 12, 178-193.

256. Pepinsky, H. B., Siegel, L., & VanAtta, E. L. The criterion in counseling: a group participation scale. *J. abnorm. soc. Psychol.*, 1952, 47, 415-419.

257. Phillips, E. L., & Agnew, J. W., Jr. A study of Rogers' "reflection" hypothesis. *J. clin. Psychol.*, 1953, 9, 281-284.

258. Porter, E. H., Jr. The development and evaluation of a measure of counseling interview procedures. Part I, the development, Part II, the evaluation. *Educ. psychol. Measmt.*, 1943, 3, 105-126, 215-238.

259. Porter, E. H., Jr. A simple measure of counselor attitudes. In E. G. Williamson (Ed.), *Trends in student personnel work*. Minneapolis: University of Minnesota Press, 1949. Pp. 129-135.

260. Porter, E. H., Jr. Understanding diagnostically and understanding therapeutically. In E. G. Williamson (Ed.), *Trends in student personnel work*. Minneapolis: University of Minnesota Press, 1949. Pp. 113-119.

261. Porter, E. H., Jr. *An introduction to therapeutic counseling*. Boston: Houghton Mifflin, 1950.

262. Porter, E. H., Jr. On the nature of psychotherapeutic interpretation. *J. consult. Psychol.*, 1952, 16, 343-346.

263. Preston, M. G., Mudd, E. H., Peltz, W. L., & Froscher, H. B. An experimental study of a method for abstracting the content of social case records. *J. abnorm. soc. Psychol.*, 1950, 45, 628-646.

264. Proff, F. C. A validity study of the distress-relief quotient as a measure of movement within the topical discussion unit. Unpublished doctor's dissertation, Univer. of Missouri, 1952.

265. Raimy, V. C. Self reference in counseling interviews. *J. consult. Psychol.*, 1948, 12, 153-163.

266. Raimy, V. C. Clinical methods: psychotherapy. *Annu. Rev. Psychol.*, 1952, 3, 321-350.

267. Rank, O. *Will therapy and truth and reality*. New York: Knopf, 1945.

268. Raskin, N. J. The development of non-directive therapy. *J. consult. Psychol.*, 1948, 12, 92-110.

269. Raskin, N. J. An analysis of six parallel studies of therapeutic process. *J. consult. Psychol.*, 1949, 13, 206-220.

270. Raskin, N. J. The development of the "Parallel Studies" project *J. consult. Psychol.*, 1949, 13, 154-156.

271. Reid, Dorothy K., & Snyder, W. U. Experiment on "recognition of feeling" in non-directive psychotherapy. *J. clin. Psychol.*, 1947, 3, 128-135.

272. Reik, T. *Listening with the third ear*. New York: Farrar, Straus, 1949.

273. Reymert, M. L. (Ed.) *Feeling and emotions*. New York: McGraw-Hill, 1950.

274. Richardson, H., & Borow, H. Evaluation of a technique of group orientation for vocational counseling. *Educ. psychol. Measmt.*, 1952, 12, 587-597.

275. Robinson, F. P. Two quarries with a single stone. *J. higher Educ.*, 1945, 16, 201-206.

276. Robinson, F. P. Are non-directive techniques sometimes too directive? *J. clin. Psychol.*, 1946, 2, 368-371.

277. Robinson, F. P. The unit in interview analysis. *Educ. psychol. Measmt.*, 1949, 9, 709-716.

278. Robinson, F. P. *Principles and procedures in student counseling.* New York: Harper, 1950.

279. Roe, Ann. Clinical practice and personality theory: a symposium. VI. Integration of personality theory and clinical practice. *J. abnorm. soc. Psychol.*, 1949, *44*, 36-41.

280. Roeber, E. C. A meaningful record of tests. *Educ. psychol. Measmt.*, 1948, *8*, 397-400.

281. Rogers, C. R. *Counseling and psychotherapy.* Boston: Houghton Mifflin, 1942.

282. Rogers, C. R. The development of insight in a counseling relationship. *J. consult. Psychol.*, 1944, *8*, 331-341.

283. Rogers, C. R. Counseling. *Rev. educ. Res.*, 1945, *15*, 155-163.

284. Rogers, C. R. Psychometric tests and client-centered counseling. *Educ. psychol. Measmt.*, 1946, *6*, 139-144.

285. Rogers, C. R. Recent research in nondirective therapy and its implications. *Amer. J. Orthopsychiat.*, 1946, *16*, 581-588.

286. Rogers, C. R. Significant aspects of client-centered therapy. *Amer Psychologist.*, 1946, *1*, 415-422.

287. Rogers, C. R. The organization of personality. *Amer. Psychologist*, 1947, *2*, 358-368.

288. Rogers, C. R. Divergent trends in methods of improving adjustment. *Harvard Educ. Rev.*, 1948, *18*, 209-219.

289. Rogers, C. R. Some implications of client-centered counseling for college personnel work. *Educ. psychol. Measmt.*, 1948, *8*, 540-549.

290. Rogers, C. R. A coordinated research in psychotherapy: a nonobjective introduction. *J. consult. Psychol.*, 1949, *13*, 149-153.

291. Rogers, C. R. The attitude and orientation of the counselor. *J. consult. Psychol.*, 1949, *13*, 82-94.

292. Rogers, C. R. *Client-centered therapy.* Boston: Houghton Mifflin, 1951.

293. Rogers, C. R. Studies in client-centered psychotherapy III: the case of Mrs. Oak—a research analysis. *Psychol. serv. center J.*, 1951, *3*, 47-165.

294. Rogers, C. R., Kell, B. L., & McNeil, Helen. The role of self-understanding in the prediction of behavior. *J. consult. Psychol.*, 1948, *12*, 174-186.

295. Rosenzweig, S. Clinical practice and personality theory: a symposium. I. the systematic intent of clinical psychology. *J. abnorm. soc. Psychol.*, 1949, *44*, 3-6.

296. Rosenzweig, S. *Psychodiagnosis.* New York: Grune & Stratton, 1949.

297. Rosenzweig, S. Frustration tolerance and the picture-frustration study. *Psychol. serv. center J.*, 1950, *2*, 109-115.

298. Rothney, J. W. M. Interpreting test scores to counselees. *Occupations*, 1952, *30*, 320-322.

299. Rothney, J. W. M. *The high school student: a book of cases.* New York: Dryden, 1953.

300. Rothney, J. W. M., & Danielson, P. J. Counseling. *Rev. educ. Res.*, 1951, *21*, 132-139.

301. Rothney, J. W. M., & Roens, B. A. *Counseling the individual student.* New York: Sloane, 1949.

302. Rotter, J. B. Clinical methods: psychodiagnostics. *Annu. Rev. Psychol.*, 1953, *4*, 295-316.

303. Rotter, J. B., Rafferty, Janet E., & Schachtitz, Eva. Validation of the Rotter Incomplete Sentences Blank for college screening. *J. consult. Psychol.*, 1949, *13*, 157-168.

304. Rotter, J. B., & Willerman, B. The incomplete sentence test. *J. consult. Psychol.*, 1947, *11*, 43-48.

305. Ruja, H. Vocational vs. emotional? *Personnel and guid. J.*, 1952, *31*, 99-100.

306. Rundquist, R. M. A comparison of the analysis of counseling interviews by topical discussion units and by the total case. Unpublished doctor's dissertation, Univer. of Missouri, 1952.

307. Saddler, L. E. A comparison of students remaining in an engineering curriculum and students transferring from engineering to other curricula. Unpublished doctor's dissertation, Univer. of Missouri, 1949.

308. Samler, J. Toward a theoretical basis for vocational counseling. *Personnel and guid. J.*, 1953, *32*, 34-35.

309. Sanford, N. Clinical methods: psychotherapy. *Annu. Rev. Psychol.*, 1953, *4*, 317-342.

310. Sanford, R. N. Psychotherapy and counseling: a symposium. Introduction and discussion. *J. consult. Psychol.*, 1948, *12*, 65-67, 88-91.

311. Sarason, S. B., & Mandler, G. Some correlates of test anxiety. *J. abnorm. soc. Psychol.*, 1952, *47*, 810-817.

312. Sarbin, T. R. The case record in psychological counseling. *J. appl. Psychol.*, 1940, *24*, 184-197.

313. Sarbin, T. R. A contribution to the study of actuarial and individual methods of prediction. *Amer. J. Soc.*, 1943, *48*, 593-602.

314. Sarbin, T. R. A preface to a psychological analysis of the self. *Psychol. Rev.*, 1952, *59*, 11-32.

315. Sarbin, T. R., & Farberow, N. L. Contributions to role-taking theory: a clinical study of self and role. *J. abnorm. soc. Psychol.*, 1952, *47*, 117-125.

316. Sargent, Helen. Non-directive counseling applied to a single interview. *J. consult. Psychol.*, 1943, *7*, 183-190.

317. Sargent, Helen. Professional ethics and problems of therapy. *J. abnorm. soc. Psychol.*, 1945, *40*, 47-60.

318. Saslow, G. Psychotherapy. *Annu. Rev. Psychol.*, 1954, *5*, 311-336.

319. Schneidler, Gwendolen G., & Berdie, R. F. Representativeness of college students who receive counseling services. *J. educ. Psychol.*, 1942, *33*, 545-551.

320. Schofield, W. Critique of scatter and profile analysis of psychometric data. *J. clin. Psychol.*, 1952, *8*, 16-22.

321. Sears, R. R. A theoretical framework for personality and social behavior. *Amer. Psychologist*, 1951, *6*, 476-483.

322. Seeman, J. A study of client self-selection of tests in vocational counseling. *Educ. psychol. Measmt.*, 1948, *8*, 327-346.

323. Seeman, J. A study of preliminary interview methods in vocational counseling. *J. consult. Psychol.,* 1948, *12,* 321-330.

324. Seeman, J. An investigation of client reactions to vocational counseling. *J. consult. Psychol.,* 1949, *13,* 95-104.

325. Seeman, J. A study of the process of non-directive therapy. *J. consult. Psychol.,* 1949, *13,* 157-168.

326. Seeman, W. A note on the "clinical practice and personality theory" symposium. *J. abnorm. soc. Psychol.,* 1950, *45,* 380-384.

327. Seeman, W. "Subtlety" in structured personality tests. *J. consult. Psychol.,* 1952, *16,* 278-283.

328. Seeman, W. Concept of "subtlety" in structured psychiatric and personality tests: an experimental approach. *J. abnorm. soc. Psychol.,* 1953, *48,* 239-247.

329. Sells, S. B. Problems of criteria and validity in diagnosis and therapy. *J. clin. Psychol.,* 1952, *8,* 23-28.

330. Shaffer, L. F. The problem of psychotherapy. *Amer. Psychologist,* 1947, *2,* 459-467.

331. Shartle, C. L. Contribution from the field of occupational adjustment. In E. G. Williamson (Ed.), *Trends in student personnel work.* Minneapolis: University of Minnesota Press, 1949. Pp. 96-104.

332. Shartle, C. L. *Occupational information, its development and application.* (2nd Ed.) New York: Prentice-Hall, 1952.

333. Shaw, F. J. A stimulus-response analysis of repression and insight in psychotherapy. *Psychol. Rev.,* 1946, *53,* 36-42.

334. Shaw, F. J. The role of reward in psychotherapy. *Amer. Psychologist,* 1949, *4,* 177-179.

335. Shaw, F. J. Counseling from the standpoint of an "Interactive Conceptualist." *J. counsel. Psychol.,* 1954, *1,* 36-42.

336. Sheerer, Elizabeth T. An analysis of the relationship between acceptance of and respect for self and acceptance of and respect for others in ten counseling cases. *J. consult. Psychol.,* 1949, *13,* 169-175.

337. Sherif, M., & Cantril, H. *The psychology of ego-involvements.* New York: Wiley, 1947.

338. Sherman, Dorothy. An analysis of the dynamic relationship between counselor techniques and outcomes in larger units of the interview situation. Unpublished doctor's dissertation, Ohio State University, 1945.

339. Sherriffs, A. C. Modification of academic performance through personal interview. *J. appl. Psychol.,* 1949, *33,* 339-351.

340. Shoben, E. J., Jr. Psychotherapy as a problem in learning theory. *Psychol. Bull.,* 1949, *5,* 366-392.

341. Shoben, E. J., Jr. A theoretical approach to psychotherapy as personality modification. *Harvard Educ. Rev.,* 1953, *23,* 128-142.

342. Shoben, E. J., Jr. Counseling and the learning of integrative behavior. *J. counsel. Psychol.,* 1954, *1,* 42-48.

343. Shostrom, E. L., & Brammer, L. M. *The dynamics of the counseling process.* New York: McGraw-Hill, 1952.

344. Small, L. A theory of vocational choice. *Voc. guid. Quart.,* 1952, *1,* 29.

345. Smith, M. B. The phenomenological approach to personality theory: some critical remarks. *J. abnorm. soc. Psychol.*, 1950, *45*, 516-522.

346. Snyder, W. U. An investigation of the nature of non-directive psychotherapy. *J. gen. Psychol.*, 1945, *33*, 193-223.

347. Snyder, W. U. Dr. Thorne's critique of non-directive therapy. *J. abnorm. soc. Psychol.*, 1945, *40*, 336-339.

348. Snyder, W. U. "Warmth" in non-directive counseling. *J. abnorm. soc. Psychol.*, 1946, *41*, 491-495.

349. Snyder, W. U. A comparison of one unsuccessful with four successful nondirectively counseled cases. *J. consult. Psychol.*, 1947, *11*, 38-42.

350. Snyder, W. U. The present status of psychotherapeutic counseling. *Psychol. Bull.*, 1947, *4*, 297-386.

351. Snyder, W. U. Clinical practice and personality theory: a symposium. IV. Some contributions of psychotherapy to personality theory. *J. abnorm. soc. Psychol.*, 1949, *44*, 22-28.

352. Snyder, W. U. Clinical methods: psychotherapy. *Annu. Rev. Psychol.*, 1950, *1*, 221-234.

353. Snyder, W. U. *et al. Casebook of non-directive counseling.* Boston: Houghton Mifflin, 1947.

354. Snygg, D., & Combs, A. W. *Individual behavior.* New York: Harper, 1949.

355. Snygg, D., & Combs, A. W. The phenomenological approach and the problem of "unconscious" behavior: a reply to Dr. Smith. *J. abnorm. soc. Psychol.*, 1950, *45*, 523-528.

356. Sopchak, A. L. College student norms for the Minnesota Multiphasic Personality Inventory. *J. consult. Psychol.*, 1952, *16*, 445-448.

357. Speer, G. S., & Jaskes, L. The influence of occupational information on occupational goals. *Occupations*, 1949, *28*, 15-17.

358. Stagner, R. *Psychology of personality.* (2nd Ed.) New York: McGraw-Hill, 1948.

359. Steinberg, A. The relation of vocational preference to emotional adjustment. *Educ. psychol. Measmt.*, 1952, *12*, 96-104.

360. Stock, Dorothy. An investigation into the interrelations between the self-concept and feelings directed toward other persons and groups. *J. consult. Psychol.*, 1949, *13*, 176-180.

361. Strang, Ruth. Use in counseling of information about vocations. *Sch. Rev.*, 1945, *53*, 526-529.

362. Strang, Ruth. Criteria of progress in counseling and psychotherapy. *J. clin. Psychol.*, 1947, *3*, 180-183.

363. Strang, Ruth. *Counseling technics in college and secondary schools.* (Rev. Ed.) New York: Harper, 1949.

364. Stromswold, S. A., & Wrenn, C. G. Counseling students toward scholastic adjustment. *Educ. psychol. Measmt.*, 1948, *8*, 57-63.

365. Strong, E. K., Jr. *Vocational interests of men and women.* Stanford, California: Stanford University Press, 1943.

366. Strong, E. K., Jr. The role of interests in guidance. *Occupations*, 1949, *27*, 517-522.

367. Strong, E. K., Jr. Interest scores while in college of occupations engaged in 20 years later. *Educ. psychol. Measmt.*, 1951, *11*, 335-348.

368. Strong, E. K., Jr. Norms for Strong's Vocational Interest Tests. *J. appl. Psychol.*, 1951, *35*, 50-56.

369. Strong, E. K., Jr. Permanence of interest scores over 22 years. *J. appl. Psychol.*, 1951, *35*, 89-91.

370. Strong, E. K., Jr. Amount of change in occupational choice of college freshmen. *Educ. psychol. Measmt.*, 1952, *12*, 677-691.

371. Strong, E. K., Jr. Nineteen-year followup of engineer interests. *J. appl. Psychol.*, 1952, *36*, 65-74.

372. Strong, E. K., Jr. Validity of occupational choice. *Educ. psychol. Measmt.*, 1953, *13*, 110-121.

373. Strong, E. K., Jr., & Tucker, A. C. The use of vocational interest scales in planning a medical career. *Psychol. Monogr.*, 1952, *66*, No. 96, (Whole No. 341).

374. Stubbins, J. The relationship between level of vocational aspiration and certain personal data: a study of some traits and influences leaning on the prestige level of vocational choice. *Genet. Psychol. Monogr.*, 1950, *41*, 327-408.

375. Stuit, D. B. Counseling methods: diagnostics. *Annu Rev. Psychol.*, 1951, 2, 305-316.

376. Sullivan, H. S. *The interpersonal theory of anxiety.* New York: Norton, 1953.

377. Super, D. E. *The dynamics of vocational adjustment.* New York: Harper, 1942.

378. Super, D. E. Strong's Vocational Interests of Men and Women. *Psychol. Bull.*, 1945, *42*, 359-370.

379. Super, D. E. Vocational interest and vocational choice. *Educ. psychol. Measmt.*, 1947, 7, 375-384.

380. Super, D. E. *Appraising vocational fitness by means of psychological tests.* New York: Harper, 1949.

381. Super, D. E. Testing and using test results in counseling. *Occupations*, 1950, *29*, 95-97.

382. Super, D. E. The criteria of vocational success. *Occupations*, 1951, *30*, 5-9.

383. Super, D. E. Vocational adjustment: implementing a self-concept. *Occupations*, 1951, *30*, 88-92.

384. Super, D. E. A theory of vocational development. *Amer. Psychologist*, 1953, *8*, 185-190.

385. Super, D. E. Career patterns as a basis for vocational counseling. *J. counsel. Psychol.*, 1954, *1*, 12-19.

386. Symonds, P. M. Securing rapport in interviewing. *Teachers Coll. Rec.*, 1938, *39*, 707-722.

387. Symonds, P. M. *The dynamics of human adjustment.* New York: Appleton-Century-Crofts, 1946.

388. Symonds, P. M. *The ego and the self.* New York: Appleton-Century-Crofts, 1951.

389. Symonds, P. M., & Dietrich, D. H. The effect of variations in the time interval between an interview and its recording. *J. abnorm. soc. Psychol.*, 1941, *36*, 593-598.

390. Taft, Jessie. *The dynamics of therapy in a controlled relationship.* New York: Macmillan, 1933.

391. Taylor, C., & Combs, A. W. Self-acceptance and adjustment. *J. consult. Psychol.*, 1952, *16*, 89-91.

392. Taylor, J. L., & Teicher, A. A clinical approach to reporting psychological test data. *J. clin. Psychol.*, 1946, *2*, 323-332.

393. Thompson, Clara. Transference as a therapeutic instrument. *Psychiat.*, 1945, *8*, 273-278.

394. Thorne, F. C. A critique of non-directive methods of psychotherapy. *J. abnorm. soc. Psychol.*, 1944, *39*, 459-470.

395. Thorne, F. C. Directive psychotherapy: III. The psychology of simple maladjustments. *J. clin. Psychol.*, 1945, *1*, 228-240.

396. Thorne, F. C. Directive psychotherapy: VII. Imparting psychological information. *J. clin. Psychol.*, 1946, *2*, 179-190.

397. Thorne, F. C. Directive psychotherapy. XI. Therapeutic use of conflict. *J. clin. Psychol.*, 1947, *3*, 168-179.

398. Thorne, F. C. Further critique of nondirective methods of psychotherapy. *J. clin. Psychol.*, 1948, *4*, 256-263.

399. Thorne, F. C. Principles of directive counseling and psychotherapy. *Amer. Psychologist*, 1948, *5*, 160-165.

400. Thorne, F. C. *Principles of personality counseling: an eclectic viewpoint.* Brandon, Vermont: Journal of Clinical Psychology, 1950.

401. Thorne, F. C. Rules of evidence in the evaluation of the effects of psychotherapy. *J. clin. Psychol.*, 1952, *8*, 38-41.

402. Thorne, F. C. Directive psychotherapy: theory, practice, and social implications. *J. clin. Psychol.*, 1953, *9*, 267-280.

403. Thorne, F. C. Editorial opinion: back to fundamentals. *J. clin. Psychol.*, 1953, *9*, 89-91.

404. Thorne, F. C., Carter, J., *et al.* Symposium: critical evaluation of non-directive counseling and psychotherapy. *J. clin. Psychol.*, 1948, *4*, 225-263.

405. Thurstone, L. L. *Multiple-factor analysis: a development and expansion of the vectors of the mind.* Chicago: University of Chicago Press, 1947.

406. Tiedeman, D. U. Problems and procedures in profile analysis. In *Proceedings, 1953 invitational conference on testing problems.* Princeton: Educational Testing Service, 1954.

407. Tindall, R. H., & Robinson, F. P. The use of silence as a technique in counseling. *J. clin. Psychol.*, 1947, *3*, 136-141.

408. Toman, W. Pause analysis as a short interviewing technique. *J. consult. Psychol.*, 1953, *17*, 1-7.

409. Torrance, E. P. The phenomenon of resistance in learning. *J. abnorm. soc. Psychol.*, 1950, *45*, 592-597.

410. Torrance, E. P. Some practical uses of a knowledge of self-concepts in counseling and guidance. *Educ. psychol. Measmt.*, 1954, *14*, 120-127.

411. Traphagen, A. L. Interest patterns and retention and rejection of vocational choice. *J. appl. Psychol.*, 1952, *36*, 182-185.

412. Travers, R. M. W. A critical review of techniques for evaluating guidance. *Educ. psychol. Measmt.*, 1949, 9, 211-225.

413. Travers, R. M. W. Rational hypotheses in the construction of tests. *Educ. psychol. Measmt.*, 1951, *11*, 128-137.

414. Tyler, Leona E. *The work of the counselor.* New York: Appleton-Century-Crofts, 1953.

415. Van Zelst, R. H. Validation evidence on the Empathy Test. *Educ. psychol. Measmt.*, 1953, *13*, 474-477.

416. Vernon, P. E. Classifying high-grade occupational interests. *J. abnorm. soc. Psychol.*, 1949, *44*, 85-96.

417. Vordenberg, W. The impact of personal philosophies on counseling. *Personnel and guid. J.*, 1953, *31*, 439-440.

418. Watson, R. I. *Readings in the clinical method in psychology.* New York: Harper, 1949.

419. Watson, R. I. *The clinical method in psychology.* New York: Harper, 1951.

420. Watson, R. I. Measuring the effectiveness of psychotherapy: Problems for investigation. *J. clin. Psychol.*, 1952, 8, 60-64.

421. Watson, R. I. Research design and methodology in evaluating the results of psychotherapy. *J. clin. Psychol.*, 1952, 8, 29-33.

422. Weingarten, E. M. A study of selective perception in clinical judgment. *J. Personality*, 1949, *17*, 369-406.

423. White, R. W. *Lives in progress: a study of the natural growth of personality.* New York: Dryden, 1952.

424. Williamson, E. G. *How to counsel students: a manual of techniques for clinical counselors.* New York: McGraw-Hill, 1939.

425. Williamson, E. G. Counseling and the Minnesota point of view. *Educ. psychol. Measmt.*, 1947, 7, 141-155.

426. Williamson, E. G. (Ed.) *Trends in student personnel work.* Minneapolis: University of Minnesota Press, 1949.

427. Williamson, E. G. A concept of counseling. *Occupations*, 1950, 29, 182-189.

428. Williamson, E. G. *Counseling adolescents.* New York: McGraw-Hill, 1950.

429. Williamson, E. G. Counseling: therapy and diagnosis. *Annu. Rev. Psychol.*, 1953, *4*, 343-360.

430. Williamson, E. G., & Bordin, E. S. Evaluating counseling by means of a control group experiment. *School and soc.*, 1940, *52*, 434-440.

431. Williamson, E. G., & Bordin, E. S. A statistical evaluation of student counseling. *Educ. psychol. Measmt.*, 1941, *1*, 117-132.

432. Williamson, E. G., & Bordin, E. S. The evaluation of vocational and educational counseling: a critique of the methodology of experiments. *Educ. psychol. Measmt.*, 1941, *1*, 5-24.

433. Williamson, E. G., & Foley, J. D. *Counseling and discipline.* New York: McGraw-Hill, 1949.

434. Wischner, G. J., & McKinney, F. Counseling. *Rev. educ. Res.*, 1948, *18*, 175-183.

435. Wolff, W., & Precker, J. A. (Eds.) *Success in psychotherapy.* New York: Grune and Stratton, 1952.

436. Wood, A. B. Transference in client centered therapy and in psychoanalysis. *J. consult. Psychol.*, 1951, *15*, 72-75.

437. Wrenn, C. G. Client-centered counseling. *Educ. psychol. Measmt.*, 1946, *4*, 439-444.

438. Wrenn, C. G. General counseling procedures. In W. S. Monroe (Ed.), *Encyclopedia of educational research.* (Rev. Ed.) New York: Macmillan, 1950. Pp. 1312-1320.

439. Wrenn, C. G. *Student personnel work in college.* New York: Ronald, 1951.

440. Wrenn, C. G. The ethics of counseling. *Educ. psychol. Measmt.*, 1952, *12*, 161-177.

441. Wrenn, C. G. Counseling methods. *Annu. Rev. Psychol.*, 1954, *5*, 337-356.

442. Wrenn, C. G., & Bell, R. *Student personnel problems.* New York: Farrar and Rinehart, 1942.

443. Wrenn, C. G., & Darley, J. G. Counseling. *Rev. educ. Res.*, 1942, *12*, 45-65.

444. Young, K. *Personality and problems of adjustment.* (2nd Ed.) New York: Appleton-Century-Crofts, 1952.

445. Zubin, J. Clinical practice and personality theory: a symposium. III. Personality research and psychopathology as related to clinical practice. *J. abnorm. soc. Psychol.*, 1949, *44*, 14-21.

446. Zubin, J. Introduction: Symposium on statistics for the clinician. *J. clin. Psychol.*, 1950, *6*, 1-6.

Index

psychological, 315
qua construction, 311
Invasion of privacy, 323–324

Kuder, G. F., 173, 176
Kuder Preference Record—Vocational:
  coding of, 92, 93, 94
  in case of Bette Morgan, 40
  in case of Bill Davis, 86, 92, 93, 94
  in case of John Battle, 217
  in case of Ruth Brook, 166
  verification score, 173

McGowan, J. F., 92
Masculinity-femininity, 65–66, 162, 176, 178–179
Minnesota Multiphasic Personality Inventory:
  in case of Bette Morgan, 41, 65–66
  in case of John Battle, 216
  in case of Ruth Brook, 167
  in case of Tom Smith, 115, 117–119
  meaning of Pd spike, 65–66
  meaning of Sc spike, 115, 118–119
Minnesota Teacher Attitude Inventory,
  in case of Bette Morgan, 37
Morgan, Bette, case of, 5, 9–76
Mowrer, O. H., 313

Needs, psychological, of clients, 312
Notes (*see* case notes)

Occupational information (*see* Information, occupational and educational)
Opening the interview, 44, 60
Opinions of counselor as a technique, 50

Porter, E. H., Jr., 311, 315, 317
Problem, development of, 18, 19, 28–29, 78, 107–108, 316–317
Problem solving, 314 ff
Proff, F. C., 3

Rapport, 56, 138
Reassurance, 99, 144, 170
Referral, 107–108, 113–114, 214–215, 321–322
Responsibility variables in counseling, 316–318
Revised Minnesota Paper Form Board, 219
Robinson, F. P., 78, 129, 318, 319

Roeber, E. C., 197
Rogers, C. R., 1, 113, 311, 315, 317, 318
Rotter Incomplete Sentences Blank:
  in case of Bette Morgan, 42–43
  in case of Ruth Brook, 168–169
Rundquist, R. M., 3

Saddler, L. E., 89, 327
Selection of tests, 15–17, 80–82, 108–113, 158, 161–162, 292–295, 316–318
Self-concept, 32, 66, 127
Silence as a technique, 24
Smith, Tom, case of, 6, 104–151
Snyder, W. U., 1, 318
Strong, E. K., Jr., 115
Strong Vocational Interest Blank:
  in case of Bette Morgan, 39
  in case of Bill Davis, 81, 85, 89–90, 96
  in case of John Battle, 218
  in case of Ruth Brook, 153
  in case of Tom Smith, 115, 116
  Interest Maturity scale, 96, 115
Structuring, 9–10, 78, 80, 81, 107–108, 110, 129, 131, 157–158, 181, 318–320
Style of counseling, 19, 28–29, 32, 44, 55, 56, 97, 106, 107, 113–114, 182, 183
Super, D. E., 32, 127

Techniques of counseling, role of theory in, 312 ff
Test selection (*see* Selection of tests)
Tests (*see* name of test)
Theory, role of, in counseling, 312 ff
Thorne, F. C., 28, 102, 313, 315, 317
Thurstone, L. L., 313
Travers, R. M. W., 91
Triggs, Frances O. (*see* Diagnostic Reading Test)

Vocational choice, 14, 32, 155, 209–210
Vocational interest:
  of engineering students, 89–90, 327
  of women, 14, 20, 155

Wechsler-Bellevue Intelligence Scale:
  in case of Bette Morgan, 44
  in case of John Battle, 219, 294
  in case of Tom Smith, 119
White, Alice M., 50
Williamson, E. G., 317, 322
Wrenn, C. G., 212, 323